The Limits of Labour

David Bright

The Limits of Labour: Class Formation and the Labour Movement in Calgary, 1883-1929

UBCPress / Vancouver

Printed in Canada on acid-free paper ∞

ISBN 0-7748-0696-6 (hardcover)
ISBN 0-7748-0697-4 (paperback)

Canadian Cataloguing in Publication Data

Bright, David
The limits of labour

Includes bibliographical references and index.
ISBN 0-7748-0696-6 (bound)
ISBN 0-7748-0697-4 (pbk)

1. Labor movement – Alberta – Calgary – History. 2. Working class – Alberta – Calgary – History. 3. Calgary (Alta.) – Social conditions. I. Title
HD8110.C352B74 1998 331.8´097123´38 C98-910609-8

This book has been published with the help of a grant from the Humanities and Social Sciences Federation of Canada, using funds provided by the Social Sciences and Humanities Research Council of Canada, and also a grant from the Chinook Country Historical Society.

UBC Press also gratefully acknowledges the ongoing support to its publishing program from the Canada Council for the Arts, the British Columbia Arts Council, and the Department of Canadian Heritage of the Government of Canada.

UBC Press
University of British Columbia
6344 Memorial Road
Vancouver, BC V6T 1Z2
(604) 822-5959
Fax: 1-800-668-0821
E-mail: orders@ubcpress.ubc.ca

To Catherine

Contents

Illustrations

Acknowledgments

'Begin at the beginning,' the King of Hearts told Alice, 'and go on till you come to the end: then stop.' With this wise injunction in mind, I wish to thank those individuals and institutions who have assisted me in my explorations of Calgary labour. In the first place, I am indebted to staff at the Glenbow Museum Archives, the City of Calgary Archives, the Provincial Archives of Alberta, and the National Archives of Canada for their professional assistance. In particular, without Doug Cass and Harry Sanders going the extra mile for me, much of what follows could not have been written. I am also grateful to librarians at the University of Calgary, who tolerated my many requests over many years with good humour and much patience.

Financial support for this study was provided by a University of Calgary Silver Anniversary Graduate Scholarship and a Killam Fellowship. The generous terms of both eased the pressures of research. David Bercuson supervised my doctoral studies, from which this book has grown, and while we rarely saw eye to eye on the meaning and nature of class, his backing and guidance over the years were invaluable. Not least, I remain grateful for his original faith in me more than a decade ago. I have also benefited greatly from the friendship and wisdom of Stephen Randall and John Ferris, while more recently Greg Kealey has been a much appreciated source of support and advice.

Publication of this book is made possible by a grant from the Humanities and Social Sciences Federation of Canada, for which I am grateful. I would like to thank the four anonymous reviewers for their critical reading of the manuscript, which stands greatly improved as the result of their recommendations. Above all, my heartfelt thanks go to Laura Macleod, editor extraordinaire at UBC Press. She not only guided me through the labyrinthine process of prepublication, but her constant encouragement and reassurance kept at bay the twin hounds of doubt and despair.

For their continuing friendship over the years, I am happy to record my debt of gratitude to Diana Mansell, John Feldberg, Scott Murray, and Harry Sanders. My thanks also go to numerous colleagues and support staff at the University of Calgary and Mount Royal College. A special mention should be made of Gordon Christie, who as executive secretary of the Calgary Labour Council introduced me to the contemporary world of local trade unionism. And for humouring my musical ambitions, I remain eternally grateful to fellow former band members Michael Lazar, Scott Oddie, and Peter Faris.

To my family in England, especially my mother, Jeanne Bright, I dedicate this book as the fruit of my decision to come to Canada all those years ago. My final but most important devotion is to Catherine Radimer, who continues to tolerate my ever changing moods. Doubtless this book would have been written without her constant support, love, and friendship, but it could never have meant as much.

The Limits of Labour

Introduction

Every summer, Calgarians gather to celebrate a mythical version of their city's history. For ten days in July, men and women from all walks of life don tight-legged jeans, wide-brimmed hats, and ornate leather boots as they cavort through the city's streets, bars, and midway. The 'world's greatest show outdoors,' as the Calgary Stampede modestly describes itself, is in fact a celebration of some ill-defined 'frontier democracy,' that is located vaguely in Calgary's distant past in a world where social equality and economic opportunity ride spiritedly across the prairies. It is a powerful myth, promoted and perpetuated by virtually all of Calgary's public institutions, including the city's media, museums, libraries, schools, and civic administration. Like all myths, it contains an element of truth. Nevertheless, this Turnerian vision of Calgary's history remains an invention of the past.[1]

Consider, in contrast to the myth of frontier equality and opportunity, the testimony of one local resident in 1919, the same year in which the Stampede was held for the first time since its inception in 1912. On the morning of 5 May, Calgary postal worker Clifford Nicholls stood up to testify before the Royal Commission on Industrial Relations. Like many of the nearly 500 witnesses who addressed that inquiry as it made its way across Canada, Nicholls spoke of the immediate conditions that lay behind the current wave of labour unrest that would soon culminate in an unprecedented series of general strikes. But he also described the grinding realities of a society that had long been divided by differences of class, differences that routinely shaped an individual's daily experiences:

> Any bitterly cold morning in this city and what will you see? You will see miserable, pale-faced men with drunken, weary-looking eyes, crawling out of their beds in the early hours of the morning, sitting down to an almost bare breakfast table and then crawling off to work with their dinner pails with a few little sandwiches in them, crawling off to the

> mills, where in the grime and misery and turmoil all day long he is worked like a beast from 7 in the morning until 5 or 6 at night. At night time it is dark again, cold and dreary and he comes out with his dinner pail and stands in the snow and sleet shivering on the corner until he can get a car where usually he again has to stand on tired, weary, blistered feet until he gets to his home, twenty minutes ride maybe away. He crawls into his home to meet his pale-faced wife, absolutely worn out with her exertions at the wash tub. They talk about finances but he finds out by the time he has paid everything which has to be paid there will be nothing left of his cheque and the consequence is he realizes that if for some reason he fails to appear at his work he will instantly be in debt.[2]

As if to underline that he was describing the condition of a class, not simply of one unfortunate individual, Nicholls then suggested what that same man might see if he were sick one day and did not go to work. 'He looks around the city and he sees men with their collars and ties on, with their fine women driving around in large McLaughlin or Studebaker cars, men that he knows do not get up before 7:30, then sit down to a comfortable meal and get the morning's paper and then go down and recline in an office chair for four or five hours a day and then go home.' Nicholls had no doubt that it was he and his fellow workers, and not 'that other man in the auto,' who were 'doing the biggest share in keeping this world going, providing food, clothing, bed and the commodities of life.' Nicholls could offer the commission no solution to this situation, but ended his testimony with the warning that 'the worker has gotten enormous ideals and he is determined to work them out.'[3]

This book is a study of the origin and nature of those ideals in Calgary and of the labour movement's flawed attempts to work them out. It approaches this subject in two stages. First, it explores the formation of Calgary's working class, and its relations with other social classes, during the city's initial era of industrialization between 1883 and 1913. Second, it assesses the limited ability of organized labour to represent and reflect the interests of that working class in the subsequent period, 1913-29, during which workers and others in the city faced a series of new, harsher economic challenges. The book's primary purpose is not so much to criticize Calgary's craft unions for failing to develop into a broader class-based movement, even if this criticism is at times difficult to avoid. Rather, its aim is to examine the specific historical circumstances that shaped the symbiotic relationship between organized labour and working-class formation in Calgary as the city underwent industrialization.

Calgary's workers have not been widely studied, either by Canadian labour historians or by historians of Calgary.[4] Their historical presence as a class, with distinct interests and demands, is peripheral to most historical accounts of the city's development, as if their impact on the economy and their participation in civic affairs were inconsequential.[5] This simply is not so, as even a brief review of Calgary labour's record indicates. During the four decades before the Second World War, Calgary ranked among Canada's leading centres of organized labour in terms of its number of trade unions. In the 1920s, Calgary was the only city other than Winnipeg that managed to send labour MPs to Ottawa. At the same time, Calgary's voters, if only briefly, elected a majority of labour candidates to their city council. Yet to date, there exists no single historical account that brings together Calgary labour's industrial and political achievements over any length of time, or that sets labour's cultural experiences within the context of class formation. This book assumes these tasks.

Calgary is a suitable location for the study of working-class formation for other reasons. First, that city has a symbolic importance within Canadian labour history, at odds with its present-day reputation as the heartland of prairie capitalism. In March 1919, for example, Calgary played host to the first Western Labour Conference, a convening of delegates unhappy with central Canada's stranglehold on the Trades and Labour Congress, and one that led eventually to the launch of the ill-fated One Big Union. Thirteen years later, in the summer of 1932, Calgary was again the scene of a historic moment for Canadian labour when trade unionists, socialists, and farmers met at the city's Labour Temple to draft a preliminary platform for a new political party, the Co-operative Commonwealth Federation. It would be interesting to know whether, or to what extent, the radical tone of such occasions reflected the temper of the host city's working class.

Calgary's reputation for working-class conservatism within a radical West requires closer study than it has so far received.[6] It is argued in the pages that follow that such a characterization of Calgary labour is not so much unwarranted as it is beside the point. The preference of most labour historians for stark opposites, such as 'radical' or 'conservative,' 'class conscious' or 'job conscious,' fails to do justice to the complexities of working-class life. This is especially true of the years surrounding the turn of the century, in which the possibilities and restrictions facing workers in the rapidly developing West placed a premium upon the flexibility of response.[7]

This book, then, is a study of Calgary's labour movement – in its industrial and political forms – within the context of class formation. In this respect, and in terms of its approach, it stands aligned with recent works such as James Naylor's study of organized workers in Ontario and Mark Leier's exploration of trade union bureaucracy in Vancouver.[8] The deep and often bitter ideological battles that divided Canadian labour historians in the 1970s and 1980s are now a distant, if well-documented, memory for many of today's younger students of Canada's working class, whose work attempts to blend the institutional focus of the so-called 'first generation' of labour historians with the class-based or culturalist approach of the 'second generation.'[9] As a result, this 'third generation' has refocused attention on the struggle between trade unions and employers, and the battle between labour parties and the state, within the context of class formation. Perhaps what most separates these proponents of 'new institutionalism,' as their approach has been characterized, from their immediate predecessors is their desire to explain, rather than explain away, the historical divisions that have fragmented the working class. As Leier writes of his own experience as a shop steward in the 1970s, 'If working-class culture was a necessary condition of organization, it was not a sufficient condition. What was noticeable and needed examination were the forces that kept workers from uniting.'[10] This book shares the ambition to explain the limits of labour to realize the potential unity of class.

A basic assumption of this study is that class remains a fruitful tool of analysis, despite its many critics and the alternative models of social change and social identity.[11] I accept the materialist premise of Marxism that a conflict of classes, or class interests, is inherent within the conditions of capitalist production. As Marx wrote in his *Contribution to the Critique of Political Economy,* 'In the social production of their life, men enter into definite relations that are indispensable and independent of their will, relations of productions which correspond to a definite stage of development of their material productive forces ... The mode of production of material life conditions the social, political, and intellectual life processes in general. It is not the consciousness of men that determines their being, but, on the contrary, their social being that determines their consciousness.'[12] From this standpoint, the working class may be identified as those men and women who work for wages, have no control or ownership of the means of production, and produce a surplus for those who do.

In adopting this approach and definition, I recognize the need to acknowledge those questions that have long dogged Marxism as an explanation of social change. What, for example, is the precise relationship between base and superstructure, or between economic determinism and human agency? In other words, are individuals and classes the subject or object of historical development? Confusion in this area, of course, may be traced back to Marx himself. 'Men make their own history,' he claimed in 1859, 'but they do not make it just as they please ... but under circumstances directly found, given and transmitted from the past.'[13] Ever since that statement, historians and other scholars have tried to clarify the exact nature of the relationship between agency and determinism, with notable contributions from Raymond Williams, E.P. Thompson, and Maurice Godelier. 'We have to revalue "determination" towards the setting of limits and the exertion of pressure,' suggested Williams, 'and away from a predicted, prefigured and controlled content.' Godelier, on the other hand, proposed that the base-superstructure relationship be thought of in functional rather than institutional terms. 'To my mind,' he wrote in 1978, 'a society does not have a top and a bottom, or even levels. This is because the distinction between infrastructure and superstructure is not a distinction between institutions. Its principle, rather, is one of distinction between functions ... If we managed to verify that social relations dominate when they function as relations of production, then we should have worked our way back to Marx's hypothesis regarding the dominant role, in the last analysis, of the infrastructure.'[14] Yet Godelier's reference to 'the last analysis' simply underlines the chicken-and-egg nature of the relationship between determinism and agency in history, a problem that has so far eluded successful resolution.[15] As Ira Katznelson has recently remarked of the most celebrated attempt to square this circle, 'Even in the hands of a master like E.P. Thompson ... it has not proved possible for Marxism within its own analytical tradition to do better than work with the formula that class formation lies at the junction of determination and consciousness, which assumes that once a working class is "made" by the impact of external conditions, the people sharing this fate will "make themselves" into a class capable of affecting history.'[16]

A modest appraisal of class formation and the labour movement in early Calgary is not the place to resolve such long-standing tensions within Marxist analysis, but neither can it ignore them entirely. The minimum obligation is to outline explicitly the model of class formation used in this book. While the influences here are many and varied, it is the theoretical work of Ira Katznelson that leaves the heaviest imprint on the pages that follow. In a number of books and articles, notably *Working-Class Formation* and *Marxism and the City,* Katznelson has developed a model of class formation that emphasizes the importance of contingency in shaping class disposition and collective action, a model that avoids the determinism frequently associated with materialist conceptions of class.[17] 'As a concept,' Katznelson argues, 'class has soaked up so much meaning that it has become bulky to use. Because it is often employed without a clearly specified definition, debates about class often become conversations in which people talk past each other because they are talking about different dimensions of class.'[18] To avoid this confusion, he proposes that the concept of class be viewed as four connected levels of theory and history: economic structure, ways of life, dispositions, and collective action. These levels are neither sequential nor hierarchical in nature. In other words, it is not necessary to realize a class identity at one level in order to move to another, nor do experiences within any one level determine those on another. Instead, as Katznelson emphasizes, 'Class formation may be thought of more fully and variably as concerned with the conditional (but not random) process of connection between the four levels of class.'[19]

The first of these four levels relates to the structure of capitalist economic development, in which privately owned, profit-maximizing firms and a wage-earning workforce constitute the necessary but not sufficient conditions for class formation at the other three levels. Katznelson acknowledges that, at this level, class formation involves features common to all capitalisms – notably the commodification of money, land, and labour – but stresses that it 'is not something that occurs as a quantitative matter, more or less. It is a contingent process whose terms and content vary from place to place.' This contingency is amplified at the second level of class formation, namely 'the patterns of life and social relations in specific capitalist societies.' As Katznelson notes, 'it is tempting to collapse the first two levels of class into the single category of the "economy,"' but he warns that doing so would mask the fact that 'the growth and expansion of capitalism has proved capable of fostering many different kinds of workplaces and work.' Instead, he argues, the first two levels should be considered in tandem, so that they 'may tell us how workers exist and live in certain circumstances, but not how they will think and act in those experienced circumstances.'[20] It is at this point that Katznelson attempts to reconcile economic determinism and human agency in the process of class formation:

> People live in spaces that are the products of specific relationships between the natural environment and human creativity ... Class formation is a process concerned with experience in a double sense: experience of the world and learning to act within and on it. No one meets with capitalism in general or directly engages the abstract commodity form whose very essence is that it is fetishized. Capitalism is lived in particular locations at particular times.[21]

This leads Katznelson to his third and fourth levels of class. The third level refers to the disposition of workers to act and behave as a class, and here he shares common ground with E.P. Thompson. 'When we speak of *a* class,' writes Thompson, 'we are thinking of a very loosely-defined body of people who share the same congeries of interests, social experiences, traditions, and value-system, who have a *disposition* to *behave* as a class, to define themselves in their actions and in their consciousness in relation to other groups of people in class ways.'[22] In that final clause, Katznelson argues that Thompson moves too quickly from the *disposition* of workers to think or behave in class ways, to their preparedness to *act collectively* on this disposition. 'Groups of people sharing motivational constructs ("disposition to behave") may or may not act collectively to transform disposition to behavior. Even where workers have close contact at work and in the residential communities; even if this interaction promotes strong collective identities; and even if these workers share common systems of meaning that incline them to act in class ways, they may not necessarily act together to produce collective action.' Accordingly, Katznelson identifies collective action as the fourth and final level of class formation. This level 'refers to classes that are organized and that act through movements and organizations to affect society and the position of the class within it,' and reflects 'more than just the common but unself-conscious shared behavior of members of a class.'[23]

In sum, Katznelson's four-level model seeks to balance the objective and subjective elements of class formation, to combine structural determinants and human agency in a manner that remains responsive to local variants in capitalist production. 'The specification of four levels of class,' he concludes, 'allows us to keep the advantages of defining class in terms of outcomes while providing a more elaborated and variable object of comparative historical analysis. The content of each of the four levels of necessity will vary from society to society; no level need be understood or analyzed exclusively in class terms; and the connections between the levels are problematical and conditional.'[24]

This model not only provides a flexible method by which to study class formation in Calgary, but does so in a way that avoids the simplistic dichotomy of radical/conservative that has long characterized the study of labour in western Canada. Instead of focusing on whether Calgary workers were radical compared to those in Winnipeg, for example, or whether they measured up to some idealized model of the working class whose 'true' goal was socialism, this book considers those conditions and circumstances that actually shaped the disposition of workers to think and behave as a class.

No model of class formation is either complete or perfect. Some feminist and labour historians have criticized Katznelson for his lack of attention to gender and family – a criticism he accepts, but one that has also been levelled at labour history more generally.[25] 'The problem ... lies in the conceptual inequality of class and gender in the discipline's paradigm-building,' argues Leon Fink. 'To put it simply, class always comes first.'[26] Numerous feminist historians have echoed and elaborated this charge, with Joy Parr noting that 'We live simultaneously, rather than sequentially, in the social relations of class and gender.'[27] Among recent contributions to the debate, one of the sharpest comes from American historian Alice Kessler-Harris. 'The sharp dichotomy between work and gender relies on formal definitions of production, wages, and labor that may not be viable in the light of recent scholarship,' she writes. 'Operating from a particular, and seemingly natural standpoint, many labor historians have perceived the world through a lens that offers only partial vision: that of the male worker.' Accordingly, Kessler-Harris calls for a 'radical reconceptualization' of class in which 'female agency can bespeak a variety of social experiences ranging from motherhood to the workplace, and male agency can be expected to reflect a continuum that extends from workplace skills to family position.' To achieve this end, it is necessary to 'challenge the notion that paid work, as a fundamentally male activity, inevitably reproduces itself in a closed system in which men derive their identity from the process of production (and then reproduce themselves by training other men), while women act in the household and in the workplace as the handmaids of the male reproductive system.' In place of production and workplace relations, Kessler-Harris locates consumption and the gendered struggle of household relations at the heart of her analysis of class formation.[28]

Many Canadian feminist historians have already produced works that incorporate the approach outlined by Kessler-Harris. Joy Parr's study of women and men in Paris and Hanover, Ontario; Suzanne Morton's book on a Halifax working-class suburb; and Joan Sangster's history of women's lives in small-town Ontario all demonstrate the gains to be made by placing gender at the heart of historical analysis.[29] Certainly there is little doubt that any model of class formation needs to attend to the question of gender, and this book – especially in Chapter 2 – goes further than Katznelson in addressing the relationship between gender and class. Yet I remain doubtful about the degree to which the two concepts can (or should) be integrated or harmonized as explanations of social change. Mari Jo Buhle states that the 'goal set by women's historians' is 'to reconceptualize basic categories of analysis to include the process of class formation *outside* capitalist production, as traditionally defined.'[30] Separated from capitalist production, however, class formation is denied its fundamental material base; what function class serves as a tool of historical analysis therefore becomes questionable. Here I agree with Bryan Palmer's reiteration that 'Class *is,* in the first instance and at its most basic, an objective, structurally determined relationship to the means of production ... Status differences and self-identification, however contradictory, are nevertheless irrelevant in this generalized class system, determined first and foremost by the homogenizing tendencies (never absolute) of modern industry and its master, capital.'[31]

Katznelson's model of class formation is also vulnerable to attack from those who favour the pervasive influence of poststructuralism on the historical discipline.[32] Gareth Stedman Jones's application of discourse theory to the politics of Chartism, and Joan Wallach Scott's championing of the techniques pioneered by Derrida and Foucault are probably the best-known examples, but recent works by Parr, Sangster, and Mariana Valverde illustrate the firm presence of poststructuralism within Canadian social history.[33] Described variously as the 'linguistic turn' or a 'descent into discourse,' one of poststructuralism's main impacts on history has been its emphasis on language, rather than material circumstances, in the construction of social identity. Scott is explicit on this point: 'Class and class consciousness are the same thing – they are political articulations that provide an analysis of, a coherent pattern to impose upon, the activities of daily life.'[34] This privileging of language or discourse in the construction of class identity has been strongly resisted by defenders of historical materialism, notably Bryan Palmer and Alex Callinicos.[35] 'Critical theory is no substitute for historical materialism; language is not life,' argues Palmer. 'Whatever insight can be gleaned from discourse theory and its privileging of language needs to be balanced with other appreciations drawn from more resolutely historical and materialist traditions.'[36] Arguing from the far left, on this question Palmer finds an unlikely ally in the conservative historian Gertrude Himmelfarb. Himmelfarb has railed against the extreme relativism and near nihilism of poststructuralism, arguing that it 'trivialize[s] history by so fragmenting it that it lacks all coherence and focus, all sense of continuity – indeed, all meaning.'[37] While a detailed review of the debate over poststructuralism would be out of place here, suffice it to say that I lean closer to the views of Palmer, Callinicos, and Himmelfarb than to those who champion its merits.

This brings us back to Katznelson and his four-level model of class formation. Katznelson himself has recently lamented the 'mutual aggression' that exists between 'traditional materialism and constructivist alternatives.' Instead, he proposes that the two approaches 'be kept in useful tension and that they should both be joined in a relationship with a once-hegemonic but now less-fashionable political, institutional, and state-focused theme within labor history.'[38] This is what his model attempts, connecting in a non-deterministic manner the economic and social structures that shape the daily lives of workers; their disposition to respond to these structures in class ways; and, finally, the degree to which they act upon this disposition via industrial organization and political struggle. While I am less convinced than Katznelson that, in any final analysis, a genuine compromise between historical materialism and poststructuralism is possible in practice, his paradigm of class formation is broadly the approach adopted in this book.

The book's first half focuses specifically on the question of working-class formation in Calgary. Chapters 1 through 4 take up the themes of structure, disposition, ways of life, and collective action in Calgary during the decades of its initial industrialization, 1883-1913, in order to trace the development of a sense of class among the city's workers. This period spans the early years of growth in the 1880s, a brief but significant depression in the 1890s, followed by the boom years of 1900-13. Chapter 1 begins with the transformation of Calgary from a small mercantile-based town on the fringe of European settlement on the prairies, into one of the region's foremost centres of industrial capitalism. Central to this transformation was the creation of a capitalist labour market and the emergence of a stable labour force consisting of men and women who were prepared to submit to the demands and disciplines of capitalist production. The chapter concludes with a look at the rise of the factory system and other concentrations of capital in Calgary, and the impact they had on the prospects for advancement of individual wage earners.

Chapters 2 and 3 then turn to the social, cultural, and political experiences of workers in this period, and to how these dimensions of their lives limited their disposition to think and act as a distinct social class. The diverse experience of work itself fractured any sense of class unity, as did divisions along lines of gender, ethnicity, and religion. Culturally, workers had much in common with other classes in society, and there is little evidence to suggest that they developed a distinct working-class culture in which they might discover refuge from or resistance to the spread of capitalist values. On the contrary, in Calgary culture acted more as a source of social cohesion than of conflict.

In contrast, Chapter 4 examines the collective actions of workers that did stress their experience as a separate class, in particular the organization of unions and the staging of labour strikes. The degree of unionization and the frequency of strikes during the years 1900-13 make Calgary comparable to cities in central and eastern Canada as a centre of working-class activism, suggesting that at this level, at least, Calgary workers were becoming well-aware of their own distinct identity.

The second half of this book looks at organized labour's industrial and political responses in the period 1913-29. A sharp economic recession in the winter of 1912-3 brought to an end Calgary's era of rapid industrial growth, years characterized by relatively full employment, steadily rising wages, and a pluralistic toleration among employers for the new trade union movement. During the next sixteen years, from the onset of the 1913 recession to the eve of a far greater depression in 1929, Calgary's economy underwent a restructuring whose hallmarks were stubbornly high unemployment, downward pressure on wages, and a new atmosphere of anti-unionism among many employers. In this respect, 1913 stands as a far more relevant turning point than 1919, the year usually selected by labour historians as the pivotal moment for western Canada's working class.

Chapter 5 begins with the end of Calgary's economic boom in 1913 and the emergence of unemployment as the key problem that would dominate labour's agenda for the next two decades. During the early years of the First World War, Calgary's labour movement reaffirmed its commitment to electoral politics rather than direct confrontation with the state, resisting demands for more radical action following the conscription crisis of 1917. Chapter 6 discusses the postwar economic slump and the subsequent restructuring of Calgary's economy in the years 1918-24. It examines the union movement's efforts to accommodate itself to these new conditions and, in particular, argues that falling wage levels and persistent unemployment helped propel the movement to seek new allies in its defensive struggle against retrenched capitalism. Chapter 7 offers a revisionist interpretation of the events of 1918-9 in Calgary, arguing that those events can best be understood not as part of a western or national labour revolt, but within the context of local political evolution and economic restructuring. Chapter 8 continues the story of labour's political advances at all three levels of government through to 1924. Despite the labour movement's considerable electoral success in these years, it nonetheless failed to build a widespread working-class base of support.

The implications of this failure are the subject of the final chapter. Chapter 9 brings together the various strands of narrative of Calgary labour's struggles in an analysis of the years 1925-9. It focuses especially on the fragmentation of labour's industrial and political organizations. Ideological, constitutional, and personal conflicts in this period destroyed any hopes that the labour movement might be able to build the class-wide base of support that had so far eluded it. As a result, in 1929 Calgary's labour movement was ill-prepared to face the tumultuous years that lay ahead. Its failure to protect working-class interests during the 1930s was a measure of the depth of that decade's depression, but it also reflected the limits of labour to develop a class-based foundation in the decades covered in this book.

Those limits require explanation, not castigation. As Ralph Miliband once noted of the left's historic tendency to suffer crippling internal divisions, there is little to be gained by 'try[ing] to apportion "blame" for a situation which had been made inevitable by the whole evolution of working-class movements in advanced capitalist countries ... More relevant ... is to note the fact of division, its debilitating effects upon the working-class movements, and the corresponding advantages which the conservative parties have derived from it.'[39] There is plenty of evidence to suggest that class differences *did* matter to workers in Calgary. What requires exploration and explanation is why and how awareness of those differences failed to translate into effective and united political action.

Part 1
Class Formation, 1883-1913

1
From Cow Town to Hub of Industry

Calgary can claim two historical beginnings, and the Canadian state played a crucial role in both. Originally, the settlement was established in 1875, following the federal government's decision to locate a North-West Mounted Police (NWMP) fort at the fork of the Bow and Elbow Rivers in order to safeguard the area's Native population against unscrupulous whisky traders. Over the next eight years, Calgary's population grew modestly to fewer than 500 residents, whose everyday needs were met by the town's two major supply stores, the Hudson's Bay Company and I.G. Baker & Co. Local industry was limited to the occasional craftsman producing high-quality luxury items, and a single sawmill – owned and managed by former NWMP officer Major James Walker – that provided timber ample to meet the demands of construction in Calgary. In short, there was no reason to believe that Calgary would, in the space of three short decades, become one of Canada's most populous cities and the largest centre of industrial capitalism between Winnipeg and the Pacific coast.[1]

Capitalism comes to Calgary. Employees stand outside James Walker's sawmill in the 1880s. The sawmill was Canada's first significant industrial establishment. Walker is seated on the far right.

Calgary's second start came in 1883 with the arrival of the Canadian Pacific Railway (CPR). That the CPR had a dramatic impact on Calgary was as evident to contemporary observers as it has been to historians.[2] In September 1882, Frank White, a ranch employee from nearby Cochrane, stood on a hill overlooking Calgary and gazed down upon '16 log shanties and houses, 9 Indian and 8 other tents besides [the] Police quarters, taking everything in site [sic].' When the CPR tracks first reached Calgary a year later, engineer Peter Turner Bone noted that the settlement still consisted 'almost entirely of tents.' This changed during the following year, as the number of permanent buildings rose to almost 250. These included 107 dwelling houses, more than 50 stores, shops, and offices, and 5 churches. Reflecting this transformation, Calgary was formally incorporated as a town towards the end of 1884. As one new resident noted with prescience in the spring of that busy year, 'From a little cluster of log buildings and shacks, which a few weeks ago on the east side of the Elbow River comprised the town of Calgary, there has sprung into existence a community which must soon put on metropolitan airs.' Turner Bone returned to Calgary in 1885, having spent the previous two years working in British Columbia, and was 'greatly struck with the growth it had made.' Expansion and development continued throughout the remainder of the 1880s, causing one visitor from Montreal in 1888 to write that Calgary's 'dwelling houses and shops have greatly increased in number, and the more recent buildings of brick and granite are handsome and very substantial.'[3]

The initial impact of the CPR was to reinforce Calgary's function as a mercantile settlement.[4] Construction crews who laid the tracks and built the roundhouse in Calgary required food, clothing, and entertainment. Enterprising merchants soon established new retail and wholesale stores to meet this demand. The CPR had subcontracted much of its construction work to other firms, many of whom subsequently placed their own orders for equipment and materials with Calgary branches of eastern-based establishments. The latter, of course, were eager to exploit the expanding markets of the Canadian West. In the mid-1880s, the first wave of settlers and ranchers further increased local demand for imported supplies.[5] As a result, by 1885 Calgary's two original wholesale companies had been joined by a host of other merchants, grocers, and butchers, as well as a dozen or so small building-contractors and two newspaper publishers. Trade in these years was brisk and substantial, totalling almost $500,000 as early as 1884.[6]

One of these traders in early Calgary was Isaac Freeze, whose experience illustrates the many commercial success stories in this period. In the spring of 1883, Freeze left his home and family in New Brunswick to establish himself on Canada's expanding frontier of opportunity. Upon his arrival in Calgary, he became somewhat despondent about his prospects. 'I don't imagine I will strike anything in this country,' he confided in a letter to his wife. 'Every branch of business is overdone and people here live more by their wits than by hard labor.' Despite these reservations, Freeze purchased four acres of land at a cost of forty dollars and built a small lumber shack from which he ran a grocer's store. Using the capital he had brought with him, he ordered $3,000 of stock from a wholesaler in Winnipeg and set about business. By August 1883, he had sold more than two-thirds of this amount and was clearing up to $300 each week. Two months later, another letter to his wife underlined the extent to which his original pessimism had been premature. 'I think the chances for making money in this country are very good,' he told her, adding the key proviso, 'that is if a person has capital to start with.'[7]

While the success of Freeze and other merchants reflected the town's rapid growth in the 1880s, Calgary's future development rested largely on the fortunes of local industrial and manufacturing concerns. The town was fortunate in this respect, for southern Alberta was blessed with a rich supply of exploitable natural resources. Canmore and Anthracite, for example, contained coalfields, large deposits of iron ore, vast timber forests, and shallow fast-running rivers that, as the *Calgary Herald* noted, 'render[ed] the utilizing of the water power most feasible for manufacturing purposes.'[8] The same point was made rather more excitedly by J.G. Fitzgerald, a local publisher and the town's deputy-sheriff, who in 1885 wrote that 'it requires no stretch of the imagination to picture the future Calgary as the manufacturing emporium of the new west, possessing as it does splendid water power and an unlimited supply of coal.'[9]

Data regarding the size of Calgary's manufacturing firms do not exist for the 1880s, but the evidence available for the district of Alberta provides some insight (see Table 1.1). By 1885, Alberta was home to some sixty firms, employing a total of 215 workers and $208,100 in capital. Wages paid that year amounted to $90,105, an average of $419 per employee, while the value of total production came to $392,740, or $1,827 per worker.

Table 1.1

Manufacturing establishments in Alberta, 1885-91

	Firms	Employees	Wages ($)	Raw materials ($)	Capital ($)	Output ($)
1885	60	215	90,000	189,000	208,000	393,000
1891	143	596	285,000	418,000	1,214,000	1,044,000

Sources: J.G. Fitzgerald, *Business Directory of Calgary, Alberta, Canada* (Calgary: Calgary Herald Publishing, 1885), 82-5; *Census of Canada* (1891), 3: 387. Figures have been rounded.

Based on these figures, the average manufacturing establishment in the mid-1880s was a small operation, with fewer than four workers, almost $3,500 in capital and an annual output of approximately $6,500. Yet such a picture is misleading, for the figures conceal the fact that a handful of large sawmills dominated the region's economy in the 1880s. Although they accounted for just 15 percent of all establishments, the nine sawmills operating in 1885 employed 50 percent of all labour and capital involved in manufacturing. As a result, whereas each sawmill employed an average of thirteen hands, firms in other industries employed fewer than two. The same contrast holds for capital investment. Sawmills represented an average investment of more than $13,000; for other industries the figure was just $1,800.[10]

Industrial development and diversification in the years after 1885 lessened the region's dependence on sawmill production. By 1891, the number of firms in Alberta had more than doubled, the manufacturing workforce had almost tripled, and total capital investment had increased virtually six-fold. Total industrial output had risen in value by 165 percent to $1 million. In the six years since 1885, Alberta's sawmills had continued to expand, but at less than the overall rate of industrial growth, with a resultant decline in their dominant position. Their share of industrial labour and capital dropped from 50 to 40 percent – still substantial, admittedly – while their contribution to total industrial output dipped slightly from 35 to 33 percent.[11]

Among the 129 other industries, size and performance varied widely. At one end of the spectrum, a dressmaker's shop and a milliner's shop between them employed just three seamstresses and had capital worth only $300. At the other end, two iron foundries provided work for fifty-five metal workers and accounted for $60,000 capital. In between were several other large firms, including a woollen factory (twelve employees, $17,000 capital), a wood-planing mill (four employees, $44,000 capital), and a meat-curing plant (twenty employees, $169,000 capital). As it had in central Canadian cities a generation earlier, industrial capitalism came to the prairies in many shapes and sizes, and the experience of work varied accordingly.[12]

Calgary's own economy was similarly developed and diversified by the early 1890s. Visiting Calgary in 1891, Conservative politician Nicholas Flood Davin remarked that 'the amount of business transacted here is greater than many towns double its size.'[13] That same year, the town's twenty-eight manufacturing firms employed some 170 individuals. Capital investment and output for these establishments amounted to $405,000 and $259,000, respectively. As with Alberta itself, a few large concerns dominated Calgary industry in these years, such as the Calgary Woollen Manufacturing Company, capitalized at $25,000. In November 1886, a large fire had burned down sixteen of the small community's wood-frame buildings, after which citizens and contractors alike preferred to use fireproof sandstone, carved from local quarries. Increased demand for new residences in the late 1880s stimulated this industry, with the result that by 1891 local entrepreneurs were spending $250,000 on construction works. One company that benefited from this early boom was the J.F. Peel brickyard, an operation that covered five acres of land on the banks of the Bow River, employed fifteen men, and produced 2,000 pressed bricks per week. Meanwhile, G.D. Hamilton had set up Calgary's first iron foundry on Atlantic Avenue, providing castings and plates for bridges and other building projects. Such enterprises in the 1880s and early 1890s provided the basis for Calgary's economic explosion after the turn of the century.[14]

As the nineteenth century neared its end, however, Calgary's economy faced its first serious setback. Homestead entries were modest before 1896, with the result that Calgary had to import the bulk of its flour and other foodstuffs. In 1892, for example, the town paid $85,000 for imported flour. A series of dry years in the early 1890s aggravated the situation, despite aggressive local efforts to promote grain growing, and resulted in a short but sharp economic depression in the town.[15] Some businesses, such as the *Tribune* newspaper, failed to survive the downturn. Calgary's population, standing at 4,000 in 1891, went into a decline and had barely recovered by the end of the century. Social effects of the depression – unemployment, poverty, inadequate housing, and increases in crime and prostitution – became issues of widespread public concern for the first time. Calgary's prospects no longer seemed so bright.[16]

The depression affected local wage earners and merchants alike. In the summer of 1896, carpenters complained that they had recently been without work for as long as four months at a time. Tradesmen who previously had freely offered credit to their customers ceased this practice as bad debts began to mount. This move to a cash-only policy hit many individuals and families already hurt by the depressed conditions, notably those who were dependent on a regular wage and who lacked any appreciable savings on which they might draw. 'The times are hard and have been hard on the working class,' complained one writer to the *Herald* in February 1895, 'and they will support any change which promises relief.' Five months later, another correspondent echoed this call for public assistance for those in need, claiming that 'The talk on the street is chiefly of the enquiring kind ... They want to know what steps the council is taking to stop the hard times becoming worse. They want to know how those out of work are going to live the coming winter.' The council, as far as it can be determined, was unable to provide an answer.[17]

Not everybody suffered as a result of the 1890s depression. Many of those firms that survived its impact emerged stronger than before, if only due to diminished competition. More importantly, the mid-1890s was also a period of readjustment and consolidation for capital. Despite the depressed conditions, external investment in Calgary industries continued and was instrumental in establishing a number of new operations, including J. Stone's pork-packing plant, Donald McLean's flour mill, A.E. Cross's Brewing and Malting Company, Brisco and Watson's tannery, and a large cold-storage plant. Each of these enterprises went on to expand and prosper in the post-1900 economic boom.[18] In addition to their reliance upon capital from central Canada and elsewhere, these new firms also all sought new markets beyond the immediate prairie hinterland, expanding into Asia and Australia, for example.[19] Their success encouraged a new wave of optimism for Calgary's prospects, with the *Herald* noting in October 1896 that there was 'no reason why we should despair of the future of our city. We have now established here a number of legitimate and excellent business institutions which look for their future support ... [to] the gradual and healthy growth of the immense ranching and agricultural country tributary to this city.'[20] The upturn in world wheat prices and the election of Wilfrid Laurier's Liberal government assisted economic recovery across western Canada in the years after 1896. Encouraged by the federal government's active promotion of settler immigration and the renewed promise of wealth on the prairies, immigrants flocked westwards in the thousands from central Canada, Britain, and Europe.[21]

Calgary, along with many other prairie urban centres, reaped the reward of this dramatic influx of labour. Table 1.2 profiles Calgary's industrial growth after 1891. The city experienced a further consolidation and concentration of its industrial capital. By 1901, Calgary factories had an average workforce of thirty-one people, compared with just six a decade earlier. Average capital investment nearly tripled from $15,000 to $43,000, while the value of output per factory rose from less than $10,000 to almost $60,000. Impressive as they were, such increases paled next to those of the decade 1901-11. While the average labour force in these years expanded only moderately to forty-six, average capitalization and output rose to $284,500 and $168,500, respectively.[22]

As Calgary's factories continued to expand and multiply, they became the source of employment for more and more of Calgary's available workers. By 1906, there were already several factories regularly employing more than 100 workers each, including the Alberta Biscuit Company, the Alberta Cigar Company, the Alberta Portland Cement Company, Cushing's sash-and-door factory, the Great West Saddlery Company, and the Gordon Nail and Wire Works. The Riverside Lumber Company joined this list in 1911, and in the following year the CPR constructed its vast new railway workshops at Ogden in east Calgary, which the company predicted would soon employ more than 1,000 men.[23]

Table 1.2

Manufacturing establishments in Calgary, 1891-1911

	Firms	Capital ($)	Employees	Wages ($)	Output ($)
1891	28	405,000	169	97,000	259,000
1901	10	432,000	307	175,000	599,000
1905	18	2,145,000	794	520,000	2,304,000
1911	46	13,083,000	2,133	1,570,000	7,752,000

Sources: Census of Canada (1911), 3: 350; *Postal Census of Manufactures Canada* (Ottawa: J. de L. Taché, 1917), 186

Historians have frequently ascribed much of western Canada's growth in this period to the success of boosterist policies – publicity campaigns to promote the general advantages, real or otherwise, of a specific location to would-be investors.[24] In the case of Calgary, Max Foran argues that a convergence of economic and political interests resulted in the formation of successive business minded administrations that shared such attitudes.[25] While this is substantially true, the argument should not be pressed too far. For example, of the 116 men elected to council in the years 1884-1912, just 25 – or 22 percent – were unquestionably members of Calgary's manufacturing class. Any political favouritism that local industrialists gained from this level of representation was balanced by the election of 26 retail merchants and 65 assorted professionals, real estate agents, and hoteliers.[26] The overall nature of this assembly may have produced an approach towards civic government that generally favoured industry and promoted the future of capital investment, but it fell short of handing manufacturers a blank cheque. In 1892, for example, a meeting of ratepayers endorsed A.E. Cross's request for a ten-year exemption from taxes on his proposed brewery. Only factory owner and Liberal supporter William Cushing opposed the idea, not so much because it offended his laissez-faire sensibilities but because he was a confirmed temperance advocate. For Cushing's lack of public spirit the *Herald* delivered the following reproach: 'Our citizens are too much in dead earnest, they are too thoroughly alive to the importance of establishing industries in the town, for any opposition to develope [sic] ... The unanimity that prevails speaks well for the public spirit of Calgary, and only a mischief maker would seek to disturb it.' Despite this display of public and press support for the brewery, the council refused Cross's application. Disappointed but not undaunted, Cross nevertheless went ahead and set up the immensely successful Calgary Brewing and Malting Company.[27]

This incident throws into question the necessity of boosterism in attracting capital investment. Although Calgary's city council certainly was

Beer break. Employees at the Calgary Brewing and Malting Company, c 1910-2. Seated front and centre is a young apprentice worker.

prepared to offer industrialists incentives – ranging from tax exemptions and cash bonuses to free land – to invest locally, it did so on the perceived merits of each case. In 1900, city clerk Charles McMillan wrote to Thomas Kennedy of Nelson, British Columbia, offering him a free site and a ten-year tax exemption if he would agree to locate a woollen factory within the city. However, when Minneapolis industrialist C.H. Mohr wrote in 1906 requesting a cash bonus and free site for his proposed flour mill, McMillan's successor, H.E. Gillis, scribbled on the request the forthright response, 'I do not see what can be done for this man.' Not all potential investors even sought such help, of course, and a few actually rejected it when offered. In 1901, Messrs. N. Bell and M. Liss turned down the city's award of a year's tax exemption for their planned cigar factory, explaining that they wanted to stand 'entirely upon [their] own merits ... [and] participate in municipal benefits without feeling that [they] have not rendered a quid pro quo.'[28] Even without the proffered handout, the Alberta Cigar Company went on to become one of Calgary's most profitable concerns.

While there is no question that urban centres across the West practised variations of boosterism in this period, there is reason to question its actual significance in the decision-making process of investment. Indeed, some historians have come to wonder 'whether communities were actually able to attract substantial outside investment' by their own actions. Calgary's council certainly appears to have been more judicious in its allocation of public money than historians of the city have sometimes implied, and the success of the Alberta Cigar Company suggests that boosterist policies were neither a necessary nor sufficient condition of local industrial growth.[29] Boosters themselves occasionally acknowledged this fact, as the writer in *Prosperous Calgary* (1908) indicated: 'Business is business and hard-headed, practical presidents and general managers of the largest and most successful farm machinery concerns in Canada and the United States don't place immense warehouses and engage large staffs for the sole purpose of pleasing the residents of any town or locality, and when Calgary is chosen it is because from a business standpoint it offers more inducements in the way of transhipment facilities, proximity to consumers, and staff accommodation.'[30] From this point of view, the long-term advantages of a particular site were far more important than any short-term incentives in influencing investment decisions. Accordingly, the practice of boosterism was important not in its absolute ability to attract new capital, but in its relative success in securing investment dollars away from other potential locations. Even then, there is room to doubt its significance, for as historian Paul Voisey argues many small towns in western Canada adopted boosterist policies and ideas identical to those in Calgary and other large centres, yet failed to enjoy the same material expansion.[31]

In any event, it is unlikely that even the best-fought booster campaign would have met with success had it not been for the accumulation of large capital surpluses in central Canada, the United States, Britain, and western Europe. The availability of these surpluses for investment was the key to the west's expansion. As the rate of profit in Britain and other industrial nations began to decline in the late nineteenth century, international capitalists sought new investment opportunities that offered comparatively high rates of return. Many such investors believed this to be true of western Canada in the fifteen or so years before the First World War.

The development of Canada's banking system in this period was a further crucial element in the growth of western cities like Calgary. The rapid expansion of financial institutions in the West after 1897 facilitated the large-scale flow of capital.[32] As the *Monetary Times* noted in 1905, central Canadian 'industry and business are quiet, and capital, being superabundant, finds difficulty in finding profitable openings for employment. In the West, the reverse condition is the fact ... The only thing needed is capital, and that is precisely what the East has to spare.'[33]

Calgary benefited from this westward tide of capital after 1900, a development that contrasted greatly with its pattern of capital accumulation in the 1880s and 1890s. In those years, most industrial investment came from local men who had amassed surpluses from the ranching business and then sought to diversify their interests and so spread their risk base. Profits made from these early ventures were reinvested and stimulated further growth. In this manner, entrepreneurs such as William Cushing

Blood, sweat, and steers. Next to the CPR workshops, the Pat Burns meatpacking plant was Calgary's major industrial operation in the years before the First World War, employing several hundred workers.

and Pat Burns built up large concerns without going into debt or having to seek additional funds on the open capital market.

This situation changed in the early years of the twentieth century. Industrialists from the United States in particular began to invest directly in existing firms and also established branch plants of American companies in the city. In 1912, for example, an Idaho brick company created a new plant that employed 100 men and had $100,000 capital. The following year, a firm from Minneapolis invested $2 million in a new traction engine manufacture. In 1904, local capitalists R.J. Hutchings, J.J. Young, and G.H. Webster convinced backers from Ontario and Scotland to support their proposal for a soap factory. That same year, Joseph Brunner of Brussels, Edward Jacobs of Antwerp, and P.Y. West of Paris each invested large sums in separate establishments in Calgary. In such fashion, Calgary became part of the international network of capitalism.[34]

Despite the growing importance of direct investment from the United States, the bulk of loan capital continued to come from British capital markets. In 1905, the Western Canada Pulp and Paper Company borrowed $300,000 in London; in 1908, the Western Canada Flour Mills borrowed $225,000 from the same source; and in 1910, the Calgary Power Company followed suit and raised $350,000. Even Pat Burns, the preeminent local success story, borrowed $200,000 in 1911 to help recapitalize his meatpacking plant. The city council itself was also heavily dependent on credit secured in London, borrowing more than $500,000 between 1905 and 1911 to help fund public enterprises such as the street railway system. Calgary ranked sixth among Canadian cities in terms of its dependence on British loans.[35]

The demand for greater capital investment produced changes in the structure of Calgary's enterprises. For example, it occasioned the emergence of the joint-stock company and the adoption of limited liability practices. By 1907, there were 161 joint-stock companies operating in the province of Alberta, with total capital worth $18.5 million. Sixty of these were the product of direct foreign investment.[36] In Calgary, many of the smaller family businesses and partnerships of the 1880s and 1890s survived into the twentieth century, but found themselves increasingly overshadowed by newer forms of organization that could boast greater capital resources and higher levels of production.[37] The Alberta Manufacturing Company, Calgary's first soap factory, was incorporated as a joint-stock company in 1904 so that it might undertake renovations and purchase new machinery. At its first annual general meeting as a limited company in October 1906, company directors confirmed the success of this move by declaring a 10 percent dividend and announcing plans to increase capitalization from $50,000 to $250,000. 'That a young company ... should have been so phenomenally successful in such a short time,' enthused the *Herald,* 'is taken as a good indication of the possibilities of Calgary from a manufacturing and distributing standpoint.'[38]

The trend towards larger concerns was unmistakable. By 1911, almost half of Calgary's firms had capital valued at $50,000 or higher. Between them, these same establishments produced 94 percent of Calgary's entire industrial output. They also accounted for 86 percent of Calgary's manufacturing labour force, employing an average of seventy-six workers per firm. By comparison, companies capitalized below $50,000 employed an average of just twelve operatives each.[39] Inevitably, this concentration of capital shaped the daily experiences of many Calgary workers as the growth of factories brought them together in larger and larger numbers than before. In doing so, it provided the context in which workers might recognize a common identity as wage earners, sharing the same basic problems and grievances above their sectional, craft-based differences.

At the same time, the expansion of factory production also intensified the division of labour and so diminished the dependency of employers and managers on the received knowledge and customary practices of their skilled craftsmen.[40] In any sizeable factory, the various tasks to be performed demanded a wide range of acquired skills. For example, a sugar beet factory established in 1904 at a cost of $800,000, ran its machinery around the clock and required the services of 100 'skilled, high salaried men' and 200 'ordinary laborers.' This combination of skilled and unskilled workers was fairly characteristic of Calgary's factories in this period. The Western Machinery and Boiler Manufacturing Company required the services of sixteen expert engineers and Shelly's Bakery employed more than forty skilled operatives, despite – or, rather, due to – both being extensively mechanized operations.[41] Factory employment involved the reskilling as much as the deskilling of workers: in itself, it neither curtailed the demand for skilled employees nor created an undifferentiated working class.[42]

In this way, factories fragmented the workforce even as they brought workers closer together in proximity and daily experience. The increased use of machinery in production enhanced this division of labour. These changes occurred unevenly in Calgary during the period 1883-1913, and their impact varied from industry to industry, from company to company. Nevertheless, by 1913 Calgary's industrial profile bore little resemblance to that of a decade or two earlier. The example of William Cushing's sash-and-door factory serves as an illustration of this transformation.

William Cushing was born in Ontario in 1852, the son of an immigrant farmer from Norwich, England.[43] He pursued his father's occupation until 1879, when he indentured as a carpenter. Four years later he moved west to Calgary, where he formed a small construction partnership with Stephen Jarrett. By 1885, the business had prospered sufficiently for Cushing to branch out on his own and start his first sash-and-door factory. He spent his first decade not only making doors but, as he later recalled, 'binding friendships, establishing business relations, in fact, building goodwill.' The original factory was a small building containing machinery worth only a few hundred dollars, and the enterprise employed just three skilled employees, who performed all of the various operations. Cushing expanded the business in 1887 and again in 1890, at which time he moved it to a larger premises after securing a contract to construct part of the new Hudson's Bay store. The new factory measured twelve by thirty metres, was powered by a twenty-five-horsepower boiler engine imported from Galt, Ontario, at a cost of $6,000, and employed a workforce of twenty. The wood was turned, planed, and moulded on the ground floor; the general workshop and factory proper were upstairs. This physical division enabled Cushing to separate and simplify the production processes and to harness them to his new power supply. As a result, he was soon able to boast of a much-improved productivity in which it took just five minutes to produce a door from start to finish.[44]

Following the influx of settlers in the late 1890s, Cushing's fortunes began to flourish. His business provided homes for both 'the needy and frugal immigrant who was erecting but a small shack' and 'the more prosperous newcomer who contemplated putting up a substantial dwelling.'

On the job. An artist's 1891 impression of the various mechanized processes performed inside William Cushing's sash-and-door factory shows the operation to be a symbol of Calgary's rapid industrial development at the turn of the century.

By the turn of the century, there were few buildings along Stephen Avenue, Calgary's main thoroughfare, that did not bear the mark of Cushing's factory. So good was business, in fact, that shortly after 1900 Cushing expanded his factory once again, this time into premises that spanned forty-two city lots and employed more than 100 workers. Three large boilers and one 150-horsepower steam engine powered the mill's machinery, while a separate electric dynamo lit the premises. The increased division of labour and degree of mechanization were such that one visitor to the factory in 1904 commented, 'All hand work is dispensed with, except the actual putting of the door together, and this is an operation of only a minute.' A power elevator connected different stages of work on the various floors, while the entire factory was joined to the CPR tracks by means of a feeder line in order to speed shipment in and out. That same year, the factory turned out 40,000 doors and windows, making it the largest sash-and-door producer in western Canada.[45] The phenomenal rise of William Cushing in just twenty years stood as a symbol of industrialism's unmistakable arrival in Calgary.

There would be no turning back; the factory had come to stay. Few Calgarians opposed the advent of industrialism outright, but occasionally a voice wistful for the preindustrial past could be heard. A whimsical piece on Calgary, published in the *Monetary Times* in 1908, captured such ambiguous feelings about the presence of the factory on the prairie frontier. 'A peculiar regretful tinge is sometimes heard in the conversation of the old timer. Gazing from his window across a pile of smokestacks, he sees sent up to the skies a sort of unending factory thanksgiving. It is the brief, periodical reign of sentiment. He starts; then writes out a wages cheque to keep wheels and a few hundred Albertan homes going.'[46] The 'reign of sentiment' was, of course, no match for the rule of the dollar. Driven by the demands of competing within regional, national, and even international markets, all of Calgary's major industrial establishments turned to mechanization as the primary means of increasing output. In 1906, for example, the *Calgary Herald* proudly displayed its own latest piece of machinery – the new Cox Duplex Perfecting Press – that produced a seamless roll of newsprint. The implementation of this device increased output to 6,000 pages per hour and was heralded by the paper's management as a great saving of time and labour.[47]

The economic and industrial growth that took place between 1883 and 1913 – scarcely more than a single generation – transformed Calgary from 'Cow-town to Hub of Industry,' in the words of one local writer.[48] The rapid increase in population stimulated building activity on a massive scale. The cultivation of wheat, beef cattle, and timber supported initial processing and manufacturing industries before 1900. The development and maturation of Calgary society supported a growing service sector. Originally attracted to the West by the magnet of high nominal wages and the promise of upward mobility, those men and women who found employment in the city's industries soon learned the harsh pervasive realities of industrial capitalism. As David Bercuson has remarked of urban workers on the prairies in general, 'for most of them the west was not a new land of opportunity with unbounded horizons; it was merely a change of scenery.'[49] But the nature of that scenery varied from one city to the next, for each was also the location of unique social conditions. If the realities of industrial capitalism necessitated the existence of a distinct working class, other social realities – including the daily experience of work, gender, and ethnicity – shaped the disposition of Calgary's workers to think and behave as a class.

2
Social Divisions and Class Disposition

The creation of a stable class of wage-earning producers was central to Calgary's industrial revolution. This process of proletarianization did not mean that the same workers necessarily had a 'disposition to behave as a class, to define themselves in their actions and in their consciousness in relation to other groups of people in class ways.'[1] Indeed, as historian Michael Hanagan notes, 'Proletarian identity does not come included as a standard accessory in the crates that bring the machine technologies to the factory; it has to be constructed using local materials drawn from the larger context of social life in which factory and machines are located.'[2] In Calgary, this larger context included the influence of gender, ethnicity, religion, and politics, influences that shaped and limited the disposition of workers to think and behave as a single class.

The identification of wage earners as the primary constituent of working-class life has been the subject of much debate and reassessment in recent years. Feminist critics, in particular, have argued that this formulation represents an unwarranted privileging of the male-dominated world of production. Alice Kessler-Harris argues that 'Operating from a particular, and seemingly natural standpoint, many labor historians have perceived the world through a lens that offers only partial vision: that of the male worker ... In the formation of class, ideas about what constitutes work play a significant, even a crucial role. Such ideas are explicitly gendered, and the identities out of which they emerge are constructed relationally: nurtured, shaped and directed by the changing household and community.'[3] In the Canadian context, recent works by Bettina Bradbury, Suzanne Morton, and Joy Parr, among others, have emphasized the centrality of the household in determining the contours of working-class experience.[4] Across industrializing Canada in the nineteenth and early twentieth centuries, the regular wages of even a skilled worker were rarely, if ever, sufficient to support himself and his family. Accordingly, the development of household strategies to supplement this source of income was essential if economic hardship and poverty were to be kept at bay. As a result, while dependency on wages was a central feature of working-class existence, it did not in itself define or determine the way in which workers regarded their own lives and situations, their disposition to think in class terms.

It might be noted here that even the shared experience of wage labour did not necessarily create a common disposition or sense of unity among Calgary workers. In objective terms, the twin processes of industrialization and concentration of capital were inseparable from the creation of a distinct class of wage-earning employees. Yet at the same time, the structural pattern of industrialization in Calgary was such that it limited the ability or potential of workers to view themselves as members of a common class. In the years before 1913, for example, the diversity and unevenness of economic development in different industries meant that substantial concentrations of labour remained the exception in Calgary, not the rule. Small workshops coexisted alongside larger factories, and so prevented any homogenization of labour.[5] By 1911, the number of men and women employed by local manufactures was more than 3,000, roughly one-sixth of the city's entire workforce, with several establishments each employing more than 100 workers. On average, however, the number of employees per factory remained fewer than thirty.[6] Thus while the experience of labour may have varied little in essentials from one factory to the next, the relatively small size of most individual plants reduced the likelihood that factory employees might develop a sense of identity commensurate to their overall strength in numbers.

The same holds true for two of Calgary's other major employers of labour, the construction industry and domestic services. In 1911, roughly one-quarter of all men employed in Calgary worked within the various building trades, a concentration of labour as promising as any for the foundation of a cohesive working-class identity. Although construction workers were certainly among the most militant in Calgary, accounting for almost two-thirds of all strikes held between 1900 and 1914, open dissent among the industry's different crafts – including a long-standing rift between stonemasons and stonecutters over job jurisdiction – intensified as mechanization and technical innovations eroded their former privileged positions.[7] Even had this not been the case, construction work itself was, by definition, temporary in nature, and bonds formed on the job typically were short-lived. This fact, together with the unavoidable seasonal restrictions upon construction activity in Calgary, made the building site a less promising location for the development of working-class awareness than might have been expected. In the case of domestic servants, who accounted for almost 2,500, or 12 percent, of Calgary's total workforce, the aggregate figure belies the typical isolation in which each individual spent most of his or her working day.[8]

Only within the local transportation industry did a large concentration of workers regularly toil alongside each other. In 1911, there were more than 2,600 workers employed by Calgary's transport services, the bulk of whom spent their days at the large Ogden CPR works in east Calgary. Accounting for some 13 percent of the city's working population, transportation workers formed the single body of labour whose daily experience afforded a glimpse of the collective power of workers as a class. It is little surprise, therefore, that railway machinists soon acquired a reputation as labour radicals in Calgary.[9]

While the structure of Calgary's workforce may have inhibited any disposition towards class outlook or behaviour, it might be argued that their common status as wage earners provided workers with a psychological bond that set them apart from other social classes.[10] Through the routine exchange of labour power in return for wages, the potential existed for workers to regard themselves as a class distinct from those who directed and compensated their efforts. Yet while the weekly wage of the head of a household – usually an adult male – remained the key source of a family's income, there is reason to suppose that few families were ever totally dependent on a single wage. Instead, the importance of wages, both in providing financial security and in shaping class attitudes, needs to be placed within the broader context of the various economic enterprises undertaken by working-class families.[11]

Wages tended to be higher in western Canada than elsewhere during this period, but higher prices for many staple goods and services offset any nominal gains enjoyed by workers in cities such as Calgary. Throughout the years before 1913, wage levels were generally inadequate to meet the monthly needs of a worker with a family of four, the size of household then adopted as the standard by the Department of Labour. Calgary was not unusual in this respect, for recent assessments of the impact of industrialization on real wages have, for all their increasing sophistication and complexity, essentially confirmed Michael Piva's early observation that 'workers did not benefit from the wealth they toiled to produce.'[12]

In the case of Calgary, evidence for the years before 1900 is patchy and provides only a bare idea of wages and the cost of living. In 1891, for example, the average daily wage for carpenters was $2.75, for bricklayers $3.50, tailors $2.00, and general labourers $1.75. Female domestic servants received just $14.00 per month, although they were usually provided with room and board. At the same time, the 'official' weekly cost of feeding a family of five was roughly $6.50, while additional expenses included rent, fuel, clothing, medical care, and perhaps some leisure activities.[13]

The years after 1900, for which more complete data are available, saw a general upward trend in hourly wage rates, although its impact on actual wage levels was lessened by a reduction in the number of hours worked per week. The overall effect, nevertheless, was to raise the amount of money a worker took home each week and to increase the amount of free time in which to spend it.[14]

With retail prices rising by 40 percent between 1903 and 1912, many workers saw their nominal wage improvements in this period wiped out completely. This was true, for example, of the skilled metal trades. Others, including skilled printers and construction craftsmen, were only marginally more fortunate, with inflation severely limiting, but not obliterating, their gains. The cumulative impact of inflation was clear by December 1911, near the peak of Calgary's prewar economic boom, when not one of the fourteen unionized trades that regularly reported wage details to the federal government recorded a monthly income sufficient to meet the Department of Labour's own recommended minimum family budget of $127. A bricklayer on union pay, for example, might earn $118.80 for a full month of employment, equal to 93 percent of the approved minimum. No other trade did even this well. At the bottom end of the scale, factory labourers and street railway employees earned, respectively, just 54 and 51 percent of the sum required to feed, house, and clothe a family of five.[15]

Given such discrepancies, few working-class households can have depended completely on a single wage. In her study of nineteenth-century Montreal, Bettina Bradbury argues that 'Families clearly attempted to shape their own economies by adjusting the number of wage-earners to meet their expenses when they were able to do so. Additional wage-earners were not only needed but were used by all fractions of the working class, with differences stemming from the economic conjuncture, the nature of the labour market, their own life cycle, and earning power.'[16] Dual incomes were probably a common feature in Calgary, although how common is difficult to assess due to the limited evidence available. Still, approximately one-half of all women employed in Calgary in 1911 were aged twenty-five or over, and it is reasonable to suppose that a fair proportion of these were married to local men and so represented a second household income. At the same time, however, how long women – either married or single – remained in the labour force was in part influenced by the late-Victorian ideal that a man should be able to support his family. This notion of the 'family wage' precluded the need for – or right of – women to work.[17]

At the same time, there is some evidence to suggest that child labour also helped to supplement the income of households in this period. Although there were only 152 youths (aged ten to fourteen) officially employed in 1911, mainly in factories, offices, and in private homes as domestic servants, many more worked in the twilight world of bootblacks, newsboys, and street vendors. City councillors viewed the rise of child labour as a serious concern, and in 1912 passed a by-law prohibiting the employment of boys under the age of ten and girls under fourteen. Where the state did not intervene was in the area of unpaid labour that many children, particularly young daughters, continued to perform inside the home, work that was invaluable at a time before labour-saving devices were common household items. The extent to which the proceeds of child labour, both paid and unpaid, contributed to household incomes remains a matter for speculation, but they serve as a further indication that a single wage was inadequate to meet the needs of a typical family.[18]

In her study of Montreal, Bradbury describes the various measures adopted by working-class families in order to 'manage and stretch' their formal incomes during the city's era of industrialization. Taking in boarders, performing odd jobs, scrounging or scavenging items discarded by others, taking advantage of the black market in stolen goods, and keeping animals for milk, meat, and eggs and a garden for vegetables and fruit were all ways in which wages could be supplemented.[19] Such was also the case in industrializing Calgary. For example, cows, pigs, and chickens were a common feature of domestic life, not merely during the frontier years of the late nineteenth century but well into the 1920s and beyond.[20] At this time, keeping backyard livestock was sufficiently widespread in the Hillhurst district of northwest Calgary that a herdsman would, for a small wage, collect cows from households each morning, walk them to nearby hills to graze, and then return them in the evening.[21] Indeed, civic officials became worried over the threat posed by livestock to public health, and in 1905 they linked a spate of recent deaths in the city to the popular practice of freely dumping pig excrement and other waste matter in alleyways. In response, city council passed a series of by-laws designed to curb the keeping of hogs in the yards of private dwellings, overlooking or ignoring their important contribution to a household's economy.[22]

For some, prostitution provided an additional, though less palatable, means of supplementing a weekly wage. Trading sex for money was almost Calgary's oldest profession, for prostitutes had been among the first arrivals in 1883, hot on the heels of the CPR construction gangs. By 1900, various red-light districts had achieved local notoriety, notably that of Nose Creek, although their existence was frequently denied by local law enforcers.[23] Prostitution was rarely a full-time occupation, and the majority of women charged with the offence also claimed employment in some other line of work. Waitresses, dressmakers, and laundry workers feature prominently on police arrest sheets for prostitution for this period, as do those in other low-paying jobs. Keepers of 'disorderly houses' were commonly women in their thirties or forties; while some men also ran such brothels, more usually they acted as pimps for single prostitutes. In 1914, Calgary's Citizens' League – a body that served as moral watchdog, among other things – learned of the case of J.W. Mercer, a twenty-eight-year-old printer who had been arrested for 'living off the avails' of a prostitute. Offended that a respectable craftsman could resort to pimping, the league was further shocked to learn that the woman in question was Mercer's own wife.[24] Two years earlier, a local railway union had charged member Philip Ritter with 'unbecoming conduct & living off earnings of a prostitute.' Ritter attempted to escape the inevitable union trial by applying for a withdrawal card, but the union refused to let him resign, insisting instead 'that he be notified to appear to answer charges preferred against him.' In this area, at least, unions were determined to keep their own house in order.[25]

One way of escaping dependency on wage labour was to engage in small-scale entrepreneurialism or 'penny capitalism.' The West, of course, had long been characterized as a land of opportunity for the working man, and many who came to Calgary continued to pursue dreams of establishing their own business. As a result, alongside the city's large capital-intensive manufacturers there proliferated a series of penny capitalist outfits, characterized by historian John Benson as those small-scale businesses in which the owner remained responsible for every facet of the enterprise.[26] While penny capitalism offered the alluring prospect of economic independence, it was also fraught with danger. The experience of Stanley Ferns is a case in point. Ferns had been more or less content working as a union bricklayer until one day in 1910, when union officials called him into the office and accused him of moonlighting on weekends. In a fit of anger, Ferns flung his union card on the desk, stormed out of the office, and promptly quit his job. Using capital that he had amassed over the years, he then set up a small contracting partnership with his friend Ed Humphries. Unfortunately for Ferns, the realities of risk involved in penny capitalism soon scuttled his hopes of success. The business remained a rather vague form of partnership with unlimited liability, a situation aggravated by the fact that early profits went into a series of increasingly questionable real estate investments. When Calgary's economic boom ended in 1913 Humphries promptly disappeared, leaving Ferns holding title to worthless undeveloped lots and a range of debts he was able to repay only by borrowing further. Caught in a downward spiral of debt, Ferns sent his wife and son back to Ontario in 1915 and, virtually bankrupt, reentered the labour market as a harvest worker.[27]

Thomas Riley, a CPR machinist and future labour city councillor, was another individual who attempted to set himself up in business without much success. Having accumulated some capital through real estate speculation in the years 1903-7, Riley quit his job at the Ogden railway works in 1908 and launched his own machine shop. 'We tried to do too much on too little,' he later confessed, citing a lack of sufficient capital as the cause of this enterprise's rapid collapse. His next, and final, entrepreneurial scheme was a pool hall in nearby Bowden. Although successful at first, the business folded during the First World War when the bulk of its patrons enlisted to serve abroad. Bloodied if not beaten by his penny capitalist endeavours, Riley returned to the Ogden railway shops where he remained irregularly employed until 1930.[28] Other would-be capitalists did not even get as far as failure. In 1906, brothers Jack and Sam Hackman arrived in Calgary via the United States, having fled the latest pogrom in tsarist Russia. They worked as rock breakers for a Calgary paving company and tried to save money in order to start their own company. However, they found that no matter how hard they worked they were always 'cut off from drawing out any capital for any business enterprise,' as they had to send what little they did manage to save back to their father in Russia.[29]

Trade union officials maintained an ambiguous and often contradictory position on the question of penny capitalism. They welcomed the sense of freedom and autonomy that it provided workers by loosening their economic dependence upon employers. Yet, they also argued that penny capitalism perpetuated the belief that workers could – and even should – achieve upward mobility by dint of their own individual efforts, a belief that ran counter to the collective aims and cooperative principles of many unions. Underpinning union concern was the basic perception that, whatever benefits if might bring the individual, penny capitalism 'served the needs of capital rather than of labour.'[30] In Calgary, a dispute within the painters' union in 1904 illustrates the labour movement's somewhat ambivalent stance. In September that year, painters at the contracting firm of Bartholomew's struck in support of a wage demand and a limit on the number of apprentices hired. Mr Bartholomew eventually conceded these demands, but not before some of his men had quit the firm to form their own workshop. Immediately, Bartholomew complained both to the painters' union and to the local press that it was 'unfair that these men should be able to be in the union and take jobs' while Bartholomew himself could not be a union member. He clearly believed that the painters' continued membership in the union was at odds with their new position as entrepreneurs in the competitive world of Calgary's building industry. The union agreed. Recording secretary John Jones told Bartholomew that 'the union ... has made it a rule that, when any of its members start contracting they shall have no vote or voice in the transaction in [sic] the business of the union.' Paint workers could be either wage-earning union members or capitalist entrepreneurs; they could not be both. In practice, the dividing line was often blurred, for as Jones somewhat sheepishly admitted to Bartholomew, he himself had recently become a contractor and so was recording secretary in acting capacity only.[31]

Subsistence measures, second and third incomes, prostitution, and penny capitalism were all symptomatic of one basic fact in Calgary before 1913. Just as in other Canadian cities undergoing industrialization, a single wage was inadequate to support the average working-class family. Even among skilled male workers this was true. As in nineteenth-century Montreal, 'Working-class survival during the period of competitive capitalism depended as much as the unpaid or informal labour of women and children in the household as it did on wages. Struggles and strategies originating in the household were as important to standards of living as those of workers on the job.'[32] Such struggles and strategies, of course, involved not only household production but also the decisions that determined consumption patterns within each family. Historians such as Bradbury are clearly right, therefore, to argue that it was the household, as much as the workplace, in which working-class perceptions, attitudes, and disposition were forged.

This shift in focus, from wage labour and immediate workplace conflicts to the household, has deepened our understanding of class formation, particularly in its emphasis on the gendered differentiation of class experience. Nevertheless, the fact remains that under capitalism the exchange of labour power for wages is the ultimate determinant of inequalities, both between and within classes. As Bradbury herself remarks, 'differences of as little as twenty-five cents a day separated men in skilled trades, those in trades undergoing rapid transformation, and the unskilled. Each fraction was potentially capable of achieving a different standard of living in good times ... Wage disparities translated into observable differences in standards of living and survival strategies.'[33] In short, an increase in wages would lessen a family's dependence on other sources of income and so enable an alteration of household consumption patterns; but that improvement could come only through either direct or indirect conflict with capital at the point of production. The formal workplace, then, remains a crucial, if not absolute, determinant of class disposition. But a return to the workplace as the crucible in which the disposition of workers to think and behave as a class was ultimately formed is not to imply that the workplace, in itself, represented a common, binding arena of experience. Just as divisions of occupation and skill fragmented Calgary's workforce, so too did important social divisions such as gender and ethnicity. Both of these shaped the structure of Calgary's emergent working class and so tempered the disposition of workers to act in class ways.

Underpinning Calgary's industrial revolution was a phenomenal rise in population. Numbering just 400 in 1883, by 1901 there were more than 4,000 residents in the city. Over the next decade, Calgary's population rose by almost 900 percent to just short of 44,000, a rate of growth faster than that in any other city in Alberta.[34] This demographic explosion was not evenly distributed between men and women. In 1891, men outnumbered women by a hundred to eighty, and this figure remained unchanged a decade later. Yet by 1911, Calgary's male population had grown to more than 26,500, compared to a female population of just 17,000, with a resulting ratio of a hundred to sixty-five. Significantly, married men exceeded married women by almost 2,000, a statistic reflecting the experience of many men who had come west to Calgary with the intention of sending home for their wives once they had established themselves.[35]

This gender imbalance was reflected, indeed exaggerated, in the composition of Calgary's formal workforce. Taken at the peak of Calgary's initial period of industrialization, the census of 1911 provides a useful snapshot of the gendered division of labour in the city. Enumerators that June recorded a total of 18,505 males (aged ten and over) who were engaged in regular employment, compared to slightly fewer than 3,000 female employees. In terms of the total population, 70 percent of all males and 16 percent of all females were employed. The actual distribution of men and women in employment varied widely from occupation to occupation, as Table 2.1 illustrates.

In the resource-extraction occupations, building trades, and transportation industry, women found themselves all but excluded from employment. Virtually the only jobs they held in these areas were clerical in nature. And, although women accounted for nearly half of all professional

Table 2.1

Calgary occupations according to gender, 1911

	Total	Female %	Male %
All occupations	21,320	13.2	86.8
Agriculture, forestry, mining	986	0.1	99.9
Building trades	4,437	0.1	99.9
Domestic and personal service	2,482	47.2	52.3
Government	1,621	3.9	96.1
Manufacturing	3,222	11.7	88.3
Professional	1,443	42.9	57.1
Trade and merchandising	4,436	11.0	89.0
Transportation	2,693	0.3	99.7

Source: Census of Canada (1911), 6: 342-51

employees as well as those in domestic and personal service, closer examination of the census data reveals this apparent parity to be misleading. Of the 1,171 women employed in domestic and personal service, 65 percent were engaged as either plain servants or laundry workers; among male employees in this category, the respective figure was just 31 percent. Similarly, among the 619 female employees classified as professionals, more than three-quarters were concentrated in teaching, nursing, or stenography, whereas men were distributed more evenly across the professions. Dressmakers, tailors, and milliners accounted for 70 percent of all women employed in the manufacturing sector, while female employment in trade and merchandising occupations was mainly limited to office and clerical positions. Women workers in Calgary, therefore, not only found themselves in a distinct minority within the overall workforce, but also were concentrated – and to some extent isolated – within a far narrower range of occupations compared to their male counterparts. This numerical inferiority and relative isolation helped to foster the impression that the workplace in Calgary remained overwhelmingly a male-oriented, if not exclusively male-dominated, environment.[36]

Calgary's female and male workforces also differed in terms of age. In 1911, half of all employed women were under the age of twenty-five, compared with less than 30 percent of male workers (see Table 2.2). The concentration of working women in their teens and early twenties presumably indicates that many eventually quit their jobs to run the household economy and to raise children. The nearly 71 percent of working men aged twenty-five to sixty-four was far greater than the proportion of

Working women on the ladder to success? Calgary's female workforce, such as these employees of Wilkins's millinery shop in 1914, tended to be concentrated in a few occupations, including domestic service, the cloth trade, clerical work, and teaching.

similarly aged women. As Bradbury notes in the case of Montreal, a mixture of pragmatism and working-class ideology helped to ensure that 'girls and women seldom entered the workforce in proportions equivalent to their brothers or boys the same age, and that over their life courses their participation was totally different.'[37] This appears also to have been the case in Calgary. Between the ages of ten and fourteen, for example, boys outnumbered girls in the workplace by roughly 2.5 to 1. In the fourteen to twenty-five age group, this ratio rose to almost 3.75 to 1, and in the decades of mature adulthood from twenty-five to sixty-four men in the workforce outnumbered women by 9.5 to 1. Fifteen- or sixteen-year-old girls earned roughly half the wages paid to boys, and it therefore made economic sense for a family to keep daughters at home to help around the house and to send sons out to work. At the same time, lingering societal fears that the male-dominated workplace was an unsuitable location for pubescent girls also limited the number of young women who entered paid employment in Calgary. As they grew older, women faced a new set of societal pressures. Working-class masculine pride in being able to support a wife and family reinforced a reluctance or refusal on the part of employers to keep women on the payroll once they married. These pressures outlasted Calgary's initial industrial transformation, for in later years, when economic conditions worsened and jobs became scarcer, the city's newspapers would often feature concerted letter-writing campaigns opposing the right of married women to hold jobs while men were unemployed.[38]

Calgary's female workers, then, were concentrated in relatively few occupations, on average were younger than their male counterparts, and could expect to remain employed in the workforce for a far shorter length of time. As such, even though they might fleetingly share a common bond as wage earners, men and women experienced the daily routine of work in different ways and within different environments. In itself, therefore, the workplace was unlikely to produce a single class disposition among men and women. Instead, gender divisions that preceded the rise of industrial capitalism in Calgary and that received reinforcement within the household were replicated at the crucial point of production.[39]

Ethnicity also played a role in limiting the way in which Calgary workers viewed themselves as a single class. At least 80 percent of Calgarians in 1901 claimed some form of British heritage, an ethnic predominance that remained virtually unaltered well into the 1920s.[40] Calgary differed from Alberta as a whole in this respect, the provincial figure being closer to 60 percent; but this greater ethnic diversity within the province did not preclude (indeed, it may have encouraged) the evolution of a virulent and enduring strain of nativism. 'Most Anglo-Albertans judged minority groups on the basis of how quickly they could be assimilated,'

Table 2.2

Calgary occupations, according to gender and age, 1911

	Female % of total				Male % of total			
Age	10-4	14-25	25-64	65+	10-4	14-25	25-64	65+
All occupations	1.5	49.0	49.0	0.5	0.6	27.9	70.9	0.6
Building trades	0.0	0.0	60.0	40.0	0.1	24.6	74.8	0.5
Domestic and personal service	2.6	50.1	46.5	0.8	0.8	27.9	70.9	0.5
Government	0.0	42.9	55.6	1.5	0.3	46.4	52.3	1.0
Manufacturing	1.9	48.2	49.9	0.0	0.9	27.5	71.2	0.4
Professional	0.2	40.5	59.1	0.2	0.4	18.3	79.7	1.6
Trade and merchandising	0.4	55.7	43.9	0.0	1.1	26.8	71.5	0.6
Transportation	1.2	68.3	30.5	0.0	0.5	28.3	71.0	0.2

Source: Census of Canada (1911), 6: 34-51

concludes Howard Palmer in his study of nativist sentiment in Alberta, 'and Europeans who were not assimilated were thought to be in need of an intensive "Canadianization" campaign.'[41] In Calgary, the local press were only too happy to support such a campaign. Ironically, their initial target for hostile scrutiny was the local Native population – the region's original inhabitants – whom the *Herald* described in 1884 as 'a nuisance generally, dirty and disgusting, and their presence is thoroughly demoralising to the community.'[42] Later, the papers switched their attention to immigrant Chinese and 'Gallicians,' both of whom they linked to the spread of disease (especially leprosy), gambling, and prostitution. Chinese immigrants also found themselves accused of operating a white slave trade in the area. Following Wilfrid Laurier's electoral victory in 1896, the pro-Conservative *Herald* criticized the new Liberal government for 'bringing in a lot of filthy Gallicians' and lamented the fact that 'Canada has become a veritable dumping ground for the refuse of civilization.' At the same time, it once more complained that Calgary was suffering 'from the Chinese plague' and suggested that 'If expulsion is impossible, why not have them collected into some quarter of the city, where they could be easy of supervision.'[43]

The idea of ethnic segregation resurfaced from time to time in public debate. In 1910, property owners in the city centre petitioned the council to have Chinese residents there 'treated like an infectious disease' and moved elsewhere.[44] A year later, the local Board of Trade wrote to Laurier informing him of 'an alarming influx of the Negro Race into the Province of Alberta, which immigration cannot but deter the incoming of the desirable White Settler.' To remedy this situation, the board requested that the federal government 'take such steps as will effectively prevent the advent of negroes to Western Canada; and that such negroes as are now in homestead lands in the country be segregated in a certain defined area or areas from which white settlers should be removed.' Such attitudes persisted among Calgarians long after settlement. In March 1920, 422 residents petitioned the council that several black families 'be compelled to move to some other locality.' Perhaps what was most alarming about this request was the city clerk's willingness to look into the possibility when he wrote to other authorities in Canada to ask how they handled the matter of segregation.[45]

Despite such disquieting requests, Calgary's ethnic minorities hardly posed a threat to the prevailing British Canadian hegemony. Before the First World War, Germans were the only ethnic group of any significant size, numbering some 2,600 or 6 percent of the city's population in 1911. Among other groups, only immigrants of Scandinavian and Polish background amounted to more than 2 percent of the whole. As for the much-maligned Chinese, the 1911 census records a total of just fifty-six Asians,

East meets West. A delegation of Calgary's small Chinese population visits city officials as part of a search for employment and social acceptance in the young city, 1910.

less than 0.2 percent of Calgary's 44,000 residents.[46] From this perspective, the frequent outbursts of nativist sentiment appear difficult to understand, but this did not prevent them from continuing, sometimes from rather unlikely sources. Even the *Albertan,* a self-proclaimed Liberal newspaper that offered a fairly progressive editorial line on many issues, declared that, 'We do not want a colored Alberta ... Shut out all colored people from homeland rights. Close out the yellow man, the red man and the black man.'[47]

The precise relationship between ethnicity and class formation has been the subject of long-standing debate among historians, with no consensus yet in sight.[48] Nevertheless, in the case of Calgary there is some evidence to suggest that ethnic considerations did influence the disposition of workers to think and behave as a single class. For example, the attitudes of Calgary's labour organizations were shaped most obviously by the demands of Anglo-conformity, identified by Palmer as the values of 'British-Canadian nationalism, citizenship, individualism, and the Protestant work ethic.'[49] Union membership lists and other records attest the degree to which immigrants of British origin dominated the local labour movement, a fact also reflected in several revealing responses to the presence of ethnic minorities in the city. In 1905, when the Laundry Workers' Union appealed to other unions to boycott Calgary's Chinese laundries, the International Typographical Union replied that its constitution already decreed 'against members supporting Chinese labor.' A few weeks later the ITU acted on this principle when its executive moved to fine members caught attending what it referred to, somewhat obliquely, as 'Chinese entertainments.' The Calgary Trades and Labour Council

(CTLC) endorsed such discrimination, commenting publicly of Calgary's Chinese that 'No one deserves them for neighbours.'[50] Even when the question of immediate neighbourhood was not at issue, the CTLC displayed its antagonism to Asian immigrants in general, as in 1907 when it petitioned the federal government to stem the influx of Japanese immigrants into British Columbia.[51] Nor were Asians the only targets of discrimination. In 1907, for example, carpenters walked off a building site rather than work alongside a black labourer. In the spring of that year, bricklayer George Howell proudly informed his union that he had seconded a CTLC motion to 'invite a deputation from the Barbers' Union, to get the facts regarding the coon barber shop' operating in downtown Calgary. While Howell's main concern related to the non-union status of the shop, his choice of language betrayed a lack of fraternalism. In early 1914, the CTLC extended its own policy of selective discrimination when it passed a resolution opposing the employment of white girls in any restaurants run by either Chinese or black proprietors.[52]

Among Anglo-Canadian workers, then, there were ways in which ethnic or racial prejudice militated against their sense of class unity. But the pressures of Anglo-conformity in Calgary also influenced the behaviour and outlook of workers from other ethnic groups, and had a bearing on their own class-oriented disposition in two main ways. First, a desire to fit in often helped the integration of those ethnic-minority workers who otherwise found themselves marginalized from mainstream society. In this case, voluntary efforts at broader cultural assimilation took precedence over the formation of working-class bonds. Second, the same wish to conform and assimilate could in itself provoke resentment and reaction against ethnic minorities on the part of workers of Anglo-Canadian background. The case of Lowrenz Hautzinger illustrates both points. Hautzinger was an employee of the Calgary Brewing Company and a part-time musician, who in 1906 applied to join the local musicians' union. He used an anglicized version of his name, 'Lawrence Haughtsinger,' to forestall any problems. The examination committee duly recommended to admit him into the union, but the general membership subsequently overruled this decision and rejected his application. Comments made in the wake of this decision suggest that, once again, ethnic prejudice had outweighed any sense of class camaraderie. Carl Tetzel, himself an immigrant from central Europe, noted sadly that his fellow union members had made 'a very poor exhibition of brotherly feeling,' while Fred Bagley, an immigrant from Jamaica but of British parentage, lamented that he 'had not believed that such a feeling could arouse [sic] in the members ... [who had] showed a very poor union spirit.' Indeed, the union's action underlined the fact that an individual's desire or willingness to conform was not necessarily enough to overcome ethnic discrimination.[53]

A desire among minorities for acceptance by the majority group also influenced relations between various ethnic groups in Calgary. As a result, discrimination did not follow any simple line dividing whites from non-whites, Anglo-Canadians from non-Anglo-Canadians. The case of Percy Adams makes this clear. In August 1908, 300 unionized mechanics struck the CPR shops in Ogden. Management responded by importing a number of Japanese labourers from outside the city in order to continue operations. Opposition to the employment of Japanese scab labour gave union and non-union workers common cause, and unorganized men who had previously remained on the job now struck work at the sheds. One of these men was Percy Adams, a black foreman who had resisted earlier union requests that he join the strike. What swayed him now was the CPR's order that he oversee a group of strike-breaking Japanese bottle-washers, and his reasoning displayed a curious mixture of class solidarity, a desire for social acceptance, and residual ethnic bias. 'I have no objection to acting as foreman of a gang of respectable white gentlemen,' Adams told a local reporter, 'but I have no desire to have anything to do with a bunch of yellow men who are attempting to undermine and take the place of my many white friends.'[54]

This comment by Adams bears out Richard Oestreicher's warning, that immigrants rarely divided their own feelings of ethnicity and class in any rigid fashion.[55] On one level, it seems clear that ethnic prejudices undermined any disposition towards a broader sense of class identity among workers. But it is perhaps more accurate to say that the formation of Calgary's working class, at the level of disposition, contained elements of nativism shared by other groups in society. 'Racism,' writes Bryan Palmer, 'finds home in some quarters of the white working class because it reasserts, among those demoralized and demeaned by commodity fetishism, the limits of which the class will tolerate.'[56] In other words, workers belonging to the dominant ethno-cultural group may discriminate against others on the basis of ethnicity as a way of compensating for their perceived loss of power and status under industrial capitalism. This may well be true, but Palmer's argument needs to be extended beyond the simple division of white/non-white, as Percy Adams's disdain for the Japanese demonstrates. In Calgary, at least, the variety of ethnic minorities and the desire for social acceptance combined to produce a mosaic of racial prejudice.

Religion also shaped the class disposition of Calgary workers, yet its precise influence is even harder to describe than that of gender or ethnicity. Indeed, labour historians have typically been reluctant to generalize about the relationship between religious affiliation and class disposition. 'It is risky to assume too close a relationship between religious sentiment and rhetoric and everyday behavior,' cautioned the late Herbert Gutman. In his study of the Chicago working class, Bruce Nelson even suggests that the 'fundamental cleavage' was not between different denominations 'but between the religious and the irreligious.'[57] This latter concern certainly played on the minds of clergy in Calgary during this period. In 1911 the Central United Church reported that the city's economic growth 'has been so remarkable that it has laid upon the Churches an almost impossible task to properly keep pace on the moral and spiritual side with this rapid material development.'[58] At best, then, remarks regarding the relationship between religion and class in Calgary must be tentative in nature.

Just as Calgary's population was overwhelmingly British in origin, so it was predominantly Protestant in denomination. Anglicans, Methodists, Presbyterians, and Baptists accounted for 80 percent of those who declared their religious affiliation in the 1911 census. Anglicans and Presbyterians each numbered more than 10,000 that year, followed closely by some 8,000 Methodists, and more distantly by the city's 2,800 Baptists. In contrast, Calgary's 4,200 Roman Catholics accounted for less than 10 percent of the city's population, and its 600 or so Jews slightly more than 1 percent.[59]

As with ethnicity, it is easier to identify Calgary's major religious divisions than it is to attribute significance to them in the formation of class relations. This problem is not peculiar to Calgary, but has surfaced regularly in other studies of Canadian labour, particularly with regard to the question of Protestant and Catholic Irish immigrants. Did this religious rivalry antagonize fellow workers and so undermine their potential class solidarity? Or did a shared sense of class interests enable these two groups to overcome their sectarian differences? Bryan Palmer argues that nineteenth-century Hamilton 'was most emphatically a Protestant city, and that this hegemony may have gone unquestioned,' but then goes on to add that workers' 'allegiance to their class may have mediated hostilities,' leaving uncertain whether the relative lack of religious strife was the result of Protestant preponderance or working-class solidarity. Gregory Kealey is equally ambiguous in his treatment of class and religion in Toronto, claiming that the 'ritualistic violence' of sectarian riots between 1867 and 1892 did not undermine the existence of a common working-class culture, although his own evidence shows that such riots occurred at an average rate of one per year during that period.[60]

Calgary's own Irish population, approximately 6,000 in 1911, escaped such sectarian conflict. In part, this no doubt reflected the general easing of relations between Irish Protestants and Catholics towards the end of the nineteenth century, but may also have been the result of the fact that the two denominations were roughly equal in size in Calgary.[61] Whatever the precise cause, it is notable that there are no recorded clashes between Protestants and Catholics in Calgary during the entire period 1883-1913.

While parades, marching bands, and public speeches made St Patrick's Day a lively and popular occasion, it lacked the intense partisanship evident in other North American cities. In fact, cross-denominational cooperation both predated and survived the impact of industrialization in Calgary. St Patrick's Day celebrations in 1890 saw a congregation of all denominations crowd into the town's Catholic church; three years later Protestants and Catholics once again joined forces to observe the occasion. This prompted the *Herald* to remark approvingly that there was 'no reason why the old hatreds and prejudices and contests that have so long separated the Irish in Ireland should be imported to this country.' In 1906, when Calgary's Orange Order staged a massive demonstration to welcome visiting lodges from elsewhere in Alberta, local industrialist and leading Orangeman Edward Crandell told the assembled crowd that the order also stood for the rights of Catholics, a remark he repeated the following year when the organization celebrated at Okotoks, Alberta.[62] Within Calgary's Irish community, then, there is no clear connection between class formation and religious division. No outbreaks of violence occurred to pit workers of differing denomination against one another, while the position of Crandell – one of Calgary's leading capitalists – suggests that the harmony between Protestants and Catholics was not a direct product of working-class solidarity, although that may have been a factor.

Among Calgary's ethnic minorities, religion may have served to reinforce a sense of isolation from the dominant Anglo-Canadian culture. By emphasizing a discrete sense of ethnic community, religion also further weakened the disposition of such immigrants to interpret their experiences primarily in terms of class.[63] Instead, already isolated at the workplace by language and habits, and often excluded from trade unions, non-British immigrants found familiarity and mutual support in the many ethnic churches established in Calgary. By the early 1900s, there were separate places of worship for Swedish Lutherans, Scandinavian and Norwegian Baptists, and German Moravians. The very existence of such churches provided alternative focal points for members of their respective communities that drew them further from any more-inclusive culture based on common class interests.[64]

The one religious organization that deliberately sought out working-class converts was the Salvation Army.[65] Combining elements of radical evangelism and democratic spiritualism, this organization enthusiastically promoted its cause at open-air meetings and parades in cities across the country in the late 1800s, and as such was ideally suited to the egalitarian temper of the 'new west.'[66] The Salvation Army first arrived in Calgary in August 1887, under the command of three female officers, Captain Mercer, Lieutenant Patterson, and Cadet Iverich. As an indication of their intention to stay, they signed a three-year lease with the town's Boynton Hall and promptly began to organize regular services. At first these proved to be popular attractions. 'Crowds followed them around the streets and filled the halls at meetings,' according to one report. 'There was no disorder and the Army was permitted to do just about as they liked.' Within the first three months, the Army recruited 24 new 'soldiers,' and by 1911 had increased the number of converts to over 330.[67]

While some individual workers no doubt responded favourably to the Salvation Army's appeal, the early organized labour movement stood squarely opposed. Union men accused the Army of collaborating with capitalist employment agencies to flood Alberta's labour markets with unskilled immigrants, many of whom were ill-suited and ill-prepared for the sort of work available. The executive of the Alberta Federation of Labor made clear its opposition in 1908 when it reported to the national Trades and Labour Congress in Halifax that year. '[We are] disgusted at the way this work has been conducted by the Salvation Army. Several labor bodies in this province have expressed themselves as opposed to any bonus being paid, directly or indirectly to this emigration agency that does its work under the cloak of religion.'[68] In Calgary, unions criticized the Salvation Army on other matters, notably its employment of non-union musicians for street parades. Eventually, the local musicians' union persuaded the Calgary Trades and Labour Council to proscribe the Army as an 'unfair' employer of labour. In 1905, Adjutant Byers of the Salvation Army earned the wrath of labour men when he delivered an address entitled 'Would Christ Belong to a Labour Union?' at a Thanksgiving dinner. Speaking at a time when plumbers, plasterers, tinsmiths, and builders' labourers had all downed tools in support of striking carpenters, and when local newspapers were running headlines like 'Labor War Wages Within Calgary Now,' Byers concluded that the Army's support lay with 'the working man,' but not the striker. In a subsequent letter to the *Albertan,* 'A Working Man' angrily denounced Byers's intervention as 'the rankest insult to union labor that I have ever heard.' In provoking such outbursts, the Salvation Army may have helped promote unity within the labour movement, but there are few signs that its presence helped to foster any broader awareness of class solidarity among Calgary workers.[69]

Reviewing the advances made by the 'new' Canadian labour history of the 1970s, Gregory Kealey once argued that 'what has emerged from this work has been an image of class surprisingly united – one in which divisions of ethnicity, skill, religion, and even sex were recognized, debated, and for a few years in the 1880s, at least, were overcome.'[70] During the years in which Calgary underwent its own industrial transformation, local workers recognized and occasionally debated these same differences, but largely failed to overcome them. With the workforce structurally divided along lines of occupation and gender, the experience of work itself did not inspire a sense of class solidarity. Wage labour may have been a central feature of working-class life, but few workers or their families were dependent solely on wages as their source of income. Instead, a variety of household strategies and struggles to make ends meet supplemented the money brought home from work each week. To admit this is not to deny the pivotal importance that workers' relations at the point of production played in shaping their aspirations and outlook, for it was the inequitable distribution of wealth that capitalism necessarily entailed that made second incomes, the taking in of boarders, the keeping of pigs and cows, and even the resort to prostitution all part of the distinct working-class experience in Calgary. At the same time, ethnic prejudice fed on and reinforced the pressures of Anglo-conformity among many workers, and so weakened their inclination to think and act along class lines.

The extent to which Calgary workers failed to overcome their own social divisions is a measure of their class disposition, their ability to define shared class interests and to act upon them. These divisive identities were not, of course, crystallized formations, but instead were the outcome of human actions and interactions. Those economic and social forces that shaped circumstances and disposition were themselves subject to change over time, and were influenced by the actions and responses of workers of Calgary. After all, disposition is not behaviour. Instead, the relevance of class disposition is best judged by a consideration of Calgary labour's cultural and political responses to industrial capitalism in the years before 1913, the subject of the next chapter.

3
Class, Culture, and Politics

A rich and diverse cultural life evolved in Calgary in the years before 1913. Theatres and opera houses frequently staged dramatic and musical productions, while saloons and pool halls offered workers and others the chance for more casual gatherings. Churches, fraternal societies, trade unions, and other institutions provided Calgarians with a network of social associations, as did the growth of organized sport in the city. If class relations were forged initially at the point of production, and the disposition to realize them tempered by conflicting social identities at work and at home, was it in the sphere of culture – a common way of life – that a full consciousness of class might be discovered? In other words, did there exist what might fairly be called a distinct working-class culture in Calgary? And if so, did it provide workers (and their spouses and families) with a base from which to resist the daily encroachments of capitalism's discipline and demands? Or did workers share in a broader, even civic culture, one that drew them closer to other Calgarians and mitigated their sense of social alienation?

Such questions came to the fore in Canadian labour history in the 1970s and continued to shape working-class studies in the 1980s. Bryan Palmer was most explicit about the possibilities of the cultural approach in his study of nineteenth-century Hamilton workers: 'Despite the irksome fact that working-class involvement in friendly society and fire-engine hall, mechanics' institute and baseball team, is shrouded in obscurity, a ubiquitous anonymity being imposed on historical knowledge by the lack of surviving sources, it is possible, and even probable, that the associational life of skilled workers cultivated a sense of solidarity that strengthened the ability of the skilled to resist the encroachments of industrial-capitalist disciplines and development.'[1]

Interest in the possibilities that a focus on working-class culture offered was inspired by the truly innovative works of E.P. Thompson, Herbert Gutman, and Raymond Williams, among others.[2] Defined by Williams as 'a description of a particular way of life, which expresses certain meanings and values not only in art and learning but also in institutions and ordinary behaviour,' culture provided these historians, and those who would follow their lead, with a means of circumventing the deterministic, and increasingly unimaginative, base-superstructure model of Marxism.[3] For them, class was not a structure to be examined, or even a category of analysis; instead it was something that 'happens when some men, as a result of common experiences (inherited or shared), feel and articulate the identity of their interests as between themselves, and as against other men whose interests are different from (and usually opposed to) theirs.' Thompson followed the logic of his own argument to conclude that 'Class-consciousness is the way in which these experiences are handled in cultural terms: embodied in traditions, value-systems, ideas, and institutional forms.' In privileging the subjective experience of workers over their objective position within the economy, Thompson moved dangerously close to a relativism that floated free from the material conditions of capitalist production. 'Class is defined by men as they live their own history,' he declared, 'and, in the end, this is its only definition.'[4]

To a great extent, the cultural moment in Canadian labour history has passed, or at least has been overshadowed by feminist and poststructuralist critiques of class analysis. Lately, Bryan Palmer himself has readily acknowledged that his former 'overly enthusiastic embrace of culture' left 'a need for more subtlety and a more nuanced appreciation of this history than originally appeared,' and his more recent work is quick to recognize the limitations and contradictions within a culturalist approach to class formation.[5] Culture, he now argues, 'is part of an interpretive framework that builds on recognition of the limitations imposed on experience by economic constraint, places the moment of self-affirmation of the working class within the context of particular stages of development and levels of conflict and struggle, and, finally, attempts to bridge the gulf between culture and the forces that are both part of it and work upon it. Such forces include those that may fragment as well as unite (family, gender, ethnicity, religion, and politics) in conjunction with those that seek to take culture to a higher level or, in their absence, mire it in the accommodation to the commonplace (class consciousness and leadership).'[6]

This need to recognize the often ambivalent cultural pressures on the formation of class relations has been a feature of recent works on Canadian labour history. In his study of Vancouver's trade union bureaucracy at the turn of the century, for example, Mark Leier argues that labour's 'culture was a mixture of class conflict and collaboration. It borrowed elements from the culture of the larger society, created some of its own, and sought to incorporate working-class traditions into day-to-day life.'[7] Leier's emphasis on class collaboration as well as class conflict is a useful reminder that culture – however defined – does not operate in a single direction at any given time. In this respect, Leier moves beyond the simple dichotomy of radical/conservative that dominates earlier studies of labour in the West. As he notes, 'we need to remember that even the most conservative union leaders were still leaders of organizations that were created to fight employers. Their actions as bureaucrats have no meaning outside the boundaries of class and class struggle.' Yet just as Ian McKay criticizes the culturalist approach for its assumption that working-class culture 'was present whenever and wherever workers gathered together,' regardless of specific historical context, so Leier weakens his own position by suggesting that class collaboration was, in itself, just another proof of class consciousness among workers. 'Even class collaboration,' he writes, 'was a tactic used to try to improve the conditions of workers. That many labour bureaucrats sought to leave the working class by becoming paid officials or starting a business is further proof that class formed the basis of their existence, for if class were irrelevant, why would these workers seek to leave one class for another? Class experience and class struggle help explain conservatism as well as radicalism, class collaboration as well as class conflict, for the fight between labour and capital takes many forms.'[8] Despite its apparent advance on the question of class and culture, then, Leier's work approaches a pre-Thompsonian perspective, in which class structure and class position determine everything, including class consciousness.

In addressing the relationship between class and culture in Calgary, and their connection to early developments in labour politics before the First World War, this chapter confronts the ways in which both conflict and collaboration were present in the cultural pursuits of workers. It does not tackle the specific issue of class consciousness and the ways in which it was, or was not, manifested in a collective working-class culture. Instead, and in keeping with Ira Katznelson's model of class formation discussed in the introduction, this chapter focuses on the extent to which the cultural 'ways of life' of workers either compounded their sense of a distinct identity or helped to incorporate them within 'mainstream' society. It is against this cultural background that the rise of 'oppositional ideologies' – labourism and socialism – is then examined.

Recently characterized by Gary Teeple as 'the main organized force arising from the working class, and its only authentic voice,' trade unions are an obvious starting point in the search for any working-class subculture in early Calgary.[9] The exclusivity of Teeple's claim is open to question, but one might fairly expect Calgary's trade unions to embody the kernel of any distinct forms of working-class culture. After all, these organizations not only defended the economic interests of their members but also represented a common cultural focal point, providing hundreds, if not thousands of members with a sense of fraternity and mutuality that the experience of work itself could not. Evening concerts, dances, banquets, 'at-home' entertainments, picnics, and parades combined to form a regular and rewarding round of social activity, and became an integral feature of Calgary's broader cultural milieu before 1913. 'This is the annual merrymaking time of the labor organizations,' announced the *Albertan* shortly after the Christmas and New Year celebrations of 1912, in which 'the members of the various unions gather together in carnival feasting and merriment.' Labour's social gatherings were popular and well-attended in this period and frequently won the press's attention. Seven hundred guests were present at the firemen's ball in 1902, an event described by the *Albertan* as 'One of the most entrancing entertainments ever held in Calgary.' The press even treated smaller occasions, such as the first carpenters' union annual ball in 1906 at which there were just seventy-five couples, as affairs of public interest.[10]

Such gatherings undoubtedly boosted camaraderie and fellowship among unionized workers, yet there is little evidence to conclude that they promoted any broader sense of class identity. Rather, as Leier points out in his study, what union leaders and delegates sought 'was not so much a spontaneous working-class culture but an official, controlled union culture that helped skilled workers come together as a class for specific ends on terms decided upon by the bureaucracy.'[11] First and foremost, this trade union culture promoted among members pride in and identification with their specific occupations, rather than with the working class as a whole. When firemen, leatherworkers, carpenters, painters, railway workers, or maintenance-of-way men congregated, they did so in order to celebrate the specific achievements of their own craft or trade. This did not, of course, preclude the possibility of broader loyalties being forged within the world of union culture, and events staged by the Calgary Trades and Labour Council (CTLC) sometimes hinted at an embryonic working-class culture. The CTLC organized several concerts as part of its efforts to boost union membership in Calgary, and officials often argued the benefits of organization against the backdrop of an evening's social entertainment. In 1903, for instance, the CTLC arranged a selection of orchestral recitals, comic songs, character sketches, and flag drill performances at the Hull Opera House. In between acts, while the audience helped themselves to assorted refreshments, CTLC leaders Bell Hardy, James Worsley, and Richard Brocklebank delivered speeches, including one on the need to patronize only union-staffed retail stores. In 1906, the CTLC staged its first successful attempt to bring union and non-union workers together at a mass rally of labour, once again at the Opera House.

As before, the occasion combined a number of speeches, this time on the 'necessity for the laboring men to stand together and achieve their independence through the polls,' with a medley of songs, dances, vaudeville acts, and the first appearance of Calgary's Citizen Band.[12]

The CTLC also held events in support of specific issues, such as the nationwide CPR strike of 1908. In August that year, it sponsored a picnic on St George's Island on the Bow River for local striking machinists and their families. Appreciative of this show of solidarity by non-union workers, unionized railway workers later donated the proceeds of their own annual ball to the machinists, who had struck in sympathy. But on occasion, even the CTLC could be a source of class division rather than unity. During the Christmas season of 1905, striking members of the musicians' union protested the lack of support received from the CTLC. Because their union frequently supplied bandsmen for CTLC concerts, the musicians were particularly annoyed. As one member complained, the CTLC 'did not seem to take any interest in the Musicians, except when they want to secure cheap music.'[13] There is room to doubt, therefore, that union social gatherings necessarily embodied a culture that was distinctively working-class in character. In form, they had much in common with contemporary bourgeois culture. At its first annual at-home concert, for example, the leatherworkers' union treated the audience to piano music, recitations of verse and poetry, and an instrumental duet. This program bespoke as much about aspiration to middle-class respectability as about working-class solidarity, and in itself reveals nothing of a unique way of life.[14]

It would be a mistake to focus exclusively on the form and content of labour's social events. Despite the structural limitations of such occasions, they still held the potential for workers to forge more inclusive bonds with one another. Workers could and did take the opportunity of these social events to discuss and promote the concerns of labour in general, untrammelled by craft sectionalism or the desire to defer to middle-class mores. An example of this occurred in March 1904, when the carpenters' union held a concert attended by most of its members. President D.D. McIntosh took advantage of the gathering to reflect upon the union's unsuccessful strike the previous summer, effectively delivering a sermon on the limitations of direct industrial action and the need for labour to engage instead in concerted political campaigns.[15]

Yet overall, the associational life of trade unions was too narrow in its embrace to constitute a distinct and separate subculture of opposition. If such a subculture existed in Calgary, it is necessary to look beyond the confines of organized labour to the broader range of pastimes and institutions that occupied the leisure time of Calgary workers, union and non-union alike. As previous studies of working-class culture have shown, such activities are vast in scope, extending from the regular and formal meetings of a Mechanics' Institute to the boozy camaraderie of a crowded saloon on a Saturday night.[16] Here, a brief exploration of local culture is restricted to a selective sample of sports, fraternal societies, holidays, and parades.

Two basic schools of thought exist among scholars on the question of sport and class formation. The first, exemplified in the work of sociologist Richard Helmes, argues that competitive sports reflect or recreate the conditions and disciplines of capitalism present at the workplace, and thus produce a social experience reinforcing that of work itself. Sports, according to Helmes, constitute 'an arena of political socialization in which system-stabilizing values are reinforced' and thereby diminish the formation of any oppositional culture among workers.[17] Historian Ross McKibbin makes the additional and complementary observation in his study of British working class formation that, in acting as 'late nineteenth-century souvenirs of country life,' sports serve to 'provide a comforting associational structure for urban life.'[18] In contrast, the second main school of thought emphasizes the fact that sports 'could illuminate class inequalities, and generate fierce opposition to the fundamental wrongs of the social order' under industrial capitalism.[19] As such, sporting occasions not only offered temporary relief from the rigours and demands of industrialism, but in their embodiment of an alternative set of values – cooperation, teamwork, and fraternalism, for example – they served as a symbolic rejection of capitalism.

Some historians reject the idea of any precise connection between sport and class formation. Alan Metcalfe suggests that sports form 'one of the sub-systems of culture that transcend socio-economic, educational and religious barriers.' Nonetheless, his own study of cricket in Canada demonstrates a clear connection between class and sport, as does Colin Howell's sophisticated analysis of baseball, class, and community in the Maritimes.[20] In short, the theoretical debate over the interrelationship between class and sport has yet to produce any sort of consensus, and – as with gender and ethnicity – the evidence for Calgary needs to be treated with caution.[21]

There is little sign that the composition of individual sports teams either reflected the emergence of class divisions in Calgary or increased the disposition of workers towards class behaviour. The earliest sporting contests were cricket and rugby matches in the 1880s between teams drawn from the NWMP, local townsmen, and the fire brigade. Before long, sports became an integral feature of Calgary's cultural life, and well before the turn of the century there were regular competitions in cricket, soccer, rugby, baseball, and lacrosse. On occasion, individual trades and companies produced their own teams, as when local printers formed the 'Press Gang' to compete in the first citywide soccer league in 1896. In July 1904, carpenters employed by two rival building contractors extended company competition on to the baseball diamond.[22] There is no evidence, however, to lend support to Palmer's view that such contests formed 'part of a culture that bred and conditioned solidarity, a prerequisite to any struggle attempting to better the lot of working men and women.'[23] On the contrary, the example of the Calgary Cricket Club suggests that it was more likely that organized sports submerged class differences and provided a force for the social integration of workers.

Formed in 1884, the Calgary Cricket Club (CCC) was originally dominated by members of the district's landed and professional middle classes – local ranchmen, merchants, and office clerks. When the team temporarily merged with that of the NWMP, the newly elected executive – a colonel, a minister, and a merchant-turned-postmaster – aptly symbolized the British Empire's cultural conquest of the prairie West, giving some support to the view that, more than any other nineteenth-century sport, cricket reflected and deliberately preserved the separation of social classes.[24] Yet within a few years, as an influx of labour greatly added to Calgary's population, the CCC became notably more democratic in its composition. By May 1901, among the eleven men who padded up for the city team to face the NWMP were three CPR employees, a carpenter, and a porter from the Alberta Hotel. Two years later, Calgary's leading batsman – with a respectable average of twenty-four runs per game – was none other than James Worsley, cofounder of the CTLC and publisher-editor of the *Bond of Brotherhood,* the first Marxist newspaper on the prairies.[25] Calgary cricket was no longer the domain of privileged settlers, if indeed it ever had been in any meaningful sense. In fact, the transformation of the Calgary Cricket Club counters the argument that cricket – and sports in general – either reproduced a pro-capitalist hegemony in the cultural sphere or else reflected existing class divisions.[26]

Historians have also identified fraternal societies as a source of working-class culture in capitalist society, but there are some serious evidential and conceptual flaws to such claims. Bryan Palmer argues that Hamilton's Acacia Lodge of the Ancient, Free, and Accepted Masons (AFAM) was largely working-class in character during the late 1800s, even though fewer than 21 percent of the identifiable members were actually skilled or unskilled workers.[27] Even had the figure been significantly higher, this need not necessarily imply a homogeneous class identity. As Mary Ann Clawson argues in her study of fraternal organizations, such an interpretation assumes 'that a constant class composition will translate into a constant class perspective, which will then be reflected in the values and actions of the organization.' Instead, concludes Clawson, 'To the extent that the fraternal order incorporated working-class men into networks that undercut class as a category, the potential for working-class organization was diminished.' More significant, perhaps, as the title of Clawson's book – *Constructing Brotherhood* – suggests, was the role of such societies in building cross-class fraternal bonds to prevent, or at least delay, the encroachment of women into their domain.[28] Such fraternal societies and kindred organizations flourished in prewar Calgary, numbering at least eighteen by 1914, many with several subordinate lodges.[29] Whether they encouraged or discouraged a disposition towards class outlook and behaviour may be judged by considering three of the city's more prominent associations: the Independent Order of Odd Fellows (IOOF), the Sons of England Benevolent Society (SOEBS), and the Ancient Order of United Workmen (AOUW).

George Murdoch, harness maker and first mayor of Calgary, founded Alberta Lodge 1 of the IOOF in December 1884. He had previously been a member of the IOOF in his native New Brunswick. The IOOF provided a valuable network of social and commercial relations for Murdoch and his fellow merchants in the 1880s, while wage labourers lacking capital resources readily welcomed the financial support it offered in time of sickness or distress, especially during the depressed 1890s. A steady increase in members led to the formation of several new Calgary lodges after 1900. Membership figures for Alberta attest to the health of the IOOF in the years before the First World War, rising from 1,000 to 5,000 between 1905 and 1911.[30]

The IOOF discriminated on the basis of gender – no women members were allowed – but not in terms of social background. 'The poor man with the rough hand and humble garb may be good and generous,' declared the *Alberta Oddfellow* in 1906, 'while another with the manner and appearance of what the world calls a gentleman may be base and mean.'[31] Available listings of executive officers in Calgary indicate that this was no mere rhetoric. Of the thirty-one officers installed in Calgary Lodges 1 and 3 in 1892, the occupations of twenty-seven may be identified. Ten were either craftsmen or labourers, including two planing-mill employees, two carpenters, one plasterer, and one CPR lineman. A decade later, among those elected to the executive of Lodge 1 were a cemetery caretaker, a school janitor, a CPR clerk, an employee of Massey-Harris, one labourer, and two teamsters. In both cases, such tradesmen accounted for more than 30 percent of all identifiable officers.[32] What impact this degree of working-class representation had on the actions and outlook of the IOOF remains a matter for speculation. Given the group's stated inclusive objectives, it seems reasonable to agree with Clawson that it represented 'a vision of unity and brotherhood among men of disparate social statuses,' rather than the viewpoint of any one social class.[33]

The origins of the Sons of England Benevolent Society date back to December 1874, when eight Toronto Englishmen – mainly clerks, artisans, and labourers – formed the organization with the aim of providing compatriots in need with mutual support and financial assistance. Being English was a condition of membership. Also, unlike the IOOF, whose commitment to Christianity was non-denominational in nature, the SOEBS excluded non-Protestants. This ethnic and religious discrimination reflected the society's declared commitment to 'the preservation and perpetuity of the British Empire, [and] loyalty to the Crown and country under Protestant rule.'[34]

In August 1890, Calgarians established the United Roses Lodge 117 of the SOEBS. By this time, the society had evolved beyond its original purpose of providing non-charitable aid to include a variety of social functions. The *Calgary Herald* predicted a secure future for the organization locally, commenting that 'The English element in the Calgary district is both numerous and influential and it may be counted upon to give the order a generous support.'[35] This was no doubt true and helped the SOEBS to prosper in Calgary. Unlike the IOOF, it counted few manual workers among its members at first. Fewer than a dozen such workers were among the 160 members listed for the years 1890-5, and virtually none featured among the early executives. By the end of the century, the SOEBS was showing signs of change. In 1901, six of the thirteen officers elected to Lodge 240 were from working-class backgrounds (four were employees at the Alberta Hotel, one was a carpenter, and the sixth was a city labourer). Yet this democratization of leadership did not produce any fundamental change in the society's function or outlook. Its formal ceremony and rituals remained unaltered: meetings continued to incorporate patriotic recitations and songs, regular toasts to the British monarch, and a closing rendition of the national anthem. These were hardly the hallmarks of a distinct working-class culture, let alone an oppositional one.[36]

The Ancient Order of United Workmen (AOUW) was a third fraternal organization that flourished in Calgary during this period. Its name hinted at proletarian origins, while its motto – 'the one needs the assistance of the other' – suggested a communitarian ethos at odds with capitalism's emphasis on competitive individualism.[37] However, Calgary's branch of the AOUW was no more working-class in character than either the IOOF or SOEBS. Thirty charter members formed Calgary Lodge 21 of the AOUW in June 1891, with the aim of providing 'a system of cheap and safe insurance' open to 'any self-respecting person.' This provision soon took second place to the AUOW's function as a social gathering, one at which men could enjoy each other's company irrespective of social or economic background. In this way, the AUOW promoted communal bonds over any class identity. The order's executive in 1892 included stonemason William Barker, carpenter Sam McComb, and the Royal Hotel's cook Frank

Marriagi, but it requires a leap of faith to infer from this that the AUOW promoted any class-based agenda.[38]

'And what the deuce is Society?' asked the *Calgary Optimist* in 1909; to which it replied, 'Calgary society? An aggregation of indifferent folks who conspire together to make each other miserable.'[39] In the brotherly world of Calgary's benevolent organizations, such cynicism would have found few supporters. Fraternal societies like the IOOF, SOEBS, and AOUW provided an arena in which men of different social classes were able to come together and socialize on a relatively equal footing. As Clawson remarks, 'the fraternal order not only created cross-class relationships, it idealized them.'[40] To go one stage further, it is even possible that such organizations encouraged a broader sense of citizenship, with their emphasis on the positive aspects of collectivism and mutualism in a society otherwise typified by a raw individualism.[41] One can view the many local festivals, carnivals, and parades held in Calgary during the years before (and after) 1913 in this light, too. Public holidays provided the most visible demonstration of the fact that class divisions forged at the workplace had little impact upon the evolution of Calgary's popular culture. Calgarians turned out by the thousand each year to witness the morning street parades on Dominion Day and Victoria Day. In the afternoon they moved on to the city's Victoria Park, where athletic contests were staged, followed by a massive public barbecue. These events were genuinely popular occasions and served to encourage a common civic identity among those in attendance. On Victoria Day in 1899, 1,500 people – roughly one-third of the city's population – participated in the afternoon festivities. For those who were unable to attend the evening's formal dinner and dance at one of Calgary's large public halls, impromptu firework displays and street entertainments rounded out the day's celebrations and further suggest the event's appeal to all classes.[42]

Dominion Day and Victoria Day were, of course, public celebrations of Canada's ties to the British Empire. As such, the enthusiastic support they received in Calgary served to underline the dominant status of Anglo-Canadian culture in that city.[43] In his Victoria Day sermon for 1902, Methodist minister the Reverend Wood emphasized the capacity of imperial bonds to overcome class divisions. 'Freedom and progress characterised the Anglo Saxons the world over,' he declared, 'and in the British empire, the poorest man that walked, was as safe as the greatest magnate.'[44] Yet the extent to which workers themselves celebrated the value of empire, and exactly what it signified to them, largely remain matters for conjecture. Still, the response of Calgary stonemason John Gillespie to the death of Queen Victoria offers one brief glimpse in this respect. Gillespie recorded the long-lived monarch's passing in the daily journal he had kept since his arrival in Calgary during the 1880s, and he subsequently set about making preparations to attend with his three sons the memorial procession planned for 3 February 1902 in Calgary. As the day neared, Gillespie's diary entries make clear his disappointment with the lack of energy being displayed by the city to commemorate the occasion. 'Went ... to see the Mayor re procession this Saturday,' Gillespie wrote on 30 January. 'Nothing was being done. He is a poor figurehead for Calgary.'[45] More routine gestures of patriotism among Calgary's workers were the various floats constructed by trade unionists for Dominion Day and Victoria Day street parades, on which Union Jacks fluttered alongside union banners in symbolic affirmation of the duality of the unionists' self-identity. Working-class participation on such occasions also included the fielding of teams drawn from CPR employees and workers at the local brewery in the holiday soccer tournament that followed the parade.[46] While it is dangerous to infer too much about collective working-class attitudes from such scattered instances, the active involvement of Calgary workers in celebrations of Canada's subordinate position within the empire suggests that many at least shared the 'inherited assumption of national superiority' of British patriotism.[47]

Surprisingly, the difficulty in locating a distinct working-class culture in Calgary is nowhere more apparent than in the case of Labour Day.[48] Although the federal government had legislated the holiday in 1894, it remained virtually uncelebrated by Calgary workers during the next few years. It was only with the formation of the Calgary Trades and Labour Council in 1901, precisely for the purpose of organizing a public parade for the next Labour Day, that the occasion achieved any social significance within the city. Consequently, the public – or at least local newspapers – quickly came to associate the holiday with the cause of trade unionism, rather than with the working class more generally. Some historians, notably Bryan Palmer, have been equally quick to contrast the 'officially sanctioned' nature of Labour Day with earlier and more spontaneous celebrations of working-class identity, arguing that 'the autonomous class activity of a self-proclaimed holiday had been shattered by government proclamation.'[49] Whatever the case elsewhere in Canada, there is no evidence in Calgary that the advent of Labour Day subverted any existing form of working-class celebration, or that the trade union movement hijacked the event from the working class. Indeed, if the complaint by one Mr McGann is any indication, had it not been for the CTLC's endeavours in 1901 and thereafter, local workers would have continued to ignore their own holiday. 'This is the day in which all those who earn their crops by the sweat of their brow, or in a sweat shop should cease work and spend the day in recreation,' McGann wrote in a letter to the *Herald* shortly after Labour Day in 1896. 'Nothing was done in Calgary to try to bring the working people together in the shape of a master picnic or anything else, and the day was spent as though very few people knew what it was built for. In fact it was a shame to see the store clerks and the school teachers labouring, as this is the one day in which the school should be closed ... If something is not done in Calgary by the labouring people in after years, Labour Day will be recognised as a day like St. Patrick's – a day for a good drink, that is if your "boss" lets you off.'[50]

Six years after McGann's warning, in September 1902, the CTLC and its constituent trade unions staged the first Labour Day parade through the streets of Calgary. Fortuitously, the holiday coincided with the opening day of the city's annual agricultural exhibition and so caught Calgarians in a ready mood of excitement. All the same, as the *Herald* noted at the time, it was 'a red letter day in the annals of Calgary labor orgnizations' and set the pattern of celebration for the next decade. Gathering at a prearranged point along Eighth Avenue on the morning of 5 September, Calgary's full complement of eleven unions began to march through the city to the brisk tempo set by the city fire brigade band at the procession's head. Many of the men – and the march consisted exclusively of male workers – wore uniforms tailored especially for the day. The typographical workers, for example, were decked out in white coats, blue trousers and caxton hats, and drew many compliments from the spectators assembled along the way 'for their splendid appearance and good marching.' Union banners and floats declared the diverse and discrete identities of the marchers, further underlining the fact that this was a celebration of unionized labour and not the working class per se. Perversely, speeches made by various of Calgary's civic and political dignitaries present at the event stressed the role and rights of labour as a class. Local lawyer and young Conservative prospect R.B. Bennett declared that 'Nothing was more dignified than labor,' and he 'was pleased to see that with a sturdy independence all classes of laboring men were rallying to defence of their rights as citizens of the world.' Similarly, *Herald* editor James Young supported 'a system of interdependency by which labor might participate in the profits of capital,' while future provincial Liberal premier Arthur Sifton remarked that 'all who came to the West were workers and anyone who came to the country with a different impression would get sadly left.' Of course, such comments may be dismissed as opportunistic vote-seeking by politicians, but the same can hardly be said of the speeches made by non-elected members of the local clergy. The Reverend Hastie of nearby Okotoks, for instance, himself the son of a weaver, dramatically told the audience that he would rather lose 'his right hand than his sympathy with the workers of the world,' and called for the implementation of a two-dollar minimum daily wage.[51]

The Labour Day celebrations of 1902 established a pattern that was amplified and reinforced over the next five years: a morning parade consisting predominantly (but not exclusively) of trade union members; an afternoon's sports card followed by a banquet and dance in the evening; displays of support and solidarity from local politicians, clergy, and city officials that transcended class lines; and tacit support from those merchants who shut up shop for the day, thereby enabling their employees to attend the festivities, and who also donated money to the CTLC's Labour Day fund. The features continued to characterize the occasion until at least 1907. Up to 3,000 marchers took part in the parade that year, while one estimate placed the number of spectators as high as 15,000, more than half the city's population. The *Albertan* captured some of the spirit of the event: 'Gaily decorated carts appeared from every direction. People threw open their doors and thronged the streets, craned their necks until they were in danger of breaking.'[52]

For all its success – or perhaps because of it – Labour Day failed to develop into an expression of a distinct working-class culture. There were two separate reasons for this failure. First, by celebrating labour's role within society and its contribution to Calgary's material growth, Labour Day helped to reduce any sense that workers might have formed a class excluded from civil society. Instead, supportive speeches by Bennett and others, together with gestures of accommodation from city merchants, nurtured the belief that Calgary was an inclusive community in which citizenship counted more than class. Strengthening this belief was the evolution – or dilution – of the character of Labour Day parades in the early 1900s. In 1906, for example, the procession included 250 local school children as well as thirty young military cadets, despite the labour movement's traditional attachment to pacifism. Four years later, the presence of two troops of boy scouts and a float from the local zoo – complete with goat and bear cub – further confused the parade's sense of identity. That the local press reported this development without comment was in part because by this time newspapers devoted their attention almost entirely to the afternoon entertainments and virtually ignored the morning parade. In its headline account of events in 1911, for example, the *Herald* managed to avoid any reference to labour: 'Very Large Crowd Attended Afternoon Celebration – Close Contest in Athletic Events – Exhibitions of Speed and Matched Horse Races – Strong Men on the Tug of War Rope – Finest Babies in the West Displayed by Admiring Parents.'[53] This dilution continued: in 1913 the *Albertan*'s coverage of the holiday gave no indication whatever that it had anything to do with labour. Instead, it described in considerable detail the record-breaking high jump of Edmontonian Ross Sheppard. 'The big day of the year in local athletics,' read the same paper's front-page headline the following year.

To the union born. A bemused looking infant poses with proud members of Calgary Lathers' Union, Local 221, as they prepare for Labour Day celebrations, c. 1908-10.

Far from being a component of any working-class culture, Labour Day had become little more than part of Calgary's sporting calendar.[54]

The second reason why Labour Day remained a communal or civic celebration, rather than a class-oriented occasion, was the fickle support of workers themselves. 'Whatever may have been the original intention,' remarked the *Albertan* in 1909 apropos of Labour Day in general, 'it has become a day belonging to organized labor.'[55] This had always been the case in Calgary, but the paper's belated recognition of the fact reflected the failure of Labour Day to develop significantly beyond its original base of trade union participation. Each September there were a number of non-union marchers in the parade, but the vast majority remained members of the local labour movement. Yet unions had difficulty ensuring a full turn-out of their members, and often had to encourage attendance by fining (or at least threatening to fine) absentees. Even this practice had little effect, and low attendance remained a problem. In 1910, for example, the 400 trade unionists who marched in that year's parade represented less than 20 percent of Calgary total union membership. The carpenters' and bricklayers' unions were particularly conspicuous by their absence, for their combined membership would have doubled the size of the procession.[56]

Struggling to maintain its core of support – male trade unionists, chiefly of British origin – Labour Day did little to break down the barriers of ethnicity and gender among Calgary workers. The CTLC took few steps to solicit the participation of ethnic minorities, although it is unclear whether the latter's reluctance to observe the holiday was a cause or effect of this attitude. Surviving photographs provide ample evidence that male workers dominated Labour Day parades. Even during its later years of dilution, the holiday remained an occasion for men to demonstrate a chauvinistic paternalism towards their female partners. The afternoon athletic contests, for example, included female heats that offered women a chance to participate in the day's celebrations, but only after the men had checked the tracks for stray garter snakes! The *Albertan* correctly, if unwittingly, captured the paternalistic and gendered nature of Labour Day in 1907 with its report that 'In the evening a dance was held in Alexander Hall, to which all labor men, married and unmarried, went, taking their wives, sweethearts and sisters along.'[57]

On the evidence of sports, fraternal societies, and the celebration of public holidays, it is difficult to conclude that there existed in Calgary any distinct working-class culture, let alone a subculture of opposition. What did exist more closely resembles McKibbin's description of the failure of British workers to develop a radical class outlook in this same period – 'a culture ... without any unified communitarian interest and incapable of giving ideological direction to working-class consciousness.'[58] As long as Calgary's economy continued to prosper and employment prospects were relatively plentiful, workers engaged in a pluralistic cultural life that emphasized cooperation, citizenship, and community over class struggle. Yet to the extent that such cultural consensus rested on the continuance of material prosperity, it remained a fragile construct subject to the vagaries of the local, national, and international economies. This became evident in the short but sharp recession of 1907-8, whose impact presaged the more serious depression of 1913. A number of store owners who had previously closed shop in recognition of Labour Day kept their doors open in September 1907 in order not to lose any further business. A few of them even fired those employees who failed to show up for work on Labour Day, even though it was a statutory holiday.[59] By themselves, such attitudes and actions do not account for the precipitous decline in popular support for Labour Day celebrations after 1907. More importantly, trade unions began to change their own estimate of the event's worth, a development that paralleled their move towards the embrace of independent political action.

Although the 1907-8 recession was short-lived, its impact was immediately apparent in halting the previously upward trend in wages among most of Calgary's unionized trades. Just as individuals and families had to tighten their belts temporarily, so trade unions were forced to reexamine the manner in which they allocated their limited funds. Labour Day was one of the first casualties, as unions began to ask what tangible benefits their continued participation in that event brought. In July 1907, the bricklayers' union cut its donation to the Labour Day sports fund from $25 to $15, and a year later reduced expenditure on its planned parade float to just $10. Even this small sum was criticized by some members, who argued that because a strike that summer had considerably depleted the union's funds, and because they were still repaying loans taken out the previous winter, the union should practise stricter economy. It is little surprise, therefore, that in 1909 the same union passed a motion 'that we are not in favor of celebrating labor day,' a decision that led the CTLC to abandon the parade entirely that year.[60]

The bricklayers' union was not alone in reevaluating its support for Labour Day. In 1912, local 449 of the printers' union voted against parading that year, preferring instead to use the money to send a delegate to the Dominion Trades and Labour Congress that October. A year earlier, a bitter dispute had broken out among members of the electrical workers' union over the relative expense of providing an engineers' cap or a white duck hat as part of the parade uniform. The CTLC itself started to dip into its Labour Day fund, at first in order to keep itself solvent, and later to pay the rent for the financially plagued Labour Temple. At the same time, a new wave of often lengthy strikes in the years 1911-2 was a serious drain on union and CTLC financial resources, as was the decision of the council to embark on an independent political course after 1912. Campaigns cost money, and the Labour Day fund became the CTLC's de facto slush fund.[61] The demise of Labour Day would prove to be a slow affair, dragging on as it did into the 1920s, but the prognosis was unmistakable well before the outbreak of the First World War. As socialist candidate Arthur Masters told a crowd on Labour Day 1911, 'Today was a day of rejoicing for organized labor all over the world. But labor would not rejoice tomorrow or for the rest of the year for there was nothing to rejoice over.'[62]

The absence of a class-based culture in Calgary limited the development of independent labour politics before 1913. Certainly there were a number of reformers, rebels, and even a sprinkling of revolutionaries – to borrow Ross McCormack's characterization of the western Canadian labour movement – who rejected the pluralistic assumptions and promises of mainstream politicians, but they failed to secure the support of anything more than a small minority of local workers.[63] Nevertheless, the political struggles of labourists and socialists alike were not without benefit, for their engagement in elections helped workers to identify, define,

A city salutes its workers. Crowds throng the sidewalk and watch from the rooftops as Local 1779 of the United Brotherhood of Carpenters and Joiners of America parades down Eighth Avenue on Labour Day, 1912.

and articulate those areas in which their interests were distinct from those of the rest of society. In this respect, the decade before 1913 may be regarded as an important transition period for labour in Calgary, bridging the partyism of workers in the 1890s and the emergence of a fully independent labour politics during the war. The limits to which either a reformist or rejectionist ideology took root among Calgary workers in this period should be viewed within this context.[64]

Organized party politics first came to Calgary in the form of a Liberal-Conservative Association in 1885. At that time, the *Herald* estimated that three-quarters of the local electorate were Tory supporters, a fact acknowledged by Prime Minister John A. Macdonald's decision to visit the town the following year. It was not until 1891 that Liberal supporters formed their own political association in Calgary. Local Grits soon developed an active following, and helped to elect Frank Oliver to Ottawa in the election of 1896, thus ending nine years of Conservative rule in the district of Alberta. A torchlit procession through the streets of Calgary on election night reflected the extent of popular support for the new Liberal government.[65]

Although candidates and officials of the two established parties were uniformly members of Calgary's merchant and professional classes, both

Liberals and Conservatives made efforts to woo the electoral and moral support of local working-class voters. They frequently succeeded, and labour votes contributed to the election of Liberals William Cushing and I.S.G. Van Wart and Conservatives Maitland McCarthy, T.M.M. Tweedie, and R.B. Bennett. It was against this background of working-class partyism that labourism and socialism emerged as political alternatives in Calgary after 1900.[66]

Residual association with the Liberals and Conservatives cast a slight shadow over the early history of Calgary's first Labour Party, originally formed in 1902 as a political club in which like-minded workers could discuss their ideas. During the federal election of 1904, party members held a campaign meeting at Norman Hall, a building that also happened to be the local Conservative Association's headquarters. The meeting itself provided further embarrassment for Labour Party officials when speeches by invited Liberal and Conservative candidates won lengthy bursts of applause. Matters were not helped the following day when the *Albertan* ran a story alleging that F.B. Cummer, party president and a printer at the pro-Conservative *Herald,* was in fact 'the *Herald*'s hired man' within the Labour Party. All in all, it was not an auspicious beginning for Calgary labour politics.[67]

More than the appearance of the new party itself, the record of elected Liberal and Conservative politicians on labour issues helped to diminish working-class support for the older parties. The rhetoric used by Bennett and others in Labour Day speeches was slow to transform into meaningful legislation that benefited labour. The Alberta executive of the Dominion Trades and Labour Congress made this point in its report of 1907, when it voiced doubts about the current provincial Liberal administration. 'We have secured certain legislation from the old party in power which is to some extent favorable to labor,' the report read, 'but we must not expect too much from either of the old parties.'[68] Working-class support for the Conservative Party in Calgary was shaken in 1911 when a rumour circulated around the city that Bennett, a candidate in that year's federal election, was using his influence at city hall to intimidate civic employees into voting for him. Although the charges were never proven, the scandal prompted Mayor J.W. Mitchell and Commissioner A.G. Graves to pledge publicly that 'no employe[e] will be discharged or his wages reduced on account of depositing his vote in harmony with his political views.'[69] By the First World War, opposition to the Conservative Party had become the official policy of the labour movement in Calgary. Accordingly, when stonecutter W.L. Webster and bricklayer George Evans wrote open letters of support for Conservative candidate Dr Thomas Blow, their respective unions issued formal reprimands against the pair.[70]

From the dwindling enthusiasm for Liberal or Conservative politics, there emerged a growing support among Calgary workers for the alternative policies espoused by labourism. Once described by historian Craig Heron as 'the neglected child of the Canadian left,' labourism owed more to nineteenth-century British Liberal radicalism than to Marxist socialism and as such was part of the cultural baggage that British immigrant workers brought with them.[71] At heart it was a moralistic ideology, advocating a kinder, fairer capitalism rather than its overthrow. 'Unlike Marxists,' writes Mark Leier, 'labourists did not divide classes according to the relationship to the means of production, that is between those who owned factories, land, or workshops and those who sold their labour to others. Instead, class was more often defined by one's relation to what was considered to be real work or socially necessary production.'[72]

Central to labourism was its faith in existing political structures and the possibility of gradually reforming capitalism's worst inequalities via the ballot box. As such, it reflected, or perhaps embodied, the privileged position that British immigrants enjoyed in the cities of the West, for they were most likely to understand and utilize the forms, language, and ideals of parliamentary politics. Labourism was the ideology of skilled craftworkers and craft unions, the latter another inheritance from the British cultural tradition, and so tended to overlook or downplay the fact that the condition of the many transient, unskilled workers in the West was unlikely to benefit from piecemeal reforms. Yet as Leier observes, while the roots of labourism may be traced back to the British tradition of parliamentary reform and radical Liberalism, it survived and thrived as a working-class ideology in Canada precisely because 'Canadian conditions and experiences also played an important role in defining labourism.'[73]

Still, there is a tendency among historians to view labourism as, at best, a weak and limited expression of working-class interests. In his study of Ontario labour in the years 1914-25, James Naylor argues that although 'the developing "labourist" political movement faithfully articulated notions of democracy and progress that were widely held by the region's workers ... labourism was perhaps too weak a vessel to contain the aspirations of its adherents.'[74] In particular, according to Naylor and others, labourism failed to adapt to the wartime economic revolution that transformed capitalist production in Canada. As a result, by the mid-1920s labourism 'had collapsed as a significant force in Canadian politics.'[75] Nowhere did it survive for as long as in Calgary, however, where the methods and ideals associated with the British tradition continued to be at least passably relevant to a sizeable number of workers well after the First World War. Yet here was the dilemma for the adherents of labourism in Calgary: while its familiarity made it a doctrine attractive to workers who shared in this British cultural heritage, its ethnic biases and assumptions almost by definition excluded or marginalized other workers. A broader, more inclusive articulation of class interests might have resolved this dilemma, and labourism might have evolved further to cope with the challenges that the 1920s and 1930s presented Calgary's working class. That this did not happen was not a failure of labourism, per se, but instead underlined the way in which specific historical circumstances fused identities of class and ethnicity into complex and unpredictable patterns.

Even with potential voters being 'discouraged' from supporting other parties, the Calgary Labour Party's existence remained fragile before 1913. It collapsed completely during the economic slump of 1907-8, and subsequently reemerged as a purely electoral organization. In part, its experience reflected the difficulty that workers across Canada faced in transforming their collective economic power – as embodied in the trade union movement – into an effective political challenge. It remained underfunded, poorly organized, and unable to overcome persistent working-class apathy in the matter of voter registration. Run by a small coterie of skilled workers of Anglo-Canadian background, the party also made little headway in appealing to the city's unskilled and ethnic minority labourers.[76] Nor did it manage to form a stable electoral partnership with either local socialists or its potential allies in the farm movement, notably the United Farmers of Alberta (UFA) and the more radical Society of Equity. All these factors helped to limit the Labour Party's electoral success in this period. A different, more specific problem was that of securing candidates who could appeal to a sufficient proportion of the electorate while remaining committed to the reformist principles of labourism. The career of Richard Brocklebank, Calgary's only elected labour candidate before the First World War, illustrates this problem.

Born in Bruce County, Ontario, in 1864, Richard Addison Brocklebank was educated at various public schools before going on to apprentice as a carpenter.[77] In 1898 he moved to Alberta, where he soon secured work with the CPR's bridge-building department. Three years later, at the age of thirty-six, he became foreman at Thomas Underwood's contracting firm, a position he held until he took over management of the business in 1907. As if to set the seal on his successful move upwards, Brocklebank's fellow contractors soon elected him president of Calgary's builders' exchange. At the same time, he was appointed vice-president of the Brick and Sewer Company. In his social life, Brocklebank was a model citizen, an active member of the Methodist church and several fraternal societies. A keen patriot and supporter of the British Empire, he volunteered to enlist in March 1915 even though, at fifty, he was well over the maximum recruitment age. Undeterred, he successfully reapplied six months later, this time claiming to be only forty-one. He served in France as a corporal, but in July 1916 was listed as missing in action. Ottawa finally closed his file in January 1918. The life of Richard Brocklebank, it seems, epitomized the combination of material success and selfless service to which so many contemporary Canadians aspired.[78]

Brocklebank also occupies a place in Calgary history as the first man elected to local office as a representative of labour. With the support of the carpenters' union and the CTLC, he first ran for election in the civic campaign of December 1902. Victory made him Calgary's first labour city councillor.[79] In April 1904, various unions endorsed his bid to run as the new Labour Party's candidate in the federal election that November.[80] As events turned out, Brocklebank declined the nomination, a decision that prompted some labour supporters to allege that 'he had been bought off by the Conservatives,' whose own candidate went on to win the election. Brocklebank angrily denied this accusation. 'There was not enough money in either [the Conservative or Liberal] party to buy him off,' he replied to his critics.[81] Perhaps with this incident in mind, it was with some reservation that Calgary unions nominated Brocklebank to run once more for his seat on city council in the civic elections of December 1904. He rewarded their support by heading the competition in Calgary's ward three, a predominantly working-class district, although his 259 votes placed him just 22 ahead of his nearest opponent. The fact that his support amounted to just 28 percent of the popular vote suggested labour's growing dissatisfaction with him.[82]

Brocklebank's own commitment to labour's cause was becoming increasingly ambiguous. In March 1906, he attacked the idea of using money donated by steel magnate Andrew Carnegie to build a new public library in Calgary. Brocklebank told an attentive audience that Carnegie would be better advised to use his profits to 'help support the widows and orphans of the men who were killed every year in the steel works of Pittsburg [sic] than to donate the money for free libraries.' A few months later, Brocklebank was among those who criticized the Labour Party's lacklustre showing, backing up his criticism by agreeing to stand as president of a revamped Independent Labor Party (ILP).[83] Yet within a matter of weeks, Brocklebank began to take steps to distance himself from the tag of being a 'labour man.' In November 1906, he rejected urgings from the ILP that he run as their candidate for mayor, claiming that he could not afford to spare the time demanded of the office. Eventually, he relented and agreed to run, but only on the condition that he do so as an independent candidate. His success at Underwood's, he reasoned, had won him many contacts and friendships with members of Calgary's professional middle class. He believed that he could deliver as much as 25 percent of the city's business vote, but only as long as he was not perceived to be an out-and-out labour candidate. While Brocklebank's reasoning may have been sound in theory, on election day it was clear that the majority of mayoral votes, including those of Calgary's middle class, had gone to merchant Arthur Cameron. Brocklebank's 338 votes represented just 23 percent of the total, a drop of five points compared with 1904 when he ran as labour's official candidate for city council.[84]

A promotion to management in 1907 effectively ended any ambiguity surrounding Brocklebank's attachment to labourism. In May that year, when the Calgary branch of the Socialist Party of Canada (SPC) discussed the trial of American labour radical Bill Haywood, Brocklebank spoke up to recommend that the party ignore calls for a public protest and instead let justice take its course, disregarding the less-than-impartial record of the American courts when it came to dealing with men such as Haywood. At the same time, Calgary labour's own growing disillusionment with Brocklebank was evident when only eleven ILP members turned up at a meeting to hear him explain his poor performance in the past campaign. It can have surprised few, then, when Brocklebank chose not to run in the civic elections in December 1907 but instead gave his formal backing to Conservative candidate James Hornby. In subsequent elections, Brocklebank continued to back Conservatives, such as 'my friend Mr. Bennett,' and was himself elected as an independent city councillor on four more occasions between 1908 and 1912. Nothing more clearly symbolized his political swing to the right than when Brocklebank outbid four other contractors in 1909 for the job of building Calgary's proposed public library, to be funded by the same Carnegie dollars he had so bitterly denounced less than three years earlier.[85]

The political career of Richard Brocklebank reveals the limits of labourism in prewar Calgary. In part, his erratic behaviour as a labour candidate reflected the lack of party discipline within the ILP, but the party was understandably more concerned with winning new members and supporters than with chastising the one man who had brought it any electoral success. As a result, at best prewar labourism in Calgary represented a compromised critique of capitalist society.

The task of criticizing capitalism therefore fell to the small but vocal group of socialists in Calgary. The first attempt at organization occurred in 1902, when Calgary's leading Marxist, James Worsley, established Local 57 of the Canadian Socialist League (CSL). In common with their colleagues across the West, Calgary socialists emphasized the need for political action to achieve their basic objectives that 'all our people shall be properly clothed, housed and fed and that all shall have the opportunity of rendering efficient service to the state, and that distributions shall be effected with justice and economy, so that none of Labor's product shall be wasted.'[86] Because the relative economic prosperity enjoyed by Calgarians in the years 1902-6 limited the appeal of radical, anticapitalist rhetoric, the socialists won few converts in these years. The CSL folded in 1904, following Worsley's temporary departure from the city.[87] Other individuals, such as Robert Burgess, sought to influence the newly formed Labour Party in favour of socialism, but it was not until the economic slump of 1907-8 that Calgary socialists once more formed an organization of their own.

Calgary's branch of the SPC was established, appropriately, on 1 May 1907. It soon drew the committed and curious alike to its regular meetings. Broadly speaking, two types of member joined the party in this period. First, there were the skilled craftsmen of British origin who resided in Calgary, whose socialism was as much a product of their cultural heritage as it was of their experience of conditions in the West. Examples of this group include Worsley himself, carpenter George Howell, stonemason Arthur Masters, and electrical worker William J. Dyson. In addition, a number of transient, often unskilled workers, whose radicalism owed more to their direct experiences in Canada, did much to organize and publicize the party. John F. Leheney, Roscoe Fillmore, Fred Hyatt, and Henri Jaxon – formerly Louis Riel's secretary during the days of the rebellion – were prominent figures within this group.[88]

The SPC combined electoral and educative activities in its sustained critique of contemporary capitalist society. Calgary socialists, recalled one party member in later years, were 'strictly against anyone who would back reforms, they being merely palliatives.' Instead, they called for a thoroughgoing revision of society, but one that fell short of outright revolution. 'The schools, churches and the legislatures,' declared Leheney to an audience at the Co-operative Hall in January 1908, 'are all controlled by the capitalist class, and the only means workingmen have of showing their power is at the polls.' The mid-decade recession gave a temporary boost to this critique, to the extent that Fillmore later recalled that 'the streets of Calgary in December 1907 were full of angry unemployed men, socialists, and radical unionists.'[89] Yet the SPC was unable to convert this discontent into electoral gains. In the federal election of October 1908, Socialist candidate Frank Sherman came a distant third with less than 6 percent of the vote. The *Albertan* offered its consolation, acknowledging the educative purpose of such campaigns and even suggesting that 'the people of Calgary will know more of the principles of Socialism before the contest is over than they do now, and they will be none the worse for that.' The paper offered no evidence to support its conclusion that 'Calgary is increasing very rapidly both in population and in its socialistic supporters.' Subsequent elections certainly contradicted the *Albertan*'s assessment. In the provincial contest of March 1909, George Howell – one of just two Socialist candidates across the entire province – garnered less than 7 percent of the vote. Charles O'Brien, the other Socialist candidate, had originally planned to run in Calgary as well, but pulled out in favour of the Rocky Mountain riding, whose large mining community offered a better prospect of success. Victory justified O'Brien's decision, although the narrow margin of thirty-five votes underlined the difficulties that socialists faced in getting elected anywhere in Alberta.[90]

Economic recovery in 1909 further eroded what little electoral support the Calgary SPC enjoyed. Arthur Masters received just 722 votes in the 1911 federal election, some 4,000 short of second-place Liberal Van Wart and almost 7,000 behind the victorious Bennett. In the provincial election of April 1913, the SPC changed tactics and attempted to secure official CTLC endorsement of its candidate, Harry Burge. At the nomination meeting of 24 March, the CTLC expected that the endorsement of its own candidate – stonemason and labour moderate Alex Ross – would be a formality; but the SPC managed to win the backing of the carpenters' union, a long-time rival of the bricklayers' union to which Ross belonged, and together with its own members this was enough to give the socialists a majority of votes at the meeting. Despite protests from CTLC officials, Burge was duly nominated the council's candidate in Calgary North, and Ross had to be content with being selected to run in another, less favourable, ward. The election results on 17 April suggest that the SPC's efforts were largely in vain, for Burge received a mere 256 votes, the worst showing by any official labour candidate to date.[91]

In sum, neither the moderate reform platform of the Labour Party nor the rejectionist ideology of the SPC met with much electoral success in prewar Calgary. In part, popular support for socialism varied inversely to economic conditions in the city, but there were also cultural factors at play that limited its appeal to working-class Calgarians. Undoubtedly, socialism's analysis of the economic iniquities of capitalist production made sense to many of those who toiled in local factories or in the Burns meatpacking plant, but experience alone was insufficient to overcome popular perceptions and prejudices regarding the doctrine and its exponents. In stark contrast to the dominant Anglo-Canadian, Protestant culture, whose emphasis on work and acquisitive individualism shaped and was shared by much of Calgary's working class, socialists were popularly identified as idlers, shiftless, 'foreign,' and Godless.[92] As long as workers believed, or at least hoped, that the upward mobility of a Richard Brocklebank was still a matter of individual effort, Calgary's immigrant workforce could regard socialism's dour-faced grousing as anachronistic. 'Socialism does not seem to have much of a chance in the West,' concluded one visitor to Calgary in 1910, 'where everybody, if he works, can soon acquire his own one hundred and sixty acres in the country, or his own lot and house in the town.'[93] Such thinking was clearly optimistic and blind to the harsher realities of capitalist production, even in the West, but as long as Calgary continued to grow, socialism – and to a lesser extent labourism – remained an expression of marginal protest within a society in which there was no tradition of a distinct working-class culture.

The absence of an alternative working-class culture hampered the development of rejectionist ideologies in Calgary, the limited support for which further restricted the chances of building such a culture, and so on. Instead, social and cultural pursuits and practices frequently cut across class lines and so encouraged the belief that, whatever the division of power at the workplace, Calgary society rested four-square on the individualistic principles of liberal democracy. Accordingly, Calgary workers were slow to respond to the class-based appeal of labourism's moderate reform proposals, and were largely indifferent to socialism's more thorough rejection of capitalist society. In consequence, no significant subculture of opposition evolved in Calgary.

Just as occupational, ethnic, and gendered divisions within the labour force limited the disposition of workers to view themselves as a class, the absence of a class-based culture suggests that many workers shared the dominant pluralistic view of society. This fact was reflected in the paltry support for the local labour and socialist parties. This is not to argue that consensus reigned supreme in Calgary before the First World War. If workers' awareness of their collective identity and strength was conspicuous by its absence in the spheres of culture and politics, it was increasingly evident in the field of industrial relations. Reacting to the demands and disciplines of industrial capitalism, workers soon learned to organize themselves. In doing so, they responded in a fashion that helped to define the emerging contours of class in Calgary, as they formed trade unions and adopted the strike as their frontline weapon.

4
Unions and Strikes

Contemporary observers were quick to recognize and praise the importance of trade unions in prewar Calgary. 'Calgary is a labor union city,' proclaimed the *Albertan* in June 1909. 'Practically every trade is unionized. The unions are strong and responsible, and in all cases the unions have been exceedingly reasonable ... The laboring man who is not a labor unionist is both unwise and ungrateful.'[1] Such declarations acknowledged the extent to which, in just a few short years, Calgary's craftsmen had successfully organized themselves in response to the conditions of rapid industrial growth. Notwithstanding praise for the 'responsible' and 'reasonable' behaviour of unions, the city's boom years were also a time of unprecedented – and, as it turned out, unrepeated – strike activity, as workers tested the strength and tolerance of their employers. The *Albertan*'s praise for what it saw as the essential moderation of the local labour movement, for example, was prompted by a month-long strike by some 270 bricklayers and stonemasons. In the years before the First World War, collective action in the field of industrial relations provided workers with the opportunity both to improve their material conditions of life and to secure recognition of their role in society.

A certain tension characterized the evolution of Calgary's early trade union movement, as the desire for social respectability and the demands of overt industrial confrontation competed for the loyalty of members. As a result, the struggle between labour and capital spilled over the boundaries of its immediate location – the workplace – and into the arena of public discourse and debate. By the same token, while industrial conflicts were generally economic in origin they also reflected workers' demands for social equality. Through such conflict the response of organized labour to the conditions of industrial capitalism was also linked to the formation of class relations more generally.

The conditions, attitudes, and behaviours characteristic of a capitalist labour market – defined by H. Clare Pentland as 'one in which the actions of workers and employers are governed and linked by impersonal considerations of immediate pecuniary advantage' – emerged only gradually in Calgary. Conditions in the 1880s and 1890s actually militated against the development of a fully functional labour market, with local business cycles, an international depression in the 1890s, and even the vagaries of Calgary's climate combining to erode any regularity in the demand for labour, skilled or otherwise. Further, Canada's western frontier continued to offer immigrant workers the prospect of geographical and occupational mobility, as well as the promise of homesteading as an alternative to wage labour. Together, the erratic nature of demand and the fluid nature of supply hindered the formation of a relatively stable capitalist labour market.[2]

Conditions before 1900 also hampered the creation of viable trade unions in Calgary. As long as individuals believed in the promise of abundant opportunities on the frontier, then the act of simply walking away from a job remained an easier option than organizing to fight for improved pay or better conditions. In 1895, a group of North-West Mounted Police constables quit the force to head north for the Yukon, where they intended to work as miners and labourers. There, they claimed, they would be able to earn as much as fifteen dollars a day, compared to their present daily police pay of a single dollar. Nor did the offer of good wages by employers – Pentland's 'impersonal considerations of immediate pecuniary advantage' – necessarily secure the services of skilled labour. In May 1885, a number of carpenters quit work without notice to help suppress the Riel rebellion. Their sudden departure from the city shook the foundations of Calgary's first construction boom and vexed the editor of the *Herald,* who attributed their decision to 'an excess of patriotism, since carpenters in Calgary command better pay than scouts.' Facing conditions in which the laws of supply and demand seemed not to apply, several Calgary employers took to hiring local Natives when they needed additional workers.[3]

Remnants of frontier individualism among workers could also take the form of singular acts of violence.[4] Such acts were usually unpremeditated and produced little remedial effect other than to bring the offender before the local magistrate. They were certainly no basis on which to build any organized resistance to prairie capitalism. In December 1891, relations between printer Thomas Smith and his employer at the *Tribune* took a turn for the worse. One night, after a heavy bout of drinking, Smith returned to the office and attacked the building. Caught in the act, he duly received a five-dollar fine and was ordered to pay costs equivalent to two days' pay. Two years later, day labourer Arthur Roberts pursued an argument with his employer over the question of wages, a dispute that ended only when Roberts pulled out a gun and attempted to shoot the other man. Despite the apparent severity of the incident, Roberts escaped with the seemingly light jail sentence of three months' hard labour. The incidence of such violence was rare, it is true, but its occurrence does suggest that the 'rules of the game,' to borrow Eric Hobsbawm's apt phrase regarding capitalistic labour markets, had yet to be fully internalized.[5]

Against this background of almost spontaneous acts of resistance and a disregard for the tenets of industrial capitalism appeared Calgary's earliest endeavours to establish labour organizations. The first attempt was Local Assembly 9787 of the Knights of Labor (KOL).[6] In December 1886, Secretary Masterman of Winnipeg's Pioneer lodge of the KOL arrived in Calgary to explain the nature and benefits of the organization. At a meeting largely attended by the town's workers, those present were undeterred by the estimated cost of $100 to form a local assembly in Calgary, and three men even signed up on the spot. Mr Bennett of the Owen Sound, Ontario, KOL remained in town to petition for further members, and the *Herald* noted with approval that, 'We have no doubt but this organization will ere long become an honour to Calgary and an object of important interest throughout the Territories.' Local Assembly 9787 went some way towards fulfilling the writer's expectations when its members produced the *Northwest Call,* the first labour paper in Alberta. They also drafted labour legislation for presentation to the territorial legislative council and continued efforts to win over new immigrants. But the KOL's activities soon fell afoul of management at local mining companies, who combined to oppose the new organization. By the 1890s Local Assembly 9787 had disappeared from Calgary.[7]

Calgary's first craft-based labour organization was Local 171 of the International Typographical Union (ITU), formed in 1887 by print workers employed at the *Herald.* Unfortunately, no details of this union have survived, but the fact that it folded within a year reinforces the idea that Calgary's labour market at this time was too fluid to permit successful organization among local workers.[8] Nonetheless, the ITU set a precedent for other workers to follow. In January 1892, Calgary's carpenters formed Local 95 of the United Brotherhood of Carpenters and Joiners of America (UBCJA). In May that year, as the economy began to slide into depression, members of this new union notified employers of their first set of demands. These included a one-hour reduction in the ten-hour work day, and wages of $2.50 per day for the 'poorest class' of carpenters and $3.00 for 'the best,' to replace the prevailing skilled rate of $2.75. Contractors were divided in their response: some refused the demand outright, while others agreed to the reduction in hours but not the increase in pay. Forced to back up its demands, the union declared a strike on 3 May 1892.[9]

The carpenters' strike is a minor milestone in the history of Calgary, for it was the first test of collective will between labour and capital.

One of the carpenters explained how his employer no longer paid wages 'calculated on a fair and honest basis,' but instead estimated 'how many men are out of work and then places his price as low as he can accordingly.' For their part, the carpenters demonstrated an awareness that the strength of the employers lay in their ownership and control of the means of production, for they quickly formed a 'Union Building Association' in a workshop above a local blacksmith's forge and offered 'to tender on all buildings and do all kinds of jobbing in a workmanlike manner.' For the first time in Calgary, a labour dispute revealed explicit acknowledgment of the division of power that necessarily resulted from capitalist production.[10]

The depression of the 1890s temporarily delayed any further advances in labour organization in Calgary, outside those CPR employees who belonged to various national railway brotherhoods.[11] Two developments made possible the establishment and expansion of a local labour movement after 1900. The first was Calgary's breathtaking rate of industrial growth, which created a seemingly endless demand for skilled workers. The majority of these newcomers accepted their status as wage earners; unlike their predecessors, they were prepared to stay and fight for their demands rather than move elsewhere, aware that opportunities were unlikely to be better in any other city in the rapidly filling West. The second development was the desire of such workers, most of whom claimed British heritage, for public recognition within Calgary society. It was this desire, for example, that fuelled the drive to make Labour Day a significant occasion in the calendar of Calgary. These two developments – the creation of a large stable workforce and the wish for social recognition – combined in the formation of the Calgary Trades and Labour Council in 1901.

Late in 1900, members of three Calgary unions – the International Association of Machinists, the Brotherhood of Railway Carmen, and the Allied Mechanics Union – met and founded the Calgary Trades and Labour Council (CTLC). Although the ostensible purpose of the new body was to set about organizing celebrations for the following year's Labour Day, from the moment of its inaugural meeting on 19 February 1901 it was evident that another – and larger – role of the CTLC would be to promote the merits of trade unionism to the growing tide of workers sweeping into the city. Calgary's first major wave of unionization came in the wake of the decision taken at the 1902 Trades and Labour Congress convention in Berlin, Ontario, to expel national or 'dual' unions, a decision that confirmed the influence of American-based international unions within the Canadian labour movement. Indeed, most of the unions formed in Calgary before 1913 were local branches of existing international unions, and received financial assistance and procedural guidance from their headquarters south of the border. Yet it was the CTLC, consisting of men whose outlook reflected the conditions and demands of labour in Calgary, that performed the day-to-day task of organizing local workers into new unions, helping them to realize their collective identity as workers. In this respect, the interests of craft and class proved to be complementary, not mutually exclusive as is sometimes suggested by labour historians.

Between 1900 and 1907, the number of trade unions in Calgary rose from three to thirty-four, with membership up from 150 to 2,000. Table 4.1 shows this growth on an annual basis. The bulk of members came from the ranks of skilled craft workers within the building industry and railway trades. Not surprisingly, then, carpenters, bricklayers, stonemasons, and CPR mechanics dominated the CTLC's executive in this period. But there were also signs that the craft-based CTLC took seriously its charter mandate to 'foster and strengthen all existing labor unions, and to endeavor to organize the skilled and unskilled workers of both sexes amongst whom no organization at present exists.'[12] For example, CTLC-led efforts to organize unskilled workers resulted in the creation of a local branch of the United Brotherhood of Railway Employees (UBRE) consisting of freighthandlers and office clerks excluded from the older railway unions. The local Allied Mechanics Unions (AMU) similarly consisted of unskilled workers from a variety of industries across the city. Both of these unions collapsed in 1903 – the UBRE due to its failed strike that spring, the AMU because many of its members quit to join newly formed craft unions – but the General Labourers Unions (GLU) and Retail Clerks Union continued the job of representing Calgary's non-apprenticed workers.[13] In the GLU's case, this work included a successful bid to unionize several German and other ethnic-minority immigrants otherwise overlooked by the labour movement.[14]

By March 1905, Calgary's overall trade union membership stood at 1,500, roughly 12.5 percent of the city's entire population and perhaps as much as 30 percent of the adult male workforce. The CTLC subsequently bolstered its claim to be Calgary's representative labour body when it formally affiliated with the Dominion Trades and Labour Congress (DTLC) later that year. At the same time, the DTLC's western organizer, W.R. Trotter, visited Calgary and proclaimed the local movement to be 'in a very satisfactory condition.' Nonetheless, the economic recession of 1907-8 took its toll upon union membership. Trotter returned to the West in 1910 and, following a tour of Alberta, reported back to the DTLC that 'Calgary and Edmonton, after a very progressive period, seemed to be resting. The various Unions were lively enough; but there was a lack of cohesion and interest in the general movement.' Calgary's labour movement, it seemed, had reached a crucial stage in its development.[15]

Table 4.1

Trade union membership in Calgary, 1900-15

	Unions	Reported membership
1900	3	150
1901	6	n/a
1902	9	1,500
1903	14	n/a
1904	19	600
1905	25	1,500
1906	28	n/a
1907	34	n/a
1908	24	2,000
1909	24	n/a
1910	31	n/a
1911	40	3,100
1912	42	3,281
1913	44	3,092
1914	43	2,424
1915	37	1,769

Sources: Department of Labour, *Labour Organization in Canada; Labour Gazette; Henderson's Calgary City Directory, Calgary Herald*

The brief but marked economic downturn of 1907-8 turned out to be a catalyst for organizational change among Calgary unions. On the one hand, the sudden deterioration in conditions was a test of their ability to retain the loyalty, commitment, and – not least – financial contributions of their members. Not all organizations proved equal to the task, and the total number of unions fell from thirty-four in 1907 to twenty-four by 1909.[16] On the other hand, the earlier drive to organize did not cease entirely, and new unions appeared in various trades, including Calgary's blacksmiths, bakers, confectioners, hotel and restaurant workers, retail clerks, brewers, and machinists' helpers. In addition, existing craft unions pooled their resources to form new umbrella organizations such as the Building Trades Council, the Carpenters District Council, and the CPR Federated Trades Council. Finally, the CTLC broadened the scope of its own activities beyond the industrial arena to encompass support for political candidates in civic and provincial politics, and lobbying the government in Edmonton on issues of concern to workers, such as technical education.[17]

The adjustment and reorganization that took place in these years won their reward in 1910, when a second burst of unionization accompanied Calgary's return to economic prosperity. The number of locals rose from twenty-four in 1909 to thirty-one in 1910, before reaching a prewar peak of forty-four in 1913. This last figure represented almost one-third of Alberta's 133 individual unions then in existence; only seven other cities across Canada were home to a greater number of labour organizations.[18]

The relationship between unions and employers was not that of equal partners but, in the words of British historian Jonathan Zeitlin, one of 'complex and shifting ties of cooperation and conflict, whose precise balance cannot be determined in advance.'[19] Among some labour historians, Calgary's early craft unions have gained the reputation for being distinctly conservative or job-conscious in their approach towards industrial relations.[20] But the historical record suggests that they were in fact a vehicle not only for important economic reforms, but also for advancing the broader political interests of workers in this period. These activities endowed craft unions with a pivotal role in the formation of class relations in Calgary, as elsewhere in Canada.[21] A brief examination of three such unions – the printers, the carpenters, and the bricklayers and stonemasons – suggests that no single characterization can do justice to the diversity of attitudes and responses of craft workers towards others unions, other workers, or the demands of industrial capitalism.

Printing, carpentry, and the brick trades accounted for more than 2,100 workers in 1911, or 10 percent of Calgary's total workforce. Within each industry the rate of unionization was close to 100 percent, and so the influence of these crafts within the labour movement itself was significantly greater than these figures suggest. The three unions consisted mainly of skilled, apprenticed men (in 1911 women accounted for less than 1 percent of workers in these trades), predominantly of British origin. Beyond these superficial similarities, each organization reacted differently to its experience of industrialization in Calgary.[22]

With the assistance of CTLC officials and other unionists, eight Calgary printers formed Local 449 of the International Typographical Union (ITU) on 27 May 1902. Growth of the ITU was slow during its first two years, with membership reaching only twenty-seven by 1904. This figure doubled over the next three years to reach fifty-six by 1907, at which time the mid-decade depression once more slowed the union's advance. A period of vigorous expansion then followed and the ITU increased in size from sixty-four at the end of 1909 to 180 by the outbreak of the First World War. By that time, the union was able to boast that 'Every shop in Calgary of any importance has a signed agreement.' Wartime enlistment hit the ITU, as it did many other unions, but with 124 members in 1921 the union still represented roughly 80 percent of Calgary's 152 printers and compositors employed at the time.[23]

In many respects, the ITU was a model craft union. Its primary concern was the exclusive and narrowly defined job-related interests of its own members. 'Eight hours for work, eight for sleep, eight to do with what they will' was the union's motto, at a time when compositors and pressmen were working a fifty-three-hour week. The union won the eight-hour day in 1906 and achieved success in persuading employers at the *Herald* and the *Albertan* to hire only union men. Weekly wages doubled during Local 449's first decade of existence, from $10.50 in 1901 to $21.00 by 1913, compared to an increase in local retail prices of approximately 40 percent.[24]

The printers' union also sought to secure improvements in working conditions. Calgary's print shops were small and stuffy, their lack of adequate ventilation remaining in the memory of linotyper R.J. Brown long after his days with the *Herald* were over. 'What a dump the composing room was,' he recalled. 'Four linotypes and presses and all the make-up equipment crowded in the basement of a building ... No air-conditioning of any sort, and the stink from the gasoline burning linotypes still seems to linger in my nostrils.'[25] Despite such conditions, worker-employer relations appear to have been remarkably amicable within the printing trade. In 1902, for example, *Herald* editor J.J. Young made an office in the paper's building available to the union, an offer that the *Albertan* matched in 1905. Indeed, such was the level of cooperation between the two sides that in 1914 the ITU was able to report that 'no untoward incident has transpired to spoil the harmony that obtains between the various employers and the members of the local. True, small differences have occasionally arised [sic], but these have always been settled amiably and to the entire satisfaction of the parties concerned.' An absence of any strike action by printers during this period may be seen as confirmation of this assessment.[26]

The history of Local 449 lends support to Sally Zerker's observation, in her study of the ITU in Toronto, that Canadian printers occupied the position of an elite within organized labour.[27] They were the aristocrats of local labour, regarding themselves on a par with white-collar professionals. This was also the public perception of printers in Calgary, to judge from one satirical account of a union social gathering in 1908: 'The long tables groaned with the good things which the committee had thoughtfully prepared. There was pâté-de-fois-gras, frogs legs, roasts of all sorts, sandwiches beautifully prepared and artfully carved to represent animals and other things pertaining to news-rooms ... Wine of the vintage of 1721 from the cellars of the Turkish sultan, dainty French liqueurs, cigars from Cuba, cigarettes especially made for the Turkish harem, and other flanking dishes too numerous to mention garnished the linen draped tables.'[28] If this alleged fancy for the finer things in life helped to set Calgary printers apart from – or above – other workers, then their own actions demonstrated a sense of *noblesse oblige* that transcended their narrow craft interests. Printers were early and active supporters of the Labour Day parades held each September; they intervened on behalf of other trades to help improve their working conditions; they supported other unions and helped to organize non-union workers, notably the city mail carriers in 1913; and they helped to realize various local social reform endeavours such as the Sunday Hospital movement, a fund-raising event held each year to help finance public health care in Calgary.[29]

The ITU was also an active participant in local labour politics, supporting early labour candidates such as Richard Brocklebank and, in later years, producing a number of successful candidates of its own. Michael Costello and Andrew Davison were both *Herald* employees and union members who went on to serve as mayor of Calgary, Costello during the First World War and Davison in the 1930s. Although each man moved closer towards the Conservative Party's position as the years passed, both managed to retain a significant personal support among Calgary workers. Local 449 also provided a number of city councillors and school-board trustees, and many of its members became keen supporters of the Dominion Labor Party in the 1920s. Fred J. White, an ITU member for more than fifty years, was the union's most successful politician. An employee with the Western Printing and Lithography Company, White was elected to city council a total of ten times between 1919 and 1941, and a labour MLA on three occasions in 1921, 1926, and 1930. Unlike Costello and Davison, he remained an ardent labour man and in 1940 joined the CCF. In each of his political roles, White persistently and consistently argued the cause of Calgary labour.[30]

Applied to the ITU, then, 'conservative' or 'job conscious' are misleading characterizations of Calgary unionism in this period. The same is true of Local 1055 of the United Brotherhood of Carpenters and Joiners of America (UBCJA). Following the demise of the short-lived Local 95 in the 1890s, Calgary's carpenters reorganized in 1902, once again with the help of CTLC officials. Twenty-nine members attended the founding meeting held at the city's Co-operative Hall on 12 April that year. Their first action was to initiate a union-shop drive by forming a committee to keep a list of all carpenters active in Calgary and to encourage non-union men to join.[31] Unlike the ITU, the UBCJA's early years were characterized by a propensity to strike in support of its demands, and between 1901 and 1914 the union struck work a total of seven times. Carpenters occupied a key position among the local building trades, and a strike by them was capable of bringing the entire construction industry to a halt. Employers were aware of this fact and during Calgary's boom years were prepared to concede many of the union's demands rather than risk a prolonged and expensive stoppage. Nonetheless, employers maintained a distinction between legitimate and illegitimate union demands, and this distinction influenced the pattern of labour relations within the industry. The two carpenters' strikes of 1902 and 1903 illustrate this delicate balance.

In May 1902, the newly organized carpenters presented a set of demands to the city's contractors. Arguing that their respective interests were 'closely allied,' the union pressed for a nine-hour day, a minimum wage of $2.50, a limit to the number of apprentices hired, and fixed rates of overtime pay. In return, it agreed that 'no carpenter [would] take work outside the contractor for less than 10% above the rate of wage paid by the contractor,' a concession that gave established businesses an advantage in the hiring of labour.[32] The contractors made no response to these proposals, and on 28 June the carpenters gave notice that they were prepared to strike in support of their demands, setting a deadline of 1 July. This ultimatum added to a sense of impending crisis within Calgary's construction industry, for stonecutters were already out on strike over wages and hours, while building labourers had recently strengthened their bargaining position by joining the General Labour Union. 'The atmosphere in the business world is dense with labor unrest,' remarked the *Albertan* of the situation. 'The sound of commerce in many centers is drowned in the noisy clamor as the forces of capital and labor clash together.'[33]

The clash intensified on 1 July when ninety carpenters struck as threatened, stopping work at thirteen separate firms. The union honoured certain existing contractual obligations, allowing a handful of carpenters and 'rough workers' to remain on those jobs begun prior to the union's original strike warning. Within two weeks local plumbers and plasterers felt the impact of the strike, as their own work was frequently dependent on that of the carpenters being completed. At least one contractor chose to sign the new agreement rather than endure any further losses. On 16 July, the CTLC staged a public display of solidarity and support in the form of a street parade and 'monster demonstration,' complete with drums, fireworks, and speeches. As one observer of the event remarked, 'it is doubtful if any public meeting, other than the political meetings in the heat of election time, and few times even then, have been better attended.' Addressing the assembled audience were not only youthful labour leaders but also two clergymen and a young R.B. Bennett. Bennett proclaimed organization to be 'the spirit of the age' and argued that if lawyers and dentists were permitted to form associations, then so should labour. He went even further, declaring the well-being of all workers to be a measure of the nation's welfare. 'So long as I live,' he told the crowd, 'I will give my best efforts to any labor organization which endeavors to uphold right causes, make better the homes of the people and tends to build up a strong and reliant race.' The Bennett who spoke to Calgary workers that summer was, it seems, a far cry from the future 'Iron Heel' prime minister of the 1930s.[34]

With public sympathies resting on the side of the carpenters, the contractors eventually conceded all of the union's demands, and the strike ended on 21 July. Building activity resumed within a few days, as did, it appears, industrial harmony. William Cushing, whose sash-and-door factory had been hit by the strike, held a garden party at his house to celebrate the return to work. Among those invited were a number of his own men, including one Mr Watson, who spoke approvingly of the 'very pleasant relations between the employer and the employees.' Public expressions of support for the carpenters helped to bolster the legitimacy of their claims and placed additional pressure on contractors to concede their substance.[35] The matter of a strike's legitimacy is significant, for while such disputes were frequently economic in terms of origin and motivation, their conduct and resolution also took place within the social arena. With no state-sanctioned arbitration process in place at the time, both sides saw the importance of appealing their case to the court of public opinion. A second strike by Calgary carpenters in 1903 further underlined the need of unions to establish the legitimacy of their demands.[36]

On 15 May 1903, 130 members of Local 1055 struck work to protest the hiring of non-union labour by certain contractors in Calgary. The employers quickly yielded on the question, dismissing all such men, and business resumed the following day. Just two weeks later, however, the carpenters once again threatened to strike, this time in support of a stoppage involving GLU-led teamsters. Contractors had attempted to break the teamsters' union by bringing in strike breakers and even operating the firms' haulage carts themselves. In response, the carpenters announced that as of 4 June they would refuse to handle any lumber hauled by non-union labour. Employers viewed this latest threat as an unwarranted challenge to their right to control the industry. To preempt the secondary strike they locked out more than eighty carpenters late on 3 June. Facing a stoppage that threatened to bring construction work to a halt, a number of Calgary's other trade unions sided with the employers and refused to lend their support to either the teamsters or the carpenters. President Savory of the bricklayers' union, for example, repeatedly stated that his own members did 'not believe in the methods of the carpenters' and refused even to boycott non-union hauled lumber. Interestingly, non-union teamsters, who had remained at work during the original dispute, now struck in sympathy with the locked-out carpenters. This gesture had little effect, as the employers had no trouble in finding replacements among the summer influx of unskilled, non-union immigrants.[37]

In contrast to the public support of the previous year, few Calgarians were prepared to the back the carpenters this time. Letters to the local press demonstrated little in the way of public sympathy, with a self-styled

'Friend of the Workingman' exhorting the carpenters to reflect 'on the gross injustice you are doing your wives and families, do not be misled by a few agitators who have their own aims in view, but act independently as free born Britons.'[38] Calgary's outspoken magistrate, Jeremiah Travis, similarly blamed the trouble on 'a few demagogues' and claimed that the union's rank-and-file members had told him that they had been averse to any strike call on this issue. 'If you are wise,' Travis counselled them, 'now you will ignore the dictation of your leaders, throw them over, cease your notion that you are ultimately going to control the universe or the Calgary portion, and go work like men ... Be men enough to act for yourselves as men and no longer as a parcel of children.'[39] Such public appeals to patriotic duty, family responsibility, and notions of masculinity all helped to undermine the legitimacy of the carpenters' cause in 1903.

In the absence of union solidarity or public support, a number of teamsters and carpenters returned to work on terms set by the contractors, while others left the city for work elsewhere. The denouement came on 14 July when, following a request from the CTLC, Deputy Minister of Labour William Lyon Mackenzie King arrived in Calgary to mediate a settlement between the employers and remaining strikers. For the carpenters the six-week dispute had been a near disaster, costing the members roughly $7,500 in lost wages and significantly draining the union's financial reserves. Perhaps more importantly, while King's compromise upheld the existing levels of union wages and hours within the industry, it ended the practice of the closed shop. In future, contractors were not to discriminate against union men, but neither would they be compelled to hire labour through the union. The union never recovered from this blow, and in the spring of 1904 Local 1055 dissolved itself, citing financial exigency. (Calgary carpenters subsequently reorganized themselves as Local 1779 of the UBCJA.)[40]

Local 2 of the Bricklayers and Stonemasons International Union (BSMIU) occupied a position between that of the printers and the carpenters in terms of militancy. Striking on just two occasions in the years before 1914, the Calgary branch of the BSMIU lived up to its 'reputation of being a level-headed and conservative union, and one which is averse to strikes and that sort of thing.'[41] Such conservatism was less the product of ideological preference or even social deference than of the technological changes then transforming the stonecutting craft across North America. Historian George Barnett details these changes in his pioneering study of the labour process, which will be briefly summarized.[42]

Although machinery to cut stone for construction had been available in the nineteenth century, it was expensive and relatively inefficient and so left intact the stonecutter's importance within the industry's labour process. This situation changed around the turn of the century, when technological advances produced machines with the capacity to perform the work of seven or eight men. Employers increasingly turned to mechanization as the frontline means of raising productivity, a choice that led to the displacement of large numbers of skilled workers. Between 1900 and 1915, the introduction of mechanical stoneplaners enabled employers in the United States to lay off half of the nation's 25,000 stonecutters.[43] As a result, although the Journeymen Stonecutters Union (JSU) continued to secure wage increases for those of its members still in employment, the stonecutters entered a steep decline relative to other trades within the construction industry. This was as true in Calgary as anywhere else on the continent. Between 1901 and 1915, union wages for local stonecutters rose by 19 percent, whereas those for bricklayers and carpenters, respectively, increased by 28 and 34 percent.[44]

The plight of the JSU in Calgary before 1914 is relevant to the attitude of the BSMIU in that it aggravated an ongoing jurisdictional dispute between local stonecutters and stonemasons. This dispute was part of a broader fraternal conflict that occurred in cities across North America wherever the two unions coexisted, but it was also shaped by local considerations. In Calgary it centred on the particular nature of the local sandstone, the primary material used for many of the city's larger buildings. The JSU's constitution claimed the right for its members to cut stone of any type or quality, while that of the BSMIU specified 'all cutting, rubbing, and grinding of all kinds of brick and all cutting, setting of cement blocks or artificial stone.' The problem was that Calgary sandstone was so soft that it was frequently classed as rubble and had to be fortified with other materials. Consequently, both the JSU and the BSMIU claimed the exclusive right to cut sandstone, and engaged in a mutually damaging price-cutting war as each tried to outbid the other for job contracts.[45] For their part, Calgary's contractors were increasingly exasperated by the instability and bitterness engendered by the dispute, and in 1912 they refused to deal with either union until the two resolved their differences. Much time was spent at the regular meetings of the BSMIU debating the need to defend and uphold the constitutional principles at stake, but with little progress towards resolution. The international headquarters of both unions were of little assistance in this respect, leaving it up to individual locals to sort out matters for themselves. Eventually, sheer numbers carried the day. In June 1912, at which time the JSU had 150 members and the BSMIU 300, both unions became embroiled in a lengthy strike. As it dragged on, the limited funds of the JSU proved insufficient to support its idle members, many of whom consequently quit the local to seek work elsewhere. This effectively won the local jurisdictional war for the BSMIU, whose larger financial base enabled it to weather the stoppage in better shape. This victory was confirmed on the international level in 1914, when the BSMIU formally absorbed the JSU.[46]

This lengthy and unproductive struggle with the JSU absorbed much of the BSMIU's energies before 1914, leaving the union on the defensive and favouring a cautious approach in other areas. The BSMIU maintained an ambivalent, arms-length relationship with other labour organizations such as the CTLC, the Alberta Federation of Labor, and the local Building Trades Council. In the case of the CTLC, the union complained that it 'did not get a square deal from that body, as the carpenters could overrule everything with their delegates as they were always there in full strength.'[47] Yet if this were true, the bricklayers themselves were largely to blame for the UBCJA's dominance: the BSMIU's own delegates were notorious absentees from CTLC meetings and so enabled the carpenters to direct council rulings. The relative conservatism of the BSMIU, in comparison with the UBCJA and ITU, may have been rooted in its material struggle with the stonecutters, but it received unnecessary reinforcement by the actions – or inaction – of its own members. In this respect, the BSMIU does lend support to the common characterization of Calgary labour as being conservative and overly job conscious.

Taken together, the experiences of the ITU, UBCJA, and BSMIU reveal a variety of concerns and attitudes as Calgary labour responded to the changes and challenges of an economy undergoing rapid expansion and transformation. In general, these unions sought to balance the interests of their own members with those of other workers in Calgary. This was not always possible, as the conflict between the BSMIU and JSU showed, but even in this case the length of fraternal strife reflected a desire for compromise rather than conquest. By 1911, the ongoing process of mutual assistance among unions had helped to charter more than forty new organizations in the city. Among these were several that consisted of unskilled workers, including hod-carriers, builders' helpers, and brewery employees. The spirit of unionism even extended to Calgary's newspaper boys, who in September 1914 organized themselves and struck for higher wages.[48] The *Albertan* was right: Calgary was a labour union city.

The existence of a union was one thing; its ability to protect and advance the interests of its members could be quite another. Employers were often willing to tolerate the presence of a union within their industry without necessarily accepting its right to make demands. The case of the American Federation of Musicians (AFM) illustrates this point. Calgary musicians formed Local 53 of the AFM in February 1905 and soon requested a wage increase for its members. One theatre manager, a Mr Tempest, replied curtly that he 'did not object to his orchestra joining the union, but he was not going to let any union dictate to him what wages he was to pay, and if the union should force him to pay more than he was paying now, he would cut out the orchestra and have the piano only.' This choice – jobs or wages – caught the union somewhat off guard, and provided the first test of its ability to enforce the union shop. Vice-president William Piper's response to Tempest underlined, with unintentional humour, the considerable distance between union rhetoric and union strength. Making a virtue out of necessity, Piper told Tempest that he was free to do as he pleased, but that if he went ahead with his threat then he had better hire a union pianist, for 'it would be better to have a union musician making a little money, than have a lot of it going into a business that catered only to society, and not to the working man.' Sadly, the historical record does not indicate whether Tempest backed down in the face of this less-than-dire ultimatum, but it seems unlikely.[49]

What this incident does demonstrate is the problem that confronted all trade unions in this period. As long as employers like Tempest felt that they could ignore unions demands with impunity, the Calgary labour movement faced a fragile and uncertain future. To attract and retain members, unions had somehow to prove that they were able to wrest concessions from employers; clearly, idle threats like that of the AFM were unlikely to do the job. As a result, during their formative years Calgary unions depended heavily on the strike weapon as a means by which to impress their employers, the public, and potential recruits with their collective strength and will. In this context, the strikes that littered the prewar decade in Calgary should be regarded not as an aberration from an otherwise peaceful norm, but as an integral feature of local industrial relations. Strikes also served a further purpose: the lessons of defeat and victory they provided workers helped to bridge the divide between craft and class.[50]

Calgary workers struck work a total of eighty-two times between 1883 and 1929. Forty-six of these strikes – 56 percent of the total – occurred in the years 1901-14, making this an unparalleled period of industrial conflict in the city. This level of strike activity was higher than that of other industrial regions in Canada. During the same time, for example, 421 strikes took place in ten cities in southern Ontario – an average of forty-two per city – while in the Maritimes workers in eleven cities struck a total of 321 times, an average of just twenty-eight strikes per city.[51] An examination of the high incidence of strikes in Calgary is merited in its own right but also contributes to the national picture of industrial tension before the First World War.[52]

Table 4.2 shows the number of strikes per year in Calgary. Their distribution lends support to the view that strikes are not simple responses to economic hardship but in fact occur more often during periods of prosperity. Workers fought sixteen of the forty-six strikes (35 percent) during Calgary's years of initial expansion, 1901-6, and a further eighteen (39 percent) during the boom years of 1910-2. In contrast, just six strikes (13 percent) took place during the economic recession of 1907-9.

The seasonal distribution of strikes further underlines this connection between strikes and periods of prosperity. As Table 4.3 illustrates, half of all strikes began in the spring months of April through June. This period marked the annual restart of the construction industry after a long winter slowdown that could last as long as seven months. At this time, contractors were particularly vulnerable to the threat of strike action, especially if they had substantial fixed capital costs to recoup. In addition, many annual wage agreements expired in May each year, and unions used the threat of strike action as a tactical weapon in contract negotiations. In March 1905, the *Herald* immediately qualified its observation that 'a labor disturbance would appear to be a very remote possibility' with the warning that, with many contracts falling due on 1 May, 'already there are reports of dissatisfaction.'[53] That the months of July to September accounted for a further quarter of all strikes may be explained in part by the summer exodus of many labourers for temporary work in the harvest fields surrounding Calgary or to tend their own homesteads, leaving those who remained in a relatively strong bargaining position with their employers.[54]

Table 4.2

Strikes in Calgary, 1901-14

	Strikes	% of total strikes for the period
1901	1	2.2
1902	1	2.2
1903	6	13.0
1904	1	2.2
1905	0	–
1906	7	15.2
1907	2	4.4
1908	2	4.4
1909	2	4.4
1910	1	2.2
1911	11	23.9
1912	6	13.0
1913	5	10.9
1914	1	2.2
Total	46	100.2

Sources: Labour Gazette; Calgary Herald; Albertan

Table 4.3

Seasonal distribution of strikes in Calgary, 1901-14

	Strikes	% of total
January-March	5	10.9
April-June	23	50.0
July-September	12	26.1
October-December	6	13.0

Sources: Labour Gazette; Calgary Herald; Albertan

Wage demands featured in at least two-thirds of all strikes in Calgary between 1901 and 1914, suggesting that workers were mainly concerned with maximizing their gains within the existing system of production. Yet even the most straightforward dispute could contain several layers of meaning for those involved. As historian Richard Price notes, 'Getting "more" implies a wider series of changes in the employer-employee relationship than that of the monetary amount involved; going on strike for more implies that workers feel they are strong enough to force concessions from the employer and immediately suggests a changed power relationship.'[55] No doubt for many of Calgary's workers who did go on strike, the prospect of winning a higher wage was a major motivation, but there is also evidence that wage demands could act as 'a convenient rallying cry,' to use Edward Shorter and Charles Tilly's phrase, that obscured other concerns.[56] A tailors' strike in 1912 revealed how the questions of wages and job control, frequently considered as separate issues by labour historians, actually shaded into one another. In April that year, thirty tailors struck for union recognition and for a 50 percent increase in wages. Their employers, the city's master tailors, conceded recognition of the new organization but limited their offer of a raise in pay to 25 percent. The tailors' demand, they argued, would fundamentally alter relations within the industry. 'We would simply have to retire from the business,' explained one master tailor. 'We told them that if they quit they might as well take their tools with them and leave the city.' In other words, the employers – and presumably the employees too – recognized that a dispute ostensibly over wages was also part of the struggle for workplace control within the local clothing industry.[57] This was true of many other strikes in Calgary in which the main issue appeared to be wages, but where in fact there were deeper working-class concerns over the nature of work itself. Three areas may be identified by way of example.

First, many of Calgary's craft workers believed that the increased mechanization of their trades enabled employers to hire relatively unskilled workers who lacked any formal training. Obviously this threatened their own status and welfare, and sapped the strength of their unions. This fear was reflected in several of Calgary's strikes. In 1905 printers at the *Herald* threatened to stop work when they discovered that their employer was using apprentices simply as cheap labour to operate the new mechanized presses. The ITU claimed that this practice denied trainee printers 'the opportunity to become proficient at job works.'[58] Other workers voiced similar complaints at different times. In 1912, 1,200 carpenters struck for six weeks in support of a wage demand, managing to bring operations to a halt at ninety-two individual firms. This show of solidarity eventually won the carpenters their increase, but diluting their sense of victory were a number of unresolved issues regarding the changing nature of the trade. As one carpenter explained, 'When a man serves his time he is supposed to know his trade ... There are men in this city that are not competent and have not got any more tools than a saw, square and hammer, and there are some men who have not learned their trade, and still they get the same wages as competent men.' A decade later, carpenter and labour alderman Robert Parkyn made much the same observation when he complained, 'I have met men in Calgary where they could no more dress or make a thing than they could fly.'[59] Plumbers also protested the deskilling of their trade when they argued that competency was 'the only issue at stake' during a strike in 1906. Although related to the matter of wage levels, this concern over the dilution of skill remained a separate and enduring worry for local workers.[60]

Related to the effect of increased mechanization was a second concern, that industrialization somehow diminished the traditional 'masculinity' of many trades.[61] For many a craftsman, work involved pride in the skills learned, a sense of camaraderie with fellow workers, and the route to socially prescribed respectability by providing the means of support for his wife and family. As American writer Whiting Williams commented in 1925, 'everywhere among the workers a man determines the social standing of himself and his family, not so much by earning power as by the NATURE of his job.'[62] Largely subliminal in nature, the masculinity of work occasionally surfaced as an issue during industrial disputes in Calgary. When a gang of labourers working on the new CPR hotel in 1913 struck for improved pay, they detailed their demands on a number of large red-lettered signs that they had erected on the building site. 'We demand 30c an hour,' stated one such placard, under which was added by way of admonition, 'Be a man and do not work for less.' Two years earlier, the question of manliness had been a feature of a strike by Calgary plasterers. The strikers had asked RNWMP superintendent R. Burton Deane to arbitrate the dispute, but to their dismay he dismissed their initial arguments for higher wages. 'It seems to me,' he ruled, 'that they should account themselves extraordinarily fortunate to have drawn such excellent pay for so long a time.' The plasterers therefore turned to what they regarded as the demeaning nature of the job itself as a justification for better pay. 'When I get down to work I strip myself to the buff and feel more like an animal than a man,' complained one of the strikers. Deane agreed that 'manliness' was indeed an important aspect of work, but deftly turned the plasterer's argument on its head. 'The stokers of a big steamship are generally stripped to the waist while working at the furnaces,' he replied, 'but they do not on that account consider themselves to be anything but MEN, made in the image of their Creator. Why should the pursuit of an honourable calling, which only a man can follow, tend to the loss of self-respect in a competent manner?'[63]

The contested authority to hire and fire personnel was a third concern illuminated by strikes in Calgary. Unions often played an important role in the recruitment process at construction sites and other workplaces, whether formally through the enforcement of a closed shop, compelling foremen to hire through the union itself, or informally by the recommendation of friends and family for vacant positions. Printers at the *Albertan* in 1904 opposed editor William Davidson's appointment of non-union man Stanley Robinson to the position of monoline operator. Even after Robinson agreed to join the union, the ITU executive continued to blackball him, claiming that he lacked sufficient experience for the job. Instead they insisted that Davidson hire an existing union member, a demand to which the editor eventually conceded.[64] Authority over hiring was also an issue in March 1910, when the foreman at the new King George Hotel building site asked union carpenters there to work a ten-hour day so that they could finish the job on schedule. The union refused his request, having fought long and hard to secure the nine-hour day. But they agreed to 'supply him with all the men needed' to complete the work, and accordingly presented him with a list of approved names. In June 1911, the King George was the scene of a more serious dispute over hiring, when the foreman hired two non-union electricians. Immediately, some ninety carpenters and other union workers struck in protest and demanded the dismissal of the two men plus the foreman himself. The contractor yielded and removed all three men, a move that tacitly confirmed not only the right of unions to direct the hiring of labour but the effectiveness of the strike as a selective weapon in industrial relations.[65]

The history of strikes in prewar Calgary accords with K.G.J.C. Knowles's observation some forty years ago, that 'since wages stand for more than can be bought with them, wage strikes tend to be symbolic of wider grievances.'[66] Concerns over the impact of mechanization, the dilution of work's masculinity, and the right to hire and fire by no means exhaust the list of labour's grievances in Calgary. Those historians who still insist on exclusively economistic – wage-related – interpretations of strikes should reflect on the fact that strikes themselves were frequently an expensive form of protest. Workers who were engaged in even a moderately lengthy dispute had to weigh the prospect of winning a future gain of a few cents an hour against an immediate loss of wages and a drain on their union's reserves. Even a victory on the question of wages held its own risk if it prompted employers to hire fewer workers in a bid to reduce their total wage bill. This, for example, had been the case in Tempest's handling of the threat by the musicians' union in 1905.[67]

On the level of class formation, the fact of labour's participation in strikes was probably more significant than the outcome of any individual dispute. Mornings spent standing on a picket line helped to produce a sense of fraternity and even solidarity among a union's members that remained only latent in the organization's more routine functions.[68] James Worsley made this point in the wake of the carpenters' defeat in 1903, when he used his *Bond of Brotherhood* to expand on the educative purposes of the strike weapon. 'Every strike, every lockout, every oppression of the workers by their masters makes every union man feel himself drawn closer and closer to this Bond, his refuge, his place of safety from the violence, greed and mastership of his employer.'[69] The fact that the *Bond of Brotherhood* collapsed within a year, due to a lack of subscribers, suggests that relatively few workers shared Worsley's more radical views of labour relations in Calgary. All the same, the prevalence of strikes in Calgary in the years 1901-14 was a measure of the relevance of his words. Victory vindicated a union's decision to strike in the first place and underlined the potential strength of labour. Defeat helped to undermine the faith of workers in boosterism's expressions of social pluralism, expressions that denied the fundamental inequality between capital and labour. In this way, strikes waged in the often narrow interests of a particular craft or union played a crucial role in the formation of wider class relations.

As in any city, of course, only a fraction of Calgary's workers belonged to trade unions, leaving the vast majority of the working class without any institutional voice or representation. Yet trade unions – especially in their combative guise – hinted at the potential strength of workers *as a class* far more convincingly than did any elements of a distinctive culture or labour's early forays into independent politics. Often criticized for their sectional interests and accommodative attitudes towards industrial capitalism, trade unions nevertheless remained fundamental to the achievement of social reforms.[70] In the years before the First World War, the emergence and development of a vital trade union movement in Calgary was largely predicated on the continuation of a buoyant economy, one that encouraged employers to tolerate the presence of 'strong and responsible' unions and concede their demands as long as they remained 'exceedingly reasonable.' In 1913, that premise was about to be rudely shaken as the onset of depression and growing threat of war thrust Calgary into a new, harsher era of industrial relations, one that would test the labour movement's ability and willingness to represent all workers.

Part 2
The Labour Movement, 1913-29

5
Depression and War, 1913-7

In the winter of 1912-3, an economic crisis sparked by events in the Balkans hit Canada much as it did other western industrial countries. 'Foreign investors, alarmed at the rapid over-expansion of Canada's economic infrastructure as well as by events in Europe,' notes historian James Struthers, 'were no longer willing to finance the frenetic pace of the nation's development. Once pricked, the balloon of credit collapsed.'[1] Among the many victims were Calgary's twin booms in construction activity and real estate speculation. The outbreak of war in August 1914 compounded their collapse. Amid the turmoil that followed, workers in Calgary struggled to adjust to the dramatically changed economic and social conditions, while a new breed of labour politicians attempted to articulate a new sense of collective class identity. 'This is a Labor war and will be won by Labor men,' declared the *Albertan* in September 1917. 'Will Labor receive its proper reward when the war is over and the battle is won, in better working conditions and a more equitable share in the fruits of production?'[2] As the war dragged on, this same question – what was the broader meaning of a victory for democracy? – came to the fore in public debate across Canada and ensured that there would be no simple return to the prewar status quo. As Calgary veteran Private Harry Fowler warned in the fall of 1917, 'Labour will demand its place in the sun. Let the Government and the members of industry prepare the way for the new men.'[3] Far more than the decade of peace and prosperity before 1913, depression and war helped to focus the minds of labour in Calgary.

The Balkans crisis of 1913 effectively ended the flow of British capital into Canada. The impact was especially severe in the West, where ten years of unprecedented economic expansion came to a grinding halt. Nowhere was this more evident than in Calgary. The depression not only exposed the fragility of the city's economic foundations, it shook the previously unquestioned faith in progress maintained by its authorities and leading entrepreneurs. Four years of war would complete this dismantling of civic ideology.

Calgary's construction industry, both the engine and barometer of the local economy, showed early and dramatic signs of the depression's impact. Always susceptible to climatic variations and seasonal fluctuations in activity, the building trades now fell victim to the tightening of capital on the world's money markets. Building permits issued in Calgary fell from a record high of almost $20.4 million in 1912 to just $8.6 million a year later. This slide continued, and by 1915 the total value of permits amounted to little more than 1 percent of the 1912 figure. Even with an improvement in economic conditions after 1915, recovery within the industry remained modest, the value of permits increasing by just 4 percent over the next two years.[4] As construction activity stalled and real estate transactions dwindled to a near standstill, many investors simply abandoned their projects and refused to pay taxes owed to the city. At the time, English financier Sir William Wiseman pointed out that 'improvements make times good and money plentiful while in course of construction, but in the depression which inevitably follows serious financial difficulties are encountered by those who have to meet Civic obligations.' Calgary was not alone in this, for all major cities across western Canada found themselves in the same predicament. By late 1914, 40 percent of the $25 million in taxes due to them remained outstanding.[5]

The situation in Calgary was further aggravated when the recently completed CPR shops at Ogden, designed to provide work for more than 2,000 mechanics, began to lay off workers in large numbers. In February 1913, the *Alberta Federationist,* a local labour newspaper, reported that it 'could not see when the Ogden shops would be able to work anything like full time with a larger working staff and modern machinery, when the old shops could not be kept on full time.' The summer of 1913 brought no significant upturn in conditions, and in August the company discharged a further 300 workers. One month later, management at the works placed all mechanics on a reduced forty-hour week, and by December a quarter of all employees had been laid off.[6]

With the construction and railway industries employing 40 percent of Calgary's workforce before 1913, it was inevitable that their decline would produce reverberations throughout the city's economy. As thousands of these workers tightened their belts, aggregate demand for goods and services diminished. Clearinghouse returns – an indicator of local retail activity – fell by more than 10 percent between 1912 and 1913, from $275 to $247 million, and by a further 31 percent over the next two years.[7] Responding to this decline, Calgary businessmen petitioned the federal government for a loan of $10 million in August 1914 'so that business can still be carried on,' and gave their support to the creation of a City Planning Commission and an Industrial Service Building, both intended to centralize and coordinate future development. Against this background, R.B. Bennett must have expressed the hopes of many Calgarians when he called on the city council to intervene and 'endeavour to concentrate our capital expenditures upon the extension of revenue-producing undertakings such as tramways, waterworks, sewers etc.'[8] But such hopes were in vain. In 1911, two years before the depression began in earnest, the city council had offered $500,000 in bonds on the London stock markets. A year later, $420,000 or 84 percent of these remained in the hands of the underwriters. As a consequence, the city entered the depression with limited capital resources, in addition to its lost tax revenues, and wartime administrations would be characterized by an austere approach towards public spending.[9]

Large-scale unemployment soon became another defining characteristic of the depression. Calgarians had long regarded seasonal unemployment as an occupational hazard and usually made provision against a temporary lay-off each winter. After 1912, however, enforced idleness became an entrenched feature of the local economy and threatened the welfare of even the most provident worker. 'Throughout the whole West the number of unemployed is considerably larger than in former years,' recorded Dominion Fair Wage Officer J.D. McNiven in December 1913, adding that 'Unemployment is not confined to any particular trade or occupation but is general.'[10] The fragmentary nature of the existing data prevents any precise calculation of the number of unemployed in Calgary, but the general magnitude of the problem is unmistakable. In January 1914, seventeen of Calgary's forty or so unions reported 1,825 of their members to be without work. By autumn, the total number of unemployed men was upward of 7,000, approximately 35 percent of the adult male workforce. Unfortunately, comparable statistics for unemployed women are not available. It should be remembered that behind those thrown out of work by the depression stood an even larger number of dependants. In January 1915, 3,061 men officially identified as unemployed claimed support for a total of 6,122 dependants, meaning that more than one person in eight among Calgary's population of 67,500 was directly affected by unemployment.[11]

The city could not ignore a problem of this size, and to its credit it undertook a number of initiatives designed both to provide relief and to put people back to work.[12] At first, these measures took the form of an increased provision of outdoor relief, the traditional means of non-charitable assistance. In 1912, the value of city-funded outdoor relief stood at $11,000; over the next year, as the depression took hold, city officials increased this figure to $16,000. By 1915, the situation had worsened so much that the city voted $25,000 to planned relief expenditures for the coming year and petitioned the provincial government for a further $7,500.[13]

While it was expanding the level of outdoor relief, the local council also looked into establishing a municipal labour bureau to help the unemployed to find available work. Private employment agencies had long been unpopular with both city officials and the Calgary Trades and Labour Council (CTLC), due to their practice of charging five dollars or more for information about potential employers rather than actual openings. In January 1912, the city enquired into the possibility of regulating these operations or, failing that, of setting up its own bureau. It eventually chose the latter course of action and opened Calgary's first Municipal Labour Bureau that September. With a fee of just twenty-five cents, the new bureau proved popular with the CTLC, the Calgary Board of Trade, and the United Farmers of Alberta. Nevertheless, it soon ran into opposition when city solicitor D.M. Moffat, Conservative alderman Harry Minchin, and the threatened private agencies all called for its termination. While the agencies' response was to be expected, that of both Moffat and Minchin stemmed from council awarding Miss G.E. Wileman, the bureau's manager, a salary of $1,000 without previously budgeting for this item. In spite of the labour movement's support for Wileman, and of the effectiveness of the bureau, which had secured work for 1,203 of Calgary's unemployed during its first four months of operation, in May 1913 Minchin won an injunction to shut the organization down. Fortunately for the city's thousands of unemployed, this proved to be but a temporary setback. Within five months, council had revived the bureau, this time placing it under the direct control of the city. In its first year, the new Municipal Labour Bureau helped 2,500 jobless men and women in their search for work. It also survived new allegations by Minchin of graft and corruption, and by the end of 1915 had helped find work for more than 7,000 people, causing the *Albertan* to hail the bureau as 'the one institution that has saved the labor situation in Calgary during the past winter.' In some ways a victim of its own success, the bureau was closed indefinitely in January 1916 when the council announced that it had fulfilled its purpose.[14]

In addition to this assistance from the state, there were, of course, a number of other institutions that also provided relief for the unemployed. Chief among these was the Associated Charities Association (ACA), an organization formed in 1909 with the aim 'not to pauperize by indiscriminate giving of material relief, but to administer in practical and yet sympathetic manner, help where it was really needed.' As economic conditions worsened during the winter of 1914-5, the ACA provided material assistance to an average of 500 families per month at a cost of $8,000. The advent of spring saw this number diminish, but as late as June 1915 more than 300 families remained dependent on aid from the ACA. Other non-state or 'civil society' sources of relief for the unemployed included the annual 'Sunshine Fund' organized by the *Herald* from 1911 onwards, and tag days run by local women's organizations.[15]

Despite all these attempts to cope with the situation, it was increasingly apparent that the depth and duration of unemployment after 1913 made it more than a local concern. Like other cities across Canada, Calgary turned for financial help to Ottawa, which – unlike the municipalities – faced no constitutional or legal restrictions in its capacity to raise tax revenues. Yet the federal government displayed a reluctance to involve itself in the question of unemployment, a reluctance that would characterize its stance over the next two decades. As Thomas Crothers, federal minister of labour, told Alberta premier Arthur Sifton in October 1914, 'the Government takes the view that responsibility for the welfare of its citizens rests, in the first place, upon the municipalities, and they have urged upon the local authorities that they should organize committees to deal with the situation.' Accordingly, on 6 November 1914, delegates representing local government, labour, and business from across Alberta convened in Calgary to discuss possible remedies. Conference organizers had invited R.B. Bennett to attend as the federal government's representative, but he declined and sent in his place Labour Adjuster J.D. McNiven. Harry Pryde, Alex Ross, Leo English, Charles Russell, and Sophie Mushkat McCluskey, all prominent Calgary labour figures, spoke on behalf of the CTLC, as for several hours the conference debated the causes of unemployment and its possible solutions.[16]

Lacking structure and direction, this unemployment conference achieved little. 'You have called a meeting to discuss the question of unemployment for men and women and have nothing definite to state,' complained McCluskey to the government delegates. 'It is an insult to the working class.' Pryde echoed this frustration during discussion of one of the well-intended but vague resolutions, explaining that 'I came here to endeavour to help the unemployed. We are not doing anything. We are simply wasting time.' Senator James Lougheed ended a long, rambling speech with the limp conclusion 'I am really at a loss to make any suggestion to you.' The general sense of futility was expressed in an uncharacteristically cynical outburst by Alex Ross, president of the Alberta Federation of Labor (ALFL) and future labour MLA. 'If we want assistance we will have to change our nationality and become aliens,' Ross unfairly suggested, 'as they are the only unemployed at the present time who are receiving assistance. As it is we are simply wasting our time.' No one present disagreed.[17]

For those Calgarians fortunate enough to remain fully employed, the depression still had an impact. After a more than a decade of steady increases, weekly wages now levelled off and in some cases declined. In part, this was the result of a tight labour market that strengthened the bargaining position of employers in wage negotiations. At the same time, many employers were prepared to initiate an eight-hour workday in order to reduce their labour costs. Ironically, they thus conceded a long-standing demand of workers at a time when they could ill-afford the reduced income it entailed. Average annual incomes reflected this decrease in weekly wages, and were further reduced as more and more workers came to experience a period of at least temporary unemployment each year.[18]

The depression of 1913-5 was as much a turning point for Calgary's labour movement as it was for workers in general. First, it ended a decade of sustained trade union growth. The decline in Calgary's trade union membership in this period was dramatic. In 1912, twenty-four of the city's forty-two unions reported a combined membership of 3,281, an average of 137 members per individual local. Over the next three years, the reported membership dropped to 1,769, and the size of the average union was just seventy-four. This was, of course, a bad time for trade unionism across the entire country, but that Calgary's slump was more than simply the reflection of a national trend was evident in its slip from eighth to tenth place among strongholds of unionism in Canada. The plight of Local 2 of the Bricklayers and Stonemasons International Union (BSMIU), one of Calgary's largest labour organizations before 1912, illustrates the extent of the decline. By May 1913, a massive 56 percent of the union's members were unemployed, and this figure increased steadily over the summer months to reach 68 percent by August. The construction industry's crisis continued over the next two years, so that by January 1915 just three BSMIU members were at work in their nominal trade. The remainder had either taken up rough, unskilled labour, such as sewer construction, or had been forced into dependency on relief payments from the union.[19]

Second, depressed conditions after 1912 sharply curtailed strike activity.[20] The 16,000 working days lost to industrial disputes between 1913 and 1917 may appear substantial, but in fact amounted to no more than half of the total lost during the months of May and June 1919.[21] With a large reserve army of unemployed willing to take the place of striking workers, and with ailing trade unions in no position to enforce strike solidarity, Calgary's labour movement was obliged to reconsider its industrial strategy and tactics. Unions began to reassess their function and purpose within the city. This reevaluation convinced them that an active and aggressive political strategy was necessary to compensate for labour's dwindling industrial strength, and consequently they embraced statist solutions to their immediate problems.

The 1913-5 economic depression was, first and foremost, a crisis of capitalism. As such, it is no surprise that one of its first political effects in Calgary was to raise the profile and influence of local socialists within the labour movement. In February 1912, the *Albertan* reported that the Socialist Party of Canada (SPC) had 'but little support among the members of organized labor and until great changes are made in their platform, or ideals ... the trade unionist and the socialists have little in common.'[22] The collapse of the local economy, however, appeared to bring many trade unionists closer to the SPC's way of thinking. In November 1913, the CTLC arranged a series of monthly meetings 'to consider means of enlightening tradesmen and laboring men on the necessity of fighting against the oppression of the "master class"' and to resist 'the oppressive iron heel of their employers,' language in stark contrast to the council's previous conciliatory emphasis on cooperation and compromise.[23]

This new radical stance proved to be superficial and short-lived. The outbreak of war revealed the CTLC's true colours and marked a sharp break in its relationship with the SPC. In July 1914 the CTLC publicly praised and endorsed the SPC's battle to secure universal suffrage, but this turned out to be its last gesture of support for the socialists. Within weeks – in fact, just three days after Britain declared war on Germany – the CTLC revoked a previous offer to help the SPC purchase tents and other equipment 'for the purpose of giving Lectures to educate the Working Classes of the City,' a traditional function of the party. The council claimed that its own financial difficulties had made this decision necessary, a dubious argument since several individual unions had already managed to provide the SPC with moral and monetary support. Whatever the true motive, the CTLC's action was a further blow to a party 'already believed to be in a state of disorganization.'[24] Growing discord between the two bodies was again evident the following spring, when the CTLC granted the SPC use of the Labour Temple for its Sunday evening lectures only on the condition that the socialists pay the nightly eight-dollar fee in advance. This demand stood in contrast to the generous terms that the CTLC continued to offer to local unions and the Alberta Federation of Labor.[25]

The CTLC was no more well-disposed to the Industrial Workers of the World (IWW), an organization that it associated, rightly or wrongly, with the SPC. On one level this is surprising, as the respective constituencies of the CTLC and IWW were mutually exclusive, the latter's membership of unskilled transient workers being precisely those who fell beyond the pale of the urban craft unions.[26] On the level of tactics, however, the clash is readily understandable, for the CTLC viewed the IWW's preference for direct action as harmful to its own commitment to achieving moderate social reforms via existing political structures. In the winter of 1912-3, the IWW and the SPC-backed Unemployed League led a series of street demonstrations, denouncing conditions at the city bunkhouse and demanding the resignation of Reverend D.A. McKillop, president of the

Associated Charities Association, for his handling of unemployment relief. The CTLC, by contrast, praised McKillop for 'satisfactorily coping with the destitution in Calgary as the result of unemployment,' and went on to state that it 'looked upon the Associated Charities as a strictly charitable institution that did not have anything to do with organized labor.' Given the extent of the depression, this last comment was disingenuous, to say the least. Nevertheless it had the desired effect, as the *Albertan* was quick to point out, of providing 'a slap in the face for the I.W.W. agitators.'[27] A year later, in January 1914, the CTLC was conspicuously silent when city authorities suppressed new demonstrations staged by the IWW, and relations deteriorated further when CTLC secretary Leo English denounced SPC delegates to the ALFL convention as 'anarchists' who wished to 'urge the "organization of the unemployed" into a force to be used for insurrection to break into the storehouses and appropriate goods and wealth wherever found.'[28]

Opposed to the prospect of direct confrontation with the state, the CTLC was no more willing to endorse pro-labour politicians of doubtful commitment and loyalty, as it had previously in the case of Richard Brocklebank. The problem of endorsing such candidates, 'friends of labour' who had risen from the ranks of the working class into positions of management and social respectability, was the subject of an article in the *Nutcracker* in 1916. 'One man proved his respect for the laborer by stating that he bosses five hundred of them, no wonder that he loved them,' remarked the pro-labour paper run by the radical William Irvine.[29] Such scepticism can only have been reinforced by the CTLC's experience

Hard times. The Reverend D.A. McKillop, president of Calgary's Associated Charities Association, reviews another application for assistance in 1911. McKillop's handling of unemployment relief became a matter of some controversy among local labour organizations in the 1920s, with the Communist Party leading a campaign for his dismissal.

with Michael Costello. Originally a printer by trade, Costello had been a founding member of Local 449 of the International Typographical Union in 1902. Two years later, he left Calgary to read medicine at Queen's University in Kingston, Ontario. After receiving his degree, he returned to Calgary to open a medical practice. Costello successfully ran for city council in 1913 and again in 1914, before going on to serve four successive terms as mayor from 1915 to 1918.[30]

In his early campaigns, Costello courted and won backing from a labour movement that remained appreciative of his record as a union man. When he addressed union meetings, those present frequently gave him a warm reception and assurances of their support at the polls. During the civic election of December 1912, the ITU noted with satisfaction that 'The doctor ... went on record as being an advocate of municipal ownership of all public utilities, and believed that Calgary should purchase a coal mine.'[31] Yet within two years, Costello's early actions as mayor won him the enmity of trade unions in the city. First, they accused him of awarding a city printing contract to a firm in Montreal, at a time when the work was badly needed in Calgary. Then they attacked his support for an 'anti-union crowd of aldermen' who had backed street railway superintendent Thomas McCauley's fight against the railwaymen's drive to organize. Finally, in April 1915 J. Ritchie, secretary-treasurer of the Carpenters District Council in Calgary, wrote to the machinists' union on the subject of Costello's opposition to union wages in the city's munition's factories. Ritchie described Costello as 'one of [the union's] bitterest enemies' and added, 'I hope and trust the boys of [Local] 348 will remember the actions of this man when the Municipal or Civic elections comes [sic] off.'[32]

As things turned out, the CTLC chose not to wait for the year-end elections, but instead initiated recall proceedings in an attempt to remove from office both Costello and James Garden, an elected city commissioner. 'General hostility to the interests of labor' was added to the CTLC's litany of grievances against the pair. Although it abandoned the endeavour in October, and Costello went on to be reacclaimed mayor, the CTLC's action illustrates the extent to which the labour movement had lost faith in its self-anointed political allies.[33]

Against this background of dissatisfaction, there emerged a new breed of labour politicians in Calgary. These men – and, for the first time, women too – shared two basic characteristics. First, they remained actively involved in the labour movement even while they ran for office, and so were more responsive to the demands of trade unionists than Brocklebank and Costello had been. Second, most of these individuals had arrived in Calgary since the turn of the century, and their attitudes reflected their immediate experience of industrial capitalism in the city, rather than any lingering notions of a pluralistic frontier democracy. Leading the resurgence of independent labour politics were machinists Robert J. Tallon, Thomas B. Riley, and Andrew J. Broatch, stonemason Alex Ross, carpenter James Rae, blacksmith John Barnecutt, electrician William J. Dyson, and printer Fred J. White. Equally important were a number of women activists, including Annie Gale, Mary Corse, Rachel Coutts, Amelia Turner, and Jean McWilliam, who all did much to promote various social reform measures benefiting workers both during and after the war. Together, these men and women represented the nucleus of what would later coalesce into Calgary's Dominion Labor Party (DLP).[34]

This loose association of labour activists – not yet a party proper – petitioned local unions for funds in support of its election campaigns and encouraged them to assist with the registration of working-class voters. Convincing workers of the importance of participating in the annual civic elections was often an uphill struggle, but it remained essential if labour were to make political headway.[35] The municipal elections of December 1914 provided the first test of their success in this area. Five labour candidates ran in these elections, with financial backing from the CTLC and seventeen unions. The *Albertan* also offered its support, endorsing the candidature of Tallon and Rae for city council, Ross for the school board, and Riley and Dyson for the hospital board. This spread of candidates fairly reflected labour's appreciation of its own interests: while the position of city councillor offered a wider sweep of influence within civic affairs, it was the school and hospital boards that were most 'closely associated with the wage earning class,' as the *Albertan* remarked. This was especially true with the rapid changes in society during the First World War. The same newspaper praised labour candidates for their emphasis on the need for social reform, and even argued that they had effectively set the political agenda in Calgary. They 'should be supported because they are labor candidates, irrespective of their platform or personal ability,' declared one editorial, adding that 'men who do not carry a labor card, and who are not usually termed wage earners, will do well to cast their ballots for labor candidates as well as the labor men, who will vote solidly for their representatives.'[36]

This forecast proved to be overly optimistic: Rae and Tallon came last and second-last in the race for council with fewer than 1,500 votes apiece. On a more positive note, Ross secured a seat on the school board, while Riley was elected on to the hospital board with an impressive 2,528 votes, and Dyson only narrowly missed joining him. Although the defeat of Tallon and Rae was disappointing, these results still represented labour's most successful mobilization of working-class support to date. And as the *Albertan* was quick to point out, despite the candidates' mixed fortunes 'labour's fight was not in vain. It was a campaign of education, and it was conducted remarkably well.'[37]

Encouraged by its performance in 1914, labour entered the next year's civic elections in good spirits. Andrew Broatch ran alongside Tallon in the contest for city council, while John Barnecutt hoped to succeed Ross as labour's representative on the school board. (Ross had resigned his seat following the outbreak of war in order to serve on the provincial commission overseeing the return of wounded veterans.)[38] The three candidates ran on the same platform of reformist policies as in 1914, although Broatch and Tallon were considerably more radical than Barnecutt in their support of a broader working-class cooperation than was currently provided by the craft union movement. The elections themselves turned out to be the quietest in Calgary's history, due largely to the enlistment in the armed forces of thousands of potential voters over the past year. Support for labour suffered a commensurate decline, with Broatch and Barnecutt going down to defeat. On the other hand, Tallon's support, while no improvement on his 1914 showing, was enough to elect him to council, making him labour's first representative on the city council since the days of Brocklebank.[39]

Tallon's election was also symbolic of an upturn in labour's fortunes, for the winter of 1915-6 marked an improvement in economic conditions across Canada. In Calgary, as elsewhere, the demands of war were creating new employment opportunities. In turn, these opportunities made possible a revival of the local labour movement's industrial wing. Yet workers did not abandon their recent political advances. Instead the political struggle for social equality and the fight for industrial democracy went hand in hand, as labour confronted an increasingly hostile interventionist state.

By the start of 1916, the war had done much to remedy the shortage of capital investment and the oversupply of labour that had prolonged the 1913-5 depression. Production of munitions and other equipment for the British Empire's war machine stimulated industrial production in Canada, while enlistment removed tens of thousands of idle men from the overstocked labour market.[40] Calgary benefited in both respects. Within six days of Britain's official declaration of war on Germany, 2,000 men from Calgary had enlisted to fight overseas. The *Albertan* captured the city's mood of jubilant and unqualified patriotism at the time. 'Calgary has enlisted for the war,' it proclaimed. 'It will be a war to the finish, with no turning backward, and no slackening of enthusiastic effort. The city responded magnificently to the summons to manifest her loyalty to the empire ... in the tremendous conflict overseas.'[41]

This response was led by members of Calgary's working class. As city commissioner Arthur Graves later recalled, 'everything stopped and hundreds of single men, they were carpenters and bricklayers and so on, went off to the war.' Within the first year of conflict, more than 9,000 Calgary men enlisted, or 42 percent of the total for Alberta.[42] The rate of enlistment was particularly high among a number of Calgary's trade unions, reflecting the lack of work available to members at the time. By August 1915, for example, 60 percent of the BSMIU had volunteered, while the entire membership of the Painters, Decorators and Paper-Hangers' Union had enlisted by July the following year. A quarter of all Calgary printers served abroad; so did 140 members of the local musicians' union. Among Calgary's civic employees, the fire brigade provided the majority of combatants. The physical demands of their work made the firemen excellent recruits in an age when many volunteers could not pass the minimal medical examination due to their poor eyesight, bad teeth, or some other defect. In December 1916, Calgary's fire chief James Smart turned down a request to send one of his men to the fire department in Prince George, British Columbia. As he explained, 'I have lost so many good men through enlistment that I find it difficult to spare such a man as I would recommend for the position.'[43]

By October 1915, this level of enlistment had produced a substantial reduction in unemployment among Calgary's skilled workers. A record Alberta wheat crop that summer assisted this recovery, with farmers increasing their demand for the construction of new buildings as a result. By the start of 1916, unemployment was virtually eliminated within the construction industry, even though some workers had simply abandoned hope of finding work at their chosen trade and instead became 'gradually absorbed in other work at greatly reduced wages.' Nevertheless, to the extent that any job was better than no job at all, the worst was over.[44]

The other factor that had ameliorated conditions was the British war machine's demand for munitions and military equipment. The West benefited only marginally from this demand, with less than 1 percent of all Canadian war contracts being placed with firms west of Ontario.[45] Still, wartime demand was responsible for breathing new life into Calgary's iron and leather industries, with the Great West Saddlery Company prospering for the first time in three years as the result of its army contracts to produce cavalry saddles. Apart from the new jobs created, workers also benefited when owner-manager R.J. Hutchings abandoned his long-standing anti-union stance after the federal government warned him that his continued opposition to a unionized workforce would jeopardize his chances of securing further government contracts.[46]

Together, enlistment and war production alleviated the worst of the depressed economic conditions in Calgary, but their very nature precluded them from forming the basis for any long-term recovery. At best they offered temporary respite, and many Calgarians feared that peace, whenever it returned, would bring with it a renewal of widespread unemployment and hardship. The local labour movement shared these fears, and took advantage of the 1916-7 economic upturn to regroup and prepare for the struggle ahead. Reported trade union membership rose from 1,769 at the end of 1915 to 2,169 a year later. In the opening weeks of 1917, a burst of organizational activity resulted in the formation of five new locals and brought the total membership up to 3,000, the movement's best showing since the start of the war.[47]

This recovery did not reflect a revitalization of Calgary's prewar craft unions, for many unions within the construction industry, such as the BSMIU, continued to flounder. Instead, it resulted from the organization of workers who previously had either resisted unionization or been excluded from existing unions. In particular, it was employees within the private and public service industries who spearheaded Calgary's second major wave of union formation. The move towards organizing such workers began in late 1915, when motion picture operators at the city's many movie theatres formed their first union. Strengthened by this new sense of solidarity, almost immediately they fought management over the issue of poor working conditions and staged a strike in rejection of a proposed 10 percent wage cut. Employers responded by hiring returned veterans to work as strike breakers. The conflict dragged on through the summer months of the following year, but in late July theatre managers across the city conceded the strikers' right to organize and signed new contracts incorporating their demands. Veterans already employed as operatives agreed to join the union.[48]

Inspired by the determination of the picture operators, workers in other service occupations followed suit and formed their own labour organizations. Hotel and restaurant employees, laundry workers, bartenders, retail clerks, and stenographers all either formed new unions or revived old ones in 1916.[49] The unionization of female domestic servants, long among the worst-paid and worst-treated of all workers in Calgary, provided special cause for celebration. The *Nutcracker* heralded the formation of the Calgary Housekeepers' Association in June 1916 as 'the first sign in Canada of a revolt of domestic workers ... against the indignities upon maids by unthinking matrons who regard their servants as chattel.' The *Albertan* agreed, if in less flamboyant terms, that the new association marked 'One of the most important steps taken by women since the beginning of the war.'[50]

Within the public sector, the imposition of a series of wage cuts in 1913-5 prompted efforts to organize workers at city hall. Wages were not the sole concern, for Calgary's civic employees also protested the cavalier approach to labour matters displayed by men such as Thomas McCauley, superintendent of the street railway system. According to the *Albertan* in September 1915, 'the management expects not merely the honest service of a honest laborer, but the cringing service of a serf ... Calgary employe[e]s do not need a union in order to keep up their wages, but they certainly need a union to protect themselves against the "hob-nailed heel of despotism" which holds autocratic sway there.'[51] Over the next two years, the CTLC successfully assisted various groups of public employees to form unions of their own, including the Calgary Federation of Civic Employees (CFCE) and associations within the city fire brigade and police force. The policemen's union, in particular, met with stiff opposition from public officials such as Police Chief Alfred Cuddy and Mayor Costello. Cuddy dismissed the Police Protective Association (PPA) as 'merely the result of agitation by a few men mainly outside the police force [which] in any other properly organized police force would not have been allowed to proceed,' but the PPA survived regardless. Finally, pro-unionist street railway men scored a victory over McCauley in April 1917, when the city council finally conceded recognition of Local 583 of the Amalgamated Transit Union.[52]

Even as unionism spread into virgin territory, Calgary's existing unions were reassessing their own function and status within the labour movement. As early as 1911, union machinist Harry Pryde had argued that 'it is self-evident that a craft union cannot retard the progress of the invention genii with their multifarious labor-saving devices,' concluding that individual craft unions within a single industry should combine their strengths by amalgamation. He cited the International Brotherhood of Electrical Workers (IBEW) and the Calgary Carpenters District Council as possible models.[53] The benefits of such amalgamation were spelled out in a memo circulated by the Tailors' Industrial Union in 1914, in which the new organization explained why it had recently supplanted the craft-oriented Journeymen Tailors' Union of America: 'Industrial changes, concentration of industry, overlapping of jurisdiction and organized scabbery forced the issue which culminated in this effort on our part to organize along such lines as will unify our forces and truly carry out the aims and objectives of the labor movement. We, the working class, must combine our efforts and forces in one organization. We must fight with a unity of action and concentration of efforts.'[54] Some of Calgary's own craft unions had reached a similar conclusion. In January 1913, only two members of Local 2 of the IBEW had attended a meeting at which organizer J.B. Pegg discussed proposals for broader industrial unionism among electricians. Eight months later, Calgary IBEW member B. Dresser reported that industrial unionism was now the chief subject of discussion among his colleagues, adding a personal note that 'as far as I can see ... it is a good thing to vote for.' Following the path of such logic, in May 1914 the IBEW called for greater cooperation between itself and non-union workers, as well as between the employed and unemployed in general.[55]

The United Brotherhood of Carpenters and Joiners of America (UBCJA) was another organization that changed its outlook. A model craft union before the war, its recognition of the need for change was evident when the union's business agent, James Rae, called for the inclusion of 'rough' or non-apprenticed workers within the local in September 1917. When the construction industry eventually recovered, Rae predicted, there would be a shortage of skilled carpenters, and employers would turn increasingly to the supply of less-qualified and cheaper men for this work. 'Having this class of men in [the] Local this Local could control them,' he argued, 'but the way conditions were at present this Local had no control of any kind over them.' It was all a question of pragmatism.[56]

There were limits to Calgary craft unions' willingness to revise their traditional outlook, however, and they certainly did not extend to the sort of nationwide, catch-all organization advocated by supporters of the IWW and later the One Big Union (OBU). Rather, Calgary unionists preferred the type of amalgamation or federation envisioned by Pryde, within which individual crafts 'could easily maintain their own identity, but would look for redress by the demand of the particular department they belonged to.' Furthermore, the resurgence and broadening of Calgary's trade unions formed only one aspect of labour's renewed struggle in the years 1916-7. If 'the exploitation of labor and greed for profits' were to end, as Pryde hoped, labour's industrial battle would have to be 'coupled with a working-class political organization (the one without the other is like a boat at sea without a rudder).'[57] As already mentioned, the election of Robert Tallon to city council in December 1915 had signalled a reaffirmation of labour's presence within and commitment to the political process at the local level. Developments in 1916-7 extended the labour movement's influence within the city council and propelled labour into the arena of provincial and federal politics.

In January 1916, Methodist minister and socialist William Irvine arrived in Calgary to take up his post at the city's Unitarian church.[58] This Scottish immigrant went on to found a number of newspapers, including the *Nutcracker* and the *Alberta Non-Partisan,* both of which he used to endorse and publicize the Alberta Non-Partisan League, a farm-based organization formed in late 1916. He also became a key figure in Calgary labour politics. Shortly after his arrival in the city, Irvine began to seek out like-minded social reformers such as *Albertan* publisher William Davidson, public school teacher Rachel Coutts and her sister Marion Carson, machinist Andrew Broatch, and carpenter Robert Parkyn, all of whom leaned towards socialism and actively supported labour's political campaigns. One of the early results of their activities was the creation of the Calgary People's Forum.[59]

Formed in February 1916, the Calgary People's Forum was modelled on its namesake in Winnipeg, itself the creation of the Reverend J.S. Woodsworth.[60] Its main purpose was to provide men and women interested in questions of social reform with an opportunity to meet and discuss their ideas. Regular meetings took place on Sunday evenings at the Empress Theatre, where speakers such as Tallon, Parkyn, and Irvine were able to refine their skills in public debate and oratory. For others, notably members of the ailing SPC, the People's Forum was one of the few venues at which free discussion of their more radical views was tolerated. The forum found itself on the receiving end of censorship in May 1917, when the management at the Empress cancelled its lease following a decision by Irvine and others to replace the traditional national anthem with a more democratic variation of 'God Save the People.' Irvine publicly defended the forum, calling it 'the one institution that is doing more to educate public opinion than any other,' and continued to offer the letters page in his *Nutcracker* as an alternative forum for debate.[61]

One of the subjects frequently discussed at the People's Forum and in the local press was the question of postwar reconstruction. For many within the labour movement, the war was no longer simply a battle against German aggression but one for democracy and social justice.[62] As such, it made sense for labour to ally itself with those who had sacrificed the most since 1914, the returned soldiers. In addition to the principle of solidarity, the CTLC also hoped that early cooperation with the Great War Veterans' Association (GWVA) might minimize any dislocation resulting from the return of thousands of soldiers after the war. At first, the GWVA was willing to reciprocate this support. 'Talk of reconstruction is fairly general, though at times vague,' wrote Private Harry Fowler in the *Alberta Non-Partisan* in October 1917. 'Men of imagination and wide sympathy are the nation's greatest need in planning any satisfactory scheme of reconstruction.'[63] Many of those who had enlisted were union men themselves and were keen to renew their association with the labour movement upon their return. There were also new axes to grind. In March 1917, for example, Private J. Pettigrew addressed the CTLC on the dissatisfaction felt by many returned veterans with the provincial and federal governments on matters relating to their reintegration. As a possible solution, Pettigrew suggested a formal affiliation between the GWVA and the labour movement. The CTLC remained cautious on this issue, preferring ex-soldiers to rejoin their former unions on an individual basis, arguing that 'the veterans were organized in the political field and not for economic effort, and were making no effort to meet the Industrial situation after the war.' All the same, relations between the two organizations remained reasonably cordial during the latter years of the war and suggested little likelihood of open conflict in the postwar readjustment.[64]

Another organization that offered to cooperate with the CTLC on the question of reconstruction was Calgary's Ministerial Association (CMA). In September 1916, this collective voice of the city's clergy proposed that it exchange non-voting delegates with the CTLC in order that the two might coordinate their efforts. The CTLC agreed in principle, but only on the condition that the CMA's membership first show 'by their action that they support us on Labor questions.' Whatever the CTLC had in mind by this demand the CMA appears to have obliged, for by October 1916 the exchange of delegates had taken place.[65] Through its links with the CMA and the People's Forum, the labour movement had forged useful connections with those members of Calgary's middle class who were sympathetic to the condition of the working class. Its subsequent alliance with the GWVA expanded this network of alliances. Whether this new sense of cooperation could translate into tangible gains for labour remained to be seen. The civic elections of December 1916 were the first test.

As in 1915, voter turnout in 1916 was low, with only 6,000 of an eligible 15,000 voters casting their ballots. On this occasion, public apathy benefited labour candidates, who managed to retain and even build upon their previous support. Tallon was reelected to city council with 3,895 votes, almost three times his total votes in 1915. Even the pro-Conservative *Herald* praised Tallon's achievement, acknowledging that 'none of his opponents denied ... his merit as an alderman, and his clean, manly stand in council or on the platform.' Broatch joined Tallon as labour's second councillor that year, while Ross and Barnecutt were both returned to the six-seat school board.[66] Another vote that favoured labour, although indirectly, was the passage of a plebiscite supporting proportional representation. The transfer of votes that this system entailed held out the promise of consolidating working class support in future elections. Finally, the election of Reverend Andrew McTaggart to city council justified the CTLC's recent alliance with the CMA. McTaggart was a Presbyterian minister whose preaching of the social gospel made him a firm ally of labour's cause. 'Only by applying the principles and teachings of Christ can we solve the problems of the unrest today,' he declared in one sermon after the war. 'Apply them to industry, to commerce, and the unrest will cease. Let it be the golden rule instead of the rule of capital.' While not all within the labour movement shared his spiritual remedy to the inequities of capitalism, McTaggart's presence on council provided them with valuable moral support.[67]

Pleased with the success of its candidates, the CTLC turned to the question of further organization. In the 1916 elections, as in previous years, both the CTLC and individual unions had provided campaign funds and personnel, but as yet there existed no formal labour electoral machinery. Early in 1917, the CTLC took steps to establish such a structure, and in March launched the Labor Representation League (LRL), loosely modelled on the British Labour Representation Committee of the early 1900s.[68] Its purpose was to coordinate and publicize the labour movement's political message, and it remained closely connected to the unions on whom it relied for the bulk of its financial support. With admirable optimism, the LRL printed 5,000 membership cards and began the task of securing subscriptions among Calgary unionists. In April 1917, it established a program of basic principles and elected its first executive, headed by Tallon as president.[69]

The LRL, indeed the entire Calgary labour movement, faced two main challenges in 1917. The first was the provincial election that June, called by the incumbent Liberal government of Arthur Sifton. The second was the federal government's implementation of conscription. Labour's response to each challenge reflected, respectively, the rapid development of its political wing and the degree of its commitment to electoral politics.

The Liberal Party had governed Alberta since the province's inception in 1905, and under Sifton had recovered from the scandal-ridden years of his predecessor, Alexander Rutherford.[70] Calgary was traditionally a Conservative stronghold: in 1913 Tory candidates had swept all three of the city's seats and hoped to do so again in 1917. The Liberals therefore formed an electoral pact with the LRL in a bid to consolidate the anti-Conservative vote. Labour agreed not to run against the Liberal candidate in Calgary North, in return for which William Irvine would remain unopposed by the Liberals in Calgary South, a seat with a high proportion of working-class voters. In Calgary Centre, labour candidate Alex Ross would face Conservative T.M.M. Tweedie in a straight fight. This pact proved to be short-lived: in May 1917 the Liberals reneged on the deal and ran a candidate in south Calgary after all. Undeterred, the LRL continued to stage an active campaign even though, as the election approached, it had only 700 paid-up members and a campaign budget of just $200. Ross, Irvine, and others spoke on a variety of issues at a series of nightly meetings, and their efforts were rewarded by Ross's surprise victory over Tweedie by 1,328 votes to 1,273. In Calgary North, pro-labour candidate William Davidson comfortably defeated Tory S.B. Hillocks, but Irvine was less fortunate. Fighting in Calgary's only three-way contest, a split in the anti-Conservative vote produced the reelection of Dr Thomas Blow. On the whole, the election represented a blow to the Conservatives, whose share of the popular vote dropped from 67 to 47 percent. Popular support for labour, on the other hand, had risen to 25 percent, a far cry from the 3 percent won by socialist Harry Burge in 1913. More importantly, the election of Ross gave Calgary labour its first representative in the provincial legislature, and some Calgarians suggested that Irvine would have joined him but for his unpopular anticonscription stance.[71]

It was the question of compulsory military service that tested labour's commitment to reform via the ballot box. In late 1916, R.B. Bennett, the newly appointed Director-General of National Service, announced his proposal for the national registration of labour, a move that labour leaders across Canada rightly interpreted as the prelude to conscription.[72] In Calgary, the CTLC did not oppose the registration scheme in principle, but instead demanded that the government also take steps to bring about the 'conscription of wealth.' The CTLC's position was set out in a letter to Prime Minister Robert Borden in December 1916: 'We have no apology to make for raising the question of profits[,] rather do we consider it a duty; the soldiers in France are asking the same question and as we cannot all be in France those who remain at home would indeed be cowards were they to permit another outrage without a single protest. The only protest at our disposal is to refuse to sign those cards until a rational scheme of National Service is presented to the country.'[73]

The CTLC did indeed go on to register its opposition to signing Bennett's cards, although the vote of seventy-five to thirty-three was far from unanimous. When the conscription bill passed in July 1917, local working-class opposition was no more solid. In Calgary, the first round of conscription stood to draft possibly 1,200 single men aged twenty to thirty-four, yet neither the CTLC nor any individual union displayed enthusiasm for a general strike of protest proposed by workers in Vancouver and Winnipeg. Instead, Calgary labour continued to exhibit a caution at odds with the standard image of western working-class radicalism. For example, Calgary carpenters declared themselves 'absolutely opposed' to conscription, but still voted twenty-eight to four against the general strike, preferring to await instructions from either the Trades and Labour Congress or the Alberta Federation of Labor. Local printers waited to see what action, if any, the federal government took regarding the conscription of wealth, while electrical workers deferred to union headquarters south of the border even though ALFL president J.A. Kinney had already said that Alberta workers could hardly expect any backing from American-based internationals.[74] Speaking at a CTLC meeting in May 1917, local unionist William Reid asked exactly what was meant by the Calgary labour movement's principled opposition to conscription. 'What would the members do if rifles were thrust in their hands and they were ordered to go to the front? Would they really oppose conscription then?' That no one had an answer for Reid was answer enough.[75]

Calgary labour's rejection of any direct or extraparliamentary action in 1917 effectively reaffirmed its commitment to the electoral route for political change. It could point to its success in municipal and provincial elections as justification for this choice. After the conscription crisis of 1917 it was never likely that the Calgary labour movement would abandon political action for direct confrontation with the state. As if to confirm its preference for due electoral process, in August 1917 the CTLC opposed the idea that the Conservative administration in Ottawa simply select a 'new' Union government. Instead it called for an immediate general election. A change of personnel rather than a change of system remained the CTLC's preference.[76]

Undaunted by his provincial defeat, the LRL again backed William Irvine as the Canadian Labor Party's (CLP) candidate in the federal election that was called for December 1917. An outspoken critic of conscription, Irvine had little chance of winning in a city where support for the

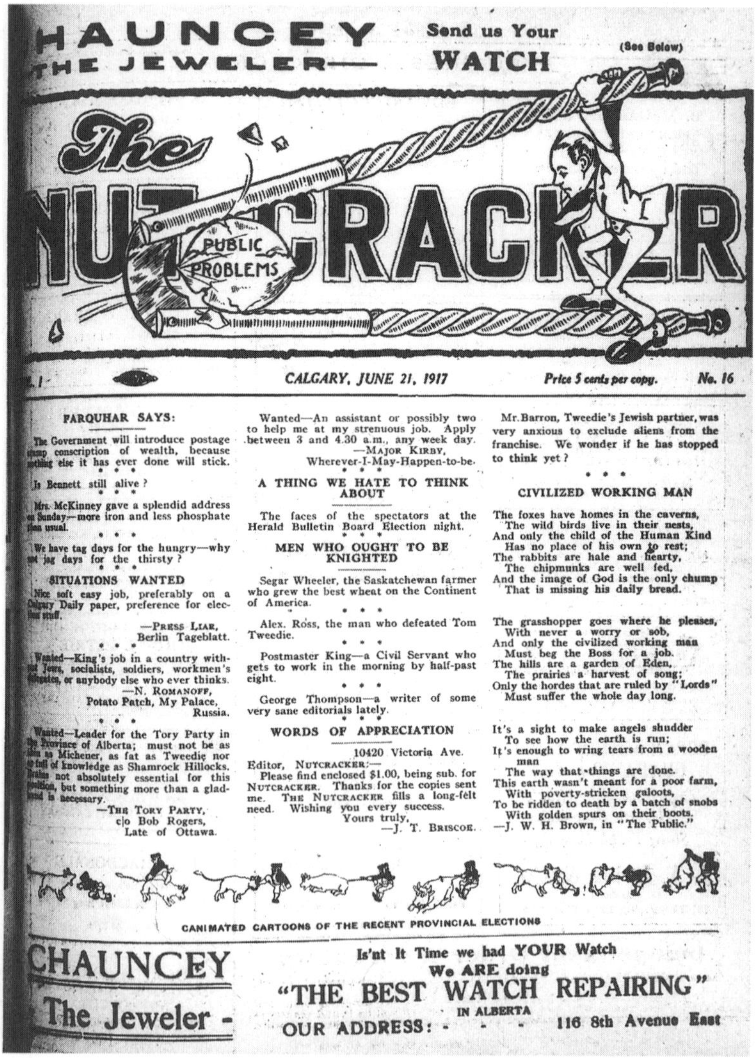

HAUNCEY THE JEWELER—— Send us Your WATCH (See Below)

The NUTCRACKER

PUBLIC PROBLEMS

.1 CALGARY, JUNE 21, 1917 Price 5 cents per copy. No. 16

FARQUHAR SAYS:

The Government will introduce postage stamp conscription of wealth, because nothing else it has ever done will stick.

* * *

Is Bennett still alive?

* * *

Mrs. McKinney gave a splendid address on Sunday—more iron and less phosphate than usual.

* * *

We have tag days for the hungry—why not jag days for the thirsty?

* * *

SITUATIONS WANTED

Nice soft easy job, preferably on a Calgary Daily paper, preference for election stuff.

—PRESS LIAR,
Berlin Tageblatt.

* * *

Wanted—King's job in a country without Jews, socialists, soldiers, workmen's delegates, or anybody else who ever thinks.

—N. ROMANOFF,
Potato Patch, My Palace,
Russia.

* * *

Wanted—Leader for the Tory Party in the Province of Alberta; must not be as thin as Michener, as fat as Tweedie nor so full of knowledge as Shamrock Hillocks. Brains not absolutely essential for this position, but something more than a gladhand is necessary.

—THE TORY PARTY,
c|o Bob Rogers,
Late of Ottawa.

Wanted—An assistant or possibly two to help me at my strenuous job. Apply between 3 and 4.30 a.m., any week day.

—MAJOR KIRBY,
Wherever-I-May-Happen-to-be.

* * *

A THING WE HATE TO THINK ABOUT

The faces of the spectators at the Herald Bulletin Board Election night.

* * *

MEN WHO OUGHT TO BE KNIGHTED

Segar Wheeler, the Saskatchewan farmer who grew the best wheat on the Continent of America.

* * *

Alex. Ross, the man who defeated Tom Tweedie.

* * *

Postmaster King—a Civil Servant who gets to work in the morning by half-past eight.

* * *

George Thompson—a writer of some very sane editorials lately.

* * *

WORDS OF APPRECIATION

10420 Victoria Ave.

Editor, NUTCRACKER:—

Please find enclosed $1.00, being sub. for NUTCRACKER. Thanks for the copies sent me. THE NUTCRACKER fills a long-felt need. Wishing you every success.

Yours truly,
—J. T. BRISCOE.

Mr. Barron, Tweedie's Jewish partner, was very anxious to exclude aliens from the franchise. We wonder if he has stopped to think yet?

* * *

CIVILIZED WORKING MAN

The foxes have homes in the caverns,
The wild birds live in their nests,
And only the child of the Human Kind
Has no place of his own to rest;
The rabbits are hale and hearty,
The chipmunks are well fed,
And the image of God is the only chump
That is missing his daily bread.

The grasshopper goes where he pleases,
With never a worry or sob,
And only the civilized working man
Must beg the Boss for a job.
The hills are a garden of Eden,
The prairies a harvest of song;
Only the hordes that are ruled by "Lords"
Must suffer the whole day long.

It's a sight to make angels shudder
To see how the earth is run;
It's enough to wring tears from a wooden man
The way that things are done.
This earth wasn't meant for a poor farm,
With poverty-stricken galoots,
To be ridden to death by a batch of snobs
With golden spurs on their boots.
—J. W. H. Brown, in "The Public."

(ANIMATED CARTOONS OF THE RECENT PROVINCIAL ELECTIONS

CHAUNCEY The Jeweler -

Is'nt It Time we had YOUR Watch
We ARE doing
"THE BEST WATCH REPAIRING"
IN ALBERTA
OUR ADDRESS: - - - 116 8th Avenue East

Applying pressure on public opinion. William Irvine's *Nutcracker* was a leading opponent of conscription in the summer of 1917. Irvine unsuccessfully ran for federal election as a member of the Canadian Labor Party that December and continued to criticize the national government in a series of outspoken publications.

war remained strong and against an opponent, Major D.L. Redman, who had been wounded in combat in 1915 and was sure to win the pro-war vote. R.B. Bennett, the architect of conscription, took no chances, leading a campaign of smears and obstruction on behalf of Redman. On one occasion Bennett told a crowd in Calgary that 'to vote for Irvine was to vote for a Traitor,' while on another he refused to let Irvine speak at a scheduled public debate. It was no surprise, therefore, that Irvine was defeated on election day, along with all sixteen other CLP candidates across the country. His share of the military vote – less than 5 percent – was less than the average for opposition candidates in Alberta, and bore out the fears that his stance on conscription would be a liability. The poor resources of the LRL had been insufficient to compensate for this, leaving Calgary labour unable to repeat at the federal level the success it had recently enjoyed in municipal and provincial elections.[77]

The 1917 civic elections, held one week before the federal contest, had highlighted this contrast. Although voter turnout was even lower than in previous years, labour managed to retain its representation at city hall. Andrew Broatch topped the poll for city council with just 855 votes, a mere quarter of his total in 1916. Annie Gale also won a seat on the council thanks to the consolidation of pro-labour votes under the new system of proportional representation. Robert Tallon narrowly failed to displace long-time incumbent commissioner Arthur Graves, losing by just 8 percent of the vote. Herbert Adshead, a respected lawyer and former Liberal, came even closer to defeating Michael Costello in the race for mayor. A mere eleven votes out of 5,255 cast separated the two men.[78]

By the end of 1917, a number of matters had been resolved. On the national level, Robert Borden's new Union government had received democratic affirmation of a sort and had a mandate to see out the war. Opponents of conscription had been defeated, and the issue was no longer a subject for debate. Instead, political attention turned to the questions of escalating inflation and postwar reconstruction. On a local level, Calgary workers had weathered the worst of the 1913-5 depression to share in an economic recovery made possible by massive enlistment and war production. By 1917, the labour movement had recovered to its prewar strength by broadening its base of support, and had established a record of independent political action that both drew on and helped to define working-class interests in Calgary. Labour had secured representation at two levels of government and thereby established a nominal working-class influence in civic and provincial affairs. Whether that influence could be anything more than nominal, and if so whether it would be tolerated by those in power, were questions that lay at the heart of events over the next few years.

6
Economic Recession and Restructuring, 1918-24

Calgary's wartime economic recovery was followed by a recession that lasted, with occasional upswings, from 1918 to 1924. At the same time, the city's economy underwent a process of restructuring as changes that had begun in the depressed conditions of 1913-5 continued and accelerated. Local events reflected developments that transformed the entire nation in the postwar era. The service and manufacturing sectors of the economy continued to grow in size and importance, to the point that they soon eclipsed Calgary's traditional industries as employers of labour. Mechanization continued to erode the demand for both skilled craftsmen and lesser-skilled manual labourers. Finally, the early 1920s also saw the emergence of a consumer-oriented culture that reflected and reproduced new social values.[1]

This was the broad context to which the Calgary labour movement had to adapt if it were to make good its claim to represent the needs and interests of the city's working class. At the same time, unions still had to confront the challenges of gender and ethnicity that had fragmented the movement in the prewar years. Their task was made more difficult by the prospect of reintegrating thousands of returning veterans into the labour force. In other words, the difficulties that local unions now faced were both old and new in nature. Those historians who emphasize the dramatic outburst of labour unrest across Canada in the spring of 1919 tend to overstate the transition from war to peace, overlooking the elements of continuity that bridged the dying months of the First World War and the early 1920s. In particular, the suggestion that labour's defeat in 1919 discredited the general strike as a tactical weapon, and so paved the way for the resumption of independent political action, overlooks the extent to which many labour movements – including that in Calgary – had remained committed to electoral politics throughout this period. The actual events of 1919 in Calgary, therefore, should be viewed within this broader context of continuity, a context that in turn was shaped by shifting economic developments.

Across North America, the 1920s confirmed capital's ascendancy over labour in the field of production. 'Layoffs came without notice, seniority was often ignored, dismissals were unregulated, and rehires were haphazard, if they occurred at all,' writes Sanford Jacoby in his study of the transformation of work in the United States. 'Although companies in the progressive minority were likely to provide stability and security to their workers, this was done only within very narrow limits.'[2] A similar pattern of development was also the case in the Canada, where American capital, technology, and production methods grew in influence during the postwar years.[3]

The United States played a crucial role in shaping Canada's postwar economic development. It not only supplied the lion's share of investment capital for new companies, but also provided new techniques to improve the efficiency of labour. The popularization of Henry Ford's mass-production techniques and F.W. Taylor's scientific management schemes helped to revolutionize the labour process still further.[4] Employers came to regard high rates of labour turnover as an obstacle to industrial efficiency and consequently devised a range of welfare benefits designed to ameliorate workplace discontent and to inspire greater worker loyalty to the company. In the course of these developments, the relationship between worker and machine changed. As the manager of one Canadian company's industrial relations department observed in 1920, 'In the past we have hired men upon the basis of education and skill. In this day ... we are beginning to realize that there is still another great factor in the hiring and placing of men. A man's mental alertness, soundness of judgment, or efficiency and skill in his trade depends to a great extent upon his physical condition. A man in poor health is like a dirty machine.'[5] Employers increasingly used such mechanistic analogies when it came to labour relations. As long as they identified their workers as a form of automaton – worthy of maintenance, but not necessarily respect – it was hardly surprising that schemes to 'democratize' production in the 1920s amounted to little. In 1919, for example, the federal government touted industrial councils as the means by which workers would gain a say in the managing of industry. In reality, the idea rarely received more than lukewarm support from employers. Even where industrial councils were implemented, at Toronto's Massey-Harris plant, for instance, they acted mainly as 'a tool of public relations for the company's management.'[6] As Stuart Brandes concludes in his otherwise sympathetic history of American welfare capitalism, such schemes 'met the human problems of industrialization in a way which at best can be termed only minimally acceptable.'[7]

Calgary was a microcosm of these industrial developments. New firms continued to set up in the city, older ones either adapted to the new economic conditions or went under. By the mid-1920s, the presence of factories manufacturing soft drinks, ice cream, and Ford automobiles was a clear sign of the industrial diversification in Calgary since the end of the war.[8] Among the prewar firms that had survived the successive impact of depression and war was the saddlery company of Riley & McCormick, for whom the 1920s proved to be a time of 'confidence and cash.'[9] One of the few local establishments to benefit from wartime federal contracts, Riley & McCormick grew and diversified in the years to 1929, branching out into the wireless and oil industries. The company's sustained growth came to a sudden stop on the eve of the 1929 stock market crash, when a fire swept through the premises, totally destroying the business.

For other established Calgary enterprises, further growth was possible only through the injection of capital from external sources. David E. Black's jewellery store is a good example. Black had opened his business in 1905 and over the next decade built up a successful operation involving the manufacture and retail of fine jewellery. In the process, he also established himself as a popular and respected citizen, serving a term as city councillor in 1919-20. By 1913, Black employed some sixty craftsmen and salespeople, but already the company was reaching the limits of growth possible on its own resources. A shortage of investment capital in the aftermath of war compelled Black to accept the offer a of merger from the national jewellers Henry Birks & Co. Black himself prospered from the arrangement, eventually becoming director and then president of the western division of Birks.[10]

With Black's departure from the Calgary firm, his personal and sympathetic style of handling labour relations also faded. It did not disappear immediately, however, and when long-time employee Tom Valentine died, Black persuaded the company to continue paying his salary to his widow for a year.[11] But such gestures became rarer. During the economic recession of 1922, Birks laid off eight of its seventy-one experienced Calgary employees, a move that prompted one local citizen to express his outrage to company headquarters in Montreal:

> Like a great many more Calgarians we are amazed and angered at your summary action in dismissing ... a number of Mr. Black's most tried and trusted assistants – men who have not been long with him, but have been instrumental in helping to build up a business that grew from nothing to what it became at its best ... You have not played the ordinary game, let alone the Christian game, in discharging men without giving them even a chance to take a cut ... If something is not done in this matter I am satisfied your business in Calgary will suffer. The talk is violently

> against you and against doing business with a firm that chooses so to misbehave.[12]

Appeals to 'the Christian game' or implicit threats of the retribution of Calgary's 'moral economy' counted for little in the new realism of postwar Canada. W.M. Birks replied to such complaints in the cold and calculating language of market-driven capitalism: he had warned Black, at the time of the takeover, that his current level of salaries was far to high, and he had advised the workforce of his intention to reduce their numbers. Birks noted that he had a business to run, and nothing more could – or should – be expected of him.[13]

In prewar Calgary, firms like Black's and Riley & McCormick had been the norm. In the 1920s, larger and more heavily capitalized establishments began to overshadow them. These larger businesses were more able to ride out the tough economic conditions of the immediate postwar years. Between 1918 and 1924, the number of middle-sized companies, whose capital ranged from $75,000 to $500,000, fell from seventy-two to forty-six, reflecting the degree to which closures and mergers prevailed in this period. Among companies with capital of more than $500,000, collapse and rationalization were far more unusual, their numbers staying roughly constant between 1918 (forty-seven) and 1924 (forty-eight).[14]

A dominant feature of Calgary's economy in the early 1920s was the appearance of new, capital-intensive operations. In the summer of 1920, Alberta Flour Mills erected in east Calgary one of the world's largest mills, producing 8,000 barrels of flour per day. In 1923, a number of important firms either located new factories in Calgary or expanded their existing plants in the city. The Totem Manufacturing Company set up an automobile body manufacture, while Imperial Oil invested in a new refinery, the construction and operation of which each gave work to 200. Also in 1923, the Riverside Iron Works moved from its original 1914 site to a new and larger plant on the city's outskirts. Covering some seven acres of land, the company claimed to be 'the largest and best equipped plant of its kind between Winnipeg and the coast.'[15]

Size alone did not guarantee economic prosperity, as the experience of the Ogden railway shops makes clear. War contracts had enabled the CPR machine works to recover from the disastrous effects of the 1913-5 depression, but this recovery soon proved to be temporary. A postwar slump in demand for rolling stock hit the works severely, with the result that the company laid off 1,000 workers or more on several occasions. Management also imposed wholesale wage reductions on its workforce and implemented a four-day work week. A slight improvement in the summer of 1923 was short-lived, and not until 1925 did conditions in the local railway trades improve significantly.[16]

The fate of the Ogden works was symptomatic of a wider economic recession in Calgary. Although the value of annual building permits recovered from the wartime low of just $150,550 in 1915, the total for the seven years 1918-24 – $13.5 million – still paled in comparison with the $20.4 million worth of permits issued in 1912. Calgary's retail sector fared better, but to some extent managed only to delay the impact of recession. Clearinghouse returns rose from $331.3 million in 1918 to $438.1 million in 1924, but then went into decline and did not recover until 1928. A further sign of the troubled times was the falling value of the livestock passing through Calgary's stockyards, from $20.9 million in 1920 to $10.5 million a year later. This economic barometer continued to drop until 1927, and even then recovery was only to a modest $10.1 million. Finally, the recession's impact was also evident within Calgary's manufacturing sector, where the number of individual firms fell from 230 in 1918 to 141 by 1924, and the total manufacturing workforce from 4,225 employees to 3,319. As these figures suggest, this period might also be interpreted as one of consolidation as well as decline for local manufacturers, with the average number of employees per firm rising from 18.4 to 23.5. Other figures support this view: average capital investment per firm rose by 88 percent, output by 40 percent, and even wages rose by an average of 28 percent over this six-year period.[17]

Calgary's captains of industry showed few signs of leadership in their collective response to the postwar recession. In his annual report for 1920, Board of Trade President T.A. Hornibrook observed that 'While the present business outlook is not as bright as we would like to see it and will require careful handling, still there is no reason for gloom. If we keep our heads and exercise due care and proper economy, I see no reason why we cannot come safely through this re-adjustment period and in the near future enjoy more cheerful and prosperous conditions.' A year later his successor, Bruce Robinson, was less optimistic about the prospects for Calgary's economy. 'We ought to face facts,' he told his fellow business leaders, 'and recognize that conditions generally have changed and that the period of reconstruction through which we have been passing, and which will probably continue for some time yet, had brought some unexpected features of a rather trying nature.' In particular, Robinson singled out taxation as a 'serious burden on business' and urged a reduction in the local rates. Subsequent reports echoed this call for lower taxes but offered few other remedies to compensate for the sluggish economy. Any tax cuts, of course, would mean a reduction in the public services provided by the city, including material support for those Calgarians most in need, but local business leaders soon made clear that they were prepared to accept this trade-off. Even David Black, whose ties to the community and sense of loyalty to his workers had been forged in the prewar era, now seemed to endorse this new, harder approach to class relations. As president of the Board of Trade in 1923, he too argued that 'The time has arrived when persistent effort must be made to adjust taxes to present conditions and find some means of reducing them. This, of course, cannot be done so long as people continue to make demands upon our various governments for additional services of one kind and another and secure them.'[18]

In general, many of Calgary's businessmen continued to regard the recession as a temporary setback, one that could be cured by a renewal of 'the oldtime confidence and hope in the future for which Calgary is noted.' At best, such hopes reflected a naïve appreciation of postwar capitalism in North America and were bound to be disappointed. Certainly, they were a poor basis for any meaningful recovery. 'Perhaps we all expected too much,' lamented a bemused H.A. Howard in his presidential report to the Board of Trade in 1925, a report that for the fifth consecutive year contained little good news for its audience.[19]

Two broad developments characterized the economic recession and restructuring of 1918-24. The first of these was an intensification of the wartime decline of those occupations and trades on which Calgary's prewar boom had largely rested. This was most evident in the case of the city's construction industry, which went from employing almost a quarter of Calgary's workforce in 1911 to less than 8 percent by 1921. The industry underwent a slight recovery in the years after 1924, but by 1931 construction workers still represented less than 9 percent of the local labour force. Calgary's transportation workers fared better, but they too experienced a relative decline in fortune. Wartime demand for machinists, boilermakers, and similar craftsmen had substantially expanded their numbers, with the result that in 1921 they accounted for 14.6 percent of the workforce, up slightly from 12.6 percent in 1911. In absolute terms, this class of workers continued to grow during the 1920s: in 1931, 57 percent more workers were employed in transportation than in 1911. Yet, in relative terms, this increase did not keep up with the expansion of Calgary's workforce as a whole in general during the 1920s.[20] A clearer sign of the decline in status of transportation workers was the shrinking size of their pay packets. During the war, machinists had managed to secure wage increases of 58 percent; by contrast, in the years 1918-24 their wages fell by 12 percent. For these workers, as for those in the construction industry, there is little doubt that the 1920s were indeed lean years.[21]

The second development, related to the first, was an increase in the size of Calgary's manufacturing and service sectors. Accounting for almost 27 percent of the workforce in 1911, these two areas grew rapidly over the next decade to reach 44 percent by 1921. The 1920s saw a slowdown in this rate of expansion, but jobs in manufacturing and service industries continued to keep ahead of the economy a whole. By 1931 they were employing almost 16,500 men and women, more than 45 percent of Calgary's working class. This represented a three-fold increase over 1911 and was twice the number of workers in the construction and transportation industries combined.[22]

Less easily quantifiable was a further development that accompanied this restructuring of Calgary's employment base, namely the emergence of a consumer-based and service-oriented economy.[23] This had a subtle impact upon both the experience and disposition of the working class. As historian Stuart Ewen argues, the new range of goods and services available in postwar society meant that, from a management perspective, workers had the 'potential [to become] "citizens" of a new industrial civilization, rather than merely "wheelhorses" in the productive process.'[24] The economies of mass production and the allure of mass advertising combined to reconstruct the working class in capitalism's own image, which emphasized labour's affinity with other social groups, notably the emergent middle class.[25] At least, this was the hope of Calgary's middle class. As the *Calgary Herald* explained in 1923, 'They [the two classes] are consumers, and it is as consumers that they need to tackle the economic problem. The consumer is essential as well as the producer in the ordered world. Given a firm understanding of this fact, much could be achieved in the way of emancipation or anything else that is making economic existence more uncomfortable each day.'[26] Such views reflected the substantive rise of Calgary's middle class in the 1920s.

To what extent did this shift in the balance of classes result in the 'embourgeoisement' of Calgary's working class? Such a question is somewhat misleading, as there is little evidence to support the view that Calgary's manual workers had ever developed a distinct and separate class-based culture. Suzanne Morton makes the important observation that 'Working-class consumption, particularly of the new consumer durables, was not simply blind obedience to the calls of middle-class advertisers but in many ways performed a similar role to saving. Goods purchased were potentially goods to sell.'[27] Yet in itself, even this motivation represents a significant shift towards archetypal middle-class values, reflecting a desire to invest for the future as well as to gratify immediate demands. Without further insight into the debates and discussions that took place in working-class households before making major purchases, it remains difficult to judge the extent to which workers internalized middle-class values in the 1920s.

Nevertheless, in the case of Calgary there is at least circumstantial evidence that labour endorsed the new shift in focus from production to consumption. In September 1920, an editorial in the *Alberta Labor News* noted that only 2,000 people had turned up for Calgary's Labour Day celebrations, the majority of workers preferring instead to spend a free day with their family. Before the war this poor turnout would have been a cause for lament; now the paper viewed it as a positive sign of the times. 'The sustaining influence and the greatest factor in the every day lives of the workers is the Home, and everything that the word implies makes it the pivot of our activities ... If then there is being shown a larger measure of pride by workmen in their homes that makes Labor Day to them a family circle affair ... then surely the highest ideals of the labor movement are functioning and becoming more permanent with the passing of time.'[28] Reflecting the centrality that pride in the home and family time played in the lives of workers, the rate of private home ownership in Calgary rose from 46 percent in 1921 to 52 percent a decade later. Another sign of the new consumption culture was the rise of the automobile. In his testimony before the Royal Commission on Industrial Relations in May 1919, building contractor and city commissioner James Garden had identified 'the lavish exhibition of people who have wealth' as one of the causes of labour unrest. 'I think these people rushing through with large automobiles has [sic] done a lot towards it,' he added. Yet just four years later, there were more than 6,000 privately owned cars licensed in the city. The number continued to rise steadily during the decade, reflecting a certain democratization of this highly visible status symbol.[29]

At the same time, the increasing popularity of movie theatres and radio shows signalled changes within Calgary's popular culture. Silent movies had first appeared in Calgary in 1904, but it was not until the 1920s that they became a prominent form of mass entertainment. Three theatres – the Allen, Bijou, and Regent – dominated the local scene, running films on a regular basis at prices affordable to virtually all pockets. Average daily attendance stood at 7,813 in 1921, or one out of every six Calgarians. In addition to their evening and matinee performances, some theatres also ran midday shows that were well-patronized by workers with an hour or so to spare on their lunch break. With 2.4 million spectators annually paying as much as fifty cents per show, the movie theatre business remained a lucrative venture in Calgary throughout the 1920s.[30] Radio programs were an even more integral feature of popular culture. By 1931, every third home in Calgary had a wireless set, offering workers some respite from the pressures or drudgery of their workday lives.[31]

Together, movies, radio shows, and the growing number of cheap magazines available in Calgary represented a democratization – or at least a levelling – of local cultural life, in that they provided regular entertainment that transcended class barriers. In this respect, the most significant feature that they shared was their relative affordability. It should not be overlooked that these new forms of entertainment, along with the automobile, could also be sources of new industrial conflict. Workers in the city's movie theatres and garages, for example, struck work on a number of occasions in order to improve their conditions and secure better wages.[32] There were also critics who viewed the new mass culture as a poor substitute for meaningful social justice in the postwar world. 'We want some of the good things in life,' labour activist Mary Corse told the 1919 Royal Commission. 'We do not want to go to the movies, we do not want a few cents more an hour, but we do want to feel we have the right to some of the good things in life,' among which she identified education, good health, and accessible health care.[33]

For one group, the diversions and distractions of the new economy were a luxury they could ill afford. The emergence of a cross-class, consumer-oriented culture was of little importance to those who became or remained unemployed in the postwar years. For them, the criterion for judging capitalism's success was not its capacity to entertain or amuse, but its ability to provide work for all who wanted it.

The spectre of prewar levels of unemployment haunted the minds of Calgary workers as hostilities neared their end. Few believed that the wartime recovery could withstand the impact of thousands of returning soldiers, and by November 1918 most expected that any 'return to normalcy' would include widespread levels of unemployment and consequent demonstrations of discontent and anger. Events were to prove them correct.

In May 1919, six months after the armistice, more than two dozen Calgarians took the opportunity to express their hopes and fears before the Royal Commission on Industrial Relations, established to investigate postwar labour unrest. Under the chairmanship of T.G. Mathers, the commission's board of inquiry heard testimony from local workers, labour leaders, employers, and other concerned citizens. Many of those who spoke argued that the cessation of Calgary's war contracts and the addition of some 5,000 veterans to an already tight labour market would inevitably result in large-scale unemployment and further trouble.[34] Other speakers looked beyond the immediate circumstances and placed the fragile nature of Calgary's wartime economic recovery within its historical context. For these witnesses, problems of reintegrating veterans or of adjusting to the termination of war contracts were simply symptoms of capitalism's failure to meet the basic needs of people; they were not, in themselves, the cause of economic dislocation. One individual who offered this interpretation was Louise McKinney, president of the Woman's Christian Temperance Union and, in 1917, the first woman to be elected to a legislature in the British Empire. 'I don't live in the City and have never lived in the City,' she told the commission, 'but it seems to me that our unrest is not new. We had it before the War, and the day was simply put forward a bit by the advent of the war.' Jean McWilliam, another prominent social reformer and women's activist in Calgary, and George Sangster, a CPR machinist and member of Calgary's Socialist Party, both expressed similar points of view. Sangster, for example, rejected the suggestion that local labour unrest had been stirred up by a handful of radicals, but instead claimed it to be 'the direct result of conditions as they were in the world before the war and which have been aggravated since. In 1914 the structure of capitalism was evidencing signs of decay.' The war had been little more than a brief interregnum of hope and superficial recovery, as the quick return of mass unemployment demonstrated.[35]

Estimates vary as to when the much-anticipated reappearance of widespread unemployment became a reality in Alberta. One contemporary writer identified the winter of 1920-1 as 'the beginning of unemployment and the reaction from the feverish activity of war,' an observation borne out by unemployment rates among trade union members, which had in recent months risen from less than 1 percent to 9.25 percent.[36] Seasonal increases in unemployment in Calgary had always been the norm, however, and there is no clear indication that this jump was unusually large. In any case, as far as Calgary was concerned unemployment had resurfaced as a serious problem well before the winter of 1920-1. In January 1919, even before the arrival of the Mathers Commission, the *Herald* had estimated the number of men without work in Calgary to be 1,500, or more than 7 percent of the available male workforce. This rate, it is true, was much lower than that of the 1913-5 depression, when unemployment levels had peaked in excess of 30 percent, but nevertheless it remained substantial enough to cause widespread hardship and much public concern.[37]

There is little doubt that Calgary suffered from unemployment disproportionately to the rest of Alberta during the postwar period. In December 1921 Calgary accounted for almost 45 percent of the province's total number of unemployed, even though the city was home to less than 10 percent of Alberta's population. By mid-1922 the figure had risen to 54 percent. Reflecting this situation were the relief payments made in Calgary, which by the winter of 1921-2 were equal in value to those of the rest of the province combined. By April 1922 they amounted to 60 percent of the total.[38] Calgary soon gained a reputation within western Canada as a place where the unemployed could expect to receive assistance in the form of food and shelter, a reputation that only aggravated matters. Civic authorities and the local police force faced an awkward dilemma. They were mandated to deal fairly with those jobless Calgarians who had legitimate claims on the city's relief system; yet it also fell to them to prevent ineligible non-residents from taking advantage of Calgary's reputed generosity.[39] As conditions worsened, officials became increasingly belligerent towards suspected abusers of the system, while public attitudes towards the unemployed hardened to reinforce preexisting distinctions between the 'deserving' and 'undeserving' poor. In 1920, Mayor R.C. Marshall responded to police reports of growing numbers of vagrants in the city by limiting relief to those who could prove six months' residency. At the same time, the police kept a close watch on those newcomers whom they deemed to be 'suspicious,' moving them on to some other location whenever possible. Under increasing pressure to reduce civic expenditure, Samuel H. Adams – Marshall's successor in office – adopted an even harder line in April 1922 when 384 unemployed men occupied city hall and demanded to meet with him. Adams refused this request and threatened to call in the RNWMP to disperse them. When labour alderman Andrew Broatch and Mary Corse, the president of the Women's Labor League, appealed to him to agree to an audience, Adams refused and, allegedly, 'told the men to starve.'[40]

Unemployment reached its peak in postwar Calgary during the winter of 1921-2. At this time, more than 2,000 men – 11 percent of the male workforce – were officially unemployed. The rate fell by half over the next year and continued to improve thereafter. By January 1924, the Board of Public Welfare (BPW) – as the Associated Charities Association had been renamed in an effort to avoid the stigma of the word 'charity' – declared the unemployment situation in Calgary to be the best in three years.[41] As in earlier years, the labour movement treated such official proclamations with a measure of scepticism. When the Provincial Labour Bureau (PLB) announced in February 1921 that unemployment was down to 900 individuals, the CTLC's own survey placed the figure nearer to 2,000. Four years later, the city council heralded an upturn in the local economy with the announcement that unemployment had dropped to 300. The Central Council of the Unemployed (CCU) – formed in December 1921 – was quick to dispute this figure. It reported to the CTLC that there were, in fact, ten times that many currently without work. It is, of course, arguable that it served the CCU's purpose to exaggerate the number of unemployed, but it is equally likely that such discrepancies simply reflected the fact that city officials counted as unemployed only those who qualified for civic relief, and that even some of those who were eligible chose not to undergo the intrusive means-testing process that a request for relief entailed.[42]

Consciously or not, Calgary's authorities and newspaper writers frequently characterized the mass of unemployed as consisting of unskilled, ethnic minority workers. Such immigrants, the *Herald* argued, had failed to absorb the values and norms of Anglo-Canadian society and so were more easily misled by communist-backed agitators within the CCU who hoped to capitalize on working-class discontent.[43] Working from similar assumptions, city officials were able to draw a line between those individuals who deserved assistance and those who were simply idlers or drunkards, fit only for chasing out of town. Some of Calgary's public shared this latter view of the unemployed, including M.D. Taylor, who expressed his opinion in a letter to the *Herald* in 1921. 'I have come into contact with a lot of this class,' he wrote, 'and found them a lazy, useless lot as a rule. All they think about is their meals, quitting time and pay day and doing as little as possible and expecting the highest wages possible for their poor labors.'[44]

This image of the unemployed fits poorly with the more objective evidence available. In December 1919 the city clerk compiled a series of reports on those men who either were unemployed or expected to become unemployed that winter. In terms of ethnic background, 92.2 percent described themselves as British in origin and a further 4.8 percent as American. Other nationalities accounted for just 2.9 percent of the total. When it came to occupation, if the handful of farmers are excluded then 58.4 percent of those listed were classified under the unskilled categories of 'laborer' and 'lightwork.' The remaining 41.6 percent belonged to a variety of skilled crafts, and as the recession deepened during the 1920s skilled workers came to account for a greater proportion of the unemployed. By March 1922, they represented more than 50 percent of the 2,205 men then officially out of work in Calgary. Contemporary portrayals of the city's unemployed as an underclass of 'dangerous foreigners' and unskilled transients thus require substantial qualification, to say the least.[45]

As James Struthers has shown, municipal, provincial, and federal authorities were largely at a loss in terms of how to deal with large-scale unemployment in the 1920s.[46] They expended much effort in a constant round of bickering and buck-passing at various conferences convened to discuss the question of responsibility. In August 1921, several of Alberta's municipal authorities met with the provincial government and came away happy with the promise of plans to extend road-digging, irrigation, and rural-work programs. The financing of this scheme remained primarily the responsibility of the cities rather than the province. In 1921, Alberta's cities provided $300,000 to underwrite relief payments, compared with just $22,000 from the government in Edmonton. City authorities regarded this imbalance as intolerable and unworkable, for as Calgary mayor George Webster complained in 1924, 'we have not the taxing power' to raise funds sufficient to meet this level of responsibility for the unemployed.[47]

Webster's remarks came some two years after western cities had staged their own conference in Calgary that concluded that 'the primal [sic] responsibility for unemployment rests upon the federal government.'[48] Although certain members of the Union Government – notably Newton

Rowell and Gideon Robertson – favoured a 'more liberal policy in relieving unemployment,' this was a minority view in Ottawa. A conference held in the nation's capital in September 1924 recommended that all three levels of government should cooperate on an equal basis in the provision of relief. Federal minister of labour James Murdock categorically rejected this conclusion. 'The Federal Government does not regard it as consistent to accept the measure of responsibility that those in attendance at the conference ... voted to place upon us,' he replied to a request for federal assistance from Alberta premier Herbert Greenfield.[49]

Throughout the early 1920s, then, municipal, provincial, and federal governments remained locked in a barren *ménage à trois* on the question of unemployment relief. It was against this background that Calgary's unemployed took matters into their own hands. Signs of organized unrest first surfaced in December 1921 in the wake of that winter's civic elections. The question of unemployment had dominated campaign debates, and public demand for some sort of action on the matter had helped to produce a labour majority on city council for the first time in Calgary's history. However, if the unemployed themselves had hoped that labour's victory would mark a significant change in municipal relief policy, they were soon to be disappointed. Labour representatives on city council pursued a cautious agenda in office, taking care not to antagonize local businessmen and investors. As machinist and new city councillor Walter Little explained to a delegation of the unemployed shortly after his election in 1921, 'even with a most progressive city council sympathetic to Labor they must not forget that they [the labour aldermen] had to run the city on business lines.'[50]

Understandably disappointed with this response, some 200 of the unemployed met at Paget Hall on 20 December 1921. This meeting marked the creation of the Central Council of the Unemployed and the launch of a campaign aimed at improving the terms and conditions of relief. The following day, representatives of the CCU met with the city commissioners to demand new supplies of clothing and shoes. Three days after that, on Christmas Eve, the CCU staged Calgary's first unemployed strike, at the Victoria Park army barracks, where many of the jobless were forced to seek shelter. Protesting the conditions of relief provided there, a number of jobless transients refused to perform the nominal (and largely menial) tasks required of them in return for a night's room and board. The CCU continued its support for such agitation into the new year, assisted by the leadership and organizational abilities of Edwin Fay. Fay was secretary of both Calgary's branch of the One Big Union (OBU) and the recently formed Workers' Party of Canada (WPC), and his interest in mobilizing the unemployed reflected his broader opposition to capitalist rule.[51] Under Fay's direction, the CCU focused its wrath upon the privately run Board of Public Welfare, which was in charge of the provision of relief. The BPW, claimed Fay, was 'an absolute insult to the intelligence of the working class and one who needs immediate relief has to go through a gruelling inquisition before he can get it, and further, any unemployed man who does not speak the English language is practically barred from obtaining relief if possible.'[52]

The CCU's cause was not helped by its volatile relationship with the local labour movement. Even as it sought support from the CTLC and Calgary's unions, the CCU continued to snipe at labour's cooperation with the city on the question of relief. In particular, it criticized the CTLC for agreeing to place delegates on the BPW, an action the CCU viewed as a tacit endorsement of the board by the labour body.[53] For its part, the CTLC was initially sympathetic to the CCU's cause, supporting the latter's demand that the administration of unemployment relief be placed directly under the city's control rather than be left to a semi-private institution. At the same time, the CTLC remained wary of forging too close a connection with an organization it associated with the Socialist Party of Canada and the OBU. In February 1921, 'large numbers' of Marxists attended a CTLC meeting held to discuss the unemployment situation. Much to the annoyance of council officials, the visitors 'vigorously opposed any measure that would bring pressure to bear on governments to undertake public works, asserting that palliatives merely bolstered up the capitalist system, a system which they were out to destroy.'[54] A year later, the CTLC drew attention to the fact that the CCU shared its headquarters at Community Hall with the remnants of Calgary's OBU. Fearful that the OBU might draw renewed support from the ranks of the unemployed, the CTLC helped to found a Federated Workers' Union that summer in an attempt to provide an alternative organization for the city's unskilled workers. Shortly thereafter, the CTLC broke all ties with the CCU, claiming that 'much of the doctrine of its leaders is inimical to the organized trade union movement.'[55]

Calgary's labour movement had enough problems of its own in the early 1920s without wishing to add to them by pursuing closer ties with the CCU. American historian Irving Bernstein once characterized these years as a time of 'weakness, internal division, and drift' for labour. This was certainly the case in Calgary, where unions struggled against a decline in membership and attempts by employers to roll back the gains made by labour during the war. As a result, the years 1918-24 were also a period of restructuring for the Calgary labour movement.[56]

The late stages of the First World War had been a boom time for Calgary's trade unions. Total membership of organization affiliated to the CTLC rose from 2,196 in January 1916 to 2,936 by December 1918, an increase of 35 percent. Some individual unions experienced far greater growth: the sheet-metal workers' union, for example, announced in September 1920 that its membership had doubled over the previous two years. Yet, even as Local 357 of the local machinists' union declared itself 'very much alive considering the fact that we have the OBU in our midst,' there were signs of trouble brewing for Calgary trade unionism.[57] In February 1919, James Rae, business agent for the carpenters' union, reported that 'conditions in the city were dull & that a great number of men were out of work.' So bleak were the prospects of winning any new members in this climate that Rae jokingly remarked that 'he would be quite willing to take a holiday' in order to save the carpenters the expense of his services.[58]

Rae's comments reflect the shift in Calgary's postwar economy described earlier in this chapter. In addition to the carpenters, other unions hit by the decline of the city's traditional industries after 1918 included the bricklayers and stonemasons. Despite its gains in the immediate postwar years, by 1923 the sheet-metal workers' union had replaced its regular fortnightly meetings first with monthly and then with bimonthly gatherings, as fewer and fewer members attended. During the following year, the union met on just three occasions.[59] This decline of Calgary's older unions more than offset the formation of new organizations in the retail and service industries, and overall union membership dropped by 10 percent between 1919 and 1921 to just 2,656. At the same time, the number of individual trade unions in Calgary rose significantly from thirty-seven in 1915 to sixty-seven by 1924, an increase that represented a considerable fragmentation of the city's aggregate union membership.[60] Following the success of retail clerks, domestic servants, and bartenders in 1917, more and more of Calgary's unskilled and semi-skilled workers had combined to form new protective associations, but frequently these faced both hostility from employers and limited support from the CTLC. Nevertheless, unions consisting of workers in the hotel and restaurant trade, local laundries, and the bookbinding, flour-milling, and meatpacking industries established their place within the labour movement, and to some extent proved themselves to be its new vanguard. Local 597 of the Hotel and Restaurant Employees Union, formed in December 1917, soon claimed to represent 75 percent of all workers in the city's hospitality industry, and in the spring of 1918 the local fought a long and successful strike for recognition.[61]

After the dramatic unrest in 1919 – discussed in the following chapter – strikes became a rare feature of labour relations in Calgary. One notable exception came in 1920, when workers at the Pat Burns meatpacking plant staged two separate (although interrelated) stoppages in support of a demand for better conditions and a 25 percent wage increase.[62] With 400 employees walking out in July and eighty more in November, these two strikes were the high point of labour militancy in a period otherwise notable for working-class quiescence on the industrial front. In total, fewer than 10,000 working days were lost to stoppages in the years 1920-4, compared to the sixty-seven days lost in 1918-9.[63]

The main problem confronting the labour movement in the immediate postwar period was the need to adjust to and evolve within the new conditions of Calgary's restructured economy. The increasing prominence of retail employees, service workers, and white-collar professionals challenged the traditional image of a workforce that consisted of skilled, manual craftworkers. Within the broader realm of the working class itself, the persistence – and even extension – of existing fragmentation further limited the potential of workers to respond to these new conditions as a class. Identities of gender and ethnicity continued to limit the disposition of workers to view themselves and behave as a unified whole whose interests and demands were distinct from those of other social classes. The return of thousands of soldiers provided a third and new source of tension.

The First World War had brought significant gains for many Canadian women. It helped to accelerate progress towards the realization of women's demands for political equality, symbolically achieved by May 1918 when women received the federal vote.[64] The demands of war production had also opened doors to greater female participation within the industrial workforce, and had produced a new sense of economic independence for many young, single women. While most women in Canada welcomed these advances, for some they represented only the first step on the road towards greater social emancipation. Such women, suggests Linda Kealey, sought to move beyond an awareness that 'remained rooted in a maternalism shared by middle-class reformers and [that was] hampered by labour and socialist acceptance of the bread-winner family model.'[65]

In Calgary, the experience of women at work in the early 1920s supports the view that gains made during the war did not, in fact, amount to genuine gender equality at the workplace, but instead women remained in a subordinate position within the local labour force. Jean McWilliam, a local boardinghouse keeper and prominent labour activist, testified to the Mathers Commission on the working conditions of many young women in Calgary. In particular, she drew attention to the problems she had faced in attempting to organize female laundry workers:

> I had the nerve to go down and organize the laborers there as a Union, I had them organized for about two weeks and my husband being overseas, I had to go out to the farm and look after my own interests and when I came back here the heads of this [municipal] labor bureau, who are running it down here, have let it go to the dogs. They went down and negotiated with the bosses. The result was, these girls had no job. The

> girls who had interested themselves with me had got fired and the employers had employed a bunch of foreigners who couldn't talk the language that is the condition here and of course when they couldn't talk the English language I couldn't talk to them and cause the employer any bother.[66]

Mary Corse, a women's representative on the CTLC, spoke similarly of her thwarted efforts to help organize the city's female cooks and waitresses, noting that 'we found conditions almost unbelievable among girls in the stores, restaurants and hotels in this City. We did everything we could, but we could move no one. I brought a resolution to the Local Council of Women and they said they could do nothing but finally endorsed a resolution which we sent to Ottawa, asking for an investigation. The reply we got was, that the Government at Ottawa could do nothing.' Speaking on the eve of Canada's greatest outburst of labour unrest, Corse warned the commission that working women, just as much as men, would not tolerate this official indifference indefinitely. 'Other girls are working in places which has [sic] not sanitary accommodation all day long and there is absolutely nothing being done about it and I want to say that is one of the reasons why there is so much unrest among the women. Almost every day, women are being added to the ranks of, shall I say the socialist party or those of socialist inclinations.'[67]

Leading by example. Jean McWilliam, third from left, emerged during the First World War as one of Calgary's most effective female labour activists, a role she continued well into the 1920s. Here she stands behind her boarding house on Seventh Avenue with some of her lodgers, her hired help, and her daughter.

As the organizing efforts of McWilliam and Corse suggest, the employment of women as paid workers in Calgary had increased dramatically during the war. As a proportion of the non-agricultural workforce, they rose from 13.6 percent in 1911 to 21 percent by 1921. The return to a peacetime economy stemmed but did not reverse this upward trend, and in 1931 women still accounted for one in five of all employed workers. Female employment remained heavily concentrated among young, unmarried women. More than 50 percent of all women employed in 1921 were under twenty-five years of age, compared to just 20 percent of employed men. The sort of jobs that women secured did not change very much. Certain industries remained virtual male monopolies. Within the construction industry, for example, there were never more than a dozen women employed, and in 1931 there were none at all. The transportation industry offered women more opportunities, but these were still relatively few in number. In 1921, more than 6 percent of all women employed in Calgary worked in transportation-related jobs, but by 1931 the figure had fallen to just under 2 percent. Even within the manufacturing sector, the proportion of female employees fell from almost 10 percent in 1921 to less than 5 percent a decade later. In contrast, gains by women were made in the fields of domestic service, commerce, and finance. In 1921, these occupations accounted for roughly half of all female workers; by 1931, the figure was nearer to three-quarters.[68]

Women's earnings remained substantially below those of their male counterparts throughout the decade. At the heart of the problem remained the notion of a 'family wage,' the idea that male workers should earn sufficient money to support their families. Mary Corse confirmed the normality of this arrangement, even if it did not entirely work in practice, when she told the 1919 commission that 'The working woman finds it practically impossible to buy the common necessities of life out of the working man's pay.' According to this view of respective gender responsibilities, the primary role of working-class women was to organize household consumption, and those women who did work for pay should not expect to receive a 'living wage' – one adequate to meet their own needs – as they could always depend on their husbands or fathers. McWilliam led the battle to reverse this official attitude, petitioning the provincial government to increase the minimum wage for female employees. In October 1920 she prepared a detailed weekly budget to support her request for a weekly minimum wage of $21.48, only to be told that many employers believed that few domestic servants – still the dominant form of female labour – could provide this value of service. McWilliam countered, somewhat surprisingly, that 'those unable to give efficient service would be discharged and forced back into those channels of employment for which they were fitted,' but she also argued that a 'living wage' was necessary not just for the physical welfare of female employees but also to safeguard 'the moral standard' of their existence. This allusion to prostitution as a supplementary form of income was spelled out more plainly by Reverend D.A. McKillop of the Board of Public Welfare a year later, when he noted the increased number of young girls that were coming before him for help. 'It has been found,' he warned, 'that unless they are given some assistance that many of them go wrong under the stress of their financial conditions.'[69] Despite such pronouncements, female wages in the 1920s would continue to lag significantly behind those of male workers.

Calgary's manufacturing sector serves as an illustration of this disparity. In 1921, the average male weekly wage of $26.28 was 93 percent more than the $13.61 received by female co-workers. Over the course of a year, men were likely to be employed for fewer weeks than women – no doubt a function of their relative employment costs – but still their average incomes remained 88 percent greater than those of women. Such disparities were not unique to manufacturing. In transportation, men's weekly wages and annual incomes exceeded women's by 59 and 55 percent, respectively, while in domestic service the margins of difference were 116 and 99 percent.[70]

Over the next decade, the wages and incomes of women declined both relatively and absolutely. Reductions in weekly wages and in the number of weeks' employment that women were able to secure each year combined to lower their average incomes in virtually every occupation by 1931. A female milliner earning $15.87 per week in 1921 received $15.33 in 1931, a reduction of 4 percent. In the same period the average length of annual employment had declined from 46.3 weeks to 44.6, resulting in an overall drop in income of 7 percent, from $735 to $683. This was a mild case. The average incomes of female cooks shrank by 18 percent, those of saleswomen by 20 percent, waitresses by 25 percent, and domestic servants by more than 30 percent.[71]

There were some exceptions to this pattern. Incomes of female teachers and telegraph operators increased by 5 and 6 percent, respectively, during the 1920s. Yet the fact remains that, within any single occupation, gender remained the most significant determinant of an individual's remuneration. The hotel and restaurant industry provides a good example. In 1921, this industry employed 125 waiters and 122 waitresses, a rare instance of gender parity within an occupation. Even ten years later, the respective figures of 279 and 228 differed by less than 20 percent. Yet the wages of male and female employees reflected anything but equality. The average income of waiters, already 37 percent higher than that of waitresses in 1921, rose by 12 percent over the course of the decade. Waitresses, on the other hand, saw their average income reduced by 24 percent over the same period. For these women and, indeed, the majority of wage-earning women in Calgary, the 'New Day,' which reformers had expected to follow the victory for women's suffrage, was slow to dawn.[72]

Ethnicity also continued to fragment the disposition of Calgary workers to behave as a class. During the war, immigrants from the belligerent nations inevitably had become targets of public hostility. In 1915, several letters to the local press denounced the city's 'enemy alien' population. 'Naturalized Germans who were born and educated outside the pale of German doctrines might be safe enough at large,' wrote 'Britisher' in July that year, 'but are they immune from contamination while associating with and influenced by those vipers who from the cradle up ... have been fed poison?' Another correspondent, despite signing the letter as 'Humanitarian,' advocated 'the Extermination of the German Nation' in its entirety.[73] The city council received petitions calling for it to discharge any 'enemy aliens' from its employ and to intern them. Although it may not have taken such requests seriously, by the end of 1915 the city had nevertheless interned a total of 124 individuals and placed a further 1,350 on parole. Even the CTLC demanded the dismissal of Germans, Austrians, and Russo-Germans from public works. Animosity erupted in February 1916, when rumours that local restaurateur Frank Nagel had dismissed a returned soldier in order to employ an Austrian sparked two nights of rioting, in which more than 500 servicemen and civilians destroyed Nagel's White Lunch cafe.[74]

Threatened by public antagonism and the possibility of internment, many Austro-Germans in Calgary did their best to play down their ethnic origins.[75] In the wake of the riots of 1916, for example, Harry Cronn removed the 'Rathskeller' sign from the front of his restaurant, while the unfortunately named Adam Kaiser transformed himself from a Russo-German into an unhyphenated Russian. Census data reflect this process of voluntary ethnic adjustment. In 1911, 2,969 Calgarians claimed German or Austrian heritage, equal to nearly 7 percent of the city's population. By 1916, their number had dropped to 996 or less than 2 percent. As late as 1921, more than two years after the signing of peace, Calgary's German population had recovered only slightly to 1,311, still just 2 percent of the total.[76]

The slow reappearance of Calgary former 'enemy aliens' after November 1918 acknowledged that the official return to peace did not suddenly produce a new era of ethnic harmony in the city. 'It was not unusual,' recalled A.J. Hooke, a future Social Credit MLA, 'to hear people with an English name speak almost contemptuously of a neighbor whose ancestors belonged to a nationality against whom we had fought during the war, even though they had neighbored with them on a very friendly basis before the war.'[77] One man, whose father had emigrated from Germany in 1900, also remembered the extent to which discrimination persisted into the 1920s and beyond, even becoming enshrined in city hiring practices. 'I'm going to tell you something and you can say what you want,' he said during an interview in 1992, 'at this particular time, in the 'twenties and 'thirties, if you were not ... English, Scotch or Irish you could not get a government job, a civic job in the city of Calgary. At that time there were real prejudice [sic].'[78]

So vehemently were such prejudices held, especially among returned soldiers, that one veteran even refused the offer of two prize horses upon learning that their former owner had christened them 'Fritz' and 'Hans.' During the provincial election of July 1921, local Conservatives attacked the Liberal Party for its use of some German-language posters, contrasting them with their own English signs, which were 'good enough [for] red-blooded Canadians.' During that same campaign, R.B. Bennett's choice of words betrayed a deeper ethnic bias when he likened both parties' scramble to win 'foreign' votes to the herding of cattle. Nor were workers themselves necessarily any more enlightened or forgiving. During Calgary's labour unrest of 1919, for example, a pro-strike newspaper charged in verse that scab workers were 'sure streaked yellow, from head to toe / They're worse than the Germans, our deadliest foe.'[79]

The hostility of veterans was also directed at those groups that had either opposed the war or remained neutral for its duration. 'The men who fought for democracy are not going to go hungry while aliens and slackers get all the jobs,' promised Arthur Haldene, president of the Calgary Great War Veterans' Association (GWVA), in January 1919.[80] Returned soldiers predictably interpreted the pacifist stance of local Hutterite and Mennonite populations as a failure of their patriotic spirit, and called on the federal government to take appropriate steps. In April 1919, the GWVA's executive formally opposed 'the decided influx of Mennonites and Hutterites and other undesirables into Canada ... who have given evidence that they do not intend to become loyal Canadian citizens.'[81] Attitudes of veterans towards organized labour were more mixed. Many Calgarians who had fought in the war were themselves former unionists, and they continued to sympathize with and support labour's demands in the years of reconstruction. But returned veterans usually rejected the more radical visions and solutions proposed by Calgary's few revolutionary figures, whom the soldiers often identified as Bolsheviks or simply 'enemy aliens.' Even during the tense spring of 1919 Calgary veterans showed no sign of support for an overthrow of capitalism. On the contrary, they were at the forefront of calls for swift and harsh treatment of socialist revolutionaries. Months earlier, the Southern Alberta branch of the GWVA had passed a resolution calling for the deportation of 'all persons maintaining Bolshevist predilections to the country of their birth while those of British nationality should be imprisoned and deprived of their franchise.'[82]

Events at James Francis Moodie's coal mine in nearby Rosedale capture the temper of local veterans. Moodie was sufficiently worried about the mood of his workforce in February 1919 that he hired a Pinkerton agent to spy on them. Posing as a fellow coal miner, the agent reported rumours 'that there is going to be a Revolution started in Calgary.' This revolution had nothing to with socialism. Instead, 3,000 veterans had recently arrived in the city and intended 'to follow the action that has been taken in Winnipeg and other places, in regard to the Austrians and Germans and Russians and all Bolshevikis and pull them off their jobs and put returned men in their places.'[83] Work, not revolution, was still the main demand among returned soldiers a few weeks later when Calgary hosted the Western Labour Conference, the gathering that resulted in the launch of the OBU. As Moodie's agent once again reported, 'any time the radical element among the miners and other crafts think that the Great War Veterans Assn. is in with them ... they are entirely wrong; ... the Veterans will never rest until all these pro-Germans and the foreign element is [sic] deported out of this country and the quicker the Government gets busy along these lines the better for everybody because the returned soldiers are not going to be idle and stand and watch these Austrians and Germans, and Russians while they have a good piece of work and plenty of money.'[84]

As elsewhere in Canada, veterans had difficulty in securing 'a good piece of work' upon their return to Calgary. During the war's closing months, the federal government had begun to devise schemes to help reintegrate soldiers into the labour market. With its own analyses predicting unemployment as high as 250,000 by Christmas 1918, Ottawa initiated the Soldier Settlement Scheme (SSS) and the Employment Service of Canada (ESC), both of which were designed to place veterans on farms, although the government soon broadened the ESC to encompass urban work too.[85] Across Alberta, the SSS had relocated 2,000 veterans by August 1920. In Calgary, the task of reintegrating an anticipated 5,000 soldiers fell to William Carnill, superintendent of the local office of the Provincial Labour Bureau (PLB). Between June and October 1918, this organization found work – mostly unskilled in nature – for 500 men and, on the surface at least, won the support and cooperation of the veterans themselves. In October 1918, the local GWVA's journal, the *Alberta Veteran,* praised Carnill's achievements to date. 'Red tape is conspicuous by its absence ... and if every department operated in the interests of the returned veteran was conducted on the same business-like, wide-awake and courteous lines, only the chronic grouch would be heard to complain.'[86]

The mood of congratulation quickly receded. In Calgary, a rift between the GWVA's official leadership and the rank and file was visible by early 1919, when the executive unsuccessfully attempted to prevent members from staging a benefit soccer match to raise money for the general strike then taking place. At the same time, pressure from its 8,000-strong membership prompted the Calgary GWVA to lead the demand for a government cash gratuity of $2,000 per veteran, the so-called Calgary resolution. This action served to bolster the Calgary GWVA's claim to be the most militant branch in Canada. (It alone in 1917 had emphasized the call to conscript wealth.) This claim gained new strength after 1919 when Calgary veterans moved away from the GWVA's original non-political stance and began to forge a tentative alliance with the local labour party. They also turned their attention away from the bonus issue and towards the broader question of unemployment.[87]

Calgary veterans' growing disillusionment with the direction in which postwar reconstruction was headed was evident at a mass meeting of the GWVA held at the Empress Theatre on 2 November 1919. Among those who addressed the audience that evening was Private George Palmer, a five-year veteran and GWVA activist. He struggled to find the words that could account for the 'class or party strife [that] was born in his heart' since his return to Canada, a country that showed little sign of being fit for heroes: 'Are we going to permit a few greed-sodden drones, men who know not, nor ever did know the meaning of the words patriotism and sacrifice to have the ruling of our lives ... No! a thousand times no! Get together, men of Canada. It's not the ignorant foreigner that we need to fear. It's not the stranger within our own gates. It's not labor, it's not the farmer. It's the rotten, corrupt system that allows men to accumulate millions while others starve.'[88] Palmer and others particularly resented the charitable nature of official measures to deal with unemployment at the time. 'Give us remunerative work and give the dole to the slacker,' demanded one veteran. 'We are sick and tired of being spoon fed.'[89] Such protests grew in frequency, with recipients complaining of psychological as well as financial impoverishment. The comments of one man, a veteran of Mons and Ypres, expressed the extremes of bitterness and resentment felt by many. 'I don't want relief: I don't want charity,' he explained. 'By — I won't have charity. By — I won't. I don't want to buy groceries on a relief ticket, and by — I won't. I'll go home and shoot my kids, my wife and myself first, by — I will.'[90]

Retraining soldiers was a necessary condition for their reintegration into Calgary's restructured workforce, but it did not itself provide any new jobs. Throughout 1919, veterans numbered disproportionately among the unemployed. In their demand for bona fide work rather than relief handouts, returned soldiers formed natural allies of discontented labour. By

1919 a local paper reported the former to be 'naturally restless to a point bordering on the rebellious.' It was a restlessness upon which the labour movement's new political organizations sought to capitalize.[91]

Calgary unions had taken the first steps to forge closer ties with returned veterans in early 1919. In January, the CTLC struck a committee of six 'to discuss plans for some kind of amalgamation with, or representation by, the Great War veterans on the council.' By May, the CTLC and GWVA, together with the Winnipeg-based Dominion Army and Navy Veterans (ANV), had agreed to cooperate on the issue of demobilization. In September, the CTLC extended its support when it participated in a parade staged by the GWVA to protest the federal government's refusal to appoint a commission on the question of the soldiers' gratuity scheme. The labour council also entered a float and various sports teams in an ANV carnival that fall. Finally, by 1921 this sort of cooperation had extended into the field of politics when the Dominion Labor Party (DLP) became the first party to include the GWVA's demands as part of its electoral platform.[92]

Even as official cooperation expanded, there were signs of friction between the returned men and those workers who had remained in Calgary during the war. This problem had been foreshadowed during the strike by motion-picture operators in 1917, when veterans acted as strike breakers before finally agreeing to join the union. It surfaced again in March 1918, when hotel workers struck in support of their demand for union recognition. Two soldiers approached one of the strikers, John C. South, as he patrolled a picket in front of the Palliser Hotel and asked him 'why he was not in the army instead of out striking for more wages.' South's reply, that he was ineligible for service, failed to satisfy his inquisitors and the altercation ended only with the intervention of the police.[93]

The problem of reintegrating veterans affected the Calgary police force itself. In 1920, police who had not fought in the war complained that they were being overlooked for promotion in favour of those who had. On the other hand, some civic employees who had served in the armed forces returned to Calgary to find themselves displaced by others who had remained behind and secured promotions in the interim. With the CTLC committed to the defence of its members regardless of their wartime record, its relations with the GWVA inevitably became more precarious as the 1920s continued and economic recovery remained elusive.[94]

Tensions between the two were greatest in the case of the Calgary Federation of Civic Employees (CFCE) and city hall employees, an estimated 67 percent of whom had been in the service. In March 1924, the CFCE announced that it would recognize in full those employees who had been taken on during the war, rather than treat them as substitute workers with no seniority rights. This move was a reversal of the union's earlier stance and came at a time when city hall was making its latest round of job cuts. Significantly, the decision placed recently hired veterans on the front line for dismissal.[95] The GWVA protested this move at a packed meeting, in which it described the CFCE's actions as a betrayal of the GWVA's own members. 'Labor has always been antagonistic and is the greatest enemy of the returned soldier,' exclaimed L.H. Russell, a member of the GWVA's executive. He went on to accuse the CFCE leadership of working in cahoots with the city even though, he claimed, the vast majority of the federation's rank and file was opposed to its action. The division of loyalties that the whole incident provoked was nowhere more evident than in remarks made at the meeting by J.W. Russell. No relation to the earlier speaker, Russell was a member of the GWVA and a labour representative on city council. Anticipating that the GWVA would appeal the CFCE's decision to the city council, Russell confessed that 'the present controversy put him in a difficult position.' As to how the conflict might be resolved, he admitted further that he 'did not know what action should be taken.'[96] Long after the last shots were fired on the western front, the experience of the First World War continued to exert a divisive influence on the hopes for working-class unity in Calgary.

The basic reality of postwar Calgary was that reconstruction – or restructuring – took place within the continuing evolution of local capitalism. Any hopes that the 1920s would bring about a new era of social justice in which labour and capital might serve as joint partners in production and society were soon dashed. As older industries declined and new ones emerged, Calgary's labour movement found itself having to adjust to the new conditions. Its traditional base of support – workers within the construction and transportation industries – had shrunk in size, and the majority of new trade union members were scattered among a larger number of small organizations in the service and manufacturing sectors. Divisions along lines of gender and ethnicity continued to fragment any prospects that local workers might confront the challenges of postwar capitalism as a united class, a situation only exacerbated by the return of Calgary's veterans. Above all else, local workers entered the 1920s under the shadow of the events of 1919, events that have gained mythic proportion in the writing of Canadian labour history. While the restructuring of Calgary's economy provides the essential context for understanding labour's political aims and achievements in the early 1920s, the tone and subtext of political discourse in this period can only be understood with reference to the legacy of 1919. Accordingly, it is necessary to reconsider the myths of 1919 in Calgary.

7
1919: Revolt Reconsidered

The Winnipeg general strike of 1919 has cast a long shadow over the writing of Canadian labour history. As a subject of inquiry, the wave of working-class unrest that swept across the country that spring continues to inspire new investigations on a regular basis. There is little disagreement among historians over the basic facts and chronology, but they remain strongly divided over the interpretation of the 1919 labour revolt.[1] Was it regional or national in nature? Were the strikers' aims revolutionary or reformist? Did the strikes represent the victory of class solidarity over divisions of ethnicity and gender, or vice versa? For Marxists, events in Winnipeg and elsewhere were a clear instance of the revolutionary potential of class solidarity, sufficient to overcome regional and sectional fragmentation. For non-Marxist historians, the ultimate defeat of the strike underlined the limitations of working-class unity and the direct-action tactics of the general strike. David Bercuson epitomizes the latter view, arguing that 'the increased class consciousness which the strike and the methods used to defeat it generated' was channelled into support for a more moderate, social-democratic political movement in the 1920s.[2] Thus, although they differ sharply in their interpretation, both schools of thought are at least agreed that the strikes of 1919 represent a major turning point in the history of Canadian workers.

Consensus also extends to the widely shared – if seldom articulated – view that Winnipeg remains the essential model of working-class experience and response in this period, a model against which the reaction of workers in all other locations should be measured. Whether historians are seeking to demonstrate the existence of a regional labour radicalism or, alternatively, a national working-class revolt, they virtually all accept Winnipeg as their central point of reference, as a 'true' expression of working-class resistance to capitalist authority. In short, not only does the Winnipeg general strike stand as the measure of working-class consciousness in 1919, but in the study of postwar class relations that city has become the norm against which historians judge the actions and response of workers in other cities, including Calgary.

In search of support for their various and often opposing hypotheses about 1919, historians have plumbed the sources for a growing number of towns and cities across Canada. Surprisingly, Calgary has escaped close scrutiny in the available published works to date – surprisingly, for the foothills city has won something of a reputation as an island of labour conservatism amid a sea of western radicalism after the First World War. This reputation deserves reconsideration, or at least closer examination. Bryan Palmer explains Calgary's opposition to the One Big Union (OBU) with dismissive references to the fact that its labour movement was dominated by 'British urban craftsmen' and that Calgary was a 'TLC stronghold.'[3] But both of these characterizations apply also to Vancouver, where support for the OBU and the general strike call in 1919 was strong. Similarly, Ross McCormack minimizes the relevance of those Calgary trade unionists who, at the March 1919 Western Labour Conference, opposed the formation of the OBU, calling them a 'handful of obscure delegates from Alberta.'[4] But were they? Delegates from urban Alberta represented one-quarter of the conference's total attendance, and those from Calgary alone nearly one-fifth. Given this level of local participation at the gathering, McCormack's choice of 'obscure' requires justification that goes beyond mere assertion. Finally, even when historians have payed close attention to the actual evidence for Calgary, their conclusions remain heavily shaped by the imposing counterpoint of Winnipeg. In her unpublished study of Calgary craft unions, for example, Elizabeth Taraska asserts that the local Trades and Labour Council 'often imitated nation-wide policies not totally connected to local conditions, and mirrored dissent flourishing in larger centres like Winnipeg and Vancouver.'[5] Again, no evidence is produced to support this claim. Yet, as was illustrated in earlier chapters, Calgary labour figures were acutely aware of local conditions and concerns and adjusted their policies and responses accordingly. Comparison with other centres – including Winnipeg – might be enlightening and valuable, but it does not explain the behaviour of Calgary's own trade union movement.

There is no doubt that Calgary's response to the call for a general strike and the formation of the OBU was ambivalent, but ambivalent is not the same as conservative. The actions of workers in Calgary in the spring of 1919, and in the following years, are best understood within their local context, not in comparison with Winnipeg or anywhere else. This context consists of the political advances that the city's labour movement had made since 1913 – discussed in Chapter 5 – and the restructuring of Calgary's economy that took place between 1918 and 1924, as detailed in the previous chapter. It is within this framework that Calgary's own so-called labour revolt of 1918-9 needs to be placed. In turn, a reconsideration of that revolt serves as the point of departure for understanding Calgary's enduring commitment to political action in the 1920s.[6]

Although the course of events leading from Canadian labour's defeat in the federal election of 1917 to the outbreak of strikes across the country in the late spring of 1919 need not be detailed here, some key points should be noted. Soon after its election in December 1917, Robert Borden's patchwork Union government added to labour's sense of political impotency when it passed a series of legislative acts that effectively curtailed the civil liberties of many citizens as well as the collective rights of workers. Escalating inflation and allegations of war profiteering by capitalist entrepreneurs fuelled working-class unease over the direction in which Canada's war effort was heading in 1918. In response, labour took steps towards broader industrial organization in order to consolidate its strength, and moved closer to embracing the general strike as a legitimate frontline weapon against the state.[7]

As part of this apparent shift from electoral politics to the tactics of direct action, there occurred in Calgary an incident that underlined the need to confront the state head-on. At least, this is how labour historians have usually interpreted the Calgary freighthandlers' strike of October 1918. This event prompted a call for a sympathy strike from other Calgary workers. Leaving no room for doubt in the reader's mind, Taraska describes the event 'as one of the catalytic events which transformed smouldering western labour radicalism into a flame of labour revolt.' In local terms it was 'a momentous event in Calgary's labour history ... a watershed for testing labour's solidarity.' Finally, she concludes, 'Calgary's general strike [of 1918] might be considered a mere bagatelle in comparison to the 1919 Winnipeg general strike, but it appeared to effectively test labour's ultimate weapon.'[8] Other historians have readily accepted Taraska's interpretation of the 1918 strike, because it neatly fits their own accounts of labour's swing from political to direct action, even if it does sit ill with their description of Calgary as a hotbed of labour conservatism.[9] Yet the actual evidence – indeed Taraska's own evidence – does not support these conclusions. Far from being an effective test of labour's 'ultimate weapon,' the strike underlined the extent to which the state held the upper hand in any direct confrontation with labour, and so by extension confirmed the wisdom of those who advocated political action as labour's best strategy. This was the lesson that many of Calgary's labour figures remembered later in 1919, when it came to the question of support for the Winnipeg general strike and the OBU.

The background to the Calgary freighthandlers' strike was a protracted series of negotiations between the federal government's Railway War Board

– created in October 1917 – and Division 4 of the Railway Employees Department of the AFL, launched by the industry's craft union in February 1918. Under the presidency of Calgary's Robert Tallon, Division 4 pursued a variety of claims during the summer of 1918, regarding wages, hours, and the recognition of unskilled employees. Eventually, on 2 September 1918, it accepted the War Board's offer of the so-called McAdoo Award, an earlier agreement that had standardized wage rates, hours, and working conditions in American government-controlled railways. In accepting this offer, Canadian union leaders – based in central Canada – overruled the objections of those western members who regarded the McAdoo Award as inadequate because it favoured workers in eastern Canada where the cost of living was lower. In addition, western representatives were concerned that the settlement failed to address the question of unorganized freighthandlers.[10]

In Calgary, where only 10 percent of freighthandlers were organized, CPR officials refused to recognize Division 4 as the employees' collective representative. This refusal contradicted the War Board's own directive and, moreover, broke with the spirit of the federal government's War Labour Policy, PC 1743. In late September, railway worker-manager relations in Calgary broke down completely. CPR superintendent D.C. Coleman fired a shed checker accused of attempting to organize non-union freighthandlers, subsequently replacing him without regard for the established protocol of seniority. In an attempt to preempt any protest action by workers against Coleman's decision, the CPR's Western Divisional Superintendent, G. Hall, invited a delegation of Calgary freighthandlers to Winnipeg to discuss the situation. At this point the dispute became transformed from a localized affair concerning a simple breach of seniority into a principled fight for the right to organize a union.[11]

Urged on by unionized Winnipeg freighthandlers, and encouraged in Calgary by assurances from Robert Tallon – also CTLC president and a labour city councillor – that 'the various trade organizations in the city were unanimously behind the men,' Calgary freighthandlers struck work in late September 1918.[12] During the days that followed, labour leaders raised the level of their rhetoric and threatened to mobilize the city's entire working class in a general strike. The federal government responded by threatening to invoke the recently enacted 'antistrike' order-in-council, PC 2525, to settle the matter.[13] This threat further inflamed matters. Many Calgary workers now saw the strike not just in terms of seniority or their right to organize, but as a test of the democratic freedoms that Canadians had fought and died to preserve. 'All we desire,' announced Calgary's labour MLA Alex Ross, 'is the right to build up our labor organizations so that at the conclusion of the war we will be able to defend ourselves against a reduction in wages rather than to depend on the state.' Tallon was less moderate in his criticism of the recent spate of orders-in-council passed by Borden's government. 'These powers are enthused by the wonderful victories being accomplished by Canadian soldiers composed mostly of men of your class,' he told a crowd of strikers, 'and they mean to use these very victories to entrench them in their arbitrary powers. If as a wage-earner I have no longer got the right to bargain with my employer or to oppose his exploiting me, but must be a slave, ... I am dead willing to come out at this time and put it to the test.' The local press appeared to have taken such threats seriously, with the *Albertan* remarking that 'The labor unions seem more ready than ever to exert their rights and bring on industrial warfare at every opportunity. There is less regard for the sanctity of contracts than ever before. There is general discontent, disturbance and dissatisfaction.'[14]

Certainly, suspicions and emotions were running high in Calgary in the fall of 1918. Strikers and authorities alike believed themselves to be in the midst of a violent class struggle. Yet it is far less clear that local support for the striking freighthandlers really did provide an effective test of 'labour's ultimate weapon,' as Taraska and others maintain. A closer examination of labour's response to the strike suggests that it did no such thing. In addition, a reconsideration of the federal government's own reaction to events belies the view that it took advantage of the Calgary dispute to test its new antistrike legislation.[15]

First, the proposed sympathy strike in Calgary won only lukewarm support from the local labour movement. Historians have exaggerated the degree to which Calgary unionists supported the idea even in principle, let alone in action. Although nineteen of the twenty-one unions that recorded a vote among their respective memberships on the question did declare their support for a sympathy strike, they represented fewer than one-third of Calgary's fifty-eight trade unions in existence in 1918. Moreover, few of these nineteen were prepared to back up their vote. At first, the only workers to down tools in solidarity were the freighthandlers' colleagues at the Ogden shops, where 1,200 men walked off the job on 12 October. Pipefitters, steamfitters, boilermakers, electricians, and blacksmiths were among those who stopped work. The Brotherhood of Locomotive Engineers and Firemen, on the other hand, refused to countenance strike action over the issue. Action spread beyond the railway shops only after rumours circulated that the federal government was preparing to invoke PC 2525. At this point, other Calgary unions ordered workers off the job, and by mid-October some 200 members of the city's public works department and other outside employees, together with 250 street railway workers, had joined the Ogden strikers.[16]

At its peak, the sympathy strike could claim the active support of perhaps 1,800 Calgary trade unionists, roughly half the total union membership of 3,500 and close to 10 percent of Calgary's overall labour force. 'The sympathetic or general strike has never come up to the expectations of its ardent supporters,' concluded Alex Ross in November 1918, 'because it is so difficult to get the unity and action of purpose necessary to carry a strike to a successful issue.'[17] That the strike drew virtually no support from the ranks of non-union labour suggests that Tallon and other leaders had failed to convince such workers that this was indeed a working-class struggle over the right to organize. Indeed, the strike's leaders actually opposed broadening the conflict to encompass non-union workers. On 17 October, unorganized women employed at the Burns meatpacking plant quit work in sympathy with the freighthandlers, only to be ordered back within ten minutes by the strike committee's chair.[18] One might read into this incident trade union paternalism rather than an absence of class solidarity. Whatever the reason, there remains little cause to regard the 1918 freighthandlers' strike as a harbinger of the nationwide revolt to come.

It is also necessary to reassess the argument that the federal government intervened in this dispute in order to test its own recent antistrike legislation. In this matter, historians have echoed contemporary conventional wisdom that the government intended to use the pristine PC 2525 as a means of prosecuting five of the Calgary strike leaders. As a result, the freighthandlers' strike has come to stand as a landmark in the larger pattern of class conflict in Canada at the close of the First World War. In the words of one such historian, Ottawa's use of PC 2525 was 'a tremendous blunder [that] ... put the government directly across the path of the unions in an open and obvious fashion.'[19] In fact, the government never actually invoked this draconian legislation in the Calgary dispute. While it is true that in October 1918 local police and military authorities expected to receive official orders to prosecute strikers under PC 2525, those orders never came. Instead, the Department of Justice charged the five Calgary men with unlawful strike action in contravention of section 56 of the Industrial Disputes Investigation Act (IDIA). This section prohibited the declaration of a strike or lockout 'prior to or during a reference of such dispute to a Board of Conciliation and Investigation.'[20] Enacted in 1907 and extended in scope in 1916, by October 1918 the IDIA was a well-established means of government intervention in labour-employer relations, whatever reservations workers may have had regarding its impartiality. The government may have been unusually assiduous in its pursuit of prosecution of the Calgary strike leaders, but it did not resort to new and overtly discriminatory legislation.[21]

In short, events in Calgary in October 1918 did not demonstrate either the effectiveness of the general strike as a tactical weapon or the government's dependence on new antilabour laws. They did convince many workers that the time had come to reorganize labour's collective strength. As one freighthandler concluded in the wake of the strike, 'The attempt that was made to unify the forces of labor showed, as no amount of theorising will ever show, the inadequacy of the Craft Organizations ... to ever be a force strong or potent enough to be a dependable factor in any struggle that does not cover a large area.' The general strike was simply too unwieldy to be used as a tactical weapon. Even Alex Ross, a seasoned supporter of craft unionism in Calgary, conceded the point. Commenting on the impossibility of conducting a sympathy strike at a purely local level, he called for broader industrial organization along national lines. 'If labor is to survive against highly organized capital it must adopt this form of organization,' he wrote in November 1918. 'The sympathetic strike is somewhat crude, it can only be regarded as a step in the development of labor organizations, the next [is] industrial unionism.'[22] Ross's remarks echoed Calgary machinist Harry Pryde's views on the necessity of amalgamation of craft unions back in 1911, and reflected Ross's own appreciation of the changes in production wrought by four years of war. But they did not represent support for an 'Owenite' organization along the lines of the OBU. This subtle but important distinction was to grow in importance over the next few months.

The example of Alex Ross underlines the problem in portraying the events of 1918-9 in the mutually exclusive terms of 'conservatism' and 'radicalism.' Ross had long been a committed supporter of existing craft unions and, as a former city councillor and MLA, was an obvious advocate of electoral politics. At the same time, he envisaged a broadening of craft unionism to accommodate the recent transformation of work and workers, and he became increasingly critical of the reformed alliance of the state and capital after the First World War. Other figures within the Calgary labour movement shared this combination of attitudes and outlook, as was evident during the Western Labour Conference in March 1919. The actions and articulated beliefs of delegates at that gathering merit reexamination. They help to explain not only why Calgary labour rejected the OBU in 1919, but also the course of labour politics in Calgary during the decade that followed.

Calgary was convention city in the spring of 1919. In quick succession, the city played host to annual conferences of District 18 of the United Mine Workers of America (UMWA) and the British Columbia Federation of Labor (BCFL), and then to the Western Labour Conference. At all three events, delegates displayed the sense of radicalism and anger that had swept much of Canada, but especially the West, over the past year. In particular, conferees vented their frustrations over the inability of craft unionism to combat the increasingly naked alliance between the state and big business. At the UMWA and BCFL conferences, delegates passed unambiguous resolutions in favour of militant industrial unionism. It fell to the Western Labour Conference – originally convened to flesh out a united front of western trade union demands to present to the eastern-dominated TLC that fall – to make plans to launch the One Big Union.

Described by Gerald Friesen as 'a combination of regional parliament and religious revival [that] recognized the ascendancy of the Socialist Party of Canada,' the Western Labour Conference represented the fullest expression of support yet seen for industrial unionism, or syndicalism, in the West.[23] Historians have rightly focused on those socialists and other radicals who led the call for the One Big Union and a corresponding abandonment of the political struggle. Yet in doing so, they have all but ignored those speakers – mainly from Calgary – who voiced contrary views, especially on the question of political action. Martin Robin, for example, notes that 'there was little vocal opposition' to the OBU and passes quickly over the arguments made by Calgary machinist Andrew Broatch. Ross McCormack and Gerald Friesen also minimize objections from the Calgary contingent, Friesen claiming that 'one can reasonably conclude that the SPC was representative of the wishes of western union members,' although he fails to demonstrate how or why this is so. Bryan Palmer's reference to the conference as 'composed of delegates not unsympathetic to radical claims and aims' is sufficiently vague to ignore the presence of any dissenting voices at all.[24] In short, historians have accepted and perpetuated the disparaging opinion expressed by Dave Rees, UMWA official and convener of the Calgary conference, that many of Alberta's labour leaders were little more than 'Lloyd George coalitionists.'[25]

There is little doubt that Calgary's delegates found themselves isolated at the 1919 conference, their stated preference for political action over direct confrontation setting them apart from the majority. This preference did not, however, preclude them from wishing to participate in the proposed new organization – indeed, it might even have strengthened their resolve to commit the OBU to some sort of political program. In the election of a central committee to organize the OBU referendum, machinist Andrew Broatch and stonemason Walter Smitten each secured just sixty-two votes out of a possible 237, placing the pair joint last. Yet that Broatch and Smitten had run for election at all is perhaps as important as their defeat; when characterizing Calgary labour in 1919, historians have often overlooked this desire to influence and direct the formation of the OBU. If Calgary fails to fit the picture of a radical western labour movement, then neither can it be dismissed as a monolith of working-class conservatism. In particular, the arguments made at the conference by men such as Broatch, John Barnecutt, William McQuoid, and J.S. Hooley need to be set not within a framework of western revolt but within the context of Calgary labour's own history of political success before 1919.[26]

Interest in the idea of industrial unionism had surfaced within the Calgary labour movement in the years before the First World War. By 1919, there were several local figures who were openly receptive to the possibility of some sort of One Big Union. Political ideology seems to have had little to do with an individual's interest in such a scheme. Socialists such as Broatch, Tallon, and Robert Parkyn publicly declared their support for the OBU, but so too did more moderate men such as Ross, Smitten, and Harry Pryde. What did set Calgary delegates apart from others at the Western Labour Conference was not their principled opposition to the OBU, but their insistence that it should not, as hardline syndicalists maintained, be formed at the expense of political action.[27] Calgary's representatives consistently argued that conflicts with capital at the workplace could not be separated from labour's broader social struggles, struggles that demanded political solutions. In March 1919, then, Broatch and company were motivated by the belief that an OBU devoid of a political component was a retrograde step.[28]

The exchange between Andrew Broatch and Jack Kavanagh illustrates the nature of these differences. A Vancouver longshoreman and member of the SPC since 1907, Kavanagh regarded the formation of the OBU as a necessary precondition for the staging of a general strike. Such a strike, in turn, was the only way in which workers could force the federal government to concede their political as well economic demands. Kavanagh had no patience for those who recommended the ballot box as an effective course of action. As he told conference delegates in Calgary, 'any time the workers imagine they can emancipate themselves merely through the gas houses of this or any other country, they have another think coming ... We have had so-called labor representatives placed in the cabinet of many administrations, all they have been used [as] was as tools to deceive the worker.'[29]

Broatch, who declared himself to be 'heartily in favor of the One Big Union' all his life, was more sanguine about the potential of political action. Indeed, he believed it to be an essential counterpart of the industrial struggle, as he explained to those at the conference:

> The fact of organizing an organization as we anticipate doing, and bringing all workers within the fold of that organization, will not eliminate the fact that laws will still exist, and the chambers where the law is made will still be a part of our social life ... To my mind we are only storming the citadel of the enemy from one angle, and that angle materially affects ourselves. When we call a general strike under this form of organization we disrupt the means of production and distribution whereby we leave the other man holding the strings of the bag; having no control of what is already produced ... [About] that I believe no delegate on the floor will offer contrary remarks.[30]

The majority of delegates did just that, of course. 'Oh! yes, lots of them,' yelled one man in response to Broatch's closing challenge. But no other speaker predicted with such accuracy the eventual outcome of the Winnipeg general strike. Other Calgary delegates echoed Broatch's views. 'Strikes have been a failure and may yet be failures,' noted CTLC representative J.S. Hooley, 'but organizing on political lines we have a chance both ways to work.' William McQuoid, a member of the Federal Labour Union and organizer for the Socialist Party of Canada in Calgary, drew attention to the gains made by workers in Britain and America through political action.[31] Despite their further protestations, Broatch, Hooley, and McQuoid failed to win the conference over to their point of view, and, as has been well documented, the OBU was launched devoid of any political agenda.[32]

Results of the referendum that led to its launch suggest that support for the OBU was not especially firm elsewhere in Alberta. Workers from across the province seemed to have shared Broatch's concerns, and away from the coalfields labour unions showed limited enthusiasm for the new organization. In Edmonton, only sixteen of the city's sixty-two unions took part in the referendum itself; of those, eight rejected the proposal outright. The remaining eight narrowly defeated it by 683 votes to 646, possibly reflecting the threat made by the Edmonton Trades and Labour Council to suspend any delegate whose union expressed even an intention to support the OBU.[33] South of Calgary, in Lethbridge, just six of that city's twenty-three unions voted on the question, and in total recorded a mere seven individual votes in favour of the OBU. Greater support was evident in Medicine Hat, where a majority of workers who voted did so in favour of the new organization. Yet even here, fewer than half of the town's eighteen unions actually participated in the referendum.[34]

In Calgary, meanwhile, the OBU proposal initially provoked a lively debate within the city's labour movement. At its meeting of 19 March 1919, just four days after the Western Labour Conference, the CTLC 'stood shivering on the brink,' according to one reporter, as it debated for two hours whether to approve affiliation.[35] Among those in favour were Broatch and Hooley, who remained committed to the idea of the OBU despite their recent failure to convince the conference of the need to give it a political dimension. Joining them as an outspoken advocate of industrial unionism was Robert Parkyn, a forty-five-year-old carpenter who had emigrated to Canada from Britain in 1907. A self-taught and widely read man, Parkyn had a local reputation as a labour radical, which would shortly be enhanced by a midnight raid on his house by the RNWMP in search of subversive literature.[36] In the OBU, Parkyn saw the potential for class solidarity that fuelled his own belief in socialism. 'Are we going to be so foolish not to get together; we, the exploited?' he asked in a letter to the *Albertan* at the time of the referendum. 'If not, then we deserve to be exploited. That is why the capitalistic class is getting together, because they know that after the war there was going to be a big fight for a greater democracy, and they do not want that ... In One Big Union is our only hope of salvation.'[37]

Parkyn's impassioned arguments left most of Calgary's unions unconvinced. Printers, bricklayers, sheet-metal workers, and even Parkyn's fellow carpenters chose not to vote in the referendum. Within the local machinists' union, one of Calgary's more radical labour bodies, the 96-46 vote in favour came only after an intense and bitter debate among members. Elsewhere, early interest in the OBU rapidly waned, and just thirty-four of Calgary's fifty-eight unions cast a vote on the matter. Of these, fourteen recorded their unanimous opposition to the OBU; members of the remaining twenty unions voted against it by a margin of 951 to 728. In Calgary, as elsewhere in Alberta, the OBU never posed a serious threat to the existing leadership of local craft-based organizations.[38]

Thus, resistance to the OBU by Alberta's urban workers was overwhelming. Just 40 percent of unions in Calgary, Edmonton, Lethbridge, and Medicine Hat participated in the referendum. Of these, 40 percent – that is, 16 percent of participating unions – voted unanimously against the idea. Added to the unions that refused to participate in the referendum, then, a full 76 percent of Alberta's city-based unions failed to record a single vote in support of the OBU in the spring of 1919, even if individual members within those unions were in favour of the proposed organization. Among the remaining 24 percent in which the vote was split, opponents outnumbered backers by 1,850 to 1,432. This last figure – the total number of votes cast for the OBU – represented less than 10 percent of Alberta's 15,272 union members, and clearly set the province apart from the rest of western Canada. Within the region as a whole, 59 percent of all trade unionists voted in favour of the OBU, and just 14 percent against. Urban Alberta unionists constituted one-third of this no vote. Given the extent of this opposition, David Bercuson's claim that the OBU 'was an aberration and not reflective of the special needs or desires of western workers' deserves reconsideration, at least in the case of Alberta.[39]

The Winnipeg general strike began in the early hours of 15 May 1919. Calgary workers struck in sympathy eleven days later and stayed out until 25 June. Gregory Kealey has calculated that the Calgary sympathy strike lasted for 31,700 worker-days, making it the third largest stoppage in western Canada behind Winnipeg and Vancouver.[40] Certainly it was Calgary's most comprehensive strike to date – the nearest thing to a precedent was the walkout by 1,200 carpenters in 1912 – yet it is difficult to regard this gesture of sympathy as a *general* strike of Calgary's working class. Only twenty-five of the city's seventy-four unions took part in the strike vote and at best they represented no more than 1,500 workers, compared to the 25,000 in Winnipeg who had downed tools on the first day of their strike. Further, the Calgary strike gained additional momentum only when it overlapped with a separate dispute involving local postal workers, at which point the city's building trades entered the fray for the first time. 'Very little mention is now made of the Winnipeg strike,' wrote Fred E. Harrison, local representative of the federal Department of Labour, to Labour Minister Gideon Robertson on 7 June. 'The attitude of the strike committee is that of one in sympathy with the postal workers. If the latter situation can be cleared, I am convinced that the strike in Calgary would cease within twenty-four hours.'[41]

Harrison's casual assessment of the strike situation in Calgary was somewhat at odds with the steps being taken by the RNWMP to monitor and repress any labour radicalism in the city. Inspector J.W. Spalding was the commanding officer in Calgary, and he was kept informed daily, sometimes hourly, by reports from Constable Frank Zaneth.[42] In September 1918, Zaneth had invented the character of 'Harry Blask,' a transient labourer and IWW member originally from northern Italy. Adopting that identity, he insinuated himself within the Calgary labour movement in the spring of 1919, and was well placed to observe and relate events as they rapidly unfolded.[43] Yet his reports to Spalding and other superior officers are notable for containing little that suggests Calgary was on the verge of a widespread labour revolt. 'Everything is very orderly and so far there has been no sign of disturbance,' recorded Detective-Corporal S.R. Waugh on 27 May 1919, based on Zaneth's clandestine observations. 'In fact if it were not for the Postal employees being out and the consequent inconvenience therefrom one would hardly realize that there was a strike in force.' On the contrary, he noted that 'The Radicals here in Calgary are down-hearted [for] they feel that the [general] strike will be lost, and it will have a great effect against the O.B.U.: they have no plans as to what they will do, they are only afraid that they will all land in jail.'[44] Reference here to the One Big Union reflected the official and deeply held belief within the RNWMP that the OBU, even though it had yet to take shape as an organization, was behind the wave of unrest across western Canada. This belief would outlast the wave itself.

If anything, the RNWMP's reliance on stool pigeons and agents provocateurs in addition to their own agents may have heightened the class tension that existed in Calgary at the time. Some of these men played both sides of the fence, and RNWMP officials could never be sure of their true loyalties. Zaneth's immediate superior, S.R. Waugh, confided such fears regarding one unnamed informant in his report of 29 May:

> I am not always sure of the veracity of [deleted] reports and I like to more or less substantiate them, the best way I can, before rendering them ... Further I have to be diplomatic with [deleted] and not let him see that I mistrust him, for fear that he turns tail on us, which I have no hesitation in saying that I think he would if he became aware of my attitude towards him. Although this man has got certain information, that has been valuable, at the same time, he does not do half he says he does and learns a lot of information from Zaneth and peddles it to me as his own; further I have found out he has said he has been to meetings he was never at ... Personally I would like to see this man transferred from here as I am nervous of him all the time, as to playing a double game and giving false information.[45]

Waugh noted that the same man had caused some unease among the strikers themselves, 'one going so far as to complain to Det. Ritchie of the City Police Force' that he was 'preaching revolution; he is a typical I.W.W. and if he had a chance would stick at nothing.'[46] Clearly a sense of mistrust and doubt pervaded the RNWMP's surveillance operations in Calgary, even as its own choice of operatives aggravated the situation they were supposed to be monitoring.

Among those who did strike work that spring, there was a sense of unity, even class consciousness, that had been missing on previous occasions. The *Calgary Strike Bulletin,* a hurriedly produced paper designed to counter what was perceived to be misleading propaganda contained in the mainstream press, featured a number of articles that celebrated this new-found solidarity. A poem entitled 'Scab or Comrade' left the reader in no doubt as to the strike's broader social relevance:

> We're proud of our comrades who stand for the right
> Our cause is a just one; we'll fight a clean fight
> Our manhood's at stake, stand firm, hand in hand
> The victory is sure – we're the salt of the land.[47]

The strike was also a moment in which divisions of ethnicity and gender appeared to dissolve in the common struggle against capitalism. 'The solidarity of the workers in the Calgary railroad roundhouse is clearly demonstrated by the fact that the Japanese wipers came out with the rest of the boys,' declared the *Strike Bulletin* on 30 May. A recently formed branch of the Women's Labor League (WLL) in Calgary was an active and enthusiastic supporter of the strike, led by its president Mary Corse and vice-president Jean McWilliam. Women were also at the centre of a tag day on 11 June to raise funds for the strike, with some collecting money on the streets and others going door to door in various districts of the city. 'The collectors for the most part were mothers of families, many the wives of returned veterans,' noted the *Strike Bulletin,* adding that 'A great deal of opposition was met with and insults were heaped upon the collector, also threats were made, which had the strikers made them would have been considered Bolshevistic.'[48] Describing this 'very hostile reception' in his report at the time, one RNWMP officer suggested 'It was with this idea in view that the City had allowed them permission to sell the tag' in the first place.[49] Nonetheless, the experience of solidarity that the tag day offered many women was probably as valuable as the $670 that they managed to raise.

Despite such moments, the strike failed to gather momentum or amass new support. Some of Calgary's major labour organizations, notably the typographical union and the freighthandlers' union, refused to throw their weight behind the strike, and even the public efforts of noted radicals such as Bill Pritchard, Joe Knight, and William Irvine did little to win new converts. Pritchard's emotive and fiery address at Calgary's Mewata Park on 7 June, for example, attracted fewer than 500 workers. When Alberta Federation of Labor president Frank Wheatley addressed a crowd of 600 a few days earlier, he stated that he was 'very much disappointed in the manner the Calgary people were carrying on the strike,' contrasting them to the nearby miners 'who would be out to a man and would never return until they got their demands.'[50] That the strike may have actually undermined any sense of class solidarity in Calgary was reflected in the remarks made by one metal trades worker upon hearing of Pritchard's subsequent arrest in Winnipeg. 'It serves him well right,' he bitterly told an undercover RNWMP agent, 'every one of your [sic] "REDS" that is keeping us from our work should be in jail, and I hope that you will all get it later or sooner.'[51]

Even among those who did actively support Calgary's sympathy strike, motives were often no more revolutionary than the hope of redressing some long-standing complaint. On the eve of the metal trades' walkout, CPR freighthandler Frank Grier rationalized the action in pragmatic terms. 'The different trades all have grievances, small and large,' he explained, 'such as the miners and the railwaymen and others, and if these different trades struck separately, no doubt they would lose out, so that our forces might as well be combined and make one issue out of the whole strike, thereby getting the respective grievances settled once and for all.'[52] Others who supported the strike found themselves frustrated by the Central Strike Committee's orders to keep certain services operating during the dispute. 'What the hell do you think I am going to do,' asked local socialist R.L. Bradshaw, 'after agitating around for ten years ... and hav[ing] been an I.W.W. for many years waiting for this moment to take place and now I have to keep at work by orders of some of those bastards of the Central Strike Committee. I will not be satisfied until I have killed somebody, especially the spotter we have in our bunch.'[53]

The strike in Calgary was eventually called off on 25 June, still 'with considerable dissension among the strikers' about whether to continue, according to one report.[54] In the end, this so-called revolt had achieved nothing and had been rejected or ignored by more than 90 percent of the city's workforce. Even those historians who argue that the war had radicalized Calgary's working class concede that its sympathy strike in 1919 was the least impressive of all those staged in the West.[55] Just as the city's unions rejected the prospect of the One Big Union, so its working class declined to escalate their various separate grievances into a single confrontation with the state.[56]

For its part, the state still had some unfinished business. Warrants to search a number of premises had been issued on 22 June, and although the Calgary strike was now over RNWMP officers went ahead with a series of raids on the night of 30 June. At the Labour Temple they seized fifty-five copies of '76 Questions and Answers on the Bolsheviks and the Soviets,' a pamphlet produced by Albert Williams, but 'found no correspondence that would show that there had been any conspiracy.' The homes of strike committee chair Hooley, Socialist Party organizer McQuoid, and a number of others were also raided, but in each case little subversive literature was discovered. The raids reached farcical proportions at the home of socialist carpenter Robert Parkyn. Police officers entered Parkyn's house at 2:30 in the morning and searched through his substantial library, seizing any volume bound in a red cover. Parkyn watched in silence until one constable removed a red-leather-bound copy of the Bible, at which point he laughed and said, 'You read that, you might be a better Mountie.' Without even pausing, the officer placed the book in a sack along with other confiscated other works. Parkyn never saw any of them again.[57]

Although they collected little evidence of any subversive activity in Calgary, these raids reflected the state's concern that revolutionary motives lay behind the wave of strikes that spring. Increasingly, this concern came to focus on the One Big Union, which in consequence continued to find itself the subject of surveillance and repression long after the strikes were over. Aware of the unwelcome attention the OBU was attracting and was likely to attract in future, some of the Calgary strikers attempted to distance themselves from the organization. Even the *Calgary Strike Bulletin*, which had run a number of articles critical of capitalism, emphasized the fact that among those who had endorsed the strike was labour city councillor Fred White, a man 'well known by all Calgarians as a Conservative rather than a Radical Trade Unionist, and a confirmed opponent of the One Big Union.'[58] Nevertheless, the OBU managed to make inroads among the city's workforce. By June 1920, 20 percent of Calgary's qualified printers had enlisted with the new organization, while the OBU's 'fair success' in recruiting at the Ogden machine shops prompted existing craft unions there to employ shop stewards in an attempt to tighten union discipline among the rank and file. By October 1920, the OBU's membership in the city included 200 transportation workers, 51 general labourers, and 23 flour millers, but even at its peak the new organization could claim no more than 1 percent of Calgary's entire workforce.[59]

Although it never won much support among Calgary's working class, the OBU did have one major lasting impact upon developments within the labour movement in the years after 1919. Popular opinion quickly demonized the organization, with people perceiving its harmful influence to be behind a variety of new critiques of capitalism in the 1920s. In February 1920, hecklers at the People's Forum shouted down orator Ambrose Tree with cries of 'Bolshevist! OBU!' during his Marxist discussion of 'The Troubles of Labour.'[60] Individuals who had been vocal supporters of the OBU in 1919 – notably Andrew Broatch, William Irvine, Annie Gale, and Sophie Mushkat McCluskey – found themselves unable to shake off the connection long after the organization itself had dwindled into insignificance in Calgary. Further, when they turned their efforts to other working-class organizations, such as the Labour Church and the Dominion Labor Party (DLP), their reputation as OBU radicals followed them and helped to taint these new endeavours.

The Labour Church was further troubled by the hostility of moderate members within the CTLC who opposed the church on principle, arguing that the widespread labour unrest of spring 1919 'had been brooded and

'Antagonistic to the ideals of honest labor.' As a wave of labour unrest swept Canada in the spring of 1919, the *Calgary Herald* appealed to the 'common interest and common effort' of labour and capital against the perceived threat of the IWW and the newly formed One Big Union.

hatched in the labor church in Winnipeg.'[61] Fears of such radicalism were fuelled when it was announced that Broatch, Irvine, Pryde, and Parkyn – all men linked to the OBU – were to form the CTLC committee struck to organize the Labour Church in Calgary. Such fears could hardly have been allayed by the subsequent announcement that among the church's goals was 'the overthrowing of the capitalist system and society.'[62] Throughout the early 1920s, many trade unionists continued to view the Labour Church as an unwelcome manifestation of the OBU's 'disruptive influence.'[63]

Similar suspicions surrounded the Dominion Labor Party, formed in September 1919 as the latest step in Calgary labour's political evolution. 'If the Labor party wants to have the co-operation of the citizens of Calgary it has got to get rid of the revolutionary people it is now putting up for office,' a returned soldier warned in opposition to the party's nomination of Andrew Broatch in November 1919.[64] The fact that Broatch had long advocated independent political action – well before he had become associated with the OBU – and had opposed revolutionary syndicalism at the Western Labour Conference was of no import to the veteran. In part, the Calgary DLP suffered from the clumsy attempts by its own leaders to assure the public that it would not be under the OBU's control. 'Exactly the opposite is the case,' stated executive member Walter Smitten, just before going on to add that 'Of course, there may be one or two members who were attracted by the O.B.U. movement propagandists, but surely a man has the right to change his opinions. It would be absurd to say once an O.B.U. advocate always an O.B.U. advocate.' Many potential supporters of the DLP remained unconvinced by this somewhat evasive assurance.[65]

Obviously the events of 1918-9 were not without influence on the Calgary labour movement, but they did not in themselves constitute a significant juncture in that movement's history, or in the formation of class relations in the city. The freighthandlers' strike of 1918 was not an effective test of the general strike weapon, nor did the government's response to that strike cause labour to lose faith in the efficacy of parliamentary politics. Calgary workers rejected the pseudo-syndicalism of the One Big Union and were lukewarm supporters of the Winnipeg general strike. Instead, the main impact of both episodes was the legacy of mistrust and suspicion that they created within the labour movement. It was against this volatile background that workers continued their fraught search for a common political identity in the years 1918-24.

8
Dissent and Descent: Labour Politics in Calgary, 1918-24

Calgary labour's rejection of the One Big Union (OBU) in 1919 reflected a continuing commitment to the reform-minded politics of labourism. Historians who emphasize the sudden but short-lived outburst of radicalism across Canada at the war's end frequently overlook the degree of continuity between labour's prewar and postwar strategies and tactics.[1] This is not to say that labour's concerns and challenges after the First World War were identical to those before 1914. The deep economic restructuring that took place after 1918 had to be confronted, and labour politicians had frequently to dispel fears and allegations that they were simply a front for the OBU. In Calgary, there were two interlocking features that marked labour's political odyssey between 1918 and 1924. The first was the attempt to form an organization that was electorally viable and, at the same time, representative of the working class's distinct interests within society. No party in Calgary had yet managed this task. The second aspect was the need to convert labour's industrial wing – the trade union movement – fully to the political cause. So far, union support for labour politics had been strictly ad hoc.

The civic elections of December 1918 provided Calgary labour with its first political test since the disappointing federal contest of 1917, in which Calgary's William Irvine had gone down to defeat along with all other twenty-six Canadian Labor Party candidates. Despite that setback, Calgary's labour candidates entered the 1918 civic campaign in good spirits, hoping to repeat the success of Andrew Broatch and Annie Gale in the previous year's elections for city council. In particular, they sought to broaden public awareness of and interest in labour's own plans for postwar reconstruction. A total of thirteen candidates ran for election in 1918, easily the record number to date in a municipal contest and a fair reflection of the aggressive optimism felt by labour at the time. Despite the strong numbers, their hopes of capturing Calgary's progressive vote were undermined by the appearance of a 'Citizens' Slate,' a loose association of business and professional candidates running on a platform that included demands for municipal ownership of public hospitals, government-assisted reintegration of veterans into civilian life, and a system of arbitration to resolve labour disputes.[2] The cross-class attraction of these policies undercut labour's more sectarian appeal, even though the two platforms were remarkably similar, and most labour candidates fared poorly as a result. Only Fred White, former president of the International Typographical Union (ITU), was elected to city council; Mary Corse, member of the ITU's women's auxiliary and co-founder of the Women's Labor League in Calgary, was the lone candidate to win a seat on the school board. All other eleven candidates were defeated.[3]

Labour's campaign committee tried to put on a brave face in its analysis of these results. 'By their earnest efforts the cause of Labor and Labor ideals have been very creditably placed before the electorate of the city,' it reported early in 1919, 'and because the principles for which we stand are progressive and humanitarian, and will in time be accepted by the majority, a candidate who promulgates those principles is not truly defeated.'[4] At the same time, the committee acknowledged the need for more rigorous organization. It recommended, first, that preparations for future campaigns begin much earlier in the year than previously had been the case and, second, that the labour movement should work all year round, not just at election time, in its efforts to increase local working-class support. To this end, the committee suggested that the Labor Representation League – formed in March 1917 – had outlived its usefulness as an organizational focus and should be replaced. Thus, even as Calgary strikers were taking to the streets in the spring of 1919, labour's political activists began planning the launch of a new party.

After a spring of distraction and a summer of preparation, the Calgary branch of the Dominion Labor Party (DLP) came into being in September 1919. Its model was the Alberta DLP, formed eight months earlier, and both branches adopted a constitution and platform loosely based on those of the British Labour Party. Local labour figures were quick to point out this connection. 'If Canada emulates the ideas and principles of the British labor movement we will not go very far wrong,' proclaimed Harry Pryde at the Calgary DLP's inaugural meeting. At the same gathering, William Irvine reiterated the need for labour to combine its industrial and political efforts, arguing that 'Labor ... had been flapping one wing for some time, with the result that it had been flying in a circle. The time had now come to stretch out the other wing and fly straight in order to achieve progress.' The meeting concluded with the election of Pryde as party president, Alice Corliss as vice-president, and Edith Patterson as secretary-treasurer.[5]

This strong representation of women in senior positions – in all, three of the seven executive officials were women – would be an enduring feature of the DLP throughout the 1920s. According to historian Pat Roome, the Calgary DLP had a core of fifty to seventy-five active female members, consisting of single working women – usually teachers or journalists – and married women belonging to union auxiliaries. Although their presence ensured that the party would continue to address issues of particular concern to Calgary working women, such as equality in the workplace and the question of a 'living wage,' labour women were divided among themselves on such subjects. In 1923, the Women's Labor League, whose leaders featured prominently within the DLP, petitioned the Calgary School Board to reduce the number of women it employed, believing that male teachers, especially married ones, should have preference when it came to hiring.[6] Such ambivalence meant that, although the DLP itself remained sympathetic to the concerns of local women, in practice its outlook reflected the views and assumptions of its male membership. In this respect, the DLP's record in the 1920s is consistent with Suzanne Morton's observation that 'men through their participation in the labour movement or labour politics may have claimed to desire a new vision of the world, but this vision was essentially one in which they remained economically, politically, and socially privileged over their mothers, wives, sisters, daughters, and girlfriends.'[7]

From the start, relations between the new DLP and the Calgary Trades and Labour Council (CTLC) were uneasy. In his study of Alberta labour politics, historian Alvin Finkel argues that the DLP was 'largely a creature of the trade unions in the province.' While this is strictly true, there were also a great many individuals within labour's industrial organizations who remained wary of embracing the new political party.[8] Despite reassuring remarks from Irvine and Pryde, the CTLC's rank-and-file membership remained hesitant about endorsing the DLP. Even endorsement of the party by the CTLC's leaders left many trade unions unconvinced: within one week of the DLP's debut meeting, delegates to the CTLC voted narrowly to reject formal affiliation. Some delegates opposed any CTLC involvement in politics at all, while others viewed the DLP as an unwelcome 'OBU outfit.' A disappointed Walter Smitten, executive member of both the CTLC and DLP, told council members that the party would press on regardless of their decision.[9]

Within weeks of its formation, the DLP entered the December 1919 municipal elections. In contrast to the previous year's shotgun approach, the new party concentrated labour's resources and backed just seven candidates, four for the council and three for the school board. Andrew Broatch and Annie Gale repeated their success of 1917 and were elected to city council, even though once again neither managed to win more than 1,000 votes. Harry Pryde and R.B. Gale were also victorious, winning seats on the school board, but James Rae, Walter Smitten, and R.J. Deachman amassed fewer than 700 votes among them on their way to defeat.[10]

These mixed fortunes reflected the DLP's two main problems at the time: how to mobilize working-class support and how to cement more fruitful relations with the CTLC. On the first issue, the pro-DLP executive on the CTLC later estimated that only 30 percent of Calgary workers had even voted in the election, and it called on unions to help increase this figure in future. On the second point, CTLC president Alex Ross argued of relations between the industrial and political wings 'I feel that the labor movement is drifting towards complete unity. The ties that will yet bind them together will be born of necessity and the program acceptable to both groups will be a synothetic [sic] program.'[11] Despite this, Ross still drew attention to the labour council's unsatisfactorily vague relationship with the DLP. Although there was no formal affiliation between the two bodies, there existed a considerable overlap among their respective memberships, especially at the executive level. The two were far from equal partners, however, for the total membership of the CTLC was ten times that of the DLP. As a result, while the DLP retained the responsibility for nominating labour's electoral candidates, the task of financing their campaigns fell generally on the shoulders of the CTLC. In the absence of any explicit agreement between the two organizations, and with many CTLC members still opposed to the idea of the DLP, the CTLC's cooperation in this regard remained voluntary in nature and largely haphazard in practice.[12]

Both sides took steps towards remedying this situation in early 1920. The CTLC urged its members to reconsider their decision of the previous September, while the DLP met with various unions in order to incorporate their demands within its official platform. Together, they agreed upon a program of social and economic demands that included the establishment of a minimum wage, the democratic control of industry, and new forms of taxation to support reform legislation. As the postwar economic recession deepened during 1920, the DLP hoped that these policies would appeal to the increasing number of workers who found themselves threatened by wage cuts and unemployment, and for whom middle-class promises of progressive reform were no longer sufficient.[13]

The civic elections of December 1920 partially fulfilled this hope. Labour's campaign started uncertainly, with organizers complaining that 'it had been impossible to persuade other persons who had been approached to enter the list [of nominations].'[14] Despite this initial reluctance, the DLP's candidates ran a vigorous campaign. Calgary voters responded by electing CPR machinist Walter Little and printer Fred White to the city council, where Broatch and Gale were serving the second year of their two-year terms. As a result, labour controlled one-third of the council's twelve seats.[15] Overshadowing this respectable showing was a controversy that erupted over Broatch's bid to replace A.J. Samis as city commissioner. Once again it was Broatch's association with the OBU that fuelled the row, and the entire incident served as a litmus test of labour's fragile sense of political unity in the postwar era. A brief summary of Broatch's life and career sets the context for this rift.

Born in 1868 in Newcastle-upon-Tyne, England, Andrew Broatch came to Canada with his parents in 1877.[16] At the age of sixteen he began an apprenticeship as a machinist, after which he embarked on an extensive period of travel across North America, including a stay in Winnipeg, where he was elected president of the local Trades and Labour Council. In 1905, at the age of thirty-seven, he moved to Calgary, where he stayed for the rest of his life. An active member of the International Association of Machinists (IAM), Broatch was also committed to the cause of labour politics, evident in his contribution to the debate on the OBU in March 1919 and in the three terms that he served as a labour representative on city council between 1917 and 1921. A large, bald man with an imposing walrus moustache, Broatch was blunt and didactic in his oratory, often to the point of causing offence. As one colleague later complained, he 'appeared to think that those who were opposed to him were a bunch of kindergarten children.'[17] Yet Broatch's principled and uncompromising stance could also inspire admiration and loyalty. William Irvine's *Nutcracker* applauded him as 'a worthy citizen, broad-minded, alert, and a real people's man.'[18] A self-proclaimed socialist and an ardent believer in the potential of working-class solidarity, Broatch counted among his close friends Vancouver radical Bill Pritchard, fellow independent thinker Robert Parkyn, and members of the local Women's Labor League, who praised him for being 'an unselfish, upright, far seeing leader of the labour cause.'[19] This mixture of ambition, perceived arrogance, and blunt openness thrust Broatch into conflict with the DLP and CTLC during the 1920 civic elections.

Already elected to a two-year term as councillor in 1919, Broatch set his sights on the more powerful position of city commissioner when it became open in November 1920. In the event, his bid ended in failure, and the incumbent A.J. Samis enjoyed a comfortable return to office. Yet, in contesting the position, Broatch garnered 2,192 votes. This support was more than double that of any other labour candidate, and it reflected the genuine popularity that he enjoyed among Calgary's working-class electorate.[20] But it was his conduct during the campaign, together with his reputation as a radical, that ruffled feathers within the labour movement's leadership and helped to undermine labour's fragile sense of unity. On previous occasions, the CTLC had selected potential election candidates – whose names it then forwarded to the DLP for formal nomination

– but this time Broatch had simply declared his intention of running for commissioner as an 'independent' labour candidate. This was despite the fact that he was a member of the DLP and so subject to its procedures. Several CTLC officials, including chair Thomas Riley and president Alex Ross, protested Broatch's action, arguing that he lacked the authority to claim to represent the interests of labour. After all, the DLP had been created precisely to focus labour's electoral efforts and to prevent such wild-card bids for office. 'In my opinion,' Ross stated, 'the industrial side of our movement is more important than the political, and Ald. Broatch's influence as a labor agitator has done more to hinder organized labor than anything else. To me the OBU is nothing else but an open shop movement.'[21]

Ross's reference to the OBU reflected a wider belief that Broatch, and those who supported his views, represented a challenge to craft unionism in Calgary. At first, it would appear that delegates to the CTLC also opposed Broatch for his breach of protocol, for they reversed an earlier council decision to canvass Calgary unions for electoral funds. But it is more likely that the CTLC was punishing Broatch for his reputation as an OBU supporter, and that his disregard for the nomination process was simply an excuse to do so. During the incident, the CTLC hierarchy made repeated references to his connections to the OBU and saw no reason why craft unions should help finance a movement 'diametrically opposed to them in principle.' Walter Smitten warned that 'Very little attempt has been made by the OBU to organize the unorganized. It finds it easier to attack the existing organizations, and that will be Ald. Broatch's continued policy.' Comments made by John Barnecutt, former president of the blacksmiths' union, were even more explicit in revealing the way in which immediate and underlying sources of animosity towards Broatch combined in the opposition to his candidacy. 'This rabble, the OBU is worse than the Socialist Party of Canada, because it is out to break and defy the law,' he explained, 'and I shall not vote for Ald. Broatch because he is not abiding by the law.'[22]

It was inevitable that the matter would also divide the DLP itself. At its meeting in early November 1920, Alex Ross, Walter Smitten, and James Rae once again attempted to block Broatch's candidature, but were opposed by socialists and OBU sympathizers within the party, such as Marion Carson and Robert Parkyn. After a long and often acrimonious exchange, the DLP eventually endorsed Broatch's nomination to run against Samis, a decision that Rae promptly announced he would refuse to recognize. Parkyn, in his role as party chair, warned Rae that this disregard for democratic order would 'tend to split the party,' to which a defeated and deflated Ross sharply rejoined, 'It is no use beating about the bush: it is split already.'[23]

The new party, barely a year old, could ill afford these disruptions. Although it had achieved a fair measure of success in the two civic elections that it had contested, it had yet to build a secure base of electoral support. Furthermore, the DLP had yet to cut its teeth at either the provincial or federal levels. This was to change in 1921, a year that proved to be an electoral landmark for both Alberta and Canada. In Alberta, the United Farmers of Alberta (UFA) defeated the incumbent Liberal Party to form the government that would dominate the province for the next fourteen years. At the national level, Mackenzie King's Liberal Party, assisted by the fledgling Progressive Party, ousted Arthur Meighen's unpopular Union government to usher in a new era of Liberal supremacy in Ottawa. Strong performances by non-traditional parties were a significant factor in both contests. In Calgary, the elections of 1921 provided an opportunity for the DLP to put its internal squabbles behind it and to demonstrate its ability to represent a broad range of labour interests.[24]

The provincial election of July 1921 supplied that year's first test of the DLP. Unlike in previous contests, Calgary was no longer divided into three separate ridings but instead was to elect a total of five MLAs from a city-wide ballot. This change resulted in an unprecedented level of political fervour in Calgary, with a total of twenty-three candidates contesting those seats. Among them were three candidates backed by the DLP and two independent labour representatives.[25] For the first time since 1913, the Socialist Party of Canada (SPC) also ran a candidate in Calgary. Frank Williams campaigned as the city's 'Revolutionary Candidate' with the unequivocal message that 'A Vote for Williams will be a vote of protest: It will show where you stand, and forward the emancipation of your class.' Dismissed by the press and other candidates alike, Williams nevertheless managed to convince 1,745 voters, a considerable advance on the 256 votes won by Harry Burge eight years before and a reminder to the DLP that support for radical labour politics was not yet dead in Calgary.[26]

In the wake of the election results of July 1921, the DLP was far too busy celebrating its own success to pay much attention to the SPC. In a contest that had swept the UFA into power in ridings across Alberta, Calgary was the heartland of support for labour. With 7,294 votes, Alex Ross came a comfortable first in the Calgary election to win his second successive term as an MLA. Fred White won 6,192 votes to take third place. Separating the two labour candidates was Bob Edwards, a man who had voiced sporadic support for labour in his various newspaper ventures, most notably the *Calgary Eye Opener*. 'Triumph of Labor,' declared the front page of the *Calgary Herald* on the day after the election. The DLP's achievement in Calgary is even more impressive when set within the context of results across Alberta. Edmonton, for example, failed to return any of its three DLP or five independent labour candidates. Indeed, there were only two other labour candidates elected in the entire province.[27]

Ross and White were both stalwarts of the labour movement in Calgary, and their election in 1921 underlined the DLP's close association with the city's trade unions. For the moment, it seemed, the DLP had chosen not to solicit the support of middle-class progressives in Calgary, but instead remained the guardian of labour's sectional interests. Five months later, in the federal election of December 1921, the party changed tack, although this had less to do with a desire to woo the middle class than to ensure the defeat of the Union government. First, the DLP formed an electoral alliance with the UFA and held similar discussions with the Liberal Party.[28] Norman Smith, editor of *The UFA,* later recalled the reasoning behind this cooperation. 'In two constituencies – East and West Calgary – there was a large urban vote, and the farmers accordingly came to an understanding with the Labor organization, and gave to the Labor people, the opportunity to contest one seat, the farmers agreeing to support the Labor man, while the other seat, West Calgary, was left open to the farmers, Labor agreeing to support the farmers' nominee.' Although divided by philosophy and policy, each of the three parties shared a determination to defeat Meighen's despised government.[29]

As Smith observed, a second change in the DLP's policy in 1921 was its decision to nominate non-union candidates. To fight the federal election, the party formally backed two men – Joseph T. Shaw and William Irvine – who had no direct connections to the local labour movement. Shaw, a lawyer, was the UFA's candidate in West Calgary, and soon after his election to Parliament he formally joined Thomas Crerar's Progressive Party.[30] Irvine was the DLP's own nomination in east Calgary, where the bulk of working-class voters lived. Through his various newspapers and his role within the Non-Partisan League and People's Forum, he had had an active presence in Calgary politics dating back to his arrival in the city in 1916. Not only could he count among his friends many of the CTLC's major figures, but his background as a carpenter lent him additional credibility as a labour candidate. Elected along with Shaw in 1921, Irvine was quick to align himself with J.S. Woodsworth, the only other Labour candidate in Parliament. However, Irvine's preference was for a non-partisan form of politics, as many of his previous endeavours had demonstrated. Consequently, he found himself increasingly at odds with those rank-and-file DLP members who stood by their belief in the class struggle and the limited value of cooperation with either farmers or middle-class allies.[31]

Doubts over Irvine's status as a true labour representative had first surfaced during the 1921 federal campaign itself. As the DLP's nominee, Irvine ran on a platform of working-class demands, including unemployment insurance, increased pensions for veterans, and the social ownership of the means of production and distribution.[32] But during the course of the election, he increasingly returned to his belief in the superiority of non-partisan politics and promoted the merits of interclass cooperation. Attending an address by Irvine to railway workers at Paget Hall, SPC member F.W. Thompson – admittedly, a biased observer – complained that he had 'heard too much bunk peddled at this meeting to sit still in his chair.' Thompson challenged Irvine's vision of non-partisan cooperation, wondering aloud if farmers would sympathize with striking threshers. 'The real issue which lies before the workingman today is this: part of the time you have too much work to do; part of the time not enough; and always too little of the necessities of life.' In a letter to the *Herald* a few days later, 'Veteran Laboring Man' echoed Thompson's criticism of Irvine and went on to denounce the latter as a 'Labor Fakir.'[33]

Shaw and Irvine remained subjects of discussion after their election to Ottawa. The 'real Labor men of Calgary are wondering how they secured a lawyer and a minister to be candidates for the organized union men of this city,' mused the *Herald*. Having raised the question, the writer suggested one possible answer, claiming that 'a small group of well-known Liberal politicians and one or two subservient [working] men' had rigged the DLP's nomination process, and so had blocked the candidacy of union men such as Harry Pryde. Pryde himself believed this to be the case. He complained that the DLP had ceased to function as a genuine labour party, but was instead 'controlled by a number of irreconcilables of the Liberal party who have used the power of the Labor vote to put them where they are. It is quite noticeable to me that the rank and file are beginning to wake up to the real situation.' The *Herald* concluded that the whole incident was a 'piece of manipulation worked so cleverly as to make an old-time politician green with envy.' Both Pryde and the paper were correct, and controversy over the DLP's nomination procedure would resurface later.[34]

At the level of civic politics, the DLP continued to back candidates more closely involved in the local labour movement and so was able to avoid this sort of conflict. In the municipal elections of December 1921, just days after the federal contest, the DLP repeated its strong performance of 1920. Four candidates – Annie Gale, Robert Parkyn, and printers George Batchelor and Andrew Davison – were elected to the city council, bringing labour's overall representation on that body to six seats out of twelve. Two more DLP candidates – Thomas Riley and R.B. Gale – won positions on the school board, providing labour with a majority there for the first time.[35] Harry Pryde, still smarting from his treatment by the DLP in the summer's provincial election, ran unsuccessfully for council as an independent, his defeat inadvertently strengthening the DLP's claim to be labour's political voice in Calgary. More significantly, the results of the

1921 election put labour on the brink of controlling the civic administration for the first time in Calgary's history.[36] The *Herald* certainly took this view, with its postelection editorial conceding that 'labor knew what it wanted, went out to get it, and did get it.' For this outcome, the paper blamed voter apathy – turnout was just 9,000 of an eligible 25,000 – but it also acknowledged the valuable promotional work performed by CTLC volunteers.[37]

The DLP could look back on the trials of 1921 with considerable satisfaction. It had fought successful campaigns in three separate elections, winning representation at all levels of government. In the process, Calgary had shown itself to be the base of labour's political strength in Alberta. Moreover, it was one of only two cities in all of Canada to have sent a Labour MP to Ottawa that year. Finally, Calgary's DLP had built on its previous success at the municipal level to make labour the single largest voice at city hall. All in all, a satisfying state of affairs for the new party.

There was still the small matter of DLP-CTLC relations to be resolved. In late 1921, active cooperation between the two organizations remained limited to the CTLC's provision of 'as many voluntary workers as possible.' In particular, the CTLC continued to stall on the question of financial assistance to the party. This situation was not peculiar to Calgary but prevailed throughout Alberta. In a bid to remedy matters, Alberta delegates to the Canadian Labor Party conference held in Winnipeg that September agreed to form a provincial branch of the CLP. Their hope in taking this step was that the provincial CLP would provide an umbrella organization under which trade unions, local labour parties (including the DLP), socialist parties, and cooperative societies could come together and work in concert without sacrificing their separate identities.[38] Such an organization would effectively bring the DLP and CTLC towards closer cooperation.

The Alberta CLP convened in Calgary's Labour Temple on 7 November 1921, under chair Thomas Riley, a DLP member and former president of the CTLC. In addition to Riley, Calgary's delegates were Fred White, Andrew Davison, Walter Smitten, and John Stark, the city's most prominent socialist at the time. There were also representatives from Edmonton, Drumheller, and Medicine Hat. The convention, much like that of the DLP in 1919, adopted a platform of objectives based on the British Labour Party's and elected a provisional executive, with Riley chosen as party president. It also agreed to hold the party's first convention immediately after the Alberta Federation of Labor's (ALFL) next annual conference, due in Lethbridge in January 1922.[39]

At that conference the ALFL endorsed the formation of the provincial CLP, but offered no material assistance to help launch the new party at the scheduled inaugural convention.[40] As a result, Alberta's CLP remained little more than a paper organization throughout the spring and summer of 1922. It was not until 30 October that the Alberta branch became officially established, when 225 delegates from across the province – representing 3,400 individual members – met in Edmonton.[41]

Calgary labour's efforts to consolidate its own forces paid off in the civic elections of December 1922. The election of bank clerk John W. Russell and the reelection of both Fred White (who was also an MLA) and Walter Little brought labour's standing on city council to seven, giving it a clear majority for the first time. 'It is doubtful,' claimed the *Alberta Labor News,* 'whether there is a city on the continent where half of the city [council] is composed of trade unionists.'[42] Yet victory proved to be a double-edged sword, for labour's representatives now found themselves charged with the running of Calgary's civic affairs. In the midst of the city's continuing economic recession, this was a heavy responsibility. Labour soon discovered that, as Walter Little had warned the Central Council of the Unemployed in 1921, getting elected was one thing, actually running the city was quite another.[43]

For two reasons, at least, labour's majority on council produced few substantive changes in policy. First, the structure of the city's administration was such that the elected commissioners could overrule council on certain matters. This had been evident in January 1922, when the council had divided on the question of cuts in unemployment relief and had deferred decision to the commissioners, who quickly endorsed the proposed reductions. As the *Herald* noted the following day, if anyone had expected the new labour-dominated council to promote more radical policies than before, 'such minds were quickly disabused' after this incident.[44] A year later, labour's majority on council blocked a motion to reduce the wages of city employees, only to see the commissioners overturn this decision. Second, shortly before the 1922 elections a group of conservative, business-oriented candidates joined together to form the Civic Government Administration (CGA), a body designed 'to combat the growing labor influence in civic affairs.' Justifying the need for such a pro-capitalist association, the *Herald* had already alleged that Fred White had 'endeavored to raise a spirit of labor bossism in the city hall' since his election as MLA in 1921. Anxious not to provide substance to such accusations, labour councillors adopted a cautious and even conservative approach towards public affairs in Calgary.[45]

By the end of 1922, then, labour had reached a turning point in its development as a political force in Calgary. For the moment, the Alberta branch of the CLP had enabled the CTLC and DLP to work together, without either the industrial or the political organization feeling subordinate to the other. Increased cooperation had provided the DLP with a majority on the city council. Yet labour's control of the council had not translated into effective power; moreover, opposition to labour in Calgary had now coalesced around the CGA. Labour's sense of political achievement and unity was therefore fragile, as three events in the following year were to demonstrate.

The first of these occurred in January 1923. Thirty-five representatives of local unions already affiliated to the Canadian Federation of Labour (CFL) met to form a Calgary and District National Trades and Labor Council as an alternative to the CTLC. This event revived secessionist memories of two decades earlier. The CFL had been formed in 1908 as the successor to the National Trades and Labour Council (NTLC), which had itself been formed in 1902 by the Knights of Labor and other 'dual' associations expelled by the Trades and Labour Congress at Berlin, Ontario, that year.[46]

Two decades later, the CTLC viewed the resurgence of dual unionism with dismay. This time, in contrast to its harsh treatment of OBU supporters in 1919, it chose to fight back with a program of 'educational propaganda' that underlined the benefits of international unionism. 'It seems to me,' said James Worsley, godfather of the Calgary labour movement and vice-president of the CTLC, 'that we should not condemn [the NTLC] too strongly at first and that we should at least try to come to an understanding and find out just what the essential difference is between that organisation and ours.'[47] Had Worsley and the CTLC been in earnest, they might easily have discovered what those 'essential differences' were. The main issue was the question of union funds. The post-1919 recession had taken its toll on the CTLC just as it had on individual unions, and as its membership declined so too did the amount of money available to finance future organizational work. In turn, this resulted in a further decline in trade union membership, and so the downward spiral continued. This situation worsened when the value of the Canadian dollar fell sharply in 1920, making it more difficult for local unions to fulfil the payment of dues that they owed – in American dollars – to their respective international headquarters in the United States. In a bid to break the cycle, in the summer of 1920 the CTLC proposed an increase in its per capita dues of five cents per member. This move served only to increase discontent among local unions.[48] The carpenters' union, citing 'the lamentable condition of the Council due largely to the inability of the Secretary [J.E.] Young,' refused to accept the increase unless the CTLC was first reorganized to operate more effectively. The whole incident revealed the emergence of new tensions within the Calgary labour movement.[49]

The second significant event of 1923 was the CTLC's support for the formation of a Calgary branch of the CLP. In February that year, Thomas

Riley chaired a CTLC meeting at which thirty delegates discussed the merits of launching a new party with the aim to coordinate labour's political efforts in the city. The meeting soon revealed the 'extremely strained' relations that existed between two factions within the Calgary labour movement. On the one side were the officials and supporters of the DLP, who were content with their own party's performance and saw no need for a new rival organization. On the other were those within the labour movement who felt that the DLP no longer represented the interests or demands of local labour and who were keen to start a fresh party. Foremost among the latter were Andrew Broatch and James Worsley. They attacked DLP president Horton H. McKim and criticized the handful of executive members who had dominated the party's affairs. Worsley complained that the 'idea of a few individuals claiming the right to dictate the Labor policy of the city was one that bore the appearance of arrogance.' Other CTLC delegates, notably labour aldermen John Russell and George Batchelor, agreed with Worsley and pressed for the launch of the new party. Eventually, and only after 'an open rupture was narrowly averted,' the CTLC appointed a committee to draw up a program and constitution for a new organization, to be based along the lines of the provincial CLP. This committee subsequently reported back with its proposals and paved the way for the creation of the Calgary CLP.[50]

McKim and other DLP supporters were furious and continued to oppose the formation of the CLP. So did five of Calgary's largest unions, who refused to believe assurances from Worsley and others that the CLP was not intended to replace the DLP but would simply coordinate labour's various political and industrial organizations. At the DLP's annual meeting in April 1923, party executive members warned of the deleterious impact that they feared the CLP would have on labour's prospects in Calgary. 'If we are not very careful,' advised John Stark, 'there will be a split in the Labour political fortunes of this city. The Dominion Labor Party has done extraordinarily well. We have put men in the city council and in the provincial and federal house. If we have two Labor organizations running candidates in opposition to each other at the next civic election we are going to fall down, and all the work that the Dominion Labor Party has done will go for nothing.' Relations between the DLP and CLP remained volatile throughout the rest of the year.[51]

The third and final development of 1923 was the emergence of a local communist movement. Its origins date back to the spring of 1921, when twenty-seven members of the Calgary SPC held a series of meetings in an upstairs room of the Palliser Hotel to discuss the twenty-one conditions of affiliation to the Second Communist International. The debate continued for six months, with Edwin Fay and John O'Sullivan leading the call for affiliation and Frank Williams opposing it. Following the July

1921 provincial election in which Williams went down to defeat, a vote for affiliation passed by seventeen votes to six, with four abstentions. This result effectively left the SPC split in two. In late 1922 and early 1923, O'Sullivan, Fay, and others confirmed this split when they broke with the moribund SPC to form a Calgary branch of the Workers' Party of Canada (WPC), itself formed in February 1922 as the public and legal face of the Canadian communist movement.[52]

Almost immediately, and in line with the 'united front' directive from Moscow, the WPC began to insinuate itself within the local CLP. Communists accounted for a number of the ninety-eight delegates attending the Alberta CLP's annual convention in April 1923. That same month, communists O'Sullivan and A.J. Boulter secured positions on the seven-person committee struck by the CTLC to compose a platform for the proposed Calgary CLP. More generally, the WPC provided a token demonstration of its solidarity with the labour movement when the party backed the traditional union demands for the open shop, the eight-hour day, and the right to picket.[53]

Even as it proclaimed its wish to cooperate with Calgary's trade union movement, the WPC could not resist sniping at established labour figures. In March 1923, it backed a demand from the Operating Engineers' Union that Alex Ross resign his position as minister of public works within the UFA government. Ross, his critics claimed, had cut the wages of government-employed engineers, a charge that he denied and that the CTLC subsequently repudiated.[54] Ross was a poor choice of target for this 'mean and cowardly piece of business,' as the *Alberta Labor News* described the attack: he had refused to condemn the OBU in 1919, risked imprisonment over his opposition to the federal government's ban on strikes, and remained enthusiastic about the Soviet Union as a model from which Canadians might learn.[55] The only result of such attacks by the WPC was the deterioration of its relations with the established union movement.[56]

The CLP and WPC therefore remained uneasy bedfellows in 1923, with many labour moderates suspicious of the communists' motives for cooperation.[57] Labour politics in Calgary, more generally, was in a state of some disarray by the summer that year. The unity of purpose that had been apparent during the previous winter's civic elections had given way to confusion and division. Calgary workers now had three separate and often antagonistic parties competing for their support – the DLP, the CLP, and the WPC. In response to this situation Hugh Bartholomew, organizer of the provincial CLP and an active WPC member, urged a consolidation of labour's political efforts in October 1923. Speaking at a meeting of the DLP in Calgary, Bartholomew renewed the call for that party to affiliate with the CLP. The time has come, he argued, for workers 'to choose between marching section by section, individually, or closing their ranks in one solid army of organized labor.'[58] The key to achieving this 'one solid army' was the CTLC, whose leading figures remained divided between supporters of the DLP and the CLP. The CTLC was still Calgary's single largest representative of labour, and any reconciliation between the DLP and CLP – and, by extension, the WPC – had to begin there. Events of 1924 first raised then dashed hopes of achieving this rapprochement.

The new year began in promising fashion. In March 1924, the CTLC finally held its long-deferred vote on whether to affiliate with the CLP. Early returns indicated that a majority – 53 percent – of all union members were in favour, with just 20 percent opposed and 27 percent undecided. As it was, a decision required only a majority of individual unions, regardless of how many members they represented. This format was obviously to the advantage of the pro-vote, and affiliation was carried by a count of twenty-seven unions to fourteen.[59] This vote paved the way for the DLP also to agree to affiliate with the CLP, and it announced its intention of doing so three weeks later at its annual general meeting. As a symbolic show of unity, former DLP president Horton McKim – the target of Worsley's scorn a year earlier – opened the third convention of the Alberta CLP that same month. This new-found amity continued when the DLP's rank and file gave its support to the formation of a Central Council of the CLP, despite the fears of some party officials that this body would fall under the influence of local communists working through the CLP. In the short run, at least, the DLP's move to cooperate with the CLP appears to have benefited the DLP, for its membership shot up from seventy-five in March 1924 to more than 300 by July.[60]

As a result of this closer coordination, by the spring of 1924 it seemed that the Calgary labour movement had finally overcome the obstacles that had long thwarted political unity. Yet, once again, appearances proved to be deceptive: the fragile unity fell apart over the summer months, and by the fall of 1924 the Calgary labour movement was more divided than ever on the question of politics. Renewed fears over the role of communists within the CLP caused the CTLC to revoke its affiliation to that party and helped to undermine the DLP's fortunes in the civic elections in December. The exact course of events leading to this breakdown remains obscure, but the CLP's nomination of communist Hugh Bartholomew in an Edmonton by-election was a contributing factor if not the precise catalyst.

In September 1924, the Edmonton CLP staged a nomination contest to select a candidate to run in an upcoming by-election. Three of the nominees were labour moderates Elmer Roper, Rice Sheppard, and Dan Knott; Bartholomew was the fourth. Roper, editor of the *Alberta Labor News* – the official journal of the provincial union movement – and a veteran of the Alberta union movement, was the clear favourite,[61] but when the votes were counted it was Bartholomew who headed the list, the three-way split in the moderate vote propelling him to victory. It was an unexpected result that 'caused something approaching consternation' within the party, and Bartholomew can have eased few minds with his acceptance speech in which he emphasized the need for the CLP to adopt a more confrontational stance. 'To abolish unemployment while the capitalistic class is supreme was unthinkable,' he declared. 'There was but one issue – class distinction – and there remained but one thing, to smash the capitalistic class into the wastepaper basket of history.'[62] Bartholomew then went on to elaborate his beliefs: 'We are living in a time when the means of production is in the hands of a small group of capitalists, and before the worker can hope for any chance of making a decent living we must get rid of this class ... We must stand shoulder to shoulder and fight for our rights, and mobilize our forces to put an end to a system that allows the few to fatten on the lives of many.'[63]

Edmonton's labour leaders were reported to be 'too dazed to move at the unexpectedness of the result,' which they blamed on the work of an active radical minority and the apathy of the more conservative majority. This was unfair and underestimated Bartholomew's considerable ability to win popular support for his outspoken position. Although he finished in third place on election day, his 4,118 votes was easily the best showing by any labour candidate in Edmonton to that time and amounted to a respectable 20.5 percent of the popular ballot.[64]

While there is no direct evidence linking the Bartholomew incident to events in Calgary, press reports and personal correspondence with their northern counterparts would have kept local labour leaders informed of the story. In particular, Bartholomew's success in securing the CLP nomination in the first place served to confirm fears that communists would use that party to strengthen their influence within the labour movement more generally. Accordingly, on 4 October 1924, the CTLC executive reversed its previous decision to affiliate with the CLP, a move subsequently endorsed by a majority of union delegates. The *Alberta Labor News* offered an unlikely explanation of this turn of events, claiming that the CTLC had been 'formed to discuss and legislate on industrial matters only and it was courting suicide to affiliate with a purely political body at this time.'[65] Since the CTLC had voted to do just that only six months before, this traditional argument no longer carried much conviction. More likely, the CTLC's action simply reflected its renewed distrust of the communists' commitment to a genuine united front.

Whatever the precise cause and exact course of events, Calgary labour's political wing was once again in a state of dissent and division by the fall of 1924. Amid this disunity and uncertainty, DLP candidates entered the civic elections that December. John Russell and Fred White secured their second and fourth terms, respectively, on the city council. Annie Gale was once again returned to the school board, but the three remaining DLP candidates were all defeated. By contrast, every candidate backed by the Civic Government Administration was elected, placing control of the council, city commissioner, and school board in the hands of this conservative association. Labour's brief flirtation with power was over. Its own failure to develop a coherent, united political identity was the key to this demise.[66]

The civic elections of 1924 signalled the end of labour's political ascent in Calgary. Since 1919, the DLP had enjoyed considerable success in local politics and had also helped to elect labour candidates to the provincial and federal governments. In this respect, at least, the years 1918-24 represent a golden age of labour politics in Calgary, never to be repeated. Labour candidates would continue to contest and win elections in the future, but never again would they have such a collective influence on the management of civic affairs.

From another point of view, the early 1920s were a time of missed opportunity for labour in Calgary. Relations between the DLP and CLP remained frosty and unstable, even though there was no issue of any real substance dividing the two. Both remained wary of the local communist movement, especially the WPC, even after it had demonstrated a nominal commitment to the policy of the united front. Indeed, the WPC acceptance of this strategy, ordered by Moscow, simply confirmed one of the main concerns of the other parties – that the first loyalty of the WPC lay outside Canada. As far as the CTLC was concerned, the WPC joined the OBU and SPC as the latest on a growing list of organizations that it regarded as disruptionist in nature. Moreover, the CTLC refused to ally itself with any political body in which the communists had – or appeared to have – a significant influence. As a result of all these concerns, Calgary labour failed to develop a single, united political voice that could articulate the interests and needs of workers as a class.

In March 1923, John W. Bruce, national president of the CLP, spoke to Calgary workers at the Ogden railway shops on the need for labour to stand together as a class. 'Because we cannot agree at the present time, or find a programme upon which we can make a united front, is it right or just or reasonable you should kick the whole works over?' he asked. 'Co-operation is the only thing leading to victory.'[67] Bruce's remarks were a timely warning to the growing alphabet of political organizations within the Calgary labour movement. Their failure to cooperate with one another compounded labour's fragmentation within Calgary's restructured economy. As a result, by the end of 1924 capital had passed through its brief postwar crisis in Calgary and was safely back in the saddle. Events of 1925-9 would confirm this fact, just as they would demonstrate labour's continuing inability to transcend its own internal schisms.

9
The Limits of Labour, 1925-9

On the surface, the late 1920s appeared to be a promising time for Calgary labour. After more than a decade of recession, war, and reconstruction, Calgary's economy underwent a spurt of renewed growth as industrial activity and investment returned close to pre-1913 levels. Workers benefited from this new prosperity: wages rose once more, unemployment dipped, and trade union membership enjoyed something of a renaissance. Yet these gains failed to translate into new victories in the field of politics, the vehicle for reform and advancement to which the labour movement had hitched its fortunes. The internal divisions and tensions that had fragmented labour politics in the years 1918-24 continued to thwart any prospects of united action after 1925. Indeed, if anything they deepened. Relations between the Dominion Labor Party (DLP) and the Canadian Labor Party (CLP) remained strained; the Communist Party's open support for a united front of working-class parties rekindled the suspicions of a Calgary Trades and Labour Council (CTLC) already wary of political involvement; and the rise of various new labour parties served only to confuse matters further. As a result, by 1929 – the eve of capitalism's worst crisis to date – there was no doubting the limits of labour's ability to serve the interests of working men and women as a class.[1]

After 1925, Calgary's economy was showing clear signs of recovery from its postwar recession.[2] Building permits that had been showing a modest improvement since 1923 more than doubled in value in 1927, and then nearly tripled during the following year. The figure for 1929 – $11.4 million – was the highest since 1912. In 1926-8, nearly 1,000 new houses were built in the city, and a number of older dwellings were converted into apartments or duplexes. Clearinghouse returns, the standard indicator of retail activity, also recovered in this period, and by 1929 stood at more than twice their 1925 level. With Calgary's hotels accommodating

300,000 travelling salespeople, company representatives, and other temporary visitors in 1926, the city proudly declared itself to be 'The Shopping Centre of Alberta,' a title symbolically confirmed three years later when the T. Eaton Company purchased a new million-dollar store in downtown Calgary. Industrial production mirrored the retail sector's return to health, with the total output of Calgary's manufacturing firms jumping by 44 percent between 1925 and 1929. Average output per establishment rose by an equally impressive 38 percent, leading the *Calgary Herald* to declare in December 1929 that 'A survey of industrial development in Calgary in the last year indicates a surprising and gratifying growth and the invasion by great industrial concerns indicates clearly that the progress of the city from the industrial standpoint is assured.' The recent stock market crash on Wall Street notwithstanding, a renewed sense of optimism pervaded commercial life in Calgary at the end of the 1920s.[3]

The changing tenor of the Board of Trade's annual reports reflected this revitalized faith in Calgary's prospects. In January 1925, retiring president H.A. Howard noted that the previous twelve months had been 'rather disappointing to the majority of merchants and manufacturers, and the anticipated improvement, in view of the immense crop of the previous year, has hardly been realized.' Just a year later, his successor, F.E. Osborne, felt able to predict that 'The outlook for the immediate future is most promising and there are good reasons for anticipating a gradual improvement in all lines of business.'[4] His hopes were confirmed by the generally positive annual reports of the next three years.

Yet even as Calgary's capitalist class declared its satisfaction with the improved conditions after 1925, there were signs that it had learned little from the preceding recession and regarded the recovery as 'back to business as normal.' This was most evident in the attitude of local entrepreneurs on the question of unemployment and unemployment relief. Unemployment was still viewed as an individual rather than social or structural problem, and individuals were held responsible for their own situation. 'Just let me say here,' said Board of Trade president W.H. Ross in January 1930, 'that while I am not lacking in sympathy for any man out of work, and especially men with young families, I can see no good reason why single men with no one to support but themselves, who have eight or nine months steady work at good wages, should be in the "bread line" a month or so after work closed down. And we have had in Calgary lately all too many of these.' A year later, with unemployment reaching unprecedented levels in Calgary, Ross remained unmoved in his appreciation of the problem. 'The pioneers of Calgary and district were noted for their fine spirit and courage and in spite of many hardships and difficulties never gave way to discouragement nor did they lose their vision. In hard times they took up another notch or two in their belts and with grim determination and undaunted courage set their faces to the task of overcoming their troubles, and they succeeded. In the same way we shall overcome the difficult times through which we are now passing and emerge before long into more prosperous and happy times.' The counterpart of this emphasis on individual responsibility was a continued demand for reduced civic expenditures on unemployment relief. Howard had made the basic argument in his annual report for 1924: 'Taxes there must be, and in view of our tremendous indebtedness they will continue to be a heavy charge upon our resources until further steps are taken to eliminate waste, to curtail expenditures and to reduce our liabilities so that the immense sums we are now paying in interest charges may be saved. And we should be prepared to do without some services, if necessary, to accomplish this.' He even argued that 'too much money is going into government and municipal bonds and not enough into industrial enterprises,' and that this diversion of funds was itself a cause of unemployment. This remained the Board of Trade's official view throughout the late 1920s, with the result that responsibility for the unemployed remained at the centre of the local class struggle.[5]

Calgary's industrial and commercial revival built upon and extended the economic restructuring that had taken place in the aftermath of the First World War. New industries continued to invest in the city, and some old ones enjoyed a new lease on life. The CPR workshops at Ogden, for example, that had suffered recurrent stoppages and lay-offs since opening in 1912, enjoyed their first long run of unbroken activity in the years after 1925. By 1929, more than 1,200 skilled craftsmen plus ninety young apprentices were employed at the works.[6] In 1926, the Board of Trade declared the decision by the English firm Spillers to purchase the old Alberta Flour Mills plant to be 'a source of much satisfaction,' not least because it confirmed Calgary's status as southern Alberta's milling centre. The future of the Pat Burns meatpacking plant was secured in 1928 when Toronto's Dominion Securities Corporation bought the operation for $15 million. At the same time, the expansion of the Riverside Iron Works together with the establishment of the Independent Biscuit Company and the Regal Oil and Refinery Company all provided further 'evidence of the present soundness of Calgary's position and its assured future.'[7] Perhaps most satisfactory of all to local business was the opening of the Royal No. 4 well in the nearby Turner Valley oilfields in 1924. Prior to this time, insufficient capital and a poor communications system had restricted the oil industry's development, with daily production between 1914 and 1923 averaging just ten barrels. With the opening of the new well, production soon shot up to 400 barrels, and by 1929 more than 200 companies were operating in Turner Valley.[8]

An increase in the demand for labour accompanied this economic upswing, but the gains for Calgarians were tempered by an influx of workers from elsewhere. In June 1927, the CTLC complained that great numbers of European immigrants were 'gradually being placed in employment in the different Industries in the City.' These newcomers, continued the council, 'had been brought out here for farm work, could not speak English, [and] were also obtain[in]g work in the different building trades, and the situation was considered serious.' The continued mechanization of production also limited the number of new jobs created, and was a problem for skilled craftsmen and lesser skilled workers alike. Again in 1927 the CTLC suggested that 'the displacement of workers by improved machinery' would soon 'eliminate the necessity of employing an large number for harvest work ... [and] in many other classes of work.'[9] Local 635 of the Brotherhood of Locomotive Firemen and Engineers had already discussed the impact of using mechanized stokers on certain locomotives; a greater challenge to traditional work practices – the introduction of the diesel engine – was just around the corner. A number of other unions argued that an increased reliance upon machinery was also eroding the apprenticeship system, by which they had previously exercised a measure of control over the supply of labour and hence wage levels.[10] In this respect, union opposition to mechanization was simply a defence of organized labour's own interests, but there were also occasions on which individual unionists expressed broader fears over the seemingly endless application of machinery. In 1929, James Worsley reflected on the changes he had seen during his three decades in the city: 'The human race, no matter the period, has always struggled by every means at its command to produce more, with less and less effort, than it did before. With the constant improvement in technique, the unlocking of nature's secrets and the application of flexible power, we are flooding the whole world with unlimited wealth, workers are no longer in absolute demand, except as hundreds, or maybe thousands, of hand workers. The problems brought to the front by changed conditions demand our earnest study.'[11]

Among the problems to which Worsley alluded was, of course, the issue of unemployment. By 1925, Calgary workers had lived with the fear and reality of widespread unemployment for more than a decade. The recovery of the late 1920s eased the situation, but a lack of work remained a stubborn feature of the lives of many Calgarians. Even in the improved conditions after 1925, there was little sign of a return to prewar levels of employment. One individual, Harry Lodge, expressed the frustration and bitterness that he felt at his inability to secure regular work. 'Three years in Canada, and this is all I have to show for it,' he told the local magistrate during his trial in 1926 for ordering a restaurant meal without having the money to pay for it. 'We would not starve and die like dogs in the street ... We couldn't go out on the prairies for there is no work. That is the result of my three years in Canada. I have less than when I came over from England. I have always been ready to work at anything that be available to earn my living at.'[12] To the extent that unemployment remained an enduring feature of Calgary's economy it continued to fragment the experience of local workers, and so dulled their disposition to think and behave as a common class. Ironically, the improved economic conditions after 1925 deepened this rift, for as unemployment among trade union members began to decline so the unions distanced themselves from the concerns of the remaining unemployed and instead returned to a narrower, even sectarian outlook. This abandonment once again opened the door for the local Communist Party and its associated organizations to become champions of the unemployed, an association that the mainstream labour movement used to justify its original decision to remain at arm's length from the unemployed. In short, well before the advent of mass unemployment in the 1930s, the Calgary labour movement's response to unemployment – with all its attendant social, economic, and political implications – had undermined any pretensions it had of representing the working class as a whole. In this respect, labour's greatest political battle of the Depression – to persuade the state to accept responsibility for the unemployed – was over before it was even begun. How this situation came to pass merits closer examination.

Across western Canada there was an easing of unemployment in the late 1920s.[13] The monthly average of employed workers in 1920 was not surpassed until July 1926, and thereafter the situation continued to improve, if seasonal fluctuations are taken into account. By August 1929, the number of workers employed was a full 45 percent higher than in 1920, while the West's population had grown by just 20 percent during the same time.[14] In Alberta, unemployment among trade unionists peaked at just over 16 percent in the summer of 1925; then it declined steeply until 1929. As in the years prior to 1914, unemployment continued to follow a seasonal pattern, reaching its height once in the lull after Christmas and again just before the spring restart of work in April and May. Apart from these regular and fairly predictable short-term swings in the demand for labour, unemployment among the province's unionized workforce never exceeded 6 percent between the summer of 1925 and the fall of 1929.[15]

In Calgary, the picture was roughly the same. Early in 1925, the local carpenters' union reported that 50 percent of its members were without work. A year later, the union could note that 'practically all men are working and work is much better than for some years.' Apart from a lengthy strike in the spring of 1928, which brought construction to a virtual halt but in itself was a sign of improved conditions, carpenters continued to enjoy near-full employment until the end of the decade, when once again almost half of the union's 800 members were without work.[16] Other unions fared similarly. Throughout 1925, rarely were there more than two dozen union bricklayers working at any one time, while poor conditions threatened to wipe the sheet-metal workers' union out of existence. Yet by the end of that year, the Board of Trade was able to report that labour in general was 'in a better condition than in 1924, employment being steadier and placements being made in more permanent positions.' In January 1925, the printers' union had narrowly defeated a proposal to impose a 2 percent levy on wages in order to create an unemployment fund, but the fact that fifty members had voted in favour suggests the extent to which the problem then existed. A year later, by contrast, the union regularly reported work to be good, and this continued to be the case as late as November 1929.[17]

It seems clear, then, that unemployment dwindled as a major issue among Calgary's trade unions as the decade wore on, as it did for organized labour elsewhere in the province. Yet for many men and women in Calgary, the lack of suitable employment remained a problem of paramount importance. With the labour movement increasingly deaf to their call for help, it was perhaps inevitable that many of the unemployed would look elsewhere for assistance. In any event, it is no coincidence that the late 1920s also saw the revival of the Central Council of the Unemployed (CCU), an organization that had first surfaced in 1921 and that had close connections with the Communist Party in Calgary. The CCU grew steadily louder in its denouncement of the city's apparent complacency on the issue of unemployment and also in its criticism of the mainstream labour movement's failure to stand up for the interests of the unemployed. For various reasons, this criticism did not result in Calgary's trade unions and the CTLC changing their views on unemployment, but instead served to reinforce the divisions that had already fragmented any sense of working-class unity.

At first, the CCU focused its attack on official estimates of the number of unemployed and on the Provincial Labour Bureau (PLB). In January 1925, the CCU rejected the city's count of 300 jobless men, declaring the true figure to be closer to 3,000. The CCU itself claimed a membership of 1,100 at the time.[18] The discrepancy in numbers largely reflected the fact that the city included only those men who applied to the PLB for assistance; the CCU continued to discourage unemployed men from registering with this body, and therefore was itself partly responsible for producing the lower official estimate. In fact, under the presidency of Communist A.J. Boulter, the CCU stepped up its earlier opposition to the PLB, arguing that it was little more than 'a stool pigeon outfit' designed to keep tabs on those without work, many of whom the city regarded as potential troublemakers. There are signs that some of Calgary's unemployed opposed the PLB for their own reasons, such as the men who said that they 'did not care to register at the Government Labor Bureau as they considered they would be sent out to under-cut those presently employed.'[19]

As in earlier years, the CCU's opposition to the PLB was at odds with the CTLC's official support for the organization. This opposition was also an embarrassment to labour representatives on city council, who had originally led the move to establish the bureau. In January 1925, labour MLA Fred White urged the CTLC not to admit delegates from the CCU into its council meetings. 'If we link up with them and give them official recognition,' he explained, 'there is a possibility of a conflict of interests.' White further added that the CTLC 'should be very careful about linking themselves with the unemployed body in view of the fact that they might have to share responsibility for actions they did not approve of.' Behind White's remarks was his residual belief that the CCU was simply a front for die-hard supporters of the OBU in Calgary, despite the absence of any evidence to support that opinion.[20]

Over the next two years, mutual mistrust continued to mar relations between the CCU and CTLC. The latter remained wary of communist and IWW influence within the CCU, while the CCU criticized craft unions for placing their desire for social respectability ahead of providing material aid for unemployed unorganized workers. A bitter letter to the *Herald* in January 1925 expressed in detail the kind of anger felt over this neglect:

> It says much for organized labor that it leaves unemployment of several workers severely alone till such time as the rabble take measures to bring it more prominently before the public eye, then they help things go along by informing the public that they are going to act very cannily regarding these unemployed, take the assertions that unemployed far exceed the labor bureau figures with a pinch of salt, and give the movement a black eye by informing us they expect the promoters are I.W.W.s and reds ... Organized labor in this city could do better than stand in the shoes of tranquility, it could obtain the sympathy of unorganized labor could it see beyond the labor temple windows.[21]

The CCU failed to produce any change in CTLC attitudes, however, in part because it lacked any formal organization that might have given it a sense of stability and continuity. In the summer months of 1925, the CCU ceased to operate after most of its members either secured work within the city or left for jobs elsewhere in Alberta. It was resurrected the following winter, as unemployment once more became widespread. Under

Boulter's leadership, the group then approached the CTLC with the demand that CCU delegates be accepted on to the labour council. The CTLC once again refused this request, saying that it would only accept unemployed trade unionists in good standing as CCU delegates. As few unemployed union members were in a position to keep up their payment of dues, the CTLC was safe in making this condition. Yet, the CCU did find allies within the CTLC in the form of Robert Parkyn and James Worsley, outspoken individuals who eventually persuaded their colleagues to reconsider their obstruction and – albeit by a single vote – admit the CCU's original delegates into future labour council meetings.[22]

The CCU also struggled to influence the provincial government's policy on unemployment. In particular, it demanded that relief be extended to include single men and not just those with wives and families. When word reached Calgary in early 1925 that the provision of such relief had been granted in Edmonton, the CCU hurriedly convened a meeting and announced that it would directly petition the government for equal treatment. Consequently, on the morning of Saturday, 21 March 1925, 125 single unemployed men left Calgary for the Alberta capital. Returned soldiers, many wearing their military decorations, accounted for three-quarters of the group. Travelling illegally on a northbound freight train – a foreshadowing of the On-to-Ottawa Trek a decade later – many of the men were arrested on their arrival in Edmonton, but three – Boulter, Alex Davison, and A. Peacock – managed to secure an interview with UFA premier Herbert Greenfield.[23]

The marchers returned to Calgary on the following Tuesday, believing that Greenfield and his ministers had relented on the question of relief for single men. This was not the case. Instead, the government offered to provide relief for just fifty of the most destitute single men currently being cared for by the Salvation Army in Calgary, perhaps 10 percent of the total number it was then assisting. At the same time, Walter Smitten – by this time provincial commissioner of labour – rather tactlessly told the local press that he expected unemployment to disappear within two weeks. 'I wouldn't be surprised if we had to send out of the province for men to fill the jobs that will be offered,' he boasted somewhat incredibly. In response to these official reactions to recent events, Boulter threatened a second march on Edmonton. Instead, a further meeting with Greenfield and representatives of the unemployed from across Alberta was set up.[24]

This meeting took place in Edmonton on 31 March 1925, but achieved little other than to underline the distance that separated each side's perception of the unemployment problem. Boulter claimed the provincial unemployed total to be five times the government's estimate of 2,000 and called on the province to provide $500,000 for the immediate needs of those without work and those in part-time jobs. In addition, he called for an investigation into the Provincial Labour Bureau with a view to abolishing it entirely. Another CCU representative dismissed Alex Ross, former CTLC president and at the time minister of public works, as 'simply a tool of the capitalist class.' The meeting ended in deadlock, with Greenfield concluding that it was 'a waste of time going over the same ground again' and Boulter muttering 'Then we may as well go home for all the good we are doing here.'[25]

With the abandonment of official talks, the CCU returned to the tactic of direct action in the winter of 1925-6. In a bid to force Calgary authorities to acknowledge the true extent of unemployment and to deal with the problem directly, CCU members began an orchestrated campaign of ordering meals at local restaurants and then refusing to pay for them. In two days in January 1926, the Calgary police court tried forty-six men for this offence. It was an effective tactic by the organized unemployed, for the cases received full coverage from local reporters and so brought the issue into thousands of Calgary homes. Calgary's unemployed at last had an opportunity to present their side of the story to the public.[26] Not satisfied with mere publicity, on 16 January 1926 a crowd of single unemployed men marched on Calgary's city hall. There, a delegation of four met with Mayor George Webster to demand that he help secure them provincial relief. After an exchange of telegrams and telephone calls, Webster announced that Ross had agreed to extend relief to cover single men. Over the next eight weeks, a relief station in east Calgary provided more than $11,000 in meals, beds, and transportation to places of work. It was a small but significant victory for the CCU.[27]

By now, the pattern had been set. The CCU disappeared from sight – or existence, even – during the summer months each year when work was relatively plentiful, only to reemerge in the winter to orchestrate demands for relief. In December 1926, Boulter once again led a parade of some 300 to city hall in a repeat performance of the previous year's demonstration. By this time, John E. Brownlee had replaced Greenfield as premier of Alberta. Brownlee, a lawyer by profession and a conservative in disposition, was less inclined than his predecessor to yield to such demands. Indeed, his government began to investigate the legitimacy of existing individual relief claims, and in January 1927 cancelled assistance to sixty men in Calgary.[28]

Boulter saw this as an opportunity to reassert his reputation among the local unemployed, for he had recently suffered a humiliating defeat in the 1926 civic elections, winning just 289 votes. On behalf of the CCU, he sent Brownlee a telegram that read, 'Situation here acute, large number of single men destitute. Big percentage returned soldiers. Immediate action by you necessary. The Central Council of the Unemployed not responsible after 4 p.m. Thursday [20 January 1927].'[29] For good measure, Boulter also told reporters who were covering a meeting of the Canadian Labor Party that 'If they arrest us they will have to feed us. The policemen's clubs and the prison bars have no further terrors for the unemployed.' Brownlee dismissed the threat, commenting merely that 'any attempt at a breach of the peace will be met by this government with the firmest hand possible.' He need not have worried. The 'slight demonstration' by the single unemployed who marched on the Calgary police station that evening 'did not create much disturbance beyond a little hollering.' There would be no storming of the winter palace that evening.[30]

Unemployment declined as a public issue over the next couple of years, but late in 1929 it returned with a vengeance. By that November, the number of Calgarians officially out of work was in excess of 5,000, a figure not seen since before the war. The Ogden works alone laid off 600 workers. Despair on the scale of that seen in 1913-4 resurfaced, with one veteran of the 10th Battalion 'confiding' his fears to the *Herald*. 'I would sooner face war with all its horrors than face the problem of looking for a job when there is none to get,' he wrote. Annual reports of the local Board of Public Welfare (BPW) recorded the magnitude of the new depression and the speed with which it struck growing numbers of Calgarians. In 1929, the BPW assisted 10,413 individuals. A year later the figure had increased by almost 70 percent to 17,472, and by 1931 had again more than doubled to 38,194, or 45 percent of Calgary's entire population. The Great Depression had arrived.[31]

Two conclusions may be drawn from Calgary's experience of and response to unemployment in the late 1920s. First, all levels of government continued their ad hoc methods of dealing with the problem. As a result, they were ill-equipped to deal with the traumatic conditions of the 1930s. The experience of Calgary confirms the observation for Canada by James Struthers that the lines of political debate over unemployment in the 1930s 'were already evident during the preceding ten years of supposed prosperity.'[32] In Calgary, it hardly mattered whether labour politicians were in office or not. 'There is only one immediate solution to the unemployment problem, and that is employment,' was the dull remedy proposed by Conservative mayor Fred Osborne in December 1929. 'It is generally admitted that the only real method of curing the present unemployment condition of our city is to provide work for those who are at present unemployed,' parroted labour mayor Andrew Davison on taking office a month later. His lack of imagination augured ill for the city's jobless in the years ahead.[33]

The second conclusion to be drawn is the fact that unemployment continued to limit the disposition of Calgary's workers to regard themselves as a single class, one with a basic core of common interests. As one local observer noted in 1925, 'Our workers who are in permanent employment are not in sympathy with the men who are unfortunate enough to be out of employment – That is one of the saddest errors of those who are assured of a salary cheque every pay day. Their interest ends when they remark at the family dinner, "Oh, I see Mr. Smith is not working yet."'[34] Another commentator made much the same point. 'The man who has been at his job for years can generally tender advice to the unemployed man, still thinking of the day when jobs could be obtained within a stone's throw of one another, and the bulk of them think of the workless as only worthy of short shrift, as lovers of their condition, and following the lines of least resistance.'[35] These were harsh words and unfair if applied to the 1930s, when those fortunate enough to have work performed countless voluntary acts of generosity to assist those in need. Yet as the aloof stance adopted by the CTLC and the lack of popular support for street demonstrations by the unemployed both suggest, they are an accurate characterization of the late 1920s. Unemployment not only highlighted the state's limited will or ability to assist those without the means to support themselves and their dependants, it also revealed a lack of communal self-help within the working class itself. As a result, the unemployed continued to exist as a separate class within a class.

For the trade union movement, the late 1920s heralded an impressive, if short-lived, recovery after more than a decade of hard times and uncertainty. Overall membership rose from less than 2,000 in 1925 to over 2,600 by 1927, and by 1930 the figure had more than doubled to almost 6,000. This last figure was roughly equal to 18 percent of Calgary's entire workforce of 32,000, an impressive achievement in a decade in which Canadian labour's gains were few and infrequent.[36] The recovery of Calgary's older unions accounted for some of this growth. After a bitter but ultimately successful strike in 1928, for example, Local 1779 of the United Brotherhood of Carpenters and Joiners of America attracted a wave of new members. By 1930, the union's membership stood at 800, a level not seen in many years. Local 348 of the International Brotherhood of Electrical Workers experienced similar growth in the late 1920s, its membership increasing by more than 50 percent in 1928 alone.[37] At the same time, new organizations emerged and established themselves, just as they had during the later stages of the First World War. These unions consisted for the most part of either lesser-skilled workers who previously had been excluded from unionization, or employees belonging to trades that were relatively new to Calgary, such as garage mechanics and auto workers. As a result of this new wave of unionization, by 1930 Calgary boasted at least seventy-seven trade unions compared with just thirty-one in 1924.[38]

While the improved economic conditions of these years may have eased the task of union organizers, it did not guarantee them success. Workers still had to be convinced of the benefits of organization, as Robert Hewitt found out in June 1926. Hewitt, the grand lodge deputy of the Railway Carmen's Union and a leading figure within the CTLC, was in charge of an organizing drive to recruit new members to the labour movement. He was under no illusions about the task he faced. 'We cannot say that the unorganized workers of the city are clamoring to be organized,' he admitted. Among the various obstacles that his campaign faced were 'the usual opposition to our efforts from some unscrupulous employees, some ten-dollar-a-week white collared employers' lackeys, whose dignity would never survive the disgrace of being classed as ordinary wage earners, as well as the usual array of organizers of dual or secessionist organizations offering their wares at any price to the end that our efforts might be obstructed.' Hewitt might also have mentioned a degree of apathy within the CTLC itself, as evident when only a quarter of its delegates attended regular council meetings.[39]

Modelled on similar campaigns in Toronto, Winnipeg, and Vancouver, the CTLC launched its organization drive to rekindle working-class interest in trade unionism. Hewitt was assisted by CTLC president George Poulton and a number of other labour leaders, including Fred White, Robert Parkyn, James Worsley, and William Irvine, and together they took their message to Calgary's workers in a series of nightly meetings held across the city. As a result of these efforts, bakery workers, beverage dispensers, sawmill employees, and several other occupations applied for union charters. Twenty-two existing local unions donated more than $300 to the CTLC to help finance its advertising expenses. Yet the campaign cannot be judged an unqualified success. Workers in many occupations stubbornly refused to embrace unionization. Despite his considerable efforts of persuasion, Hewitt confessed that soap-factory employees, flour-mill men, and laundry workers continued to show little interest in the idea, and he 'deemed it best to leave them until we have dealt with those who have a better realization of organization.' In other cases, workers were keen to organize a union but found it difficult to maintain a critical mass of members that would provide the continuity and stability necessary to survival.[40]

Calgary's labour movement also faced a new structural problem in the late 1920s: its leadership was ageing and in danger of stagnation. A small clique of men had come to dominate both labour's industrial and political organizations, in some cases exercising seemingly proprietary rights over the positions that they held. Almost without exception, these men were now in their late forties or fifties. Consequently there was a generation gap between them and many of the younger rank-and-file union members. Moreover, many labour leaders had effectively become career unionists, their long tenure in office distancing them from the immediate experiences and concerns of those on the shop floor. Firm in convictions and conceptions of trade unionism forged in an earlier period, these men had some difficulty in adapting to the many new challenges that now faced them.

This bureaucratization of labour is the focus of Mark Leier's recent study of the Vancouver Trades and Labour Council (VTLC), in which he argues that the crucial line separating trade union officials from the rank-and-file membership was one of power rather than ideology. According to Leier, 'The control of information, elevated status, authority over members, and control of union policy and structures – all of which tend to remove union leaders from the shop floor and the workers they represent – offer clues to the development of unions.'[41] Leier's emphasis on power and authority instead of ideology enables him to demonstrate how little practical difference it made whether labourists or socialists dominated the VTLC, as both groups believed 'that the working class must be managed, that the masses cannot determine their struggle.'[42] The conviction that they alone understand and can defend the true interests of the working class leads labour bureaucrats to make the promotion and preservation of their own position of power their top priority, which in turn necessitates a working accommodation with other social classes. In this way, Leier offers an alternative to the 'incorporatist' or 'labour aristocracy' explanations of trade union conservatism.[43] Yet while Leier's study represents a significant advance in this respect, his own explanation raises a number of questions. *How* did labour bureaucrats exercise their power over the rank and file, given the relatively democratic nature of trade unions? The VTLC, like the CTLC, was hardly a despotic organization and would certainly have yielded to the popular will of the membership had large numbers expressed serious dissatisfaction with the rule of bureaucrats. At the same time, Leier downplays the broader context of capitalism as the major power structure, although he does admit, 'When we speak of the power of the labour leader ... we do well to remember that it is weak compared with that of capital and the state.'[44] Given this simple fact, surely there were far more important and overwhelming obstacles in the path of socialism than the restrictive influence of labour bureaucrats.

The consolidation of a small clique of leaders in Calgary was a reflection, rather than a cause, of the problems that beset the labour movement in the 1920s. When open dissent did occur, it was aimed not at the existing leadership but at the continental orientation and obligations of Canadian trade unions. There were few signs that Calgary's rank-and-file unionists were unhappy with the leadership they received, either in terms of ideology or of any abuse of power. On the contrary, the fact that so many union officials were reelected – or more commonly reacclaimed – to their position each year reflected an unhealthy apathy or indifference among the general membership.

There were several prominent examples of Calgary's greying leadership in the 1920s. When he retired due to ill health in July 1927, forty-seven-year-old John Young – originally a carpenter by trade – had been the CTLC's secretary-treasurer for fifteen consecutive years. In that same year, machinist George Poulton was serving his fifth term as president of the CTLC, having first been elected in 1922. Like Young, only illness prevented him from extending this record (he died shortly after standing down in 1928). The *Alberta Labor News* noted that the period of Poulton's presidency had coincided with declines in membership, finance, and morale, from which it deduced that the 'most conservative policies in all undertakings were thus forced upon Mr. Poulton, and his associated executives during that critical period.' Yet while this interpretation may have been a fair comment on the years prior to 1925, there is no evidence that he changed either his policies or beliefs during the subsequent period of economic recovery.[45] The CTLC confirmed its dependence on figures from the past when it elected James Worsley as Poulton's successor. Worsley, sixty-three years old when first elected, remained president until 1933. The credentials of Worsley, a founder and former president of the CTLC, were beyond question. For years he had helped to establish new unions in Calgary, while his *Bond of Brotherhood,* published in 1903-4, was an early and uncompromising advocate for the working class. By the same token, it might be argued that Worsley's most significant achievements lay behind him and that the CTLC was merely avoiding some hard questions about its own future by electing him president at this time. Indeed, Worsley's election in 1928 was notable not so much for the fact that it represented a break with the more conservative-minded Poulton, but because it underlined the extent to which the CTLC remained a hostage to its own past.[46]

This preference for the known rather than the new can be seen elsewhere within the labour movement. For example, Alex Ross served as president of the Calgary Labour Temple from its inception in 1912 until 1922, at which time he was succeeded by carpenter James Rae, who in turn held the position until 1928. Both men were well-respected within the movement, but neither was able to prevent the Labour Temple from sliding deeper into financial crisis during their tenure. An outstanding $10,000 mortgage from the city hung ominously over the temple's future, and schemes backed by Ross and Rae to raise revenue to pay off this sum – such as the creation of an unlicensed Labour Club – proved to be less than successful. Ross and Rae were only indirectly responsible for the

Labour Temple's financial troubles, for it was John Young who held the key position of secretary-treasurer for sixteen years from 1912 to 1928, just as he did within the CTLC. Whatever its benefits may have been, this continuity of leadership stifled innovation and threatened the very existence of the Labour Temple. It was only after the relatively youthful Fred White, then aged forty, took over management of the Labour Club in 1926 and promptly introduced entertainments that embraced the values of the new consumer-oriented society – the raffling of a Chrysler motor car, for example – that the Labour Temple's fortunes turned around. Perhaps in recognition of his rescue work, White was elected president of the organization in 1928.[47]

While these men – Poulton, Rae, Ross, White, Worsley, Young, and a handful of others – represented a strong line of continuity within the trade union movement, one that stretched back to the turn of the century, they also figured prominently within Calgary labour's political organizations. In 1925, for example, the local Canadian Labor Party elected Worsley as vice-president and Young as financial secretary, despite the latter's unimpressive record. Party president that year was machinist Thomas Riley, another man whose involvement in the Calgary labour movement dated back a quarter of a century. A year later, Riley was succeeded by Worsley. In April 1927, the Dominion Labor Party elected Young as its treasurer, consolidating his position as labour's undisputed financier.[48]

That this small group of men – fewer than a dozen in number – exercised virtually complete control of Calgary's labour movement did not go unnoticed by contemporaries, even if few were prepared to mount a direct challenge. In January 1927, in one of his regular columns for the *Alberta Labor News,* union musician J.I. Fish drew the attention of readers to the length of time that the CLP's current executive had been in office and called for their replacement at the party's forthcoming convention. Eight months later, Poulton himself admitted the danger of labour's leadership becoming complacent over time. 'There is no room for lax officers in an organization of live wire members,' he warned.[49] The trouble was, it seems, that very few such 'live wires' ever rose to positions of power within Calgary's labour movement in this period.

When it did come, the challenge to the CTLC's middle-aged and bureaucratically minded leadership took the form of a renewed breakaway movement. As already seen, in 1923 the formation of the Calgary and District National Trades and Labor Council had signalled local dissatisfaction with the CTLC and its affiliated international unions. The secessionist movement gained new momentum in the late 1920s, culminating in 1927 with the formation of the All-Canadian Congress of Labour (ACCL). Leaders of the CTLC were determined not to let this new wave of oppositional or 'dual' unionism take root in the city. As a result, the two sides of the divide spent much time and energy fighting a civil war of uncivil words.[50]

The first signs of organized labour's renewed discord in Calgary occurred in February 1925, when one-third of the members of Local 583 of the Amalgamated Association of Street and Electric Railway Employees of America (AASEREA) quit to form a new national union. This new organization – Local 2 of the Canadian Street Railway Employees Union – immediately applied to city council for recognition. Council complied, ignoring protests from the Calgary Federation of Civic Employees (CFCE), with whom the AASEREA was affiliated. Two months later, Calgary representatives of the Canadian Federation of Labour began to organize a series of meetings to form other breakaway unions. In response, the CTLC sent delegates – including the ubiquitous White, Worsley, and Riley – to these meetings in an attempt to disrupt proceedings. The war was on.[51]

In the weeks that followed, the CTLC and its political allies did their best to obstruct the new organizations. The Labour Temple Company, for example, turned down a request from the CFL to rent hall space for its meetings, citing the threat of disruption posed by the latter's dual union affiliates. After the CFL became absorbed within the ACCL in 1927, leaders of Calgary's established labour movement reiterated their opposition to any organization that challenged their authority. James Worsley, then president of the CLP in Calgary, published an article in which he described the ACCL as an 'enemy we have to fight ... that insiduously [sic] sows dissention [sic] in our ranks, continually attacking the elected officers of the organizations.' He dismissed the newly formed Canadian unions as 'purely nominal, and totally inadequate to provide the necessary protection', arguing that they were little more than paper organizations that provided few of the basic material functions of a trade union. With unintended irony, Worsley titled his page of vitriol 'Toward Unity.'[52]

Confronted by such unequivocal opposition, the ACCL gained few long-lasting affiliates in Calgary. In 1927, there were but four such unions in the city, of which only one – the General Workers Union of Canada, Unit 1 (Building Construction Labourers) – was still extant in 1930. The fact that this union was led by communists A.J. Boulter and Phil Luck cannot have endeared it to the CTLC. All told, by the end of the 1920s there were just three unions with links to the ACCL operating in Calgary.[53] Still, the revival of national unions in the late 1920s had drawn attention to the continued subordination of Canadian interests to those south of the border. At the same time, the revival in membership of trade unions affiliated to the CTLC could not mask the fact that a growing gap separated leaders from the rank and file. This was perhaps reflected in the apathy and absenteeism that remained features of CTLC meetings in this period. Overall, there was a sense of uncertainty and lack of direction among Calgary unions after 1925, and nowhere was this more evident than in the strike record.

Strike activity continued its postwar decline in the late 1920s, with days lost to industrial disputes falling from roughly 10,000 in 1920-4 to fewer than 6,000 in 1925-9. In the last five years of the decade, there were just seven work stoppages, with a single strike by carpenters in 1928 accounting for almost 90 percent of total days lost. Five of the strikes occurred in 1928-9, with workers recording one outright victory, three compromise settlements, and one clear defeat. The two strikes fought in 1925 and 1927 ended in victory for the employers.[54]

Confusion characterized the objectives and tactics in labour's use of the strike weapon in this period. Two disputes in particular underline this fact. First, in August 1925, unionized motion-picture operators struck in an attempt to enforce the closed shop at the city's Palace Theatre. Two of the striking men kidnapped non-unionist Guy McAllan at the end of a ten-hour shift, forced him into a car, and then drove him around the city for several hours. Eventually they took him to a house where they argued the merits of unionism with him until six o'clock the next morning. McAllan finally signed union papers – 'They were making a good many arguments, and I felt so tired and weary,' he later confessed – but quickly recanted his allegiance once freed. The incident had nevertheless rattled him enough to quit his job and return to his former trade of motor mechanic. In addition to this strange and rather desperate action, the striking operators also hired unemployed members of another union to picket the Palace, a clear breach of labour law at the time. No official of the motion-picture operators' union was later able to offer a satisfactory explanation for this action. 'There was no particular reason,' union operator Joseph Aaron later admitted. 'We decided to picket the theatre and when the hour came to do so, there were none of our own members available, so we sent down to the Salvation Army home and employed two men.' The only practical effect that this action had was to allow the theatre's management to request and secure police assistance.[55]

The second strike, by biscuit factory operatives in 1929, also offered a less than compelling demonstration of labour solidarity. In June that year, management at the Independent Biscuit Company suspended one of its female packing-plant employees. As she collected her belongings and left the factory, six other young women quit in sympathy and demanded her immediate reinstatement. Beneath this apparent display of principled unity among non-union workers was the rather less noble fact that the woman in question had been teasing a deaf-mute co-worker for the past two weeks, and it was this behaviour that had prompted factory management to suspend her for two weeks. Most of the factory's forty other employees sided with management in this case: they agreed to work with the disciplined woman upon her return but 'were through with the girls that walked out.' Management in turn heeded shop-floor sentiment and dismissed the six who had struck work.[56]

Such incidents did little to enhance the strike's public image as a legitimate form of labour protest. Moreover, their outcome underlined the extent to which labour remained essentially on the defensive in the late 1920s, despite the recovery in trade union membership. In the face of a resurgent capitalism, Calgary unions were unable to convert their returning strength in numbers into real might at the bargaining table. 'Defeat was a structural consequence of the increasing power of employers,' notes Bryan Palmer of Canada in the 1920s, 'a power that was, for the most part, unmatched in working-class circles.'[57] This is no doubt true but overstates labour's inability to direct its own fortunes, for one result of labour's industrial weakness was to elevate the importance of the political struggle in the 1920s. In Calgary, it was within the political arena – more specifically, that of electoral politics – that the limits of labour would be tested. Once again the search for effective political representation challenged the disposition of Calgary workers to think, act, and respond as a class.

Calgary labour's political record in the years 1925-9 should be judged within the context of external challenges and internal dissent. The former came from mainly from the local Communist Party, which hoped to capitalize on its leadership of Calgary's organized unemployed and once again embarked upon a twin campaign of infiltration and opposition in its relations with the labour movement. Meanwhile, internal dissent took the form of several prominent CLP members who criticized the party leadership's continuing manipulation of the nomination process and subsequently quit to form a new Independent Labor Party (ILP). Against this background of division and dissent, leaders of the CLP and the DLP strove to keep their own uneasy alliance intact and to justify their increasingly singular concentration on legislative solutions to labour's economic and social concerns.

When Prime Minister Mackenzie King called a federal election for October 1925, the Calgary CLP hoped that the reelection of labour MP William Irvine might shake off the disappointment of the previous December's civic contest in which labour had lost its majority on city council. Running in working-class east Calgary, Irvine defended his seat against Liberal candidate William Davidson and Conservative challenger Fred Davis. Writing to Mackenzie King after the election, Davidson confessed that he had entered the contest without much expectation of winning, but nonetheless had hoped that he might steal perhaps 20 percent of Irvine's vote. Davidson believed, correctly as it turned out, that Irvine was 'not as strong with labor as before' and calculated that enough disaffected labour voters would transfer their support to give him with an outside chance of victory.[58]

The election results of 1925 proved Davidson right in his analysis but wrong in his forecast. He had misjudged the changing mood of the electorate. Irvine's share of the popular vote did indeed drop by twelve points to just 31.5 percent of the total, but Davidson's own support also fell from 26 to 21.5 percent. Calgary workers had clearly shown little inclination to switch their support to the Liberals, and in fact had heckled Davidson during the campaign over his own record on labour issues. Combined support for Davidson and Irvine amounted to just over 6,000 votes, down a full third on the Labour-Liberal total for 1921, when an effective campaign against the Union government had served to focus working-class discontent. No such focal point existed in 1925, and any switch in allegiance that did occur worked to the benefit of the Conservative candidate, who with 5,560 votes – 47 percent of the total – claimed victory in east Calgary that year.[59]

Irvine's defeat shook the CLP, and the party's troubles only worsened during the civic elections later that year. Problems were first evident when no one could be persuaded to run against the incumbent mayor George Webster. In other contests, the CLP met with mixed fortune. Two of its four candidates for city council – printer Andrew Davison and carpenter Robert Parkyn – were elected, joining Fred White and John Russell, who were in their second year of office. Three labour candidates ran for the school board, but only Thomas Riley managed to secure a seat. These results may have confirmed the strong support that still existed for labour candidates at the municipal level, but they also left control of the civic administration firmly in the hands of the conservative Civic Government Administration.[60]

Shortly after these elections, an incident occurred that sparked a serious rupture within the CLP. It concerned the seemingly innocent matter of school textbooks. As part of the city's ongoing efforts to limit public expenditure, in January 1926 the school board announced that it would cease its practice of providing pupils with free books. In doing so, the board ignored protests from Riley that it had no mandate to take such action, and it dismissed arguments from the women's section of the DLP that local taxes had already paid for the books in question. Robert Parkyn was determined to fight the decision. In letters to the *Herald,* he had long championed the importance of education and he feared the consequences that would follow the school board's action. Assisted by fellow radical Andrew Broatch and others, Parkyn – then in his sixty-fourth year –

led a campaign of popular agitation for the reinstatement of the textbooks. This campaign quickly evolved into a demand for the recall of F.S. Selwood and Geoffrey Sylvester, the pair of school board trustees who had originally proposed the change in policy. In March 1926, the recall campaign selected two candidates to run against Selwood and Sylvester: William Ewart Turner, a CPR baggage handler and editor of the *Calgary Labor Weekly*, and the unrelated Amelia Turner, who worked for the official newspaper of the United Farmers of Alberta. A month later, the two made provincial history when they each won a clear majority in Alberta's first recall contest.[61]

While the outcome of the recall election was a clear victory for the champions of direct democracy in Alberta, it was also something of a slap in the face for the CLP in Calgary. Although the two Turners had run as official CLP candidates in the past, on this occasion the party had offered them no financial or moral assistance. 'All credit goes to the people outside the Labor Temple,' Parkyn commented somewhat bitterly after the election, noting that among labour's formal leaders only Fred White had publicly supported the recall effort.[62] On an issue of direct concern to hundreds of working-class families, the CLP had been curiously silent.

Parkyn's own disaffection from the CLP grew stronger in 1926 when he sought a party nomination to contest that year's provincial election. In June, shortly before the election was due, fifty delegates to the Calgary CLP met to select three candidates from a possible five. The names before them were A.J. Boulter, Alex Ross, John Russell, Fred White, and Parkyn. Assured that he had the unanimous support of all fifteen DLP delegates present at the meeting, Parkyn fully expected to be among those chosen. As it turned out, he managed only to tie with Russell for third place on the first vote, behind party favourites Ross and White. A second vote held to decide the third candidate was won by Russell by twenty-five votes to Parkyn's twenty-two. Parkyn could not believe that he had been rejected. Almost immediately his supporters protested the result, claiming that it ignored the DLP's unanimous preference for their man as a CLP candidate. What they did not know was that the DLP vote had been a little less than solid, for two delegates had switched their support from Parkyn to Russell on the second vote, providing the latter with the crucial margin of victory. Parkyn himself was less inclined to pursue the protest. 'The matter would have been dropped there as far as I was concerned,' he later claimed. But pressure from his friends and colleagues prevailed: Parkyn resigned from the CLP and agreed to run in the provincial election as an Independent Labor candidate.[63]

Within the CLP, reaction to Parkyn's departure was mixed. The man who had beaten him, John Russell, was generally bemused. 'I regret a possible split in the Labour movement,' he said, adding that he was 'unconscious of having done anything wrong' and had actually voted for Parkyn himself. 'Anything I can do to avoid any unpleasantness on the eve of an election, I will gladly and willingly do,' he offered, even volunteering 'to step out of the contest if the Canadian Labour [sic] Party wishes me to do so.' Others within the party were less magnanimous. 'What is the use of holding a convention if a disgruntled candidate can afterwards seek to disrupt the organized machinery of the party?' one official grumbled in clear reference to Parkyn.[64] Of more immediate concern was how the CLP would fare in the election in the wake of this open rift with one of its more popular figures.

The election results of 28 June 1926 suggest that dissatisfaction with the CLP ran deeper than the feelings of one 'disgruntled candidate.' Assisted by Andrew Broatch and other like-minded radicals, Parkyn ran under the old socialist slogan of 'Work for use, and not for profit' and campaigned hard in Calgary's working-class districts. He contrasted his own record of activism with that of the 'clique at the Labor temple [who] sit around too much and do not mix with the masses. They will not go to the [People's] Forum because they think that the people there are too red,' he taunted.[65] CLP candidates Ross, Russell, and White staged their own public meetings, but emphasized the need for new labour legislation rather than any more thorough-going social reforms. They also continued the CLP's policy of praising the UFA government – in which Ross, of course, had been an important minister – despite its poor record on unemployment relief in the 1920s. Thus, labour voters were presented with two fairly distinct choices in the provincial election of 1926 – the left-leaning radicalism of Parkyn or the moderate platform of reforms offered by the CLP. Their preference was clear. Parkyn's 2,167 first-round votes were more than twice the number received by either Ross or White, while Russell was far behind with fewer than 500 votes. However, this was the first Alberta election to be held on the basis of proportional representation, a fact that favoured parties running more than a single candidate, and the final results emerged only after ten rounds of vote transference. White benefited most from this system, picking up sufficient votes from Ross and Russell to secure his reelection to the legislature. Ross's defeat ended ten years of service as an MLA and five as a cabinet minister, and was a warning to the CLP that it could not take its past support for granted. On the other hand, Parkyn's election as Alberta's first Independent Labor MLA vindicated his break with the CLP.[66]

Disappointment over the results soon turned to bitterness and recrimination within the labour movement. 'There is only one conclusion that one can come to if the vote of the people is any indication,' remarked the *Alberta Labor News* in reference to Ross's defeat. 'That is, the workers do not want a cabinet minister, and that Calgary does not want a cabinet minister.'[67] Yet the CLP could not afford the luxury of self-pity. On the same day that the provincial votes were being counted, Conservative prime minister Arthur Meighen dissolved Parliament and announced a federal election for 14 September 1926. Here, it seemed, was a chance for the CLP to repair some of the damage done in recent elections.

Any hopes that the CLP might have had for a campaign of labour unity soon received a setback. The party planned a mid-August convention to select candidates and requested that Calgary's various labour organizations submit their own nomination lists to this gathering. From these recommendations, the CLP would make the final choice of candidate to contest Calgary East, won the previous year by the Conservative Fred Davis. The DLP complied and on 3 August selected, by a narrow margin, Thomas Riley over Herbert Adshead as its nomination to the CLP convention. Keen that the DLP should present a united front to the CLP, Adshead graciously urged his own supporters to make Riley the party's unanimous choice, which they did. There still remained a problem. Leaders of the CLP still hoped to have Adshead run as their candidate, believing that his background as a farmer and teacher would help secure the necessary Liberal and UFA votes needed to win an 'anything but Meighen' campaign. Therefore, at its nomination convention on 18 August, the CLP once again ignored the DLP's democratic decision and instead selected Adshead to run in Calgary East.[68]

As a strategic move, the CLP's disregard for the labour movement's due process was justified when Adshead defeated Davis by a comfortable margin of 12 percent. Furthermore, the party could point to the fact that Adshead's 6,870 votes were more than the total amassed by Irvine and Davidson in 1925, and so were proof that labour could win on its own merits without resorting to questionable alliances. But perhaps most significantly, after a year of internal division and disappointing results, the Calgary CLP could claim credit for having achieved Canadian labour's sole victory in the 1926 federal election.[69] Despite Adshead's remarkable victory, the election had still managed to provide the CLP with cause for concern. During the campaign itself, a number of Calgary trade unionists had publicly declared their support for the Conservative Party, whose protectionist policies, they argued, would safeguard Canadian jobs. Workers in the district of Sunnyside and at Ogden announced that they were 'prepared to put the Conservative party into power with a working majority' and give them the benefit of five more years. More positively enthusiastic was the card-carrying unionist of thirty-five years' standing who told the *Herald* that 'I honestly believe that every Labor man and his wife should give Messrs. Bennett and Davis their vote and influence to get this big breadwinner across, and give your boys and girls a chance to enjoy real prosperity at home.'[70] Sentiments such as these had not prevented the CLP from winning the local election, but they did reveal the measure of the work yet to be done.

Adshead's victory had, in any event, been achieved at the expense of worsening relations between the CLP and DLP, and division and dissent continued to dominate Calgary labour politics after the 1926 federal election. Arguments soon broke out inside the CLP, mostly centred on party member A.J. Boulter, who also remained a card-carrying communist and president of the Central Council of the Unemployed. In October 1926, Boulter clashed with Fred White over alleged safety infractions at the Spillers Mill, where Boulter was employed. A month later, he challenged rulings made by CLP president James Worsley, whom he denounced as 'quite a Mussolini.' A well-disciplined cadre of communists within the CLP ensured that moderates could not easily dismiss Boulter as a marginal figure or a crank. In November 1926, communists within the CLP secured Boulter the party's nomination to run in the civic elections that year, much to the surprise and dismay of the CLP's leadership. At the same time, a group of former CLPers solidified their discontent with the party with the launch of a new Independent Labor Party (ILP) in November 1926. Formed by Robert Parkyn, Andrew Broatch, Jean McWilliam, and other radicals, the ILP added a further ingredient to the melange of labour parties competing for votes in Calgary and thus served to further confuse the electoral choice before the city's working class.[71]

This sense of fragmentation and confusion helped to produce labour's worst result in years in the civic elections of December 1926. Among CLP candidates, John Russell and Edith Patterson won seats on the city council, but both Worsley and Boulter lost badly, with fewer than 300 votes apiece. Broatch ran as the ILP's candidate for council, but also lost with just 605 votes. Andrew Davison ran for mayor on the CLP platform, but failed to oust CGA-backed incumbent F.E. Osborne. Just 221 votes out of more than 10,000 cast separated the two men, and Davison blamed this narrowest of defeats on the inclusion of Boulter on the CLP slate. Boulter's reputation as a known communist, Davison claimed, had enabled the CGA to scare many potential voters from supporting anyone who shared the same platform with him. Angry and bitter, Davison soon quit the CLP, and began a trek towards the right that would eventually end in his endorsement of R.B. Bennett in the 1935 federal election.[72]

In January 1927, the Calgary CLP had a chance to take stock of its position when it hosted the provincial party's annual general meeting. It was not a promising occasion, with concern over apathy and internal rifts within the membership prevailing. Only one-third of Alberta's 464 CLP delegates attended the meeting, a marked decline from previous conventions. Calgary's branch of the party had an affiliated membership of almost 600, but recording-secretary William Ewart Turner remarked that 'he could see no ground for hope that the number would be appreciably increased for some time to come.' In particular, the labour movement had been unable to parlay the successful union drive of 1926 into increased support for its political parties.[73]

The matter that most urgently demanded attention was the delicate relationship between the CLP and the DLP. Despite the fact that there was a considerable overlap in membership and executive officers, the alliance between the two parties remained uneasy and uncertain. The CLP's recent lack of support for the Turners' recall campaign and its disregard for the DLP's choice of election candidates had only aggravated matters. When the DLP held its own annual convention in April 1927, party members voiced their discontent with the state of affairs. The DLP was the meat of the political labour movement in Calgary, claimed party supporter J.I. Fish, compared to which the CLP was merely the dry bones. 'The DLP ran things and ran them well, before the CLP was in existence,' he added, 'and I was glad to find that there was a rambunctious feeling that they would as a party inside a party, again reassert themselves and take over the reins, if need be.' The two parties moved nearer to some sort of reconciliation over the summer of 1927, when, as a sign of goodwill, the CLP accepted all three of the DLP's nominations for that year's civic elections.[74]

Elsewhere within the labour movement, there was less sign of unanimity as those elections approached. The CLP attempted to block Boulter from securing another nomination for city council in 1927, and in response the Communist Party promptly withdrew its support for the CLP. Two years later, Calgary communists would abandon all pretence of a united front when they adopted the Comintern's new 'social fascist' critique of reformist labour parties; at that point, the Alberta CLP finally decided that enough was enough and expelled all known communists from its ranks. In 1927, the CLP also faced continued opposition from a number of rival labour candidates. The ILP supported Robert Parkyn's run for council, while the ACCL entered the fray when it gave its backing to Andrew Broatch and W.F. Dorward in the same contest. That brought the total of labour candidates for city council to six, a record for Calgary. But the greater selection of candidates failed to result in increased representation: of the six only W.H.A. Thomas of the CLP and Parkyn of the ILP were elected. Labour's overall standing on the twelve-seat council remained at four, with the remaining eight seats still belonging to the CGA. This was the pattern for the remainder of the decade. Although the CLP and DLP continued to work together in closer harmony than before, they failed to increase their representation on city council, let alone loosen the CGA's grip on power. Fred White and Edith Patterson were elected in December 1928, joining Parkyn as labour's representatives on council, and a year later John Russell once again secured a seat on the same body as a CLP candidate. Parkyn was reelected in December 1929. His victory would have brought labour's total on council back up to four, but he had dropped the labour tag altogether and had run simply as an independent. This decision effectively ended almost two decades of Parkyn's close association with the Calgary labour movement, marking the exit of one the movement's most distinguished and principled members. It was also a sad but appropriate comment on the CLP-DLP's failure to achieve any meaningful political unity.[75]

Workers in Calgary continued to elect labour candidates to city council after 1929, but never again would labour representatives dominate the civic government as they had in the mid-1920s. Labour's brief taste of power was history. Historians sometimes point to Andrew Davison's lengthy tenure as mayor from 1930 to 1945 as evidence of labour's enduring influence at city hall, but there is little evidence to support this interpretation.[76] Arriving in Alberta in 1894, Davison had apprenticed as a printer and was employed by the *Calgary Herald* in 1911. He soon became the typographical union's secretary-treasurer, served with the 82nd Battalion during the First World War and later edited the *Alberta Veteran,* and then returned to his chosen trade. He held a number of elected positions in the 1920s, including that of union president and two terms as a city councillor.[77] Despite this background, by 1928 Davison was declaring in his campaign literature that 'It seems to me that the annually recurring battle between Labor on the one hand and the CGA on the other is beginning to pall on many of our citizens.' At the relatively young age of forty, Davison remained politically ambitious and did not wish his aspirations to be caught in the crossfire of class politics. As a result, and despite Davison's own background as a printer and experience in local trade unionism, labour won few favours from a man who in 1935 declared Canada to be 'fortunate to have a man like Prime Minister Bennett at the head of the ship of state.'[78]

There remains one fundamental question for consideration: did labour – the party, the movement, the people – expect success at the polls to produce any meaningful change, whether political, economic, or social? As the *Alberta Labor News* remarked in 1926, 'we cannot secure a civic utopia by electing a Labor Mayor. A Mayor of a city like Edmonton or Calgary is very much a creature of circumstances.' The CLP itself acknowledged that electoral success alone would not achieve the party's ultimate goal of the 'abolition of class and privilege based upon economic power.' To those who hoped that politics would produce quick solutions, the CLP further warned that it was unlikely 'that these ideals can be achieved in one generation.'[79]

The success of the CLP, or any other labour party in Calgary for that matter, is not to be judged simply by its electoral record. Electing candidates was only the first step towards achieving the sort of remedial legislation that would alleviate the 'evils which ... sprout out of the capitalist system as naturally as the fungi of decomposition out of a damp and airless basement.'[80] In Alberta, such legislation included the Factories Act (1917), a new Workers' Compensation Act (1918) to replace that of 1908, and the Minimum Wage Act (1922). Throughout the 1920s, pressure and lobbying from labour's elected representatives secured improvements and advances in each of these areas. In 1926, the provincial government amended the Factories Act to bring oil and gas workers within its scope. Labour also won an increase in the level of compensation for injuries under the Workers' Compensation Act, from 55 percent of an individual's average earnings in 1922 to 66.6 percent by 1929. In a province where, in 1928, industrial accidents occurred at the rate of almost 1,000 per month, the importance of such legislation is not easily dismissed.[81]

In the prosaic arena of labour legislation, then, the CLP and its elected representatives won many small victories for workers in Alberta.[82] Their success extended well beyond the confines of party headquarters and even the organized labour movement. Yet the reformist nature of this remedial legislation made it less and less plausible that the CLP would ever 'bring about a wider distribution of private ownership in the instruments of well-being and happiness than has ever yet been seen,' as promised in its own platform.[83] Unable to overcome its own internal divisions and always limited in popularity among the working class, the CLP's main achievement in the 1920s was to keep alive a vision of a parliamentary route to the 'co-operative commonwealth.' Whether the game was worth the candle was a question to be answered in the decade that followed.

How, finally, is labour's political record in Calgary best characterized? There are two possible interpretations. On the one hand, the election of its candidates at the municipal, provincial, and federal levels of government justified the Calgary labour movement's commitment to electoral action. Alongside Winnipeg, Calgary spearheaded labour's electoral success in Canada during the 1920s. On the other hand, the proliferation of labour parties – the CLP, DLP, ILP, WPC, and ACCL – both reflected and aggravated the fragmentation of working-class political support in Calgary. Competition among these organizations limited any one party's ability to represent more than a fraction of the local workforce. In this respect, labour politics in Calgary proved to be one more source of division and dissent.

Despite three decades of struggle with the reality and implications of industrial capitalism in Calgary, the labour movement had failed to forge a sense of unity either with or among the city's working class. In late 1929, the distance between the two remained as wide as ever. This was evident in the wake of the civic elections that December, in which voters returned only two labour candidates to city hall. At a meeting of the CTLC, which had backed the CLP candidates, several speakers 'decried the laxity of the voters in failing to register or for being too preoccupied in their own affairs.' Even Robert Parkyn, who had just been elected, complained that his own campaigners had met many workers on polling day who were unaware even that an election was being held. Once again, these speakers implied, the people had let the party down.[84]

Some of the people, at least, saw things rather differently. 'It is not so much a case of Labor's neglect in visiting the poll,' wrote 'W.B.J.' to the *Herald,* 'as it is the leaders' neglect in visiting the forces of Labor.' The writer's denunciation of the CLP continued: 'To carry on the work of the Labor movement entails not only hard work but sacrifice as well, and I have not yet seen those, among the leaders of the movement, who are prepared for that ... In spite of the fact that these men have been in office for years, there are hundreds of citizens who do not understand the policy of the Labor party. This is a terrible indictment against those who assume to condemn the workers for not visiting the polls, and with them rests the responsibility and they only, for the disaster that overtook them in the civic election.'[85]

In the 1920s, conditions of economic recession, capitalist restructuring, and persistent unemployment provided the soil in which the Calgary labour movement – and in particular its political organizations – might have sown the seeds of a unitary working-class identity. Instead, factional squabbling and fraternal strife squandered the opportunity to forge a united political front. As a result, politics joined ethnicity and gender as a further line of fracture that revealed the limits of labour to think, act, and respond as a class. The decade ahead – the 1930s – would provide plenty of opportunity for Calgary workers to rue this irony.

Epilogue

The 1930s mark a separate and distinct period in the history of the Calgary labour movement. The rise of mass unemployment, the renewed debate over responsibility for the unemployed, and the reinvigoration of the local Communist Party combined to lend a new sense of urgency to the notion of class conflict, an urgency that challenged the gradualist principles and assumptions of the Calgary Trades and Labour Council (CTLC) and its political affiliates. Workers took to the streets in a series of parades and demonstrations, while the unemployed confronted local and federal police officers in a series of violent and bloody clashes. In response to such threats to civil order, the state – via the criminal justice system – effectively suspended the right to free assembly, arrested those who insisted on exercising that right, and even deported those whom it deemed to be the ringleaders. All this was a far remove from the relative quiet that had characterized class relations in previous decades.[1]

Yet while the unrest of the 1930s was the product of immediate circumstances, it also had deeper roots that lay in developments since the end of the First World War. The mainstream labour movement's uneasy relationship with the Communist Party, its ambiguous and less than wholehearted support for the unemployed, and its failure to unite its own industrial and political wings had all been key features of the 1920s. In turn, the limits of labour in the 1920s can only be understood if they too are placed within a broader context – the historical formation of class relations in Calgary since the closing years of the nineteenth century. The failure of the Canadian Labor Party (CLP) to retain its base of working-class support in the 1930s and its virtual collapse in the election of 1935 illustrate the importance of these long-term historical connections.

On 22 August 1935, Albertans went to the polls in unprecedented number and elected William Aberhart's Social Credit Party as their new provincial government. For the incumbent and much-troubled United Farmers of Alberta, it was a complete rout: not one sitting government member was reelected. Volumes have been written on the events surrounding this election, and it would be difficult to overstate the significance of Social Credit's victory as a landmark in Alberta's politics.[2] Public interest in the election was at an unprecedented level, with voter turnout at an all-time high of 82 percent (compared with 67 percent in the previous two contests). For the first time in the province's history, the government won a clear majority of the popular vote, with Social Credit taking fifty-six of the sixty-three seats available.

Yet for the Calgary labour movement, all this was of secondary importance. Instead, the 1935 election stood as a final repudiation of the CLP's claim to be the preferred choice of local workers. A total of twenty candidates – including four labour and one communist – contested Calgary's six seats. When the voting was over, Calgarians had elected four Social Crediters, one Liberal, and one Conservative. Labour's most successful candidate, Fred White, had come twelfth in the first round, and his 1,024 votes were a mere fraction of the 3,192 that had secured him a third successive term as MLA in 1930. Robert Parkyn, running once again as an independent labour candidate, fared even worse. His electoral support, which had previously jumped from 1,544 votes in 1930 to 2,003 in a 1933 by-election, plummeted to just 224 votes. A.J.E. Liesemer and W.G. Southern, labour's two other candidates, mustered a paltry 621 votes between them. All told, labour's share of the popular vote fell from 26 percent in 1926 and 22 percent in 1930 to 6 percent in 1935.[3] For the first time since 1913, Calgary labour failed to secure any representation in the provincial legislature. It has never since regained it.[4]

There is little doubt where labour's former support went. As studies by Edward Bell and others have shown, working-class votes were vital to the triumph of Social Credit in 1935.[5] This was especially true in Calgary's industrial districts. In Ogden, for example, where the CPR stockyards remained the major employer, 87 percent of the vote went to Social Credit. In Ceepear, another industrial area, the figure was 93 percent.[6] One union worker later explained how Aberhart had effected this mass conversion. 'He gave me to understand that in all matters of labour policy, the elected members of labour would be consulted and he would welcome any people from labour groups. So then our shops formed a Social Credit group, and eventually our whole plant was organized into the — group for Social Credit. We had hundreds of members.'[7] For other working-class Calgarians, Aberhart's appeal was more elemental. 'I was unemployed,' said one worker, 'and he made me feel I could really be somebody again if I got behind him. He had a wonderful brain and a wonderful knowledge of the whole depression situation. He seemed to know better about the problems of labour than we did ourselves.' This remained a dominant impression in the minds of those who lived through

The beginning of the end? Working-class support for Social Credit in the provincial election of 1935 ensured the defeat of the Canadian Labor Party in Calgary, and the CLP never recovered from this blow. Here workers proclaim their support for William Aberhart and Social Credit at the CPR railway yards in Ogden, the traditional heartland of Calgary labour unionism, thereby symbolizing the extent of the CLP's failure that year.

the 1930s. Almost six decades after Aberhart's election, Calgarians still recall his 'socialistic' appeal to 'the poor people of a have-not province.' As one man explained, 'this guy pushed the right buttons.'[8]

If Aberhart's populist, even messianic, appeal struck a genuine chord with Calgary's working class, employed and unemployed alike, then the labour movement's own response to the Depression was a further factor in explaining the mass desertion of its political support. The CTLC and CLP remained ambivalent in their direct support for the unemployed, just as they had throughout the 1920s. As a result, it was left to the Communist Party to organize and mobilize the city's jobless in their struggle for recognition and relief.[9] Led by energetic men such as Pat Lenihan and E.H. Starr, the local Communist Party was only too willing to assume this role, helping Calgary's unemployed to stage various relief strikes, street demonstrations, and other public protests. Through a series of court judgments, local state authorities responded to this unrest by terminating the 'right' of free assembly and prosecuting those who persisted in protest. The last open clash between Calgary's unemployed and the state came in the summer of 1935, a month before the provincial election, by which time there was little hope of repairing relations between the jobless thousands and the labour movement. At the same time, there was never any likelihood that the Communist Party, whose commitment to electoral politics had never been better than questionable, would usurp the CLP as a viable political force, even in the extreme conditions of the 1930s. Nevertheless, the fact that Lenihan amassed 820 votes in the 1935 election – more than the combined total for Parkyn, Southern, and Liesemer – was symbolic of how low support for mainstream labour candidates had slumped.[10]

Working-class disillusionment with the CLP in 1935 reflected a deeper malaise that affected the entire labour movement in Calgary. There was a growing sense, already evident in the 1920s, that an unbridgeable gap separated the interests of the organized movement from workers as a class. In a long letter to the *Calgary Herald* just two days before the provincial election, one local worker detailed his accumulated grievances with the CTLC:

> I am firmly convinced that their principal motive is to look out for themselves on every occasion. Take the craft unions for instance, say over a space of 15 or 20 years, and what do you find? All advances received were at the expense of unorganized labor and the consuming public ... If organization causes some workmen to thrive at the expense of others who belong to less favored classes, it is impossible to give security and happiness to those who are forever in the rear. This continual preaching of universal brotherhood does not have the clear ring to it [that] it should have, and when one makes a comparison between the payments received for work done by organized skilled labor and other branches of labor which is just as important for the welfare of society, any right thinking person must come to the conclusion we have kept silent for too long on these matters of importance.[11]

This was a damning indictment of the Calgary labour movement in 1935, but an accurate one. In January that year, printers at the *Albertan* newspaper began a bitter dispute that dragged on into 1936 and achieved little but to underline the fragile nature of solidarity even among fellow craft trade unionists.[12] As the above writer implied, organized labour might pay lip service to the notion of 'universal brotherhood,' but its failure to defend the unskilled and the unemployed at a time when they needed protection more than ever betrayed the notion of a single working class in Calgary.

As the correspondent also indicated, this troubled state of affairs was not new to 1935, or even to the 1930s. Aberhart's charismatic presence as a political option and the widening impact of austerity precipitated the CLP's reversal of fortune that year, but in themselves they were not its cause. The historical course or pattern of events in the 1920s prevented the CLP from becoming an enduring social democratic party with a broad base of working-class support. Its volatile relations with the Dominion

Labor Party (DLP) and the CTLC, despite their considerable overlap in members and interests, absorbed too much of the party's time and attention. Unable to present itself as the undisputed political voice of the labour movement, the CLP had always struggled to convince Calgary workers that it could either understand, represent, or defend their best interests. To the extent that this debilitating fragmentation was, as previous chapters have shown, rooted in the historical evolution of the Calgary labour movement, the collapse of working-class support for the CLP in 1935 cannot be separated from this longer history. The connections may be summarized here briefly.

Calgary's labour movement had originally come into being at a time of extraordinary economic growth, relative prosperity, and expectations that these circumstances would continue indefinitely. In the decade before 1913, workers frequently used strike action to back their demands for a greater share of the wealth that they produced. Employers were generally willing to concede these demands rather than risk a prolonged interruption of production. Ironically, such conflicts – and in essence they *were* class conflicts – encouraged the popular belief in the mutuality of interests of labour and capital, the belief that any differences night be resolved on the basis of reasonable compromise. The dominance of Anglo-Canadian cultural forms and values reinforced this notion by providing a common social milieu in which worker and boss could occasionally meet as equals. Within the emergent labour movement, even when workers argued that their interests were in fact *distinct* from those of their employers, there were few that claimed that they were necessarily *opposed*. As long as wages continued to rise and jobs continued to be relatively plentiful, organized labour could reasonably claim that its preference for cooperation and compromise with capital paid dividends.

It became harder to maintain this claim after 1913, when Calgary's economy went into a sudden and sharp decline. Following a decade in which the city's rate of growth was virtually unrivalled throughout Canada, the perceived impact of this recession was all the greater. While unemployment was not an unknown phenomenon before 1913, it now became a characteristic and enduring feature of Calgary's economy. Enlistment and wartime production eased conditions temporarily by 1916, but labour's experience during the years of postwar economic restructuring suggested that full employment would not be part of capitalism's return to normality. At the same time, the federal government's wartime antilabour legislation, its repression of the Winnipeg general strike, and its laggard efforts to assist those out of work all undermined any notion that the state was simply an impartial umpire when it came to dealing with labour.

In response to the changed conditions after 1913, Calgary's labour movement intensified, but did not significantly alter, the policies and practices that it had pursued in the prewar years. The majority of its members continued to be organized along craft lines in proudly exclusive unions, although some of these unions were also affiliated to broader federations. In the political arena, the Labor Representation League was formed in 1917 and signalled an organizational advance over the ad hoc campaigns of previous years. It also provided valuable experience for those men and women who later founded the DLP and CLP in Calgary. Together, Calgary's unions and labour parties pursued the goal of economic and social reform within the existing state system, rather than attempt to reform or overthrow that system itself.

In line with Marx's observation that the 'tradition of all the dead generations weighs like a nightmare on the brain of the living,' the Calgary labour movement was unable to jettison its own historical traditions as it confronted the new circumstances after 1913. Most of those who led the movement in the 1920s and beyond had helped to establish it during the prewar years, and their attitudes and beliefs were inevitably shaped by their experience of this period. Alex Ross, Fred White, Robert Parkyn, and John Young were among those influential figures who were either unwilling or unable to abandon the belief that electing labour representatives to local, provincial, and national governments was the best way to advance to the interests of all workers. Like Samuel Johnson's observations on an over-hasty remarriage, perhaps this represented the triumph of optimism over experience. In May 1919, for example, shortly after the RNWMP had, with government sanction, raided his own home in the small hours of the morning, Robert Parkyn stood before the Mathers Commission to deliver his testimony on class relations in Calgary. 'I believe humanity is good at heart,' he told the commission. 'We are all kin. We are all trying to create a better condition, and I believe that we will eventually come to it.'[13] This faith in a sense of humanity that transcended divisions of class – and the hope that capitalism's representatives shared in it too – was one of the Calgary labour movement's strengths before the First World War. In the 1920s and 1930s, it proved to be one of its major weaknesses, but by then it was too late to convert to a more radical, class-oriented outlook.

Why this was so brings us back to the question of class formation in Calgary. The phrase 'working class' has recurred frequently in these pages, yet it begs the question to what extent there actually existed an identifiable working class in Calgary. Although the term itself assumes the existence of some common interest or concern among those who sold their labour power in return for wages, it is less than clear whether Calgary workers ever experienced or exhibited such a bond. On the contrary, it has been suggested here that other identities – those of occupation, gender, ethnicity, and possibly religion – may have divided the workforce and weakened any latent sense of class. In the realm of politics, factionalism and fragmentation similarly undermined efforts to build a party that might serve as a focal point for working-class demands. In what way, then, does it make sense to talk of a single working class in Calgary? And, by extension, what value – if any – does class analysis retain as an explanation of social change in the Canadian West in this period? These are questions that, in an often roundabout way, this study has attempted to tackle, and to which it now devotes its closing comments.

Such reservations over the use of class as a model or method of inquiry depend on how the term is conceptualized in the first place. As long as the model employed maintains (more or less) the orthodox distinction between 'class in itself' and 'class for itself,' Calgary workers might at best be described as constituting a class in their 'objective' economic experiences – that is, in their daily routines on the job, in their diminishing control over production – but largely lacking any sense of class consciousness in their 'subjective' social or political behaviour. Within this framework, therefore, there appears to be no particular reason for privileging class over other plausible explanations as a cause of historical change. A different picture emerges if we return to the four-level model of class formation – structure, ways of life, disposition, and collective action – developed by Ira Katznelson and discussed in the introduction.[14] The application of this model to Calgary, I would suggest, underlines the ways in which class was both a meaningful factor in the everyday lives of workers in the city and the key to understanding Calgary's broader social, economic, and political evolution in these years.

At the first level, that of structure, the expansion of privately owned and profit-maximizing enterprises was dependent upon a relatively stable and predictable supply of skilled labour. In turn, the dependence of these workers on wages as their main (though by no means sole) source of income explicitly identified them as a distinct class of citizens within the capitalistic labour market. No amount of social interaction, shared cultural experiences, or individual aspirations of upward mobility could hide this basic fact of life in Calgary at the time, and it makes no sense now to deny that, at this level, the working class existed as a very real phenomenon.

The structure of wage labour in Calgary shaped the patterns or ways of life of Calgary's working class, the second level of analysis in Katznelson's model. The man whose words open this study, postal worker Clifford Nicholls, made this point abundantly clear when he addressed the Mathers Commission in 1919. His reference to the working man who 'has to stand on tired, weary, blistered feet until he gets to his home' and 'his pale-faced wife, absolutely worn out with her exertions at the wash tub' may appear somewhat melodramatic, but it is a forceful reminder that ten hours of manual toil each day left workers with little time or energy for leisure pursuits in the evening. As Nicholls also implied in his testimony, a single wage was unlikely to meet even the basic needs of a family in Calgary, with the result that working-class households had to adopt a variety of strategies to make ends meet. Second incomes, subsistence measures, forays into penny capitalism and even prostitution were all integral, not incidental, features of Calgary's developing capitalist economy. Finally, class relations, formed at the point of production, intersected with non-capitalist relations – notably those of gender and ethnicity – to influence the ways in which workers interacted with each other and with society more generally. In this manner, the daily demands and dictates of capitalism helped to shape the basic patterns of life for workers in Calgary, compounding their structural identity as a distinct class.

The third level of Katznelson's model is the disposition of workers to think and behave in class terms, and it is here that the formation of class relations in Calgary was at its weakest. The same ambition and initiative that drove thousands of men and women westwards in the first place also, in many cases, nurtured their hopes of achieving economic independence. As such, it is understandable if they were reluctant to identify themselves primarily in terms of the wages they received. As in every other city in Canada, individuals viewed themselves and their interests as much in terms of occupation, gender, and ethnicity as in terms of class differences, and any search for a generic or homogeneous working-class viewpoint is a forlorn endeavour. In addition, it seems clear that Calgary's dominant Anglo-Canadian culture did at times blunt any working-class disposition that may otherwise have prevailed. In the first instance, it provided workers of the same background with a sense of equality absent in their other experiences and so helped to integrate them into the social status quo. Second, it emphasized differences between such workers and those of cultural minorities, regardless of their shared objective or structural position in society. As a consequence of both, culture retarded the disposition of workers to view themselves as a united force and left many of Calgary's cultural minority workers as a vaguely identified 'class apart.'

The weakness of class disposition among Calgary workers influenced class formation at the fourth level, that of collective action. Attempts by the DLP and CLP to articulate and defend the interests of workers as a class met with limited success, largely because they were unable to convince workers that such collective interests actually existed. With workers for the most part unwilling to regard themselves as members of a single class, only a minority ever gave their support to Calgary's labour parties. Had the CLP, DLP, and CTLC managed to provide a clear display of concord and cooperation in the 1920s, more workers might have accepted and endorsed the view that were indeed fundamental interests that united them. Instead, discord and factionalism within labour politics became a further source of internal division and did little to win new converts to the cause. William Aberhart pounded the final nail into the CLP's coffin in 1935, but party activists had been busy with their own hammers throughout the previous decade.

It is the dialectic between disposition and collective action that explains the limits of working-class support for labour politics in Calgary during the 1920s and 1930s. Collectively, workers did not, in E.P. Thompson's phrase, 'define themselves in their actions and in their consciousness in relation to other groups of people in class ways,' and so they were not predisposed to back a party that preached the politics of class.[15] In turn, Calgary's various labour parties failed to inspire the mass of their potential supporters to adopt a class-based perspective on society, due largely to the parties' own ideological, constitutional, and personal conflicts during the 1920s. The demise of the CLP in 1935 was not, in any true sense, predetermined or inevitable. Rather, the party was an active and culpable participant in its own downfall.

Class shaped the lives of Calgary workers far more than it did the ways in which they thought about their lives. The decline in support for the class-based politics of the CLP during Calgary capitalism's deepest crisis in the 1930s was symbolic of this fact. Yet it is impossible to understand or write the history of labour in Calgary outside the context of class formation. It was in response to the demands and conditions of *capitalist* production that workers first began to organize unions in the late nineteenth century, and it was a reaction to the increasingly pro-capital nature of both state intervention and public discourse in the early 1900s that led them to engage in political action. As noted in 1904 by James Worsley, cofounder of Calgary's labour movement and its most enduring advocate of political action, 'class conflict exist[s] here as naked and unashamed as in the older cities most of us have but recently left, and no matter how local circumstances may have obscured the fact for a time, sooner or later it must assert itself to the worker's sorrow.'[16] These words still rang true in 1935, the year in which the limits of labour became all too apparent in Calgary. Yet as Calgary workers would find out for themselves in the unsettled years after the Second World War, it was one thing to deny the relevance of class but quite another to dismiss it as a fact of life.

Notes

Introduction

1 See Colin Campbell, 'The Stampede: Cowtown's Sacred Cow,' in *Stampede City: Power and Politics in the West,* ed. Chuck Reasons (Toronto: Between the Lines, 1984), 103-22.

2 Canada, Royal Commission on Industrial Relations, 1919, Minutes of Evidence, testimony of Clifford Nicholls (Calgary, 3 May 1919).

3 Ibid.

4 Previous studies of the Calgary labour movement include Elizabeth Ann Taraska, 'The Calgary Craft Union Movement, 1900-1920' (MA thesis, University of Calgary, 1975); Alimohamed Damji, 'From Militancy to Passivism: The Calgary Labour Movement, 1919-1924' (MA thesis, University of Calgary, 1987); David Bright, 'Bonds of Brotherhood? The Experiences of Calgary Labour, 1903-1919' (MA thesis, University of Calgary, 1990). See also Warren Caragata, *Alberta Labour: A Heritage Untold* (Toronto: Lorimer, 1978).

5 Prime examples of this neglect are Max Foran and Sheilagh Jameson, eds., *Citymakers: Calgarians after the Frontier* (Calgary: Historical Society of Alberta, Chinook Country Chapter, 1987), and *Centennial City: Calgary, 1894-1994* (Calgary: University of Calgary, 1994).

6 For example, see Bryan D. Palmer, *Working-Class Experience: Rethinking the History of Canadian Labour, 1800-1991,* 2nd ed. (Toronto: McClelland and Stewart, 1992), 190. Key statements of western labour radicalism include H. Clare Pentland, 'The Western Canadian Labour Movement, 1897-1919,' *Canadian Journal of Political and Social Theory* 3 (1979): 53-78; David Jay Bercuson, *Confrontation at Winnipeg: Labour, Industrial Relations, and the General Strike* (Montreal: McGill-Queen's University Press, 1974), *Fools and Wise Men: The Rise and Fall of the One Big Union* (Toronto: McGraw-Hill Ryerson, 1978), and 'Labour Radicalism and the Western Industrial Frontier, 1897-1919,' *Canadian Historical Review* 58, 2 (1977): 154-77; and A. Ross McCormack, *Reformers, Rebels, and Revolutionaries: The Western Canadian Radical Movement, 1899-1919* (1977; reprint, Toronto: University of Toronto Press, 1991), and 'The Western Working-Class Experience,' in *Lectures in Canadian Labour and Working-Class History,* ed. W.J.C. Cherwinski and Gregory S. Kealey (St John's: Committee on Canadian Labour History, 1985), 115-26.

7 For other studies that make this point, see Robert A.J. McDonald, 'Working-Class Vancouver, 1886-1914: Urbanism and Class in British Columbia,' *BC Studies* 69-70 (1986): 33-69; Allen Seager, 'Workers, Class, and Industrial Conflict in New Westminster, 1900-1930,' in *Workers, Capital, and the State in British Columbia: Selected Papers,* ed. Rennie Warburton and David Coburn (Vancouver: UBC Press, 1988), 117-40; Jeremy Mouat, 'The Genesis of Western Exceptionalism: British Columbia's Hard-Rock Miners, 1895-1903,' *Canadian Historical Review* 71, 3 (1990): 317-45; John Douglas Belshaw, 'The British Collier in British Columbia: Another Archetype Reconsidered,' *Labour/Le Travail* 34 (1994): 11-36.

8 James Naylor, *The New Democracy: Challenging the Social Order in Industrial Ontario, 1914-1925* (Toronto: University of Toronto Press, 1991); Mark Leier, *Red Flags and Red Tape: The Making of a Labour Bureaucracy* (Toronto: University of Toronto Press, 1995).
9 See Bryan D. Palmer, 'Working-Class Canada: Recent Historical Writing,' *Queen's Quarterly* 86 (1979): 594-616; Kenneth McNaught, 'E.P. Thompson vs Harold Logan: Writing about Labour and the Left in the 1970s,' *Canadian Historical Review* 62, 2 (1981): 141-68; David J. Bercuson, 'Through the Looking Glass of Culture: An Essay on the New Labour History and Working-Class Culture in Recent Canadian Historical Writing,' *Labour/Le Travailleur* 7 (1981): 95-112; Gregory S. Kealey, 'Labour and Working-Class History in Canada: Prospects in the 1980s,' ibid., 116-35, and 'Writing about Labour,' in John Schultz, ed., *Writing about Canada: A Handbook for Modern Canadian History* (Scarborough, ON: Prentice-Hall, 1990), 145-74; James Naylor, 'Working-Class History in English Canada in the 1980s,' *Acadiensis* 19, 1 (1989): 156-69; Joanne Burgess, 'Exploring the Limited Identities of Canadian Labour: Recent Trends in English-Canada and in Quebec,' *International Journal of Canadian Studies/Revue internationale d'études canadiennes* 1-2 (1990): 149-73.
10 Leier, *Red Tape and Red Flags,* 9.
11 For example, see Peter Calvert, *The Concept of Class: An Historical Introduction* (London: Hutchinson, 1982); Ellen Meiksins Wood, *The Retreat from Class: A New 'True' Socialism* (London: Verso, 1986); and Lenard R. Berlanstein, ed., *Rethinking Labor History: Essays on Discourse and Class Analysis* (Urbana: University of Illinois Press, 1993).
12 Karl Marx, *A Contribution to the Critique of Political Economy* (1859), reprinted in *The Marx-Engels Reader,* ed. Robert C. Tucker, 2nd ed. (New York: W.W. Norton, 1978), 4.
13 Karl Marx, *The Eighteenth Brumaire of Louis Bonaparte* (1859; reprint, New York: International Publishers, 1963), 15.
14 Raymond Williams, 'Base and Superstructure in Marxist Cultural Theory,' *New Left Review* 82 (1973): 4; Maurice Godelier, 'Infrastructures, Societies, and History,' *Current Anthropology* 19, 4 (1978): 763. See also E.P. Thompson, *The Making of the English Working Class* (Harmondsworth: Pelican, 1963).
15 See Alex Callinicos, *Making History: Agency, Structure, and Change in Social Theory* (Oxford: Polity Press, 1987).
16 Ira Katznelson, *Marxism and the City* (Oxford: Clarendon Press, 1992), 237-8. For other examples of the substantial debate over Thompson's legacy, see William H. Sewell, Jr, 'How Classes Are Made: Critical Reflections on E.P. Thompson's Theory of Working-Class Formation,' in *E.P. Thompson: Critical Perspectives,* ed. Harvey J. Kaye and Keith McClelland (Philadelphia: Temple University Press, 1990), 50-77. See also Ellen Meiksins Wood, 'The Politics of Theory and the Concept of Class: E.P. Thompson and His Critics,' *Studies in Political Economy* 9 (Fall 1982): 45-75; Paul Buhle, 'E.P. Thompson and His Critics,' *Telos* 49 (Fall 1981): 127-37; Kay Trimberger, 'E.P. Thompson: Understanding the Process of History,' in *Vision and Method in Historical Sociology,* ed. Theda Skocpol (Cambridge: Cambridge University Press, 1984), 211-43; and Marc W. Steinberg, 'The Re-making of the English Working Class?' *Theory and Society* 20, 2 (1991): 173-97.
17 See the following works by Ira Katznelson: *Marxism and the City;* 'Working-Class Formation: Constructing Cases and Comparisons,' in *Working-Class Formation: Nineteenth-Century Patterns in Western Europe and the United States,* ed. Ira Katznelson and Aristide R. Zolberg (Princeton: Princeton University Press, 1986), 3-44; *City Trenches: Urban Politics and the Patterning of Class in the United States* (New York: Pantheon Books, 1981); 'Working-Class Formation and the State: Nineteenth-Century England in American Perspective,' in *Bringing the State Back In,* ed. Peter Evans, Dietrich Rueschemeyer, and Theda Skocpol (Cambridge: Cambridge University Press, 1985), 257-84; 'The "Bourgeois" Dimension: A Provocation about Institutions, Politics, and the Future of Labor History,' *International Labor and Working-Class History* 46 (1994): 7-32.
18 Katznelson, 'Constructing Cases and Comparisons,' 14.
19 Ibid., 21.
20 Ibid., 14-6.
21 Katznelson, *Marxism and the City,* 203-4.

22 Quoted in Katznelson, 'Constructing Cases and Comparisons,' 18, emphasis in original.
23 Ibid., 17-20.
24 Ibid., 21-2.
25 Alice Kessler-Harris, 'A New Agenda for American Labor History: A Gendered Analysis and the Question of Class,' in *Perspectives on American Labor History: The Problems of Synthesis,* ed. J. Carroll Moody and Alice Kessler-Harris (De Kalb: Northern Illinois University Press, 1990), 234, n. 16; Katznelson, 'Constructing Cases and Comparisons,' 4, n. 2.
26 Leon Fink, 'Culture's Last Stand? Gender and the Search for Synthesis in American Labor History,' *Labor History* 34, 2-3 (1993): 181.
27 Joy Parr, *The Gender of Breadwinners: Women, Men, and Change in Two Industrial Towns, 1880-1950* (Toronto: University of Toronto Press, 1990), 8.
28 See Alice Kessler-Harris, 'Treating the Male as "Other": Redefining the Parameters of Labor History,' *Labor History* 34, 2-3 (1993): 192, 193, 194, 195.
29 Parr, *Gender of Breadwinners*; Suzanne Morton, *Ideal Surroundings: Domestic Life in a Working-Class Suburb in the 1920s* (Toronto: University of Toronto Press, 1995); Joan Sangster, *Earning Respect: The Lives of Working Women in Small-Town Ontario, 1920-1950* (Toronto: University of Toronto Press, 1995).
30 Mari Jo Buhle, 'Gender and Labor History,' in *Perspectives on American Labor History,* ed. Moody and Kessler-Harris, 68 (emphasis in the original). See also Catharine A. MacKinnon, *Toward a Feminist Theory of the State* (Cambridge: Harvard University Press, 1989).
31 Bryan D. Palmer, *Descent into Discourse: The Reification of Language and the Writing of Social History* (Philadelphia: Temple University Press, 1990), 138.
32 For a review of poststructuralism, see Peter Dews, *Logics of Disintegration: Post-Structuralist Thought and the Claims of Critical Theory* (London: Verso, 1987). Also useful are George G. Iggers, *Historiography in the Twentieth Century: From Scientific Objectivity to the Post-modern Challenge* (Hanover: Wesleyan University Press, 1997), and Keith Jenkins, ed., *The Postmodern Reader* (London: Routledge, 1997).
33 Gareth Stedman Jones, *Languages of Class: Studies in English Working-Class History, 1832-1982* (Cambridge: Cambridge University Press, 1983); Joan Wallach Scott, *Gender and the Politics of History* (New York: Columbia University Press, 1988); Mariana Valverde, *The Age of Light, Soap, and Water: Moral Reform in English Canada, 1885-1925* (Toronto: McClelland and Stewart, 1991). In addition to works by Parr and Sangster cited above, see Joan Sangster, '"Pardon Tales" from Magistrate's Court: Women, Crime, and the Court in Peterborough County, 1920-1950,' *Canadian Historical Review* 74, 2 (1993): 161-97; Joy Parr, 'Gender History and Historical Practice,' ibid., 76, 3 (1995): 354-76, and Gail Cuthbert Brandt, 'Postmodern Patchwork: Some Recent Trends in the Writing of Women's History in Canada,' ibid., 72, 4 (1991): 441-70.
34 Scott, 'On Language, Gender, and Working-Class History,' in *Gender and the Politics of History,* 56.
35 Palmer, *Descent into Discourse*; Alex Callinicos, *Against Postmodernism: A Marxist Critique* (Oxford: Polity Press, 1989).
36 Palmer, *Descent into Discourse,* 138.
37 Gertrude Himmelfarb, 'Postmodernist History,' in *On Looking into the Abyss: Untimely Thoughts on Culture and Society* (New York: Vintage Books, 1995), 154.
38 Katznelson, 'The "Bourgeois" Dimension,' 9. Various critics offered their responses to Katznelson's propositions in the same issue of *International and Working-Class History.*
39 Ralph Miliband, *The State in Capitalist Society* (London: Quartet Books), 177.

Chapter 1: From Cow Town to Hub of Industry

1 On Calgary's history before 1883, see Hugh A. Dempsey, *Calgary: Spirit of the West* (Saskatoon: Glenbow/Fifth House Publishers, 1994), 3-36.
2 Lawrence H. Bussard, 'The Early History of Calgary' (MA thesis, University of Calgary, 1935), 44; David H. Breen, *The Canadian Prairie West and the Ranching Frontier, 1874-1924* (Toronto: University of Toronto Press, 1983), 93-5; Max Foran, *Calgary: An Illustrated History* (Toronto: Lorimer, 1978), 16-24.

3 Glenbow Museum Archives (GMA), M1302, Frank White diaries, 21 Sept. 1882; P. Turner Bone, *When the Steel Went Through: Reminiscences of a Railroad Engineer* (Toronto: Macmillan, 1947), 49, 116; *Calgary, Alberta, Canada. Her Industries and Resources* (Calgary: Burns and Elliott, 1885), 23; Hugh A. Dempsey, ed., 'Calgary: A Century Ago,' *Alberta History* 32, 3 (1984): 28; *Calgary Herald,* 17 Sept. 1888.

4 See James M. Francis, 'Montana Business and Canadian Regionalism in the 1870s and 1880s,' *Western Historical Quarterly* 12, 3 (1981): 291-304; Henry C. Klassen, 'I.G. Baker & Co. in Calgary, 1875-1884,' *Montana* 35, 3 (1985): 40-55; A.A. den Otter, 'Transportation, Trade and Regional Identity in the Southwestern Prairies,' *Prairie Forum* 15, 1 (1990): 1-23.

5 Lewis G. Thomas, 'The Rancher and the City: Calgary and the Cattlemen, 1883-1914,' in *Ranchers' Legacy: Alberta Essays by Lewis G. Thomas,* ed. Patrick Dunae (Edmonton: University of Alberta Press, 1986), 39-60.

6 *Calgary, Alberta,* 25-76, 86.

7 GMA, M6141, I.S. Freeze papers, letters to wife Evelyn, 2 June 1883, 5 Aug. 1883, 2 Sept. 1883, 29 Sept. 1883, 24 Oct. 1883.

8 *Calgary Herald,* 2 Jan. 1884.

9 J.G. Fitzgerald, *Business Directory of Calgary, Alberta, Canada* (Calgary: Calgary Herald Publishing, 1885).

10 *Census of the Three Provisional Districts of the North West Territories, 1884-1885* (1885), 82-5.

11 *Census of Canada* (1891), 2: 181-5; 3: 387.

12 See Bryan D. Palmer, *A Culture in Conflict: Skilled Workers and Industrial Capitalism in Hamilton, Ontario, 1860-1914* (Montreal: McGill-Queen's University Press, 1979); Gregory S. Kealey, *Toronto Workers Respond to Industrial Capitalism, 1867-1892* (1980; reprint, Toronto: University of Toronto Press, 1991).

13 Nicholas Flood Davin, *Homes for Millions: The Great Canadian Northwest, Its Resources Fully Described* (Ottawa: Brown Chamberlain, 1891), 84.

14 *Census of Canada* (1911), 3: 350; *Calgary Herald,* 25 July 1890, 1 June 1891; Fitzgerald, *Business Directory of Calgary.*

15 Foran, *Calgary,* 25-8. For the broader context, see Charles Hoffman, 'The Depression of the Nineties,' *Journal of Economic History* 16, 2 (1956): 137-64; and Edward J. Chambers, 'Late-Nineteenth-Century Business Cycles,' *Canadian Journal of Economics and Political Science* 30, 3 (1964): 391-412. See also S.B. Saul, *The Myth of the Great Depression, 1873-1896,* 2nd ed. (London: Macmillan, 1985).

16 Henry C. Klassen, 'Social Troubles in Calgary in the Mid-1890s,' *Urban History Review* 3-74 (1974): 8-16.

17 *Calgary Herald,* 4 Aug. 1896, 3 Feb. 1896, 4 Feb. 1895, 3 July 1895. For an account of relations between Calgary's merchant class and its early council administration, see Maxwell Laurence Foran, 'The Civic Corporation and Urban Growth: Calgary, 1884-1930' (PhD diss., University of Calgary, 1981).

18 *Calgary Herald,* 26 April 1893, 31 July 1895. GMA, M109, P. Turner Bone papers, file 3, contain a full prospectus for Stone and Company pork packers.

19 Alfred J. Sproule, 'The Role of Patrick Burns in the Development of Western Canada' (MA thesis, University of Alberta, 1962), 106.

20 *Calgary Herald,* 8 Oct. 1896.

21 There has been an enduring debate over the timing, nature, and extent of economic growth in the late nineteenth century. Differing interpretations are offered by W.A. Mackintosh, 'Economic Factors in Canadian History,' *Canadian Historical Review* 4, 1 (1923): 12-25; Penelope Hartland, 'Factors in Economic Growth in Canada,' *Journal of Economic History* 15 (March 1955): 13-22; Gordon W. Bertram, 'Economic Growth in Canadian Industry, 1870-1915: The Staple Model and the Take-Off Hypothesis,' *Canadian Journal of Economics and Political Science* 29, 2 (1963): 162-84; Duncan McDougall, 'Canadian Manufactured Commodity Output, 1870-1915,' *Canadian Journal of Economics* 4, 1 (1971): 21-36; Morris Altman, 'A Revision of Canadian Economic Growth: 1870-1910 (A Challenge to the Gradualist Interpretation),' ibid., 20, 1 (1987): 86-113.

22 *Census of Canada* (1911), 3: 350; *Postal Census of Manufactures Canada* (Ottawa: J. de L. Taché, 1917), 186.
23 *The Story of Calgary, Alberta, Canada: Progress, Resources, Opportunities* (Calgary: n.p., 1914), passim.
24 Alan F.J. Artibise, 'Boosterism and the Development of Prairie Cities, 1871-1913,' in *Town and City: Aspects of Western Canadian Urban Development,* ed. Alan F.J. Artibise (Regina: Canadian Plains Research Center, 1981), 209-35; Max Foran, 'The Boosters in Boosterism: Some Calgary Examples,' *Urban History Review* 8, 2 (1979): 77-82.
25 Foran, 'The Civic Corporation and Urban Growth,' 25-44.
26 Ging G.G. Wong, *Calgary's Civic Government: A Structural History* (Calgary: Glenbow Archives Institute, 1978), 21-9.
27 *Calgary Herald,* 15 March 1892; Henry C. Klassen, 'Entrepreneurship in the Canadian West: The Enterprises of A.E. Cross, 1886-1920,' *Western Historical Quarterly* 22, 3 (1991): 327.
28 Calgary City Archives (CCA), City Clerk files, box 4, file 7, Chas. McMillan to Thomas Kennedy, 24 Aug. 1900; box 11, file 97, C.H. Mohr to President of the Business Men's Association, 3 Dec. 1906; box 4, file 8, M. Liss and N. Bell to Mayor, 4 April 1901.
29 Gilbert A. Stelter, 'The City-Building Process in Canada,' in *Shaping the Urban Landscape: Aspects of the Canadian City-Building Process,* ed. Gilbert A. Stelter and Alan F.J. Artibise (Ottawa: Carleton University Press, 1982), 1-29; Dean Beeby, 'Industrial Strategy and Manufacturing Growth in Toronto, 1880-1910,' *Ontario History* 76, 3 (1984): 199-232.
30 *Prosperous Calgary* (Calgary: n.p., 1908), n.p.
31 Paul Voisey, 'Boosting the Small Prairie Town, 1904-1931: An Example from Southern Alberta,' in *Town and City,* ed. Artibise, 147-76.
32 Ian Drummond, 'Financial Institutions in Historical Perspective,' *Canadian Banker* 74 (1967): 150-8.
33 *Monetary Times,* 16 June 1905.
34 *Calgary Herald,* 20 July 1912, 11 Jan. 1904; *Industrial Canada,* March 1913.
35 Frank W. Field, *Capital Investments in Canada* (Montreal: Monetary Times, 1912), 74. See also Matthew Simon, 'New British Investment in Canada, 1865-1914,' *Canadian Journal of Economics* 3, 2 (1970): 238-54.
36 *Monetary Times,* 28 Sept. 1907.
37 Henry C. Klassen, 'Family Businesses in Calgary to 1939,' in *Citymakers: Calgarians After the Frontier,* ed. Max Foran and Sheilagh Jameson (Calgary: Historical Society of Alberta, Chinook Country Chapter, 1987), 303-19.
38 *Calgary Herald,* 11 Jan. 1904, 29 Oct. 1906.
39 *Census of Canada* (1911), 3: 322.
40 See Anna Bezanson, 'Skill,' *Quarterly Journal of Economics* 36 (1922): 626-45; George E. Barnett, *Chapters on Machinery and Labor* (1926; reprint, Carbondale: Southern Illinois University Press, 1969). More recently, see the essays in Patrick Joyce, ed., *The Historical Meanings of Work* (Cambridge: Cambridge University Press, 1987).
41 *Calgary Herald,* 14 July 1904; *The Story of Calgary* (Calgary: n.p., 1914), 46-7.
42 See Raphael Samuel, 'Workshop of the World: Steam Power and Hand Technology in Mid-Victorian Britain,' *History Workshop* 3 (1977): 6-72.
43 Details on Cushing's life and career are based on the following sources: Archibald Oswald MacRae, *History of the Province of Alberta: Biographical* (Canada: Western Canada History, 1912), 1: 486-8; B.M. Greene, ed., *Who's Who and Why* (Toronto: International Press, 1921), 468; *Prairie (Illustrated),* 18 April 1891; *Calgary Herald,* 12 April 1899, 20 April 1904, 9 Dec. 1904, 14 Jan. 1905, 12 March 1921; *City of Calgary Year Book* (1919), 6; 'A Western Manufactory,' in *Why Go to Canada* (Calgary: Calgary Herald, 1910), 15.
44 *Prairie (Illustrated),* 18 April 1891.
45 'A Western Manufactory,' 15; *Calgary Herald,* 19 Dec. 1904.
46 *Monetary Times,* 31 Oct. 1908.
47 *Calgary Herald,* 5 May 1906.
48 Ibid., 11 June 1924.
49 David Bercuson, *Fools and Wise Men: The Rise and Fall of the One Big Union* (Toronto: McGraw-Hill Ryerson, 1978), 21.

Chapter 2: Social Divisions and Class Disposition

1 E.P. Thompson, 'The Peculiarities of the English,' reprinted in his *The Poverty of Theory and Other Essays* (London: Merlin, 1978), 295. See also Ira Katznelson, 'Working-Class Formation: Constructing Cases and Comparisons,' in *Working-Class Formation: Nineteenth-Century Patterns in Western Europe and the United States,* ed. Ira Katznelson and Aristide R. Zolberg (Princeton: Princeton University Press, 1986), 3-44; Jacques Rancière, 'The Myth of the Artisan: Critical Reflections on a Category of Social History,' and responses by William H. Sewell and Christopher H. Johnson, *International Labor and Working Class History* 24 (1983): 1-25.

2 Michael Hanagan, 'New Perspectives on Class Formation: Culture, Reproduction, and Agency,' *Social Science History* 18, 1 (1994): 78.

3 Alice Kessler-Harris, 'Treating the Male as "Other": Redefining the Parameters of Labor History,' *Labor History* 34, 2-3 (1993): 192, 194. See also Harold Benenson, 'Victorian Sexual Ideology and Marx's Theory of the Working Class,' *International Labor and Working Class History* 25 (1984): 1-23, with responses from David Montgomery and Ellen Ross, ibid., 24-36.

4 Bettina Bradbury, *Working Families: Age, Gender, and Daily Survival in Industrializing Montreal* (Toronto: McClelland and Stewart, 1993), and 'Gender at Work at Home: Family Decision, the Labour Market and Girls' Contributions to the Family Economy,' in *Canadian and Australian Labour History: Towards a Comparative Perspective,* ed. Gregory S. Kealey and Greg Patmore (St John's: AASLH/CCLH, 1990), 119-40; Suzanne Morton, *Ideal Surroundings: Domestic Life in a Working-Class Suburb in the 1920s* (Toronto: University of Toronto Press, 1995); Joy Parr, *The Gender of Breadwinners: Women, Men, and Change in Two Industrial Towns, 1880-1950* (Toronto: University of Toronto Press, 1990). See also Neil Sutherland, '"We Always Had Things to Do": The Paid and Unpaid Work of Anglophone Children between the 1920s and the 1960s,' *Labour/Le Travail* 25 (1990): 105-41.

5 See Raphael Samuel, 'Workshop of the World: Steam Power and Hand Technology in Mid-Victorian Britain,' *History Workshop* 3 (1977): 6-72; Richard Edwards, *Contested Terrain: The Transformation of the Workplace in the Twentieth Century* (New York: Basic Books, 1979); David M. Gordon, Richard Edwards, and Michael Reich, *Segmented Work, Divided Workers: The Historical Transformation of Labor in the United States* (Cambridge: Cambridge University Press, 1982).

6 *Census of Canada* (1911), 4: 344.

7 This is discussed in Chapter 4.

8 *Census of Canada* (1911), 6: 342-50. On domestic servants, see Alice Kessler-Harris, *Out to Work: A History of Wage-Earning Women in the United States* (Oxford: Oxford University Press, 1982), 136-7.

9 *Census of Canada* (1911), 6: 342-50.

10 Whiting Williams, *Mainsprings of Men* (New York: Charles Scribner's Sons, 1925), 17-30.

11 The best discussion of this facet of working-class life is Bradbury, *Working Families,* especially 80-181.

12 Michael J. Piva, *The Condition of the Working Class in Toronto, 1900-1921* (Ottawa: University of Ottawa Press, 1979), 58. See also Joseph Harry Sutcliffe, 'Economic Background of the Winnipeg General Strike: Wages and Working Conditions' (MA thesis, University of Manitoba, 1972); Terry Copp, *The Anatomy of Poverty: The Condition of the Working Class in Montreal, 1897-1929* (Toronto: McClelland and Stewart, 1974), 30-43; Gordon Bertram and Michael B. Percy, 'Real Wage Trends in Canada, 1900-26: Some Provisional Estimates,' *Canadian Journal of Economics* 12, 2 (1979): 299-312; Michael J. Piva, 'Urban Working-Class Incomes and Real Incomes in 1921: A Comparative Analysis,' *Histoire sociale/Social History* 16, 32 (1983): 143-65; Edward J. Chambers, 'New Evidence on the Living Standards of Toronto Blue Collar Workers in the Pre-1914 Era,' ibid., 18, 36 (1985): 285-314, and 'Addendum on the Living Standards of Toronto Blue Collar Workers in the 1900-1914 Era,' ibid., 20, 40 (1987): 357-62; John Douglas Belshaw, 'The Standard of Living of British Miners on Vancouver Island, 1848-1900,' *BC Studies* 84 (1989-90): 37-64; David Gagan and Rosemary Gagan, 'Working-Class Standards of Living in Late-Victorian Urban Ontario: A Review of the Miscellaneous Evidence on the Quality of Material Life,' *Journal of the Canadian Historical Association* (1990): 171-93.

13 Canada, *Sessional Papers* 7 (1892): 129-30. Where food items for Calgary were not given, those for the Regina district are substituted. Ibid., 126.

14 Wage figures are based on Department of Labour, *Wages and Hours of Labour in Canada, 1901-1920* (Ottawa: J. de L. Taché, 1921). On the fight for shorter hours, see Bryan D. Palmer, *A Culture in Conflict: Skilled Workers and Industrial Capitalism in Hamilton, Ontario, 1860-1914* (Montreal: McGill-Queen's University Press, 1979), 131-52; John Battye, 'The Nine Hours Pioneers: The Genesis of the Canadian Labour Movement,' *Labour/Le Travailleur* 4 (1979): 25-56. Important discussions of the division between work time and 'free' time include E.J. Hobsbawm, 'Custom, Wages, and Work-load,' in his *Labouring Men: Studies in the History of Labour* (London: Weidenfeld and Nicolson, 1964), 344-70; E.P. Thompson, 'Time, Work-Discipline, and Industrial Capitalism,' reprinted in his *Customs in Common* (London: Merlin Press, 1991), 352-403; Richard Whipp, '"A Time to Every Purpose": An Essay on Time and Work,' in *The Historical Meanings of Work,* ed. Patrick Joyce (Cambridge: Cambridge University Press, 1987), 210-36; Tamara K. Hareven, *Family Time and Industrial Time: The Relationship between the Family and Work in a New England Industrial Community* (Cambridge: Cambridge University Press, 1982).

15 Department of Labour, *Board of Inquiry into Cost of Living: Report of Board* (Ottawa: J. de L. Taché, 1915), 1: 137, 141, 209, 210, 212.

16 Bradbury, *Working Families,* 115.

17 *Census of Canada* (1911), 6: 342-3. On social attitudes towards working women, see Sonya O. Rose, '"Manliness, Virtue, and Self-Respect": Gender Antagonism and Working-Class Respectability,' in her *Limited Livelihoods: Gender and Class in Nineteenth-Century England* (Berkeley: University of California Press, 1992), 126-53; Elizabeth Roberts, *Women's Work, 1840-1940* (London: Macmillan, 1988), 44-54; Joan Sangster, 'Canadian Working Women in the Twentieth Century,' in *Lectures in Canadian Labour and Working-Class History,* ed. W.J.C. Cherwinski and Gregory S. Kealey (St John's: CCLH/Hogtown Press, 1985), 60; Gail Cuthbert Brandt, '"Weaving it Together": Life Cycles and the Industrial Experience of Female Cotton Workers in Quebec, 1910-1950,' *Labour/Le Travailleur* 7 (1981): 113-26; Christina Burr, 'Defending "The Art Preservative": Class and Gender Relations in the Printing Trades Union, 1850-1914,' *Labour/Le Travail* 31 (1993): 47-74; Linda Kealey, *Enlisting Women for the Cause: Women, Labour, and the Left in Canada, 1890-1920* (Toronto: University of Toronto Press, 1998). On the question of the 'family wage,' see Jane Humphries, 'Class Struggle and the Persistence of the Working-Class Family,' *Cambridge Journal of Economics* 1 (1977): 241-58; Hilary Land, 'The Family Wage,' *Feminist Review* 6 (1980): 55-77; Michèle Barrett and Mary McIntosh, 'The "Family Wage": Some Problems for Socialists and Feminists,' *Capital and Class* 11 (Summer 1980): 5-72; Alice Kessler-Harris, *A Woman's Wage: Historical Meanings and Social Consequences* (Lexington: University of Kentucky Press, 1990).

18 *Census of Canada* (1911), 6: 342-33; Glenbow Museum Archives (GMA), M1883, City of Calgary Civic Government papers, file 213. See also Henry C. Klassen, 'In Search of Neglected and Delinquent Children: The Calgary Children's Aid Society, 1909-1920,' in *Town and City: Aspects of Western Canadian Urban Development,* ed. Alan F.J. Artibise (Regina: Canadian Plains Research Center, 1981), 375-92; John Bullen, 'Hidden Workers: Child Labour and the Family Economy in Late-Nineteenth-Century Urban Ontario,' *Labour/Le Travail* 18 (1986): 163-87; Bradbury, *Working Families,* 118-51, and 'Gender at Work at Home,' 119-40.

19 Bradbury, *Working Families,* 152-81.

20 *Calgary Herald,* 13 Feb. 1890; various interviews conducted by David Bright and Shane Carmody, deposited with GMA, RCT 879, as 'The Working People of Calgary Oral History Project' (1992).

21 Interviews conducted by David Bright and Shane Carmody; GMA, M3126, Ada Ryan papers, letter to unnamed cousin, 1962; Elsie Kneeshaw, 'As Memory Serves,' in *Reminiscences* (Calgary: Century Calgary Publications, 1975), 3-6.

22 *Calgary Herald,* 25 Feb. 1905; Calgary Civic Government papers, file 86. See also Bettina Bradbury, 'Pigs, Cows, and Boarders: Non-Wage Forms of Survival among Montreal Families, 1861-1891,' *Labour/Le Travail* 14 (1984): 9-46.

23 See Judy Bedford, 'Prostitution in Calgary, 1905-1914,' *Alberta History* 29, 2 (1981): 1-11; S.W. Horrall, 'The (Royal) North-West Mounted Police and Prostitution on the Canadian Prairies,' *Prairie Forum* 10, 1 (1985): 105-27; James H. Gray, *Red Lights on the Prairies* (Toronto: Macmillan, 1971), 149-83.
24 Calgary Police Archives, Charge Books, 1906-14.
25 GMA, M2201, Brotherhood of Locomotive Firemen & Enginemen, Local 635, minutes, 19 Jan. 1912, 2 Feb. 1912. See also David Bright, 'The Cop, the Chief, the Hooker, and Her Life,' *Alberta History* 45, 4 (1997): 16-26.
26 John Benson, *Entrepreneurism in Canada: A History of 'Penny Capitalists'* (Lewiston, NY: Edwin Mellen Press, 1992).
27 S.J. and H.S. Ferns, *Eighty-Five Years in Canada* (Winnipeg: Queenston House, 1978), 71.
28 GMA, M3973, George Gooderham interviews, file 7, interview with T.B. Riley.
29 GMA, M3978, Jack Hackman papers, 28. See also the failed attempts of Arthur Turner at penny capitalism, in GMA, M1255, Arthur J. Turner papers.
30 Benson, *Entrepreneurism in Canada,* 127-47, quote from 127.
31 *Calgary Herald,* 9 and 11 April 1904.
32 Bradbury, *Working Families,* 14.
33 Ibid., 215.
34 *Census of Canada* (1911), 1: 535.
35 Figures quoted in Max Foran, *Calgary: An Illustrated History* (Toronto: Lorimer, 1978), 174. See also J. Burgon Bickersteth, *The Land of Open Doors* (1914; reprint, Toronto: University of Toronto Press, 1976), ix-xix; Lewis H. Thomas, *The Making of a Socialist: The Recollections of T.C. Douglas* (Edmonton: University of Alberta Press, 1981), 12.
36 *Census of Canada* (1911), 6: 342-51. For discussion of this question, see Bryan D. Palmer, 'Most Uncommon Common Men: Craft and Culture in Historical Perspective,' *Labour/Le Travailleur* 1 (1976): 5-31, and Sonya O. Rose, '"Maintaining the Industrial Supremacy of the Country": Industrialists and Gendered Work,' in her *Limited Livelihoods,* 22-49.
37 Bradbury, 'Gender at Work,' 133.
38 For example, see *Calgary Herald,* 24 Aug. 1921, 26 Aug. 1921, 31 Aug. 1921, 4 Sept. 1921.
39 See Gita Sen, 'The Sexual Division of Labor and the Working-Class Family: Towards a Conceptual Synthesis of Class Relations and the Subordination of Women,' *Review of Radical Political Economics* 12, 2 (1980): 76-86.
40 Foran, *Calgary,* 174.
41 Howard Palmer, *Patterns of Prejudice: A History of Nativism in Alberta* (Toronto: McClelland and Stewart, 1982), 5-60. See also Ross McCormack, 'Cloth Caps and Jobs: The Ethnicity of English Immigrants in Canada, 1901-1914,' in *Ethnicity, Power, and Politics in Canada,* ed. Jorgen Dahlie and Tissa Fernando (Toronto: Methuen, 1981), 38-55. See also Allen Seager, 'Class, Ethnicity, and Politics in the Alberta Coalfields, 1905-1945,' in *'Struggle a Hard Battle': Essays on Working-Class Immigrants,* ed. Dirk Hoerder (De Kalb: Northern Illinois University Press, 1986), 304-24.
42 *Calgary Herald,* 7 May 1884.
43 Ibid., 24 Aug. 1892, 24 Jan. 1899, 24 Feb. 1899, 28 June 1904; *Nor'wester,* 28 March 1891; *Calgary Annual Report* (1913), 'Health Report'; National Archives of Canada (NAC), Records of the Immigration Branch, vol. 403, file 585245, part 1, Mayor W.F. Orr to Hon. J.M. Daly, 1 June 1894.
44 *Eye Opener,* 4 Oct. 1910, 14 Oct. 1910. See also the letter from 'Mother' calling for a ban of Chinese laundries, *Calgary Herald,* 3 March 1903. See also Gillian Creese, 'Class, Ethnicity, and Conflict: The Case of Chinese and Japanese Immigrants, 1880-1923,' in *Workers, Capital, and the State in British Columbia: Selected Readings,* ed. Rennie Warburton and David Coburn (Vancouver: UBC Press, 1988), 55-85.
45 NAC, Wilfrid Laurier papers, microfilm 905, J. Dawson to Wilfrid Laurier, 6 June 1911; City Clerk papers, box 132, file 997, petition dated 31 March 1920, outgoing correspondence from City Clerk Charles Miller, dated 13 April 1920. For a contemporary comment on the question of Chinese labour, see C.E. Fryer, 'The Opposition to Oriental Labour,' *Journal of the Canadian Bankers' Association* 15, 3 (1908): 241-9.
46 Foran, *Calgary,* 178.

47 *Albertan,* 6 April 1911, 20 Sept. 1906.

48 For example, see Christopher McCall, *Class, Ethnicity, and Social Inequality* (Montreal: McGill-Queen's University Press, 1990); Bruno Ramirez, 'Ethnic Studies and Working-Class History,' *Labour/Le Travail* 19 (1987): 45-8; A. Margeurite Cassin and Alison I. Griffith, 'Class and Ethnicity: Producing the Difference That Counts,' *Canadian Ethnic Studies* 13, 1 (1981): 109-29; James R. Barrett, 'Unity and Fragmentation: Class, Race, and Ethnicity on Chicago's South Side, 1900-1922,' *Journal of Social History* 18, 1 (1984): 37-55.

49 Palmer, *Patterns of Prejudice,* 46. On the relationship between organized labour and ethnic minorities, see Robert Asher, 'Union Nativism and the Immigrant Response,' *Labor History* 23, 2 (1982): 325-48; Barrett, 'Unity and Fragmentation'; John Bodnar, *Immigration and Industrialization: Ethnicity in an American Mill Town, 1870-1940* (Pittsburgh: University of Pittsburgh Press, 1977), 76-101.

50 GMA, M7070, International Typographical Union Local 449, minutes (ITU mins.), 30 May 1905, 25 July 1905; *Calgary Herald,* 3 March 1905.

51 Wilfrid Laurier papers, vol. 483, p. 130300, CTLC to Wilfrid Laurier, 14 Oct. 1907.

52 *Labour Gazette* 12 (1911-2): 39; GMA, M2198, Bricklayers and Stonemasons International Union Local 2, minutes (BSMIU mins.), 20 March 1907, 3 April 1907; GMA, M4743, Calgary Trades and Labour Council, minutes (CTLC mins), file 2, 6 March 1914.

53 GMA, M2193/M2937, American Federation of Musicians Local 53, minutes (AFM mins), 9 Sept. 1906.

54 *Calgary Herald,* 7 Aug. 1908.

55 Richard Jules Oestreicher, *Solidarity and Fragmentation: Working People and Class Consciousness in Detroit, 1875-1900* (Urbana: University of Illinois Press, 1989), 211.

56 Bryan Palmer, '"What the Hell": Or Some Comments on Class Formation and Cultural Reproduction,' in *Popular Cultures and Political Practices,* ed. Richard B. Gruneau (Toronto: Garamond Press, 1988), 38.

57 Herbert G. Gutman, 'Protestantism and the American Labor Movement,' in his *Work, Culture, and Society in Industrializing America* (New York: Alfred A. Knopf, 1977), 107; Bruce C. Nelson, 'Revival and Upheaval: Religion, Irreligion, and Chicago's Working Class in 1886,' *Journal of Social History* 25, 2 (1991): 233-53.

58 GMA, M1363, Calgary Central United Church papers, box 8, file 97, Annual Report, 1911.

59 Foran, *Calgary,* 178.

60 Palmer, *Culture in Conflict,* 45; Gregory S. Kealey, *Toronto Workers Respond to Industrial Capitalism, 1867-1892* (1980; reprint, Toronto: University of Toronto Press, 1991), 98-123. For a critique of Palmer's research in this respect, see David Bercuson, 'Through the Looking Glass of Culture: An Essay on the New Labour History and Working-Class Culture in Recent Canadian Historical Writing,' *Labour/Le Travailleur* 7 (1981): 102-3.

61 David A. Wilson, *The Irish in Canada* (Ottawa: Canadian Historical Association, 1989), 17. The 1911 census counts 4,200 Catholics in Calgary in 1911, of whom 800 were likely to have been French or Italian. Assuming the bulk of the remaining 3,400 were Irish in background, this suggests a rough parity with Protestant Irish.

62 *Calgary Herald,* 17 March 1890, 8 Feb. 1893; *Albertan,* 21 Feb. 1902, 12 July 1906, 13 July 1906, 13 June 1907. See also Hereward Senior, 'Orangemen on the Frontier: The Prairies and British Columbia,' in *The Untold Story: The Irish in Canada,* ed. Robert O'Driscoll and Lorna Reynolds (Toronto: Celtic Arts of Canada, 1988), 1: 417-22.

63 Jean R. Burnet with Howard Palmer, *'Coming Canadians': An Introduction to a History of Canada's People* (Toronto: McClelland and Stewart, 1988), 125-50.

64 *Henderson's Calgary City Directory* (n.p., 1906). See also 'The Lutheran Legacy,' in *The Search for Souls* (Calgary: Century Calgary Publications, 1975), 287-95, and 'Ukrainian Rite Catholic Church,' ibid., 629-42.

65 Lynne Marks, 'The Knights of Labor and the Salvation Army: Religion and Working-Class Culture in Ontario, 1882-1890,' *Labour/Le Travail* 28 (1991): 89-128, and 'The "Hallelujah Lasses": Working-Class Women in the Salvation Army in English Canada,' in *Gender Conflicts: New Essays in Women's History,* ed. Franca Iacovetta and Mariana Valverde (Toronto: University of Toronto Press, 1992), 67-117.

66 Phyllis D. Airhart, *Serving the Present Age: Revivalism, Progressivism, and the Methodist Tradition in Canada* (Montreal: McGill-Queen's University Press, 1992), 72.
67 *Calgary Tribune,* 19 Aug. 1887; *Calgary Herald,* 26 Aug. 1887; William E. Mann, *Sect, Cult, and Church in Alberta* (Toronto: University of Toronto Press, 1955), 9; *Census of Canada* (1911), 2: 149.
68 Trades and Labour Congress of Canada, *Annual Report of Proceedings,* 1908, 'Report of Alberta Executive.' For background on this question, see Desmond Glynn, '"Exporting Outcast London": Assisted Emigration to Canada, 1886-1914,' *Histoire sociale/Social History* 15, 29 (1982): 209-38.
69 BSMIU mins, 30 Oct. 1908; AFM mins, 11 Feb. 1908; *Albertan,* 28 Sept. 1905, 1 Oct. 1905, 5 Oct. 1905.
70 Gregory S. Kealey, 'Labour and Working-Class History in Canada: Prospects in the 1980s,' *Labour/Le Travailleur* 7 (1981): 89.

Chapter 3: Class, Culture, and Politics

1 Bryan D. Palmer, *A Culture in Conflict: Skilled Workers and Industrial Capitalism in Hamilton, Ontario, 1860-1914* (Montreal: McGill-Queen's University Press, 1979), 39.
2 Standard works include E.P. Thompson, *The Making of the English Working Class* (1963; reprint, Harmondsworth: Penguin, 1980); Herbert G. Gutman, *Work, Culture, and Society in Industrializing America: Essays in American Working-Class and Social History* (New York: Pantheon, 1976); Raymond Williams, *Culture and Society, 1780-1950* (Harmondsworth: Penguin, 1958), and *The Long Revolution* (Harmondsworth: Penguin, 1961). For a valuable review of this subject, see Tony Bennett, Graham Martin, Colin Mercer, and Janet Woollacott, eds., *Culture, Ideology, and Social Process: A Reader* (London: B.T. Batsford, 1981).
3 Williams, *The Long Revolution,* 57.
4 Thompson, *Making of the English Working Class,* 9, 10, 11.
5 Bryan D. Palmer, *Working-Class Experience: Rethinking the History of Canadian Labour, 1800-1991,* 2nd ed. (Toronto: McClelland and Stewart, 1992), 16. See also Bryan D. Palmer, *Descent into Discourse: The Reification of Language and the Writing of Social History* (Philadelphia: Temple University Press, 1990), especially 120-44, and *Capitalism Comes to the Backcountry: The Goodyear Invasion of Napanee* (Toronto: Between the Lines, 1994).
6 Palmer, *Working-Class Experience,* 21-2.
7 Mark Leier, *Red Flags and Red Tape: The Making of a Labour Bureaucracy* (Toronto: University of Toronto Press, 1995), 108.
8 Ibid., 10-1; Ian McKay, 'Historians, Anthropology, and the Concept of Culture,' *Labour/Le Travailleur* 8/9 (Autumn/Spring 1981/2): 24.
9 Gary Teeple, *Globalization and the Decline of Social Reform* (Toronto: Garamond Press, 1995), 72.
10 *Albertan,* 20 Jan. 1912, 24 Jan. 1902, 20 March 1906.
11 Leier, *Red Flags and Red Tape,* 108.
12 *Calgary Herald,* 25 Feb. 1903.
13 Ibid., 30 March 1908, 13 August 1908, 19 Aug. 1908; *Albertan,* 30 March 1908; Glenbow Museum Archives (GMA), M2193/M2397, American Federation of Musicians, Local 53, minutes (AFM mins), 24 Dec. 1905.
14 *Calgary Herald,* 21 Feb. 1903. On middle-class culture in Calgary, see Henry C. Klassen, 'Life in Frontier Calgary,' in *Western Canada: Past and Present,* ed. A.W. Rasporich (Calgary: McClelland and Stewart West, 1975), 42-57.
15 *Calgary Herald,* 17 March 1904.
16 For example, see Palmer, *Culture in Conflict,* and his 'Most Uncommon Common Men: Craft and Culture in Historical Perspective,' *Labour/Le Travailleur* 1 (1976): 5-31; Peter DeLottinville, 'Joe Beef of Montreal: Working-Class Culture and the Tavern,' ibid. 8-9 (1981-2): 9-40; Judith Fingard, *Jack in Port: Sailortowns of Eastern Canada* (Toronto: University of Toronto Press, 1982), 82-139; Leier, *Red Flags and Red Tape,* 108-24.
17 Richard C. Helmes, 'Ideology and Social Control in Canadian Sport: A Theoretical Review,' in *Sport in the Sociocultural Process,* 3rd ed., ed. Marie Hart and Susan Birrell

(Dubuque, IA: W.C. Brown, 1981), 209. See also Gary Cross, *A Social History of Leisure since 1600* (N.p.: Venture Publishing, 1990).

18 Ross McKibbin, 'Why Was There No Marxism in Great Britain?' *English Historical Review* 99, 391 (1984): 306-7.

19 Palmer, *Culture in Conflict,* 58.

20 Alan Metcalfe, *Canada Learns to Play: The Emergence of Organized Sport, 1807-1914* (Toronto: McClelland and Stewart, 1987), 13-4, 83-4; Colin D. Howell, 'Baseball, Class, and Community in the Maritime Provinces, 1870-1910,' *Histoire sociale/Social History* 22, 44 (1989): 265-86 and *Northern Sandlots: A Social History of Maritime Baseball* (Toronto: University of Toronto Press, 1995). For an overview of the subject, see Bruce Kidd, *The Struggle for Canadian Sport* (Toronto: University of Toronto Press, 1996), especially 146-83.

21 Other useful studies include Steven Gelber, 'Working at Playing: The Culture of the Workplace and the Rise of Baseball,' *Journal of Social History* 16 (1983): 3-20; Melvin L. Adelman, 'Baseball, Business, and the Work Place: Gelber's Thesis Reexamined,' ibid. 23, 2 (1989): 285-301; Richard Gruneau, *Class, Sports, and Social Development* (Amherst: University of Massachusetts Press, 1983); Allen Guttman, *From Ritual to Record: The Nature of Modern Sports* (New York: Columbia University Press, 1978); Ian Day, *'Sorting the Men Out from the Boys': Masculinity, a Missing Link in the Sociology of Sport* (Sheffield: PAVIC, 1990).

22 *Calgary Herald,* 17 June 1884, 22 July 1884, 18 Aug. 1890, 25 Aug. 1890, 20 Oct. 1890, 22 June 1891, 29 June 1891, 6 July 1891, 27 July 1891, 12 April 1894, 8 May 1896, 13 May 1901, 26 July 1904; *Prairie (Illustrated),* 13 Dec. 1890, 16 Dec. 1890. See also William M. McLennan, *Sport in Early Calgary* (Calgary: Fort Brisebois Publishing, 1983).

23 Palmer, *Culture in Conflict,* 58.

24 *Calgary Herald,* 22 July 1884. See Keith A.P. Sandiford, 'Cricket and the Victorian Society,' *Journal of Social History* 16 (Winter 1983): 311.

25 *Calgary Herald,* 17 June 1884, 22 July 1884, 13 May 1901, 28 May 1903; *Prairie (Illustrated),* 16 Dec. 1890. Occupations of members of the Calgary Cricket Club are from *Gronlund's Calgary City Directory* (n.p., 1902), while details on Worsley may be found in Henry C. Klassen, '*The Bond of Brotherhood* and Calgary Workingmen,' in A.W. Rasporich and Henry C. Klassen, *Frontier Calgary: Town, City and Region* (Calgary: McClelland and Stewart West, 1975), 267-71.

26 Cf. Leier, *Red Flags and Red Tape,* 121-2. See also Metcalfe, *Canada Learns to Play,* 133-80; Morris K. Mott, 'The Problems of Professionalism: The Manitoba Amateur Athletic Association and the Fight against Pro Hockey, 1904-1911,' in *Winter Sports in the West,* ed. E.A. Corbet and A.W. Rasporich (Calgary: Historical Society of Alberta, 1990), 132-42; Joan Sangster, 'The Softball Solution: Female Workers, Male Managers and the Operation of Paternalism at Westclox, 1923-1960,' *Labour/Le Travail* 32 (1993): 167-99.

27 Palmer, *Culture in Conflict,* 41. John Cumbler makes similar claims in *Working-Class Community in Industrial America: Work, Leisure, and Struggle in Two Industrial Cities, 1880-1930* (Westport, CT: Greenwood Press, 1979), 44-6.

28 Mary Ann Clawson, *Constructing Brotherhood: Class, Gender, and Fraternalism* (Princeton: Princeton University Press, 1989), 107-8. See also Alice Kessler-Harris, 'Treating the Male as "Other": Re-defining the Parameters of Labor History,' *Labor History* 34, 2-3 (1993): 202.

29 *Henderson's Calgary City Directory* (n.p., 1914), 147-9.

30 GMA, Margaret Maw, 'George Murdoch Biography, 1850-1910' (unpublished paper, 1968), 4; Patricia Jasen, 'Oddfellows in Early Calgary,' *Alberta History* 35, 3 (1987): 8-12.

31 Quoted in Jasen, 'Oddfellows,' 10. See also *Constitution of the Grand Encampment of Manitoba IOOF and of Subordinate Encampments* (n.p., 1891).

32 *Calgary Herald,* 13 Jan. 1892, 22 Jan. 1901; *Henderson's Northwest Territories Gazetteer and Directory* (n.p., 1892); ibid. (1894).

33 Clawson, *Constructing Brotherhood,* 6.

34 Dr John S. King, *The Early History of the Sons of England Benevolent Society* (Toronto: Thos. Moore, 1891), 10-33.

35 *Calgary Herald,* 5 Aug. 1890.
36 Ibid., 5 Aug. 1890, 6 Jan. 1903; GMA, M1660, Sons of England Benevolent Society, United Roses Lodge (SOEBS), Charter Member List and History; *Henderson's Northwest Territories Gazetteer and Directory* (n.p., 1890-8).
37 Quoted in Palmer, *Culture in Conflict,* 40.
38 *Calgary Herald,* 17 June 1891, 17 June 1892; *Subordinate Lodge Constitution: General Laws and Standing Regulations* (Woodstock: Sentinel-Review Print, 1890).
39 *Calgary Optimist,* 27 Nov. 1909.
40 Clawson, *Constructing Brotherhood,* 109.
41 See John Patrick Diggins, 'Comrades and Citizens: New Mythologies in American Historiography,' *American Historical Review* 90, 3 (1985): 614-39.
42 *Calgary Herald,* 25 May 1899, 23 May 1901, 24 May 1902, 23 May 1903, 26 May 1903, 23 May 1904, 26 May 1904, 23 May 1905, 25 May 1905, 23 May 1907, 25 May 1909, 24 May 1913.
43 See David Cannadine and Elizabeth Hammerton, 'Conflict and Consensus on a Ceremonial Occasion: The Diamond Jubilee in Cambridge in 1897,' *Historical Journal* 24 (1981): 111-46; and David Cannadine, 'The Context, Performance, and Meaning of Ritual: The British Monarchy and the "Invention of Tradition," c. 1820-1977,' in *The Invention of Tradition,* ed. Eric Hobsbawm and Terence Ranger (Cambridge: Cambridge University Press, 1983), 101-64.
44 *Calgary Herald,* 24 May 1902.
45 GMA, M273, John Gillespie diary, various entries.
46 J.A. Irvine, *Souvenir of the Dominion Day Pageant* (Calgary: J.A. Irvine, 1908).
47 Richard Hoggart, *The Uses of Literacy* (1957; reprint, London: Penguin, 1992), 103.
48 For background details on Labour Day, see Leier, *Red Flags and Red Tape,* 108-11; Michael Kazin and Steven J. Ross, 'America's Labor Day: The Dilemma of a Workers' Celebration,' *Journal of American History* 78, 4 (1992): 1294-1319.
49 Palmer, *Culture in Conflict,* 57-8.
50 *Calgary Herald,* 8 Sept. 1896.
51 *Calgary Herald,* 2 Sept. 1902; *Albertan,* 6 Sept. 1902.
52 *Albertan,* 3 Sept. 1907.
53 *Calgary Herald,* 4 Sept. 1906, 6 Sept. 1910, 5 Sept. 1911; *Albertan,* 4 Sept. 1906, 6 Sept. 1910.
54 *Albertan,* 2 Sept. 1913, 7 Sept. 1914.
55 Ibid., 6 Sept. 1909.
56 Ibid., 6 Sept. 1910; *Calgary Herald,* 6 Sept. 1910.
57 *Albertan,* 3 Sept. 1907. The Glenbow Museum Archives contain a number of photographs of Labour Day parades from this period.
58 McKibbin, 'Why Was There No Marxism?' 306.
59 GMA, M2198, Bricklayers and Stonemasons International Union, Local 2, minutes (BSMIU mins), 6 Sept. 1907; *Calgary Herald,* 3 Sept. 1907.
60 BSMIU mins, 12 July 1907, 14 Aug. 1908, 2 Oct. 1908, 11 June 1909.
61 GMA, M7070, International Typographical Union, Local 449, minutes (ITU mins), 7 Aug. 1912; GMA, M2214/M2215, International Brotherhood of Electrical Workers, Local 410, minutes (IBEW mins), 11 Aug. 1911, 15 Aug. 1911, 18 Aug. 1911; GMA, M4743, Calgary Trades and Labour Council, minutes (CTLC mins), file 4, 21 July 1916, 18 Oct. 1918.
62 *Albertan,* 5 Sept. 1911.
63 A. Ross McCormack, *Reformers, Rebels, and Revolutionaries: The Western Canadian Radical Movement, 1899-1919* (1977; reprint, Toronto: University of Toronto Press, 1991).
64 For a useful discussion of partyism among the working class, albeit within a different context, see Gregory S. Kealey, *Toronto Workers Respond to Industrial Capitalism, 1867-1892* (1980; reprint, Toronto: University of Toronto Press, 1991), 216-36.
65 *Calgary Herald,* 21 May 1885, 24 July 1886, 22 April 1891, 25 June 1896; Max Foran, *Calgary: An Illustrated History* (Toronto: Lorimer, 1978), 60. Until 1903, Alberta was a single federal constituency.

66 *Calgary Herald,* 5 Sept. 1901, 21 Feb. 1902, 4 Nov. 1904, 3 Oct. 1909, 14 Sept. 1911, 22 Sept. 1911, 31 Oct. 1911; *Albertan,* 2 Feb. 1911, 5 Sept. 1911, 12 Sept. 1911. For the broader context of labour politics in this period, see Bernard Ostry, 'Conservatives, Liberals, and Labour in the 1880's,' *Canadian Journal of Economics and Political Science* 27, 2 (1961): 141-61.

67 *Calgary Herald,* 17 Oct. 1904, 18 Oct. 1904; *Albertan,* 17 Oct. 1904.

68 Trades and Labour Congress of Canada, *Annual Report of Proceedings* (n.p., 1907), 24.

69 *Albertan,* 14 Sept. 1911, 15 Sept. 1911.

70 *Calgary News-Telegram,* 17 April 1913; BSMIU mins, 25 April 1913.

71 Craig Heron, 'Labourism and the Canadian Working Class,' *Labour/Le Travail* 13 (1984): 45.

72 Leier, *Red Flags and Red Tape,* 92-3.

73 Ibid., 98.

74 James Naylor, *The New Democracy: Challenging the Social Order in Industrial Ontario, 1914-1925* (Toronto: University of Toronto Press, 1991), 76.

75 Heron, 'Labourism and the Canadian Working Class,' 70.

76 For details of Calgary's first Labour Party, see David Bright, 'Bonds of Brotherhood? The Experiences of Labour in Calgary, 1903-1919' (MA thesis, University of Calgary, 1990), 71-5. See also Errol Black and Tom Mitchell, 'Labour in Brandon Civic Politics: A Long View,' *Manitoba History* 23 (Spring 1992): 3; and Tom Mitchell, '"A Square Deal for All and No Railroading". Labour and Politics in Brandon,' *Prairie Forum* 15, 1 (1990): 47-8.

77 Sources on Brocklebank's life are C.W. Parker, ed., *Who's Who and Why* (Toronto: Canadian Press Association, Ltd., 1912), 2: 61; *Calgary News-Telegram,* 7 July 1916; *Calgary Herald,* 29 Jan. 1918.

78 See John English, *The Decline of Politics: The Conservatives and the Party System, 1901-1920* (Toronto: University of Toronto Press, 1977), 106-22.

79 *Calgary Herald,* 10 Jan. 1903.

80 Brocklebank had beaten the socialist James Worsley in the candidacy election by seventy-two votes. Ibid., 6 Nov. 1903, 27 April 1904.

81 Ibid., 17 Oct. 1904, 4 Nov. 1904.

82 Ibid., 5 Dec. 1904, 13 Dec. 1904.

83 *Albertan,* 20 March 1906, 8 Aug. 1906. For Calgary union opposition to Carnegie's philanthropy, see ITU mins, 24 Feb. 1906; BSMIU mins, 3 April 1907.

84 *Albertan,* 14 Nov. 1906, 17 Nov. 1906, 20 Nov. 1906, 4 Dec. 1906, 10 Dec. 1906.

85 *Calgary Herald,* 1 Feb. 1907, 2 Dec. 1907, 26 Oct. 1908, 2 Sept. 1909, 3 Sept. 1909; *Albertan,* 27 Feb. 1907, 15 May 1907.

86 *Albertan,* 28 Feb. 1902, 4 March 1902. On the CSL, see Palmer, *Working-Class Experience,* 181.

87 *Calgary Herald,* 16 Aug. 1948.

88 *Albertan,* 25 Jan. 1908, 27 Jan. 1908, 16 Jan. 1908, 20 April 1908; *Calgary Herald,* 22 Feb. 1908, 1 March 1908, 8 March 1908, 11 March 1908, 20 March 1908, 29 March 1908. See also Nicholas Fillmore, *Maritime Radical: The Life and Times of Roscoe Fillmore* (Toronto: Between the Lines, 1992), 37-41; W.J.C. Cherwinski, 'Honoré Joseph Jaxon, Agitator, Disturber, Producer of Plans to Make Men Think, and Chronic Objector ...,' *Canadian Historical Review* 46, 2 (1965): 122-33; Donald B. Smith, 'Honoré Joseph Jaxon: A Man Who Lived for Others,' *Saskatchewan History* 34, 2 (1981): 81-101; Smith, 'Rip Van Jaxon: The Return of Riel's Secretary in 1884-1885 to the Canadian West, 1907-1909,' in *1885 and After: Native Society in Transition,* ed. F. Laurie Barron and James B. Waldram (Regina: Canadian Pains Research Center, 1985), 211-23.

89 Public Archives of Alberta, 80.218, Warren Caragata research papers, box 2, Fred S. Faulkner to Florence L. Riley (n.d.); *Albertan,* 25 Jan. 1908; Fillmore, *Maritime Radical,* 38.

90 *Albertan,* 7 Sept. 1908, 28 Oct. 1908; *Calgary Herald,* 28 Oct. 1908; McCormack, *Reformers, Rebels, and Revolutionaries,* 64; Kenneth A. Wark, *A Report on Alberta Elections, 1905-1982* (Edmonton: n.p., 1983), 22-3.

91 *Calgary Herald,* 22 Sept. 1911, 25 March 1913, 26 March 1913, 4 April 1913, 10 April 1913, 18 April 1913; *Albertan,* 25 March 1913; Wark, *Alberta Elections,* 25.

92 For example, see Hon. J.W. Longley, 'Socialism: Its Truths and Errors,' *Canadian Magazine* 6, 4 (1896): 297-304; Hugh A. Dempsey, ed., 'Confessions of a Calgary Stenographer,' *Alberta History* 36, 2 (1988): 9. See also Paul W. Fox, 'Early Socialism in Canada,' in *The Political Process in Canada,* ed. J.H. Aitchison (Toronto: University of Toronto Press, 1963), 79-98, and McCormack, *Reformers, Rebels, and Revolutionaries,* 71-6.

93 John Burgon Bickersteth, *The Land of Open Doors* (1914; reprint, Toronto: University of Toronto Press, 1976), 62.

Chapter 4: Unions and Strikes

1 *Albertan,* 6 June 1909.

2 H.C. Pentland, 'The Development of a Capitalistic Labour Market in Canada,' *Canadian Journal of Economics and Political Science* 24, 4 (1959): 450. For a discussion of Pentland's approach, see Paul Deprez, 'Pentland's Scarcity of Labour and the Industrial Revolution,' *Canadian Journal of Political and Social Theory* 3, 2 (1979): 95-100, and Alan Greer, 'Wage Labour and the Transition to Capitalism: A Critique of Pentland,' *Labour/Le Travail* 15 (1985): 7-22.

3 *Calgary Herald,* 10 Sept. 1884, 7 May 1885, 22 July 1897; Hugh A. Dempsey, ed., 'Calgary and the Riel Rebellion,' *Alberta History* 3, 2 (1985): 7-18. See also John Lutz, 'After the Fur Trade: The Aboriginal Labouring Class of British Columbia, 1849-1890,' *Journal of the Canadian Historical Association* (1992): 69-93.

4 See Louis A. Knafla, 'Violence on the Western Canadian Frontier: A Historical Perspective,' in *Violence in Canada: Sociopolitical Perspectives,* ed. Jeffrey Ian Ross (Don Mills, ON: Oxford University Press, 1995), 10-39.

5 *Calgary Herald,* 19 Dec. 1891; Canada, *Sessional Papers* 15 (1895), 'Annual Report of Inspector Z.T. Wood, (1894),' 146. See E.J. Hobsbawm, 'The Machine Breakers,' in his *Labouring Men: Studies in the History of Labour* (London: Weidenfeld and Nicolson, 1964), 5-22.

6 The standard work on the Knights of Labor in Canada is Gregory S. Kealey and Bryan D. Palmer, *Dreaming of What Might Be: The Knights of Labor in Ontario, 1880-1900* (Toronto: New Hogtown Press, 1982).

7 *Calgary Herald,* 31 Dec. 1886; Provincial Archives of Alberta (PAA), Lorne Thompson research notes, box 2, Eugene Forsey to Lorne Thompson, 23 Nov. 1965.

8 Gregory S. Kealey, 'Work Control, the Labour Process, and Nineteenth-Century Canadian Printers,' in *On the Job: Confronting the Labour Process in Canada,* ed. Craig Heron and Robert Storey (Montreal: McGill-Queen's University Press, 1986), 95.

9 *Calgary Herald,* 4 May 1892; *Calgary Tribune,* 4 May 1892; *Sessional Papers* 6 (1891), 87; 7 (1892), 129.

10 *Calgary Herald,* 9 May 1892. Unfortunately, no record exists of the strike's outcome.

11 Elizabeth Ann Taraska, 'The Calgary Craft Union Movement' (MA thesis, University of Calgary, 1975), 13-28. See also J.H. Tuck, 'The United Brotherhood of Railway Employees in Western Canada, 1898-1905,' *Labour/Le Travailleur* 11 (1983): 63-88.

12 *Rules of the Calgary Trades and Labour Council,* rev. ed. (Calgary: n.p., 1911).

13 Thomas B. Riley, 'Sketch of Trade Unionism in Calgary,' *Alberta Labor News,* 'Labor Annual,' 3 Sept. 1921; Glenbow Museum Archives (GMA), M3973, George Gooderham interviews, file 7, interview with Thomas B. Riley.

14 For example, see *Calgary Herald,* 25 Oct. 1902.

15 Ibid., 22 Feb. 1905; 'Labour Annual,' 3 Sept. 1921; Trades and Labour Congress of Canada, *Annual Report* (1910), 37.

16 *Labour Gazette* 8 (1907-8), 66; 11 (1910-1), 1090.

17 Ibid. 7 (1907-8), 980-3; 9 (1909), 963; 10 (1910-1), 998-1,000. On the local debate over technical education, see *Albertan,* 22 Oct. 1910, 7 Oct. 1911, 5 Oct. 1912.

18 *Census of Canada* (1911), 6: 342. This calculation excludes agricultural workers, owners, managers, foremen, superintendents, government officials, and professionals, few of whom were potential union members. Their inclusion would bring the proportion of unionized workers to roughly 22 percent.

19 Jonathan Zeitlin, '"Rank and Filism" in British Labour History: A Critique,' *International Review of Social History* 34 (1989): 60-1. See also Leo Panitch and Donald Swartz, *The*

Assault on Trade Union Freedoms: From Wage Controls to Social Contract (Toronto: Garamond Press, 1993), 7-43; and Bob Russell, *Back to Work? Labour, State, and Industrial Relations in Canada* (Scarborough, ON: Nelson, 1990).

20 For example, Taraska, 'Calgary Craft Union Movement,' 1; Bryan D. Palmer, *Working-Class Experience: Rethinking the History of Canadian Labour, 1800-1991,* 2nd ed. (Toronto: McClelland and Stewart, 1992), 190.

21 For example, Bryan D. Palmer, *A Culture in Conflict: Skilled Workers and Industrial Capitalism in Hamilton, Ontario, 1860-1914* (Montreal: McGill-Queen's University Press, 1979); Gregory S. Kealey, *Toronto Workers Respond to Industrial Capitalism, 1867-1892* (1980; reprint, Toronto: University of Toronto, 1991); Ian McKay, *The Craft Transformed* (Halifax: Holdfast Press, 1985).

22 *Census of Canada* (1911), 6: 342-6. The census identifies 436 bricklayers and stonemasons, 1,430 carpenters, and 268 engravers and printers.

23 R.J. Brown, 'Sixty Years in the I.T.U.,' in *Calgary Typographical Union No. 449, 1902-1952* (n.p., n.d.); 'Typos Are Strong,' in *Souvenir Program and Union Directory: Official Program and Souvenir of Labor Day 1914* (Calgary: Calgary Trades and Labor Council, 1914). See also David Bright, 'A Lack of Brotherly Love: The Printers' Conflict in Calgary, 1935,' *Prairie Forum* 19, 2 (1994): 208-12; and Kealey, 'Nineteenth-Century Canadian Printers,' 83-97.

24 Canada, Department of Labour, *Wages and Hours of Labour in Canada, 1901-1920* (Ottawa: J. de L. Taché, 1921); Department of Labour, *Board of Inquiry into Cost of Living: Report of the Board* (1915), 1: 209-12, 1141.

25 Brown, 'Sixty Years in the I.T.U.'

26 GMA, M7070, International Typographical Union, Local 449, minutes (ITU mins), 26 Aug. 1902, 27 Dec. 1904, 3 Jan. 1905, 14 Feb. 1905, 4 Aug. 1905; 1914 report appears in Brown, 'Typos Are Strong.'

27 Sally Zerker, *The Rise and Fall of the Toronto Typographical Union, 1832-1972: A Case Study of Foreign Domination* (Toronto: University of Toronto Press, 1982), 9.

28 *Calgary Herald,* 8 April 1908. Calgary printers' reputation as labour aristocrats drew comment earlier, in *Calgary Tribune,* 16 March 1982.

29 ITU mins, 28 Oct. 1902, 29 March 1903, 3 Jan. 1905, 21 Aug. 1905, 27 Dec. 1914; *Calgary Herald,* 3 Oct. 1893.

30 Ging G.G. Wong, *Calgary's Civic Government: A Structural History* (Calgary: Glenbow Archives Institute, 1978), 31; Kenneth A. Wark, *A Report on Alberta's Elections, 1905-1982* (Edmonton: n.p., 1983), 33-55.

31 GMA, M2241/M7227, United Brotherhood of Carpenters and Joiners of America, Local 1055/1779, minutes (UBCJA mins), 8 April 1902, 10 June 1902, 19 May 1903, 26 May 1903; *Albertan,* 18 Sept. 1906.

32 Ibid., 3 May 1902.

33 Ibid., 25 June 1902.

34 Ibid., 8 July 1902, 15 July 1902, 18 July 1902. For an account of Bennett's career in Calgary, see James Gray, *R.B. Bennett: The Calgary Years* (Toronto: University of Toronto Press, 1991).

35 *Albertan,* 22 July 1902.

36 See Gaston V. Rimlinger, 'The Legitimation of Protest: A Comparative Study in Labor History,' *Comparative Studies in Society and History* 2 (1959-60): 329-43.

37 *Labour Gazette* 2 (1903), 969; *Calgary Herald,* 30 May 1903, 1 June 1903, 4 June 1903, 8 June 1903.

38 Ibid., 10 June 1903.

39 Ibid., 16 June 1903. On Travis's earlier controversial history in Calgary, see Max Foran, 'The "Travis Affair,"' *Alberta Historical Review* 19, 4 (1971): 1-7.

40 *Bond of Brotherhood,* 4 June 1903, 5 June 1903, 10 June 1903, 26 June 1903; *Labour Gazette* 4 (1903-4), 140-3.

41 *Albertan,* 19 May 1904.

42 George Barnett, *Chapters on Machinery and Labor* (1926; reprint, Carbondale: Southern Illinois University Press, 1969).

43 Ibid., 30-64.
44 *Wages and Hours of Labor in Canada, 1901-1920.*
45 Taraska, 'Calgary Craft Union Movement,' 6-7; National Archives of Canada (NAC), Department of Labour, 'Strikes and Lockouts,' vol. 300, file 3541; *Calgary Herald,* 24 Aug. 1904.
46 *Calgary Herald,* 1 June 1912; Taraska, 'Calgary Craft Union Movement,' 7.
47 BSMIU mins, 17 Aug. 1904, 26 July 1907, 22 Nov. 1911.
48 *Labour Organizations in Canada* (1913), 121-2; *Calgary Herald,* 3 Sept. 1914.
49 AFM mins, 12 March 1905.
50 See Walter Korpi and Michael Shalev, 'Strikes, Industrial Relations, and Class Conflict in Capitalist Society,' *British Journal of Sociology* 30, 2 (1979): 164-87.
51 Craig Heron and Bryan D. Palmer, 'Through the Prism of the Strike: Industrial Conflict in Southern Ontario, 1901-1914,' *Canadian Historical Review* 57, 4 (Dec. 1977): 425; Ian McKay, 'Strikes in the Maritimes, 1901-1914,' *Acadiensis* 13, 1 (1984): 14.
52 For example, Stuart Jamieson totally ignores strikes in Alberta cities in his *Times of Trouble: Labour Unrest and Industrial Conflict in Canada, 1900-1966* (Ottawa: Task Force on Labour Relations, 1968), 62-157.
53 'Strikes and Lockouts,' vol. 296, file 3119; *Calgary Herald,* 9 March 1905.
54 For example, *Calgary Herald,* 16 Aug. 1897.
55 Richard Price, *Masters, Unions, and Men: Work Control in Building and the Rise of Labour, 1830-1914* (Cambridge: Cambridge University Press, 1980), 6.
56 Edward Shorter and Charles Tilly, *Strikes in France, 1830-1960* (Cambridge: Cambridge University Press, 1974), 1-20. See also Peter N. Stearns, 'Measuring the Evolution of Strike Movements,' *International Review of Social History* 19, 1 (1974): 1-27.
57 'Strikes and Lockouts,' vol. 299, file 3463. As an example of this overlap, Robert McDonald's study of Vancouver labour shows that the number of strike issues (102) exceeded the number of recorded strikes (68) by 50 percent. Robert A.J. McDonald, 'Working-Class Vancouver, 1886-1914: Urbanism and Class in British Columbia,' *BC Studies* 69-70 (1986): 55.
58 ITU mins, 3 Jan. 1905; 31 July 1920, 25 Sept. 1920.
59 'Strikes and Lockouts,' vol. 300, file 3536; *Calgary Herald,* 18 July 1904; Royal Commission on Industrial Relations, Evidence (Calgary, 3 May 1919), testimony of Robert H. Parkyn.
60 *Calgary Herald,* 8 Jan. 1906, 9 Jan. 1906.
61 See Mercedes Steedman, 'Skill and Gender in the Canadian Clothing Industry, 1890-1940,' in *On the Job,* ed. Heron and Storey 152-76; Shirley Tillotson, '"We May All Soon Be 'First-Class Men'": Gender and Skill in Canada's Early-Twentieth-Century Urban Telegraph Industry,' *Labour/Le Travail* 27 (1991): 97-125; Christina Burr, 'Defending "The Art Preservative": Class and Gender Relations in the Printing Trades Unions, 1850-1914,' *Labour/Le Travail* 31 (1993): 47-73. Also useful is J.A. Mangan and James Walvin, eds., *Manliness and Morality: Middle-Class Masculinity in Britain and America, 1800-1940* (New York: St Martin's Press, 1987).
62 Whiting Williams, *Mainsprings of Men* (New York: Charles Scribner's Sons, 1925), 58.
63 *Calgary Herald,* 8 March 1913; GMA, M311, Richard Burton Deane papers, 'Reminiscences of a Mounted Police Officer' (1911). For more details on Deane and his experience with labour in the West, see William M. Baker, ed., *Pioneer Policing in Southern Alberta: Deane of the Mounties, 1888-1914* (Calgary: Historical Society of Alberta, 1993), 46-55, 164-5, 171-3.
64 ITU mins, 28 June 1904, 29 June 1904.
65 UBCJA mins, 17 March 1910; 'Strikes and Lockouts,' vol. 299, file 3394; *Labour Gazette* 12 (1911-2), 39.
66 K.G.J.C. Knowles, *Strikes: A Study of Industrial Conflict* (Oxford: Basil Blackwell, 1954), 219. See also Alvin Gouldner, *Wildcat Strike* (Yellow Springs, OH: Antioch Press, 1954).
67 Knowles also makes this point in *Strikes,* 240.
68 Tom Langford, 'Strikes and Class Consciousness,' *Labour/Le Travail* 34 (1994): 107-37.

69 *Bond of Brotherhood,* 12 June 1903.

70 Gary Teeple, *Globalization and the Decline of Social Reform* (Toronto: Garamond Press, 1995), 72.

Chapter 5: Depression and War, 1913-7

1 James Struthers, *No Fault of Their Own: Unemployment and the Canadian Welfare State, 1914-1941* (Toronto: University of Toronto Press, 1983), 12-3.

2 *Albertan,* 1 Sept. 1917. See also Robert Craig Brown and Ramsay Cook, *Canada, 1896-1921: A Nation Transformed* (Toronto: McClelland and Stewart, 1974), 198-203; David Jay Bercuson, *Confrontation at Winnipeg: Labour, Industrial Relations, and the General Strike* (Montreal: McGill-Queen's University Press, 1974), 22-31; R.T. Naylor, 'The Canadian State, the Accumulation of Capital, and the Great War,' *Journal of Canadian Studies* 16, 3-4 (1981): 26-55; Kenneth Norrie and Doug Owram, *A History of the Canadian Economy* (Toronto: Harcourt Brace Jovanovich, 1991), 411-40.

3 *Alberta Non-Partisan,* 26 Oct. 1917. See also John Herd Thompson, *The Harvests of War: The Prairie West, 1914-1918* (Toronto: McClelland and Stewart, 1978), 30-1, 167-8; R. Matthew Bray, '"Fighting as an Ally": The English-Canadian Patriotic Response to the Great War,' *Canadian Historical Review* 61, 2 (1980): 141-68.

4 *Industrial Canada,* April 1913, May 1913, Jan. 1914; *Henderson's Calgary City Directory* (n.p., 1920); *Calgary Municipal Manuals* (n.p., 1910-20).

5 Wiseman quoted in *Canadian Annual Review* (1913), 29. On outstanding taxes, see 'Report of Unemployment Conference at Calgary, Alberta' (6 Nov. 1914), testimony of Mayor H.A. Sinnott; and H.L. MacLeod, 'Properties, Investors, and Taxes: A Study of Calgary Real Estate Investment, Municipal Finances, and Property Tax Arrears, 1911-1919' (MA thesis, University of Calgary, 1977), 8-42.

6 *Alberta Federationist,* 28 Feb. 1913; *Labour Gazette* 14 (1913-4), 258, 417; 'Report of Unemployment Conference at Calgary,' J.D. McNiven to Gerald Brown, 26 Dec. 1913.

7 *Calgary Municipal Manuals*; Calgary Board of Trade, *Annual Reports.*

8 *Labour Gazette* 14 (1913-4), 35; Glenbow Museum Archives (GMA), M2260, Calgary Chamber of Commerce, box 13, file 30, Annual Report (1913); Bennett quoted in *Canadian Annual Review* (1913), 30; see also Calgary City Archives (CCA), RG 26, City Clerk files, box 65, file 514, William H. Willson (Secretary of the Board of Trade) to J.M. Miller (City Clerk), 3 Jan. 1914.

9 *Canadian Annual Review* (1912), 154.

10 *Labour Gazette* 14 (1913-4), 675; 'Report of Unemployment Conference at Calgary,' correspondence, McNiven to Brown, 26 Dec. 1913.

11 *Labour Gazette* 14 (1913-4), 949; 15 (1914-5), 915; 'Unemployment Conference at Calgary,' correspondence, unidentified memorandum dated 5 Sept. 1914; National Archives of Canada (NAC), RG 27, Department of Labour, vol. 3134, file 152, 'Summaries of Reports from Labour Gazette Correspondents re Unemployment, 15 September 1914-15 April 1915.' See also David Schulze, 'The Industrial Workers of the World and the Unemployed in Edmonton and Calgary in the Depression of 1913-1915,' *Labour/Le Travail* 25 (1990): 47-75.

12 For background, see Judy Blanche Bedford, 'Social Justice in Calgary: A Study of Urban Poverty and Welfare Development in the 1920s' (MA thesis, University of Calgary, 1981), 48-96.

13 'Report of Unemployment Conference at Calgary,' correspondence, estimate of unemployed dated 16 Sept. 1914; *Labour Gazette* 15 (1914-5), 790.

14 *Albertan,* 11 Aug. 1908, 10 March 1909, 1 June 1909, 30 Jan. 1911, 6 Feb. 1911, 19 July 1912, 1 Oct. 1912, 3 Oct. 1912, 4 Oct. 1912, 12 Oct. 1912, 12 March 1913, 9 May 1913, 4 Dec. 1914; *Labour Gazette* 13 (1912-3), 216, 309, 600; GMA, M1883, City of Calgary Civic Government papers, file 113, D.S. Moffat to F. Kerr, 27 Jan. 1912. As a postscript, Harry Minchin, the alderman who has opposed Wileman's 'petticoat rule' on the grounds that it broke the city's financial guidelines, was himself later arrested and convicted for embezzling $8,000 while in office. *Albertan,* 1 Oct. 1912, 21 March 1913.

15 GMA, M2118, Associated Charities Association papers, file 1, Executive Committee report, 1914; *Labour Gazette* 15 (1914-5), 46; *Calgary Herald,* 26 Feb. 1921. See also John Keane, *Democracy and Civil Society* (London: Verso, 1988).
16 'Report of the Unemployment Conference at Calgary,' correspondence, T. Crothers to A.L. Sifton, 3 Oct. 1914. See also Struthers, *No Fault of Their Own,* 9.
17 *Calgary Herald,* 6 Nov. 1914; 'Report of the Unemployment Conference at Calgary,' transcript of meeting.
18 John Blue, *Alberta, Past and Present: Historical and Biographical* (Chicago: Pioneer Historical Publishing, 1924), 2: 292.
19 Canada, *Sessional Papers* 36 (1914), 85; (1915), 111; (1916), 67; (1917), 63; GMA, M2198, Bricklayers and Stonemasons' International Union, Local 2, minutes (BSMIU mins), 9 May 1913, 15 Aug. 1913, 29 Jan. 1915, 26 Feb. 1915.
20 The four wartime strikes were: 80 Grand Trunk Pacific track layers working six miles north of Calgary on 7 March 1913; 250 plumbers in the city from 2 June to 7 July 1913; 300 construction workers from 15 July to 2 August 1913; and 35 construction workers from 2 July to 31 July 1917. NAC, Department of Labour, 'Strikes & Lockouts,' vol. 301, file 21; vol. 302, files 85 and 97; vol. 306, file 80.
21 Gregory S. Kealey, '1919: The Canadian Labour Revolt,' *Labour/Le Travail* 13 (1984): 29; Douglas Cruikshank and Gregory S. Kealey, 'Canadian Strike Statistics, 1891-1950,' ibid. 20 (1987): 85-145.
22 *Albertan,* 10 Feb. 1912.
23 Ibid., 24 Nov. 1913.
24 GMA, M4743, Calgary Trades and Labour Council, minutes (CTLC mins), 24 July 1914, 7 Aug. 1914, 21 Aug. 1914.
25 GMA, M2204, Calgary Labour Temple, minutes, 5 April 1915, 14 Sept. 1915.
26 Schulze, 'The Industrial Workers of the World'; Ross McCormack, 'Wobblies and Blanketstiffs: The Constituency of the IWW in Western Canada,' in *Lectures in Canadian Labour and Working-Class History,* ed. W.J.C. Cherwinski and Gregory S. Kealey (St John's: CCLH/New Hogtown Press, 1985), 101-14; Mark Leier, *Where the Fraser River Flows: The Industrial Workers of the World in British Columbia* (Vancouver: New Star Books, 1990).
27 *Albertan,* 24 Jan. 1913.
28 Schulze, 'The Industrial Workers of the World,' 72.
29 *Nutcracker,* 2 Dec. 1916.
30 GMA, M7070, International Typographical Union, Local 449, minutes (ITU mins), 24 May 1902, 26 July 1904; *Calgary Herald,* 27 April 1908; Ging G.G. Wong, *Calgary's Civic Government: A Structural History* (Calgary: Glenbow Archives Institute, 1978), 22.
31 ITU mins, 30 Nov. 1912.
32 *Albertan,* 28 Jan. 1915, 17 Feb. 1915; GMA, M2214/2215, International Brotherhood of Electrical Workers, Local 348, minutes (IBEW mins), box 2, file 12, J. Ritchie to J.L. Broeckx, 12 April 1915.
33 *Albertan,* 28 April 1915, 29 April 1915; CTLC mins, 15 Oct. 1915.
34 Heather Foran, 'Annie Gale,' in *Citymakers: Calgarians After the Frontier,* ed. Max Foran and Sheilagh Jameson (Calgary: Historical Society of Alberta, Chinook Chapter, 1987), 196-207; Patricia Roome, 'Amelia Turner,' ibid., 225-46, and 'Amelia Turner and Calgary Labour Women, 1919-1935,' in *Beyond the Vote: Canadian Women and Politics,* ed. Linda Kealey and Joan Sangster (Toronto: University of Toronto Press, 1989), 89-117; Linda Kealey, 'Women in the Canadian Socialist Movement, 1904-1914,' ibid., 171-95.
35 CTLC mins, 16 April 1915, 9 July 1915.
36 *Albertan,* 7 Dec. 1914; CTLC mins, 8 Jan. 1915.
37 Ibid., 15 Dec. 1914, 16 Dec. 1914.
38 Ibid., 25 Nov. 1915, 27 Nov. 1915.
39 Ibid., 14 Dec. 1915.
40 A. Ross McCormack, *Reformers, Rebels, and Revolutionaries: The Western Canadian Radical Movement, 1899-1919* (1977; reprint, Toronto: University of Toronto Press, 1991), 120-1; Thompson, *Harvests of War,* 27-44.
41 *Albertan,* 9 Sept. 1914.

42 GMA, M3973, interviews conducted by George Gooderham, file 2, interview with Arthur G. Graves; *Canadian Annual Review* (1914), 664; (1915), 704; City Clerk papers, file 873, S.G. Petley to L.A. Campbell, 25 Feb. 1919.

43 IBEW mins, 9 Dec. 1914; *Labour Gazette* 16 (1915-6), 165; *Calgary Herald,* 13 July 1916; Fred White, 'Where the Trail Leads,' *Calgary Typographical Union No. 449, 1902-1952* (Calgary: n.p., 1952); GMA, M1881, City of Calgary Fire Brigade Department papers, box 3, file 59, Smart to Gillett, 8 Dec. 1916.

44 Thompson, *Harvests of War,* 61-2; Leonard D. Nesbitt, *Tides in the West* (Saskatoon: Modern Press, n.d.), 20-2; *Labour Gazette* 16 (1915-6), 562.

45 Department of Labour, vol. 125, file 601.3, 'memorandum re conditions of labour in Canada as affected by the war' (n.d.). See also Michael Bliss, 'War Business as Usual: Canadian Munitions Production, 1914-1918,' in *Mobilization for Total War,* ed. N.F. Dreisziger (Waterloo: Wilfrid Laurier University Press, 1981), 45-55; Naylor, 'The Canadian State,' 33-8; Thompson, *Harvests of War,* 55.

46 CTLC mins, 19 Sept. 1915.

47 *Albertan,* 18 Jan. 1917.

48 CTLC mins, 17 March 1916, 14 April 1916, 7 July 1916, 21 July 1916.

49 Ibid., 11 May 1916, 6 July 1917.

50 *Nutcracker,* 17 Nov. 1917; *Albertan,* 6 June 1916, 17 Oct. 1916. See also Linda Kealey, 'Women and Labour during World War I: Women Workers and the Minimum Wage in Manitoba,' in *First Days, Fighting Days: Women in Manitoba History,* ed. Mary Kinnear (Regina: Canadian Plains Research Center, 1987), 76-99.

51 *Albertan,* 18 Sept. 1915.

52 IBEW mins, 29 May 1917, 31 May 1917; *Nutcracker,* 3 Feb. 1917, 2 March 1917, 14 April 1917, 24 April 1917; *Calgary Herald,* 16 Jan. 1917, 23 Feb. 1917, 28 Feb. 1917, 12 March 1917, 10 April 1917, 12 April 1917, 4 May 1917; *Albertan,* 14 Jan. 1917, 16 Jan. 1917, 20 Jan. 1917, 6 Feb. 1917, 12 March 1917, 30 March 1917, 18 April 1917, 20 April 1917, 12 May 1917. See also Greg Marquis, 'Police Unionism in Early Twentieth-Century Toronto,' *Ontario History* 81, 2 (1989): 109-28, and Barbara Grinder, *Local Colour: A Commemoration of the 75th Anniversary of the Amalgamated Transit Union Local 583* (Calgary: n.p., 1990), 121-33.

53 H. Pryde, 'Is the Industrial Union in Sight?' in Souvenir of the 27th Annual Convention, *Trades and Labour Congress of Canada* (Calgary: Calgary Trades and Labour Council, 1911).

54 IBEW correspondence, box 2, file 12, Tailors' Industrial Union circular.

55 IBEW correspondence, box 2, file 10, circular from J. Fitzgerald, President of General Office, 25 May 1914.

56 GMA, M7227, United Brotherhood of Carpenters and Joiners of America, Local 1779, minutes (UBCJA mins), 12 Sept. 1917.

57 Pryde, 'Is the Industrial Union in Sight?' For background, see David J. Bercuson, *Fools and Wise Men: The Rise and Fall of the One Big Union* (Toronto: McGraw-Hill Ryerson, 1978), 252-64.

58 For details of Irvine's career and background, see Anthony Mardiros, *William Irvine: The Life of a Prairie Radical* (Toronto: Lorimer, 1979), and Howard Palmer, 'William Irvine and the Emergence of Political Radicalism in Calgary, 1916-1921,' *Fort Calgary Quarterly* 7, 2 (1987): 2-19.

59 See Richard Allen, *The Social Passion: Religion and Social Reform in Canada, 1914-1928* (1971; reprint, Toronto: University of Toronto Press, 1990), 3-80; Paul F. Sharp, *The Agrarian Revolt in Western Canada* (Minneapolis: University of Minnesota Press, 1948), 77-104.

60 Allen, *The Social Passion,* 83; Kenneth McNaught, *A Prophet in Politics: A Biography of J.S. Woodsworth* (Toronto: University of Toronto Press, 1963), 44.

61 *Nutcracker,* 25 May 1917, 21 June 1917; Mardiros, *William Irvine,* 40.

62 Thompson, *Harvests of War,* 30-1.

63 *Albertan Non-Partisan,* 26 Oct. 1917.

64 CTLC mins, 4 Aug. 1916, 30 March 1917.

65 Ibid., 29 Sept. 1916, 13 Oct. 1916.

66 *Calgary Herald,* 11 Dec. 1916, 12 Dec. 1916.
67 Ibid., 12 Dec. 1916; *Albertan,* 5 Sept. 1916; *Alberta Labor News,* 11 Sept. 1920. Proportional representation passed by 3,223 votes to 1,383. Labour figures such as Robert Parkyn quickly took advantage of the People's Forum to explain how workers should use the system to maximize the chances of electing labour candidates. *Calgary Herald,* 4 Jan. 1917.
68 See Ralph Miliband, *Parliamentary Socialism: A Study in the Politics of Labour,* 2nd ed. (London: Merlin Press, 1972), 17-38.
69 CTLC mins, 16 March 1917, 30 March 1917, 13 April 1917; UBCJA mins, 23 March 1917. The LRL's platform is reprinted in Mardiros, *William Irvine,* 59-60. Union affiliation was twenty-five cents per member per year. *Nutcracker,* 30 March 1917.
70 See L.G. Thomas, *The Liberal Party in Alberta: A History of Politics in the Province of Alberta, 1905-1921* (Toronto: University of Toronto Press, 1959), 58-133; D.R. Babcock, *Alexander Cameron Rutherford: A Gentleman of Strathcona* (Calgary: University of Calgary Press, 1989), 57-66.
71 *Nutcracker,* 25 May 1917; *Calgary Herald,* 24 April 1917, 23 May 1917, 29 May 1917, 15 June 1917; Kenneth A. Wark, *A Report on Alberta Elections, 1905-1982* (Edmonton: n.p., 1983), 25-9; *Canadian Annual Review* (1917), 806; Mardiros, *William Irvine,* 45-8, 275.
72 See Martin Robin, *Radical Politics and Canadian Labour, 1880-1930* (Kingston: Queen's University Industrial Relations Centre, 1968), 121.
73 NAC, Robert Borden papers, vol. 68, J.E. Young to Sir Robert Borden, 22 Dec. 1916. See also McCormack, *Reformers, Rebels, and Revolutionaries,* 128-9.
74 McCormack, *Reformers, Rebels, and Revolutionaries,* 129-31; UBCJA mins, 7 July 1917; ITU mins, 30 June 1917; IBEW mins, 8 Aug. 1917; CTLC mins, 20 July 1917, 3 Aug. 1917.
75 CTLC mins, 22 June 1917; *Calgary Herald,* 26 May 1917.
76 CTLC mins, 17 Aug. 1917.
77 Mardiros, *William Irvine,* 66; CTLC mins, 23 Nov. 1917; *Calgary Herald,* 28 Nov. 1917; Desmond Morton, 'Polling the Soldier Vote: The Overseas Campaign in the Canadian General Election of 1917,' *Journal of Canadian Studies* 10, 4 (1975), 55.
78 *Calgary Herald,* 11 Dec. 1917. Labour's relative success in Calgary may be compared to its bungled performance in Brandon, Manitoba, that year. See Errol Black, 'Labour in Brandon Civic Politics: A Long View,' *Manitoba History* 23 (1992), 4.

Chapter 6: Economic Recession and Restructuring, 1918-24

1 For background, see Robert Craig Brown and Ramsay Cook, *Canada, 1896-1921: A Nation Transformed* (Toronto: McClelland and Stewart, 1974); John Herd Thompson with Allen Seager, *Canada, 1922-1939: Decades of Discord* (Toronto: McClelland and Stewart, 1985); Robert Bothwell, Robert Drummond, and John English, *Canada, 1900-1945* (Toronto: University of Toronto Press, 1987).
2 Sanford M. Jacoby, *Employing Bureaucracy: Managers, Unions, and the Transformation of Work in American Industry, 1900-1945* (New York: Columbia University Press, 1985), 167-205, quote on 204. See also David Montgomery, *The Fall of the House of Labor* (Cambridge: Cambridge University Press, 1987), 411-64.
3 See Bryan D. Palmer, *Working-Class Experience: Rethinking the History of Canadian Labour, 1800-1991,* 2nd ed. (Toronto: McClelland and Stewart, 1992), 214-36.
4 Ibid., 214-9; Reginald Whitaker, 'Scientific Management Theory as Political Ideology,' *Review of Radical Political Economics* 2, 3 (1979): 75-108; Samuel Haber, *Efficiency and Uplift: Scientific Management in the Progressive Era, 1890-1920* (Chicago: University of Chicago Press, 1964); Peter F. Meiksins, 'Scientific Management and Class Relations: A Dissenting View,' *Theory and Society* 13, 1 (1984): 177-209. For details of working-class resistance to the new management techniques, see Bryan Palmer, 'Class, Conception, and Conflict: The Thrust for Efficiency, Managerial Views of Labor, and the Working Class Rebellion, 1903-22,' *Review of Radical Political Economics* 7, 2 (1975): 31-49; Charles S. Maier, 'Between Taylorism and Technocracy: European Ideologies and the Vision of Industrial Production in the 1920s,' *Journal of Contemporary History* 5, 2 (1970): 27-61, and 'The Factory as Society: Ideologies of Industrial Management in the Twentieth

Century,' in *Ideas into Politics: Aspects of European History, 1880-1950,* ed. R.J. Bullen (Totowa, NJ: Barnes and Noble, 1984), 147-63.

5 A.A. Bureau, 'Making Employees 100 Per Cent Efficient,' *Industrial Canada* (Oct. 1920).

6 Bruce Scott, 'A Place in the Sun: The Industrial Council at Massey-Harris, 1919-1929,' *Labour/Le Travailleur* 1 (1976): 158-92.

7 Stuart D. Brandes, *American Welfare Capitalism, 1880-1949* (Chicago: University of Chicago Press, 1970), 147. See also Jacoby, *Employing Bureaucracy,* 195-204; Robert Ozanne, *A Century of Labor-Management Relations at McCormick and International Harvester* (Madison: University of Wisconsin Press, 1967); Margaret E. McCallum, 'Corporate Welfarism in Canada, 1919-39,' *Canadian Historical Review* 71, 1 (1990): 46-79; Robert Storey, 'Unionization versus Corporate Welfare: The "Dofasco" Way,' *Labour/Le Travailleur* 12 (1983): 7-42; Craig Heron and Robert Storey, 'Work and Struggle in the Canadian Steel Industry, 1900-1950,' in *On the Job: Confronting the Labour Process in Canada,* ed. Craig Heron and Robert Storey (Montreal: McGill-Queen's University Press, 1986), 225-7. For a contemporary view, see William G. Colgate, 'Reducing the Cost of Labour Turnover by Advertising,' *Industrial Canada* (Aug. 1920).

8 *Henderson's Calgary City Directory* (1924), 42.

9 Glenbow Museum Archives (GMA), M.M. Guichon, 'Riley & McCormick' (unpublished paper).

10 For details of Black's early years in Calgary, see David Bright, 'Bonds of Brotherhood? The Experiences of Labour in Calgary' (MA thesis, University of Calgary, 1990), 51-3, and GMA, M98, David E. Black papers, passim. See also Max Foran, *Calgary: An Illustrated History* (Toronto: Lorimer, 1978), 120.

11 Author's interview with Lillian Valentine (4 March 1992).

12 Black papers, box 2, file 49, A.O. MacRae to W.M. Birks, 27 Jan. 1922.

13 Ibid., W.M. Birks to A.O. MacRae, 1 Feb. 1922. E.P. Thompson discusses the moral obligations of capitalism in his two essays, 'The Moral Economy of the English Crowd in the Eighteenth Century' and 'The Moral Economy Revisited,' both in his *Customs in Common* (London: Merlin Press, 1991), 185-351.

14 *Dun and Bradstreet Reference Book* (Jan. 1918); ibid. (Jan. 1924).

15 *Calgary Herald,* 28 June 1920, 9 June 1923, 11 July 1923, 13 Oct.1923, 21 Jan. 1924; *Canadian Annual Review* (1923), 748; *Calgary Municipal Manual* (n.p., 1923); *Industrial Canada* (Nov. 1923).

16 *Calgary Herald,* 21 Dec. 1920, 31 Jan. 1921, 5 April 1921, 2 May 1921, 23 Sept. 1922, 9 July 1923, 10 Aug. 1923, 19 June 1924, 22 Aug. 1924, 20 Sept. 1924, 22 Oct. 1924.

17 Figures taken from *Calgary Municipal Manuals*; GMA, Chamber of Commerce, M2260, box 13, file 30, Annual Reports. See also R. Bruce Wilson, 'Business, Industry, and Commerce in Calgary, 1920-1930' (unpublished paper, University of Calgary, 1976).

18 GMA, Chamber of Commerce, M2260, box 13, file 38, Annual Reports, 1920, 1921, 1923.

19 Ibid., Annual Reports for 1922, 1924, and 1925.

20 *Census of Canada* (1911), 6: 342; (1921), 4: 354; (1931), 7: 232.

21 During the war, the weekly wages of Calgary machinists – as reported to the Department of Labour – had risen by 58 percent, from $24.30 to $38.40. Between 1918 and 1924 they fell by 25 percent to reach $33.88. Canada, Department of Labour, *Wages and Hours of Labour in Canada, 1901-20* (Ottawa: King's Printer, 1921), and *Wages and Hours of Labour in Canada, 1920 to 1930* (Ottawa: King's Printer, 1931).

22 *Census of Canada* (1911), 6: 342; (1921), 4: 354; (1931), 7: 232.

23 Stuart Ewen provides useful context for this transformation in *Captains of Consciousness: Advertising and the Social Roots of the Consumer Culture* (New York: McGraw-Hill, 1976). See also Niels Thorsen, 'The Traditional and the Modern Understanding of Consumption,' in *Consumption and American Culture,* ed. David E. Nye and Carl Pedersen (Amsterdam: VU University Press, 1991), 5-17. A valuable debate was sparked by Michael Denning's article, 'The End of Mass Culture,' *International Labor and Working Class History* 37 (Spring 1990): 4-40, and his own rejoinder in ibid., 38 (1990): 63-7. There is relatively little work on the emergence of consumer capitalism in Canada, but see Palmer, *Working-Class Experience,* 229-36; Keith Walden, 'Speaking Modern: Language, Culture,

and Hegemony in Grocery Window Displays, 1887-1920,' *Canadian Historical Review* 70, 3 (1989): 285-310; Cynthia Wright, '"Feminine Trifles of Vast Importance": Writing Gender into the History of Consumption,' in *Gender Conflicts: New Essays in Women's History,* ed. Franca Iacovetta and Mariana Valverde (Toronto: University of Toronto Press, 1992), 229-60; and the chapter 'The 1920s: An Era of Drift,' in David B. Marshall, *Secularizing the Faith: Canadian Protestant Clergy and the Crisis of Belief, 1850-1940* (Toronto: University of Toronto Press, 1992), 181-204.

24 Ewen, *Captains of Consciousness,* 14.

25 However, see Suzanne Morton's discussion of class and consumption in *Ideal Surroundings: Domestic Life in a Working-Class Suburb in the 1920s* (Toronto: University of Toronto Press, 1995), 44-50.

26 *Calgary Herald,* 12 May 1923.

27 Morton, *Ideal Surroundings,* 48.

28 *Alberta Labor News,* 18 Sept. 1920.

29 *Census of Canada* (1921), 3: 57; (1931), 5: 988; Canada, Royal Commission into Industrial Relations, 1919 (Calgary, 3-5 May 1919), testimony of James H. Garden; *Calgary Herald,* 6 April 1924. See also Henry Klassen, 'Bicycles and Automobiles in Early Calgary,' *Alberta History* 24, 2 (1976): 1-8; Alfred A. Hunter, *Class Tells: On Social Inequality in Canada* (Toronto: Butterworths, 1981), 69.

30 *Canadian Annual Review* (1921), 829; *Henderson's Calgary City Directory* (1911).

31 *Census of Canada* (1931), 5: 980.

32 *Alberta Labor News,* 20 Aug. 1921, 10 Sept. 1921, 17 Sept. 1921.

33 Royal Commission into Industrial Relations, testimony of Mrs George [Mary] Corse.

34 Ibid., testimonies of R.C. Marshall and F.J. White.

35 Ibid., testimonies of Louise McKinney, Jean McWilliam, and George Sangster. On McKinney, see Paul Voisey, 'The "Votes for Women" Movement,' *Alberta History,* 23, 2 (1975): 22; Una MacLean, 'The Famous Five,' *Alberta Historical Review* 10, 2 (1962): 1.

36 John Blue, *Alberta, Past and Present: Historical and Biographical* (Chicago: Pioneer Historical Publishing, 1924), 1: 396. See also David J. Bercuson, *Fools and Wise Men: The Rise and Fall of the One Big Union* (Toronto: McGraw-Hill Ryerson, 1978), 216.

37 *Calgary Herald,* 6 Jan. 1919; David Schulze, 'The Industrial Workers of the World and the Unemployed in Edmonton and Calgary in the Depression of 1913-1915,' *Labour/Le Travail* 25 (1990): 54.

38 National Archives of Canada (NAC), Department of Labour, vol. 209, file 617:9.1, 'Unemployment Relief Measures – Correspondence with the Province of Alberta' (1922-1926), passim; *Calgary Herald,* 21 April 1922.

39 On Calgary's reputation, see ibid. *Calgary Herald,* 9 September 1921.

40 *Alberta Labor News,* 8 April 1922.

41 *Canadian Annual Review* (1920-6), passim; GMA, Associated Charities Association papers, M2118, file 1, 7 Jan. 1924. The organization changed its name in April 1921. Ibid., file 2, 20 April 1920.

42 *Calgary Herald,* 4 Feb. 1921, 28 Aug. 1919, 10 Aug. 1920, 1 March 1921. See also K.B. Conn, 'Employment and Unemployment in Canada: Its Measurement, with Special Reference to 1919,' *Canadian Historical Review* 6, 3 (1925): 237.

43 *Calgary Herald,* 15 April 1921.

44 Ibid., 8 Dec. 1920, 21 Dec. 1921, 28 Dec. 1921.

45 City of Calgary Archives (CCA), City Clerk papers, file 914, 'Registration Reports,' 27 Oct. 1919, 8 Nov. 1919, 15 Nov. 1919, 6 Dec. 1919; *Calgary Herald,* 6 March 1922. See also Donald Avery, *'Dangerous Foreigners': European Immigrant Workers and Labour Radicalism in Canada, 1896-1932* (Toronto: McClelland and Stewart, 1979), and *Reluctant Host: Canada's Response to Immigrant Workers, 1896-1994* (Toronto: McClelland and Stewart, 1995).

46 James Struthers, *No Fault of Their Own: Unemployment and the Canadian Welfare State, 1914-1941* (Toronto: University of Toronto Press, 1983), 12-43.

47 *Calgary Herald,* 24 Aug. 1921, 12 Jan. 1921. Webster quoted in Struthers, *No Fault of Their Own,* 36.

48 *Calgary Herald,* 4 Aug. 1922.

49 Department of Labour, vol. 209, file 617.9, H. Greenfield to James Murdock, 23 Dec. 1924; Murdock to Greenfield, 23 Dec. 1924.

50 *Calgary Herald,* 17 Dec. 1921. Little's warning was borne out when, in January 1922, labour aldermen failed to block the city commissioners' recommendation to cut unemployment relief payments by more than 15 percent. Ibid., 10 Jan. 1922.

51 Ibid., 24 Dec. 1921, 16 March 1922. See also E.R. Fay, 'The Early Years,' *Marxist Quarterly* 1 (Spring 1962): 13-21.

52 *Alberta Labor News,* 4 April 1922.

53 *Calgary Herald,* 24 Jan. 1922, 20 March 1922.

54 *Alberta Labor News*, 12 Feb. 1921.

55 Ibid., 4 April 1922, 27 May 1922, 19 Aug. 1922; *Calgary Herald,* 3 June 1922, 17 June 1922.

56 Irving Bernstein, *The Lean Years: A History of the American Worker, 1920-1933* (Boston: Houghton Mifflin, 1960), 42; Alimohamed Damji, 'Militancy to Passivism: The Calgary Labour Movement, 1919-1924' (MA thesis, University of Calgary, 1987), 122-53. See also Frank Stricker, 'Affluence for Whom? – Another Look at Prosperity and the Working Classes in the 1920s,' *Labor History* 24 (Winter 1983): 5-33; Montgomery, *Fall of the House of Labor,* 449-64. The notion of restructuring is normally applied to North American labour in the post-1945 era, especially the 1970s and 1980s. While historians and economists have paid relatively little attention to Canadian labour in the 1920s, the concept of restructuring appears to be of valid application and is useful in the questions that it both answers and raises. For an overview of the concept, see Jane Jenson and Rianne Mahon, eds., *The Challenge of Restructuring: North American Labor Movements Respond* (Philadelphia: Temple University Press, 1993).

57 *Alberta Labor News,* 4 Sept. 1920.

58 GMA, M7227, United Brotherhood of Carpenters and Joiners of America, Local 1779, minutes (UBCJA mins), 6 Feb. 1919.

59 GMA, M2198, Bricklayers and Stonemasons International Union, Local 2, minutes (BSMIU mins), 18 July 1924; GMA, M2230, Sheet Metal Workers Union, Local 254, minutes (SMW mins), file 5, entries for 1923 and 1924, passim.

60 *Albertan,* 4 Dec. 1918; *Hendersons' Calgary City Directory* (1923); Blue, *Alberta, Past and Present,* 1: 381; *Labour Organizations in Canada* (1927).

61 *Albertan,* 4 Jan. 1918; *Alberta Labor News,* 29 Jan. 1921; SMW mins, 13 May 1920. Jean McWilliam provides details in the local laundry industry in her testimony to the 1919 Royal Commission. See also Star Rosenthal, 'Union Maids: Organized Women Workers in Vancouver, 1900-1915,' *BC Studies* 41 (1979): 36-55; Dorothy Sue Cobble, *Dishing It Out: Waitresses and Their Unions in the Twentieth Century* (Urbana: University of Illinois Press, 1991).

62 David Bright, 'Meatpackers' Strike at Calgary, 1920,' *Alberta History* 44, 2 (1996): 2-10.

63 Figures cited in Damji, 'Militancy to Passivism,' 113. In all, Calgary workers struck on just seven occasions between the spring of 1919 and the end of 1924.

64 Kathryn Kearney, 'Canadian Women and the First World War,' *Canadian Woman Studies* 3, 1 (1981): 95-6; Alison Prentice, Paula Bourne, Gail Cuthbert Brandt, Beth Light, Wendy Mitchinson, and Naomi Black, *Canadian Women: A History* (Toronto: Harcourt Brace Jovanovich, 1988), 203-26; Voisey, 'The "Votes for Women" Movement,' 10-23; Brown and Cook, *A Nation Transformed,* 296-9.

65 Linda Kealey, '"No Special Protection – No Sympathy": Women's Activism in the Canadian Labour Revolt of 1919,' in *Class, Community, and the Labour Movement: Wales and Canada, 1850-1930,* ed. Deian R. Hopkins and Gregory S. Kealey (Wales: LLAFUR/CCLH, 1989), 136. See also Veronica Strong-Boag, *The New Day Recalled: Lives of Girls and Women in English Canada, 1919-1939* (Toronto: Copp Clark Pitman, 1988), 1-6; Jill McCalla Vickers, 'Feminist Approaches to Women in Politics,' in *Beyond the Vote: Canadian Women and Politics,* ed. Linda Kealey and Joan Sangster (Toronto: University of Toronto Press, 1989), 16-36.

66 Royal Commission into Industrial Relations, testimony of Jean McWilliam.

67 Ibid., testimony of Mary Corse. See also Cobble, *Dishing It Out,* and Kealey, 'No Special Protection.'

68 *Census of Canada* (1911), 6: 342; (1921), 4: 340; (1931), 7: 232.

69 *Alberta Labor News,* 9 Oct. 1920, 17 Dec. 1921.

70 *Census of Canada* (1931), 5: 60-2, 72.

71 Ibid.

72 *Census of Canada* (1921), 3: 152-4; (1931), 5: 60-2. This example may be multiplied to include female cooks, teachers, and retail personnel, among others. See also Strong-Boag, *The New Day Recalled,* 41-80.

73 *Calgary Herald,* 14 May 1915, 19 May 1915, 7 July 1915. See also Thompson, *Harvests of War,* 75; Joseph A. Boudreau, 'Western Canada's "Enemy Aliens" in World War One,' *Alberta Historical Review* 12, 1 (1964): 1-9; Gerhard P. Bassler, 'The Enemy Alien Experience in Newfoundland,' *Canadian Ethnic Studies* 20, 3 (1988): 42-62; Art Grenke, 'The German Community of Winnipeg and the English-Canadian Response to World War I,' ibid. 20, 1: 21-44.

74 Canada, *Sessional Papers* 28 (1916), 'Annual Report of Supt. F.J. Horrigan, Commanding "E" Division, Calgary,' 133; *Labour Gazette* 15 (1915): 1402; *Calgary Herald,* 11 May 1915, 24 Aug. 1915, 28 Aug.1915, 11 Feb. 1916, 12 Feb. 1916, 14 Feb. 1916, 21 Feb. 1916, 22 Feb. 1916, 24 Feb. 1916. On local troop disturbances, see also Wilbur F. Bowker, 'The Honourable Horace Harvey, Chief Justice of Alberta,' *Canadian Bar Review* 32, 9 (1954): 933-7. Desmond Morton provides the broader context in '"Kicking and Complaining": Postwar Demobilization Riots in the Canadian Expeditionary Force, 1918-1919,' *Canadian Historical Review* 64, 2 (1983): 334-60.

75 Cf. Thompson, *Harvests of War,* 76-7; Terence L. Craig, 'Frederick Philip Grove and the "Alien" Immigrant in the West,' *Journal of Canadian Studies* 20, 2 (1985): 92-100.

76 *Calgary Herald,* 24 Feb. 1916; census figures cited in Damji, 'Militancy to Passivism,' 166.

77 Alfred J. Hooke, *30 + 5: I Know, I Was There* (Edmonton: Co-op Press, 1971), 22.

78 Author's interview with Al Leinweber, 5 March 1992.

79 Hooke, *30 + 5,* 22-3; *Calgary Herald,* 16 July 1921, 18 July 1921; *Calgary Strike Bulletin,* 11 June 1919.

80 *Manitoba Free Press,* 29 Jan. 1919.

81 *Calgary Herald,* 20 March 1919; CCA, City Clerk papers, file 873, S.G. Petley to City Council, 17 April 1919. See also *G.W.V.A. of Calgary Yearbook* (n.p., 1919), 195.

82 *G.W.V.A. of Calgary Yearbook* (n.p., 1919), 205; Desmond Morton and Glenn Wright, *Winning the Second Battle: Canadian Veterans and the Return to Civilian Life, 1915-1930* (Toronto: University of Toronto Press, 1987). See also Desmond Morton, *When Your Number's Up: The Canadian Soldier in the First World War* (Toronto: Random House, 1993).

83 GMA, M861, James Francis Melville Moodie papers, file 5, Operator #3 reports, 1 Feb. 1919.

84 Ibid., 30 March 1919.

85 Struthers, *No Fault of Their Own,* 16-22.

86 *Calgary Herald,* 26 Aug. 1920; *Alberta Veteran,* 12 Oct. 1918. See also Walter S. Wood's account of his experience as Assistant Superintendent of the Soldier Settlement Scheme in Calgary in *The Men Who Came Back: A Book of Memories* (Toronto: Ryerson Press, 1956), 61-92.

87 *Calgary Strike Bulletin,* 14 June 1919; *Searchlight,* 5 Dec. 1919; Morton and Wright, *Winning the Second Battle,* 73. See also Desmond Morton and Glenn Wright, 'The Bonus Campaign, 1919-21: Veterans and the Campaign for Re-establishment,' *Canadian Historical Review* 64, 2 (1983): 147-67.

88 *Searchlight,* 14 Nov. 1919.

89 *Calgary Herald,* 15 Aug. 1921.

90 H.B. Adshead, 'Smelly People,' in his *Pioneer Tales and Other Human Stories* (Calgary: n.p., 1924).

91 *Calgary Herald,* 15 July 1919; Royal Commission into Industrial Relations, testimony of F.J. White; *Searchlight,* 5 Dec. 1919.

92 GMA, M4743, Calgary Trades and Labour Council minutes, 12 Sept. 1921; *Calgary Herald,* 26 Sept. 1919.
93 *Calgary Herald,* 4 April 1920.
94 Ibid., 28 Jan. 1920.
95 Ibid., 30 March 1924.
96 Ibid.

Chapter 7: 1919

1 The essential account remains David Jay Bercuson, *Confrontation at Winnipeg: Labour, Industrial Relations, and the General Strike* (Montreal: McGill-Queen's University Press, 1974), while Bryan Palmer provides a recent, alternative interpretation in *Working-Class Experience: Rethinking the History of Canadian Labour, 1800-1991,* 2nd ed. (Toronto: McClelland and Stewart, 1992), 200-5. Other important works on the strike include Gerald Friesen, '"Yours in Revolt": The Socialist Party of Canada and the Western Labour Movement,' *Labour/Le Travailleur* 1 (1976): 139-57; Gregory S. Kealey, '1919: The Canadian Labour Revolt,' *Labour/Le Travail* 13 (1984): 11-44; Allen Seager, 'Nineteen Nineteen: Year of Revolt,' *Journal of the West* 23, 4 (1984): 23-61; James Dubro and Robin Rowland, *Undercover: Cases of the RCMP's Most Secret Operative* (Toronto: McClelland and Stewart, 1991), 39-86; Nolan Reilly, 'The General Strike in Amherst, Nova Scotia,' *Acadiensis* 9, 2 (1980): 56-77; James Naylor, 'Toronto 1919,' Canadian Historical Association *Historical Papers* (1986): 33-55; James R. Conley, 'Frontier Labourers, Crafts in Crisis, and the Western Labour Revolt,' *Labour/Le Travail* 23 (1989): 9-38. Among the more recent contributions to the literature on the subject are Chad Reimer, 'The Counterhegemonic Challenge of the 1919 Winnipeg General Strike,' *Prairie Forum* 18, 2 (1993): 219-37; Tom Mitchell, '"To Reach the Leadership of the Revolutionary Movement": A.J. Andrews, the Canadian State, and the Suppression of the Winnipeg General Strike,' ibid., 239-55; J.M. Bumsted, '1919: The Winnipeg General Strike Reconsidered,' *Beaver* 74, 3 (1994): 27-44 and *The Winnipeg General Strike of 1919: An Illustrated History* (Winnipeg: Watson and Dwyer, 1994); Craig Heron, ed., *The Workers' Revolt in Canada, 1917-1925* (Toronto: University of Toronto Press, 1998).
2 Bercuson, *Confrontation at Winnipeg,* 194. See also Martin Robin, *Radical Politics and Canadian Labour* (Kingston: Queen's University Industrial Relations Centre, 1968), 199-267; A. Ross McCormack, *Reformers, Rebels, and Revolutionaries: The Western Radical Labour Movement, 1899-1919* (1977; reprint, Toronto: University of Toronto Press, 1991), 170-1.
3 Palmer, *Working-Class Experience,* 190.
4 McCormack, *Reformers, Rebels, and Revolutions,* 159.
5 Elizabeth Ann Taraska, 'The Calgary Craft Union Movement, 1900-1920' (MA thesis, University of Calgary, 1975), 62.
6 Further elaboration of this argument may be found in David Bright, '"We Are All Kin": Reconsidering Labour and Class in Calgary, 1919,' *Labour/Le Travail* 29 (1992): 59-80.
7 Desmond Morton with Terry Copp, *Working People: An Illustrated History of the Canadian Labour Movement,* rev. ed. (Toronto: Deneau, 1987), 113-24; Palmer, *Working-Class Experience,* 196-213.
8 Taraska, 'Calgary Craft Union Movement,' 71-2.
9 For example, see David J. Bercuson, *Fools and Wise Men: The Rise and Fall of the One Big Union* (Toronto: McGraw-Hill Ryerson, 1978), 71-2; Kealey, '1919,' 31-2; M. Ann Capling, 'The Communist Party of Canada in Alberta, 1922-1929' (MA thesis, University of Calgary, 1983), 19.
10 Taraska, 'Calgary Craft Union Movement,' 65-8.
11 Ibid., 62-72.
12 For details of Tallon's career, see *Canadian Congress Journal* 10, 3 (1931): 28-9.
13 Bercuson, *Confrontation at Winnipeg,* 81; Kealey, '1919,' 31. For details of federal anti-labour legislation passed in this period, see also Gregory S. Kealey, 'State Repression of Labour and the Left in Canada, 1914-1920: The Impact of the First World War,' *Canadian Historical Review* 73, 3 (1992): 281-314.

14 *Albertan,* 11 Oct. 1918, 14 Oct. 1918.
15 Taraska's account of events – by far the fullest and most attentive to detail – runs into trouble when she tries to explain how such an expression of militant class consciousness folded so quietly in the face of limited government opposition. Taraska, 'Calgary Craft Union Movement,' 69-70.
16 *Calgary Herald,* 8 Oct. 1918, 10 Oct. 1918, 11 Oct. 1918, 12 Oct. 1918, 16 Oct. 1918, 18 Oct. 1918; *Albertan,* 16 Oct. 1918, 19 Oct. 1918, 19 Oct. 1918. See also Ross's analysis of the strike in *Alberta Non-Partisan,* 6 Nov. 1918.
17 *Alberta Non-Partisan,* 6 Nov. 1918.
18 Ibid., 18 Oct. 1918.
19 Bercuson, *Fools and Wise Men,* 71-2.
20 *Albertan,* 18 Oct. 1918. The text of the IDIA is reproduced in Dave de Brou and Bill Waiser, eds., *Documenting Canada: A History of Modern Canada in Documents* (Saskatoon: Fifth House Publishers, 1992), 206-13. Confusion over this point is particularly surprising given that Martin Robin had made the correct interpretation in 1968. See Robin, *Radical Politics and Canadian Labour,* 167-8.
21 Palmer, *Working-Class Experience,* 205-6; Paul Craven, *'An Impartial Umpire': Industrial Relations and the Canadian State, 1900-1911* (Toronto: University of Toronto Press, 1980), 279-317; Reginald Whitaker, 'The Liberal Corporatist Ideas of Mackenzie King,' *Labour/Le Travailleur* 2 (1977): 137-69.
22 *Alberta Non-Partisan,* 6 Nov. 1918.
23 Friesen, 'Yours in Revolt,' 144.
24 Robin, *Radical Politics and Canadian Labour,* 175; McCormack, *Reformers, Rebels, and Revolutionaries,* 159; Friesen, 'Yours in Revolt,' 145; Palmer, *Working-Class Experience,* 189.
25 Quoted in Friesen, 'Yours in Revolt,' 143.
26 *The Origin of the One Big Union: A Verbatim Report of the Calgary Conference, 1919* (Winnipeg: One Big Union, 1919), 42.
27 On western Canadian syndicalism, see McCormack, *Reformers, Rebels, and Revolutionaries,* 113, 116-7, 143-5; Mark Leier, *Where the Fraser River Flows: The Industrial Workers of the World in British Columbia* (Vancouver: New Star Books, 1990), 1-31. On the relationship between moderate trade unionists and socialists, see Mark Leier, 'Workers and Intellectuals: The Theory of the New Class and Early Canadian Socialism,' in *Making Western Canada: Essays on European Colonization and Settlement,* ed. Catherine Cavanaugh and Jeremy Mouat (Toronto: Garamond Press, 1996), 133-53.
28 Martin Robin makes this observation in *Radical Politics and Canadian Labour,* 175-7, as does David Bercuson in *Fools and Wise Men,* 85-6. Neither author, however, pays much attention to the considerations and conditions that shaped the stand taken by Calgary's delegates, a stand sharply at odds with the otherwise unanimous outpouring of western radicalism.
29 *Origin of the One Big Union,* 47. See also David Akers, 'Rebel or Revolutionary? Jack Kavanagh and the Early Years of the Communist Movement in Vancouver, 1920-1925,' *Labour/Le Travail* 30 (1992): 9-44.
30 *Origin of the One Big Union,* 47.
31 Ibid.
32 Bercuson, *Fools and Wise Men,* 127-8.
33 Public Archives of Alberta (PAA), Edmonton Trades and Labour Council, minutes, 21 April 1919, 5 May 1919. On the ETLC's history, see William R. Askins, 'Labour Unrest in Edmonton and District and Its Coverage by the Edmonton Press, 1918-1919' (MA thesis, University of Alberta, 1973).
34 Bercuson, *Fools and Wise Men,* 107.
35 *Calgary Herald,* 19 March 1919, 20 March 1919.
36 Author's interviews with Parkyn's son, Reginald Parkyn, 25 Jan. 1992, 18 April 1992.
37 *Albertan,* 20 March 1918.
38 *Calgary Herald,* 17 April 1919; *Albertan,* 31 March 1919; GMA, Bricklayers and Stonemasons International Union, Local 2, minutes (BSMIU mins), 24 April 1919; GMA, International Typographical Union, Local 449, minutes (ITU mins), 29 March 1919, 26 April

1919; GMA, Sheet Metal Workers Union, Local 254, minutes (SWM mins), 1 May 1919; John Blue, *Alberta, Past and Present: Historical and Biographical* (Chicago: Pioneer Historical Publishing, 1924), 1: 386.

39 Blue, *Alberta, Past and Present,* 381, 386; Bercuson, 'Western Labour Radicalism and the One Big Union: Myths and Realities,' in *The Twenties in Western Canada,* ed. S.M. Trofimenkoff (Ottawa: Queen's Printer, 1973), 32.

40 Kealey, '1919,' 29.

41 National Archives of Canada (NAC), RG 27, Department of Labour, vol. 313, file 151A, ms 72699, F.E. Harrison to Gideon Robertson, 7 June 1919.

42 See NAC, RG 146, CSIS files, vol. 1, file 1025-9-99028, part 12.

43 Zaneth's story is told more fully in James Dubro and Robin Rowland, *Undercover: Cases of the RCMP's Most Secret Operative* (Toronto: McClelland and Stewart, 1991).

44 NAC, RG 146, vol. 1, file 1025-9-9028, part 12, Det.-Corpl. S.R. Waugh to 'K' Division, Lethbridge, 27 May 1919.

45 Ibid., Waugh to 'K' Division, 29 May 1919.

46 Ibid.

47 *Calgary Strike Bulletin,* 11 June 1919.

48 Ibid.

49 NAC, RG 146, vol. 1, file 1025-9-9028, part 12, Inspector J.W. Spalding to 'K' Division, 11 June 1919.

50 Ibid., Spalding to 'K' Division, 3 June 1919.

51 Quoted in ibid., report by RNWMP officer FWZ[aneth], 20 June 1919.

52 Ibid., report by J.W. Spalding, RNWMP Inspector, Calgary Sub-Division, 21 May 1919.

53 Ibid., quoted in Waugh to 'K' Division, 29 May 1919.

54 Ibid., Spalding to 'K' Division, 24 June 1919.

55 For example, see Alimohamed Damji, 'Militancy to Passivism: The Calgary Labour Movement, 1919-1924' (MA thesis, University of Calgary, 1987), 89.

56 *Calgary Herald,* 28 May 1919.

57 Interview with Reginald Parkyn.

58 *Calgary Strike Bulletin,* 30 May 1919.

59 *Edmonton Free Press,* 21 June 1920; *Searchlight,* 3 Sept. 1920; *Calgary Herald,* 15 March 1921; Jack Masson and Peter Blaikie, 'Labour Politics in Alberta,' in *Society and Politics in Alberta: Research Papers,* ed. C. Caldarola (Toronto: Methuen, 1979), 272-3. On shop stewards, see James Hinton, *The First Shop Stewards Movement* (London: Allen and Unwin, 1973).

60 *Calgary Herald,* 2 Feb. 1920.

61 Ibid., 23 Dec. 1919, 10 Dec. 1920, 15 March 1921, 22 Nov. 1921; GMA clippings file for Sophie McCluskey. On the formation of labour churches in western Canada, see Richard Allen, *The Social Passion: Religion and Social Reform in Canada* (1971; reprint, Toronto: University of Toronto Press, 1990), 159-74; Kenneth McNaught, *A Prophet in Politics: A Biography of J.S. Woodsworth* (Toronto: University of Toronto Press, 1963), 136-9; Howard Palmer, 'William Irvine and the Emergence of Political Radicalism in Calgary, 1916-1921,' *Fort Calgary Quarterly* 7, 2 (1987): 10-2; Anthony Mardiros, *William Irvine: The Life of a Prairie Radical* (Toronto: Lorimer, 1979), 38-42.

62 *Edmonton Free Press,* 20 March 1920. The committee consisted of Andrew Broatch, Harry Pryde, Robert Parkyn, Mrs A. Corliss, Rachel Coutts, William Irvine, Edith Patterson, A. Nicholson, S. Lunnan, and R. Gosett. The last is probably Robert Gosden, a police spy operating in Calgary in 1919. See Dubro and Rowland, *Undercover,* 44; Gregory S. Kealey, 'The Surveillance State: The Origins of Domestic Intelligence and Counter-Subversion in Canada, 1914-1921,' *Intelligence and National Security* 7, 3 (1992): 201-2. My thanks to Mark Leier for providing further insights into the career of Gosden.

63 This was the view of the CTLC's Labour Temple Company, which continued to deny the OBU permission to rent hall space in 1920 for this reason. GMA, M2204/M4743, Labour Temple Company, minutes, 17 April 1920.

64 *Edmonton Free Press,* 1 Nov. 1919.

65 *Calgary Herald,* 27 Sept. 1919.

Chapter 8: Dissent and Descent

1 For example, Desmond Morton with Terry Copp, *Working People: An Illustrated History of the Canadian Labour Movement,* rev. ed. (Toronto: Deneau, 1984), 113-24; Bryan D. Palmer, *Working-Class Experience: Rethinking the History of Canadian Labour, 1800-1991,* 2nd ed. (Toronto: McClelland and Stewart, 1992), 200-13. Studies that attempt to place the events of 1919 within a continuum of experience include James Naylor, *The New Democracy: Challenging the Social Order in Industrial Ontario, 1914-1925* (Toronto: University of Toronto Press, 1991), and Gregory S. Kealey, 'The Surveillance State: The Origins of Domestic Intelligence and Counter-Subversion in Canada, 1914-1921,' *Intelligence and National Security* 7, 3 (1992): 179-210. Despite his own somewhat teleological approach to the western Canadian labour movement before 1919, Ross McCormack also suggests the degree to which a sense of continuity was as important as any abrupt shift in tactics ascribed to the impact of the failed general strikes that year. See A. Ross McCormack, *Reformers, Rebels, and Revolutionaries: The Western Canadian Radical Movement, 1899-1919* (1977; reprint, Toronto: University of Toronto Press, 1991), 170-1.

2 *Calgary Herald,* 6 Dec. 1918.

3 *Albertan,* 15 Nov. 1918; *Calgary Herald,* 2 Dec. 1918, 3 Dec. 1918, 4 Dec. 1918, 6 Dec. 1918, 10 Dec. 1918. The eleven defeated labour candidates were: William Groves (machinist); Edward Geehan (machinist); Thomas McLaughlin (railway carman); Robert Parkyn (carpenter); Walter Smitten (bricklayer); David Davidson (occupation unknown); Joseph Harris (machinist); William McPhee (blacksmith); David Ormond (stonecutter); James Petrie (machinist); and Joseph Hooley (boilermaker). For more details on Corse, see Patricia Roome, 'Amelia Turner and Calgary Labour Women,' in *Beyond the Vote: Canadian Women and Politics,* ed. Linda Kealey and Joan Sangster (Toronto: University of Toronto Press, 1989), 94-8.

4 Glenbow Museum Archives (GMA), M2204/M4743, Calgary Labour Temple Company, minutes, box 6, file 132, Reports of Campaign Committee, 1918.

5 *Calgary Herald,* 23 Sept. 1918.

6 Roome, 'Amelia Turner and Calgary Labour Women,' 98.

7 Suzanne Morton, *Ideal Surroundings: Domestic Life in a Working-Class Suburb in the 1920s* (Toronto: University of Toronto Press, 1995), 154.

8 Alvin Finkel, 'The Rise and Fall of the Labour Party in Alberta, 1917-1942,' *Labour/Le Travail* 16 (1985): 69.

9 *Calgary Herald,* 27 Sept. 1918.

10 Ibid., 6 Dec. 1918, 11 Dec. 1918.

11 *Alberta Labor News,* 18 Sept. 1920.

12 Ibid., 9 Oct. 1920. By Sept. 1921, DLP membership in Calgary stood at 270, compared with more than 3,000 CTLC members. *Calgary Herald,* 21 Sept. 1921.

13 *Calgary Herald,* 9 Feb. 1920.

14 *Alberta Labor News,* 13 Nov. 1920.

15 *Calgary Herald,* 11 Dec. 1920, 13 Dec. 1920, 14 Dec. 1920, 16 Dec. 1920.

16 Biographical details of Broatch are from GMA, clippings file for Andrew Broatch, and the profile in *Calgary Herald,* 6 Dec. 1919.

17 Ibid., 17 April 1916.

18 *Nutcracker,* 2 Dec. 1916.

19 *Red Flag,* 21 June 1919; *Searchlight,* 2 Jan. 1919.

20 *Calgary Herald,* 16 Dec. 1920.

21 *Alberta Labor News,* 20 Nov. 1920, 27 Nov. 1920.

22 *Calgary Herald,* 13 Nov. 1920; *Alberta Labor News,* 27 Nov. 1920.

23 *Calgary Herald,* 8 Dec. 1920.

24 On the success of non-traditional parties, see John Herd Thompson with Allen Seager, *Canada, 1922-1939: Decades of Discord* (Toronto: McClelland and Stewart, 1985), 14. Elsewhere, Seager similarly emphasizes the importance of 1921 for labour in Canada. See Allen Seager, 'Workers, Class, and Industrial Conflict in New Westminster,' in *Workers, Capital, and the State in British Columbia: Selected Papers,* ed. Rennie Warburton and David Coburn (Vancouver: UBC Press, 1988), 130.

25 Kenneth A. Wark, *A Report on Alberta Elections, 1905-1982* (Edmonton: n.p., 1983), 33.

26 *Calgary Herald,* 9 July 1921; Wark, *Alberta Elections,* 25, 33. Williams's share of the popular vote was four times that of the combined total for the seven Communist Party candidates who ran in the provincial election of March 1975. Ibid., 109-10.

27 *Calgary Herald,* 19 July 1921; Wark, *Alberta Elections,* 33-6. The two were William Johnson in Medicine Hat and P.M. Christophers in Rocky Mountain House.

28 *Calgary Herald,* 9 Sept. 1921, 23 Sept. 1921. See also Martin Robin, *Radical Politics and Canadian Labour, 1880-1930* (Kingston: Queen's University Industrial Relations Centre, 1968), 200-3. However, for labour's suspicions of both the Liberals and UFA, see *Alberta Labor News,* 2 April 1921, 16 April 1921.

29 GMA, M1157, Walter Norman Smith papers, box 1, file 5, Norman Smith to Rex R. Smith, 22 Aug. 1922; *Alberta Labor News,* 23 April 1921. For an account of Meighen and the 1921 federal election, see Roger Graham, *Arthur Meighen,* vol. 2, *And Fortune Fled* (Toronto: Clarke, Irwin, 1963), 165-201.

30 For Shaw's political views, see *Alberta Labor News,* 29 Oct. 1921.

31 Walter D. Young, *Democracy and Discontent: Progressivism, Socialism, and Social Credit in the Canadian West* (Toronto: Ryerson, 1969), 29-39; Francis A. Carman, 'The Labour Party in Parliament,' *Dalhousie Review* 2, 4 (1923): 444-56; Kenneth McNaught, *A Prophet in Politics: A Biography of J.S. Woodsworth* (Toronto: University of Toronto Press, 1963), 167-8. Irvine's performance in Ottawa is discussed in Leif Gordon Stolee, 'The Parliamentary Career of William Irvine, 1922-1935' (MA thesis, University of Alberta, 1969)

32 *Alberta Labor News,* 12 Nov. 1921, 26 Nov. 1921, 10 Dec. 1921.

33 *Calgary Herald,* 21 Sept. 1921, 2 Nov. 1921, 22 Nov. 1921.

34 Ibid., 30 Nov. 1921, 1 Dec. 1921, 7 March 1923.

35 *Alberta Labor News,* 24 Dec. 1921.

36 Labour councillors soon demonstrated their power when they blocked the reappointment of Mrs E.P. Newhall to the library board, thus forcing Mayor Samuel Adams to cast his deciding vote in favour. Ibid., 3 Jan. 1922.

37 Ibid., 15 Dec. 1921; *Alberta Labor News,* 26 Nov. 1921.

38 Ibid. This account contrasts with Finkel's observation that 'The close relationship of the Dominion Labor Party with the trade unions insured that the DLP would be well-funded and was unlikely to have rifts with the trade union movement.' Finkel, 'The Labor Party in Alberta,' 70. For details on the Winnipeg conference and labour's divisions elsewhere in Canada, see Robin, *Radical Politics and Canadian Labour,* 213-4.

39 *Alberta Labor News,* 26 Nov. 1921. This issue also contains an outline of the CLP's platform.

40 *Alberta Labor News,* 21 Jan. 1922.

41 Robin, *Radical Politics and Canadian Labour,* 252.

42 *Alberta Labor News,* 14 Dec. 1922.

43 See Maxwell Laurence Foran, 'The Civic Corporation and Urban Growth: Calgary, 1884-1930' (PhD diss., University of Calgary, 1981), 255-352.

44 *Calgary Herald,* 10 Jan. 1922. See also *Alberta Labor News,* 17 June 1922.

45 Ibid., 7 Oct. 1922, 20 March 1923; *Alberta Labor News,* 21 Oct. 1922. On the importance of class divisions within municipal politics in the post-1919 era, see J.E. Rea, *Parties and Power: An Analysis of Winnipeg City Council, 1919-1975* (Winnipeg: University of Manitoba, n.d.), 1-14.

46 Palmer, *Working-Class Experience,* 168; Robert H. Babcock, *Gompers in Canada: A Study in American Continentalism before the First World War* (Toronto: University of Toronto Press, 1974), 72-97.

47 *Calgary Herald,* 25 Jan. 1923, 10 Feb. 1923.

48 Ibid., 5 June 1920.

49 GMA, M4743, Calgary Trades and Labour Council, minutes, 27 Aug. 1920, 8 Oct. 1920, 30 Dec. 1920.

50 *Calgary Herald,* 1 Feb. 1923.

51 Ibid., 6 April 1923; Robin, *Radical Politics and Canadian Labour,* 252; Roome, 'Amelia Turner and Calgary Labour Women,' 93.

52 Edwin Fay, 'The Early Years,' *Marxist Quarterly* 1 (Spring 1962): 19-21; M. Ann Capling, 'The Communist Party of Canada in Alberta, 1922-1929' (MA thesis, University of Calgary, 1983), 5-29, 110-42; Robin, *Radical Politics and Canadian Labour,* 147. See also William Rodney, *Soldiers of the International: A History of the Communist Party of Canada, 1919-1929* (Toronto: University of Toronto Press, 1968); and Ian Angus, *Canadian Bolsheviks: The Early Years of the Communist Party of Canada* (Montreal: Vanguard Publications, 1981).

53 *Workers' Guard,* 1 Feb. 1923, 15 March 1923; *Canadian Congress Journal* 3, 5 (1923): 15; Finkel, 'Labour Party in Alberta,' 75-81; David Akers, 'Rebel or Revolutionary? Jack Kavanagh and the Early Years of the Communist Movement in Vancouver, 1920-1925,' *Labour/Le Travail* 30 (1992): 35, 41. For background details on the move to the united front, see Larry Peterson, 'The One Big Union in International Perspective: Revolutionary Industrial Unionism, 1900-1925,' *Labour/Le Travailleur* 7 (1981): 115-31; Ralph Miliband, *Parliamentary Socialism: A Study in the Politics of Labour,* 2nd ed. (London: Merlin Press, 1972), 82-92. See also V.I. Lenin, *'Left-Wing' Communism, an Infantile Disorder* (Moscow: Progress Publishers, 1950).

54 *Calgary Herald,* 2 March 1923; *Alberta Labor News,* 3 March 1923, 17 March 1923.

55 On Ross's outspoken defence of labour, see *Alberta Labor News,* 4 Sept. 1920.

56 Finkel, 'The Labour Party in Alberta,' 73; *Calgary Herald,* 30 Dec. 1919, 31 Dec. 1919, 2 Dec. 1920, 18 Oct. 1923; *Alberta Non-Partisan,* 20 Nov. 1919.

57 Roome, 'Amelia Turner and Calgary Labour Women,' 100.

58 *Calgary Herald,* 24 Oct. 1923. For details on Bartholomew, see Capling, 'Communist Party of Canada in Alberta,' 8.

59 *Calgary Herald,* 23 March 1924; CTLC mins, 21 March 1924; *Alberta Labor News,* 29 March 1924, 12 April 1924.

60 Roome, 'Amelia Turner and Calgary Labour Women,' 98; *Calgary Herald,* 16 April 1924, 19 April 1924, 21 April 1924, 7 May 1924; *Alberta Labor News,* 26 July 1924. For comparison, see Ian McKay, *The Craft Transformed* (Halifax: Holdfast Press, 1985), 74.

61 *Edmonton Bulletin,* 11 Sept. 1924. For biographical details of Roper, see *Canadian Congress Journal* 11, 1 (1932): 9; *Calgary Herald,* 16 Nov. 1994.

62 *Alberta Labor News,* 16 Aug. 1924.

63 *Edmonton Bulletin,* 11 Sept. 1924. On Bartholomew's talent as an orator, see Ivan Avakumovic, *The Communist Party in Canada: A History* (Toronto: McClelland and Stewart, 1975), 24. Bartholomew's career was cut short after party members brought child molestation charges against him, and he committed suicide in 1931.

64 Wark, *Alberta Elections,* 177; *Edmonton Bulletin,* 31 Oct. 1924.

65 *Alberta Labor News,* 13 Sept. 1924, 11 Oct. 1924; *Calgary Herald,* 4 Oct. 1924. See also Capling, 'Communist Party of Canada in Alberta,' 117.

66 *Calgary Herald,* 24 Nov. 1924, 10 Dec. 1924, 11 Dec. 1924; *Alberta Labor News,* 22 Nov. 1924, 13 Dec. 1924. In her study of Calgary female labour activists, Patricia Roome also regards the end of 1924 as a turning point in labour's fortunes. Roome, 'Amelia Turner and Calgary Labour Women,' 102-3. More generally, Craig Heron concludes that 'labourism had collapsed as a significant force in Canadian politics by 1925.' Craig Heron, 'Labourism and the Canadian Working Class,' *Labour/Le Travail* 13 (1984): 70. See also James Naylor, 'Ontario Workers and the Decline of Labourism,' in *Patterns of the Past: Interpreting Ontario's History,* ed. Roger Hall, William Westfall, and Laurel Sefton MacDowell (Toronto: Dundurn Press, 1988), 278-300.

67 *Calgary Herald,* 3 March 1923.

Chapter 9: The Limits of Labour, 1925-9

1 For a regional comparison, see Jim W. Warrian, 'From Pluralism to Pluralism: The Political Experience of Organized Labour in Saskatchewan from 1900 to 1938' (MA thesis, University of Regina, 1985). James H. Gray provides an account of the decade in *The Roar of the Twenties* (Toronto: Macmillan, 1975). See also Gerald Friesen, *The Canadian Prairies: A History* (Toronto: University of Toronto Press, 1987), 339-411; Bryan D. Palmer, *Working-Class Experience: Rethinking the History of Canadian Labour, 1800-1991,* 2nd ed.

(Toronto: McClelland and Stewart, 1992), 214-40; Desmond Morton with Terry Copp, *Working People: An Illustrated History of the Canadian Labour Movement,* rev. ed. (Toronto: Deneau, 1987), 125-38; James Naylor, *The New Democracy: Challenging the Social Order in Industrial Ontario, 1919-1924* (Toronto: University of Toronto Press, 1991). For comparative work in the United States, see David Montgomery, *The Fall of the House of Labor* (1987; reprint, Cambridge: Cambridge University Press, 1989), 411-64; Robert H. Zeiger, *American Workers, American Unions, 1920-1985* (Baltimore: Johns Hopkins University Press, 1986), 3-25; Alan Dawley, *Struggles for Justice: Social Responsibility and the Liberal State* (Cambridge: Belknap Press, 1991), 295-333.

2 Michael Bliss provides the context for this recovery in *Northern Enterprise: Five Centuries of Canadian Business* (Toronto: McClelland and Stewart, 1987), 381-409.

3 Statistics are based on various volumes of the following: *Henderson's Calgary City Directory; Calgary Municipal Manuals*; Calgary Board of Trade, *Annual Reports; Canadian Year Book.* See also Maxwell Foran, *Calgary: An Illustrated History* (Toronto: Lorimer, 1978), 120; *Calgary Herald,* 8 Jan. 1927, 12 Dec. 1929.

4 Glenbow Museum Archives (GMA), M2260, Calgary Chamber of Commerce, Annual Reports for 1924-30.

5 Ibid.

6 Ibid., 9 July 1929.

7 Calgary Chamber of Commerce, Annual Reports for 1925 and 1928; *Calgary Herald,* 5 Aug. 1926, 10 May 1928; *Canadian Annual Review* (1928), 284.

8 Foran, *Calgary,* 124.

9 GMA, M4743, Calgary Trades and Labour Council, minutes, (CTLC mins), 10 June 1927.

10 GMA, M2201, Brotherhood of Locomotive Firemen and Enginemen, Local 635, minutes (BLFE mins), 14 March 1926; GMA, M7070, International Typographical Union, Local 449, minutes (ITU mins), 25 Jan. 1930, 22 Feb. 1930.

11 *Alberta Labor News: Labor Annual,* 2 Sept. 1929. See also Donald M. Marvin, 'Review of Modern Business Methods,' *Canadian Congress Journal* 7, 7 (July 1928), and Herman Frank, 'Does the Machine De-Humanize?' ibid., 7, 12 (Dec. 1928).

12 *Calgary Herald,* 13 Jan. 1926.

13 For a contemporary survey of conditions, see Scott Nearing, 'The Labour Situation in Western Canada,' *Labor Monthly* 7, 5 (May 1925): 288-93.

14 *Canadian Annual Review* (1920-9); Friesen, *Canadian Prairies,* 512.

15 *Canadian Annual Review* (1924-31).

16 GMA, M7227, United Brotherhood of Carpenters and Joiners of America, Local 1779, minutes (UBCJA mins), 26 Feb. 1925, 30 July 1925, 14 Jan. 1926, 22 April 1926, 6 May 1926, 29 May 1930.

17 GMA, M2198, Bricklayers and Stonemasons International Union, Local 2, minutes (BSMIU mins), 6 Feb. 1925, 13 March 1925, 27 March 1925, 24 April 1925, 8 May 1925, 22 May 1925, 19 June 1925, 3 July 1925, 17 July 1925; GMA, M2230, Sheet Metal Workers' Union, Local 254, minutes (SMW mins), 8 Jan. 1925, 18 Aug. 1926, 10 July 1927; ITU mins, 31 Jan. 1925, 28 Feb. 1925, 27 March 1926, 24 April 1926, 29 May 1926, 30 Nov. 1929; Calgary Chamber of Commerce, Annual Report for 1925.

18 *Alberta Labor News,* 28 Feb. 1925; *Calgary Herald,* 21 March 1925.

19 *Calgary Herald,* 12 Jan. 1925, 23 Jan. 1925, 21 Feb. 1925, 26 March 1925; *Alberta Labor News,* 17 Jan. 1925; CTLC mins, 4 Feb. 1927.

20 *Calgary Herald,* 12 Jan. 1925, 24 Jan. 1925; *Alberta Labor News,* 31 Jan. 1925.

21 *Calgary Herald,* 30 Jan. 1925.

22 Ibid., 9 Jan. 1926.

23 Ibid., 30 March 1925.

24 Ibid., 23 March 1925, 26 March 1925.

25 Public Archives of Alberta (PAA), *Report of the Conference Between the Unemployed Association of Alberta and the Provincial Government* (31 March 1925), 1-8.

26 *Calgary Herald,* 12 Jan. 1925, 13 Jan. 1925.

27 Ibid., 16 Jan. 1926, 13 March 1926.

28 Ibid., 8 Dec. 1926, 18 Jan. 1927. On the growing conservatism of the UFA administration,

see Susan M. Kooyman, 'The Policies and Legislation of the United Farmers of Alberta Government, 1921-1935' (MA thesis, University of Calgary, 1981), 12-23.
29 *Calgary Herald,* 18 Jan. 1927.
30 Ibid., 20 Jan. 1927, 21 Jan. 1927. Boulter frequently overestimated the revolutionary sentiment among Calgary's unemployed, as when he predicted that 1,200 individuals would attend the planned Communist Party's commemoration of Lenin. Ibid., 20 Jan. 1925.
31 Ibid., 12 Nov. 1929, 13 Nov. 1929, 23 Nov. 1929; GMA, M2118, Associated Charities Association papers, file 2, Board of Public Welfare Annual Reports (1929-31).
32 James Struthers, *No Fault of Their Own: Unemployment and the Canadian Welfare State, 1914-1941* (Toronto: University of Toronto Press, 1983), 42.
33 Calgary City Archives (CCA), RG 26, City Clerk papers, box 209, file 1403, Mayor Osborne to ?, 16 Dec. 1929; ibid., circular from Andrew Davison, R.C. Thomas and T.A. Hornibrook, 7 Jan. 1930.
34 *Calgary Herald,* 24 Jan. 1925.
35 Ibid., 30 Jan. 1925.
36 Membership figures are based on the annual reports of the president of the CTLC, reproduced in part in the local press. *Calgary Herald,* 24 Jan. 1925, 22 Jan. 1927, 25 May 1928; *Alberta Labor News,* 28 Jan. 1928. These figures do not always tally with those published in other sources, such as *Labour Organization in Canada* and *Canadian Congress Journal.*
37 UBCJA mins, 29 May 1930; *Calgary Herald,* 8 Dec. 1928.
38 *Labour Organization in Canada* (1930), 77. For a listing of Calgary unions in this period, see A.J. Heide, ed. *Union Label Guide of Calgary,* vol. 2 (Calgary: n.p., 1928).
39 *Alberta Labor News,* 12 June 1926; *Calgary Herald,* 24 July 1926. See also Robert Hewitt, 'A Labor Day Message on Organization,' *Alberta Labor News: Labor Annual,* 2 Sept. 1929, 29-30.
40 *Alberta Labor News,* 22 May 1926, 26 May 1926; CTLC mins, 21 Jan. 1927, 1 April 1927.
41 Mark Leier, *Red Flags and Red Tape: The Making of a Labour Bureaucracy* (Toronto: University of Toronto Press, 1995), 41.
42 Ibid., 34.
43 See ibid., 13-42 for a detailed discussion of the relevant historiography. See also John Foster, 'British Imperialism and the Labour Aristocracy,' in *The General Strike 1926,* ed. Jeffrey Skelley (London: Lawrence and Wishart, 1976); A.E. Musson, 'Class Struggle and the Labour Aristocracy, 1830-1860,' *Social History* 1, 3 (1976): 335-56; H.F. Moorhouse, 'The Marxist Theory of the Labour Aristocracy,' ibid. 3, 1 (1978): 61-83; Alistair Reid, 'Politics and Economics in the Formation of the British Working Class: A Response to H.F. Moorhouse,' ibid. 3, 3 (1978): 347-61; John Field, 'British Historians and the Concept of the Labor Aristocracy,' *Radical History Review* 19 (Winter 1978-9): 61-85; and Robert Gray, *The Aristocracy of Labour in Nineteenth-Century Britain, c. 1850-1900* (London: Macmillan, 1981).
44 Leier, *Red Flags and Red Tape,* 35.
45 *Calgary Herald,* 24 Jan. 1925, 22 Jan. 1927, 15 July 1927, 3 Oct. 1951; *Alberta Labor News,* 31 Jan. 1925, 29 Jan. 1927, 2 July 1927, 10 Sept. 1927, 4 Feb. 1928.
46 *Alberta Labor News,* 28 Jan. 1928, 8 July 1928; *Calgary Herald,* 16 Aug. 1948.
47 GMA, M2204, Calgary Labour Temple Company, minutes, 14 March 1922, 31 Dec. 1922, 31 Dec. 1923, 4 Feb. 1924, 31 Dec. 1924, 31 Dec. 1925, ? Dec. 1926, 1 Feb. 1927, 12 Sept. 1927, 24 Feb. 1928, 11 Feb. 1929, 3 Feb. 1929.
48 *Alberta Labor News,* 31 Jan. 1925, 20 April 1929; *Calgary Herald,* 18 Nov. 1926, 10 Nov. 1928, 13 Nov. 1929.
49 *Alberta Labor News,* 22 Jan. 1927, 5 Sept. 1927.
50 See Palmer, *Working-Class Experience,* 252-3.
51 *Calgary Herald,* 28 Feb. 1925, 16 May 1925.
52 Calgary Labour Temple Company, minutes, 12 May 1925; J.E. Worsley, 'Toward Unity,' *Alberta Labor News: Labor Annual*, 3 Sept. 1928; Canadian Labor Party, *Building Alberta for the People on the Labor Plan* (n.p., 1930).

53 *Labour Organization in Canada* (1927), 145-7; ibid. (1929), 137-9.

54 National Archives of Canada (NAC), RG 27, Department of Labour, 'Strikes and Lockouts,' vol. 335, file 69; vol. 338, file 2; vol. 340, files 31, 33; vol. 341, file 66; vol. 343, file 48. See also *Labour Gazette* (1925-9), passim.

55 'Strikes and Lockouts,' vol. 335, file 69.

56 Ibid., vol. 343, file 48.

57 Palmer, *Working-Class Experience,* 221.

58 NAC, microfilm C2275, William Lyon MacKenzie King papers, vol. 129, William Davidson to William Lyon Mackenzie King, 10 Nov. 1925, 30 Nov. 1925.

59 *Calgary Herald,* 23 Oct. 1925; Howard A. Scarrow, *Canada Votes: A Handbook of Federal and Provincial Election Data* (New Orleans: Hauser Press, 1962), 44, 53.

60 *Calgary Herald,* 12 Nov. 1925, 9 Dec. 1925, 11 Dec. 1925, 17 Dec. 1925. The seven candidates who ran in 1925 were Andrew Davison, Donald Macpherson, Robert Parkyn, Thomas Vickers (council); Thomas Riley, William Ewart Turner, Amelia Turner (school board).

61 Ibid., 9 Jan. 1926, 28 Jan. 1926, 4 Feb. 1926, 10 Feb. 1926, 16 March 1926, 1 April 1926; *Alberta Labor News,* 26 Sept. 1925, 3 April 1926; author's interview with Reginald Parkyn, Robert Parkyn's son (18 April 1992).

62 *Calgary Herald,* 25 June 1926. On radical democratic populism in the west, see David Laycock, *Populism and Democratic Thought in the Canadian Prairies, 1910 to 1945* (Toronto: University of Toronto Press, 1990), 69-135.

63 *Calgary Herald,* 14 June 1926, 18 June 1926, 25 June 1926; *Alberta Labor News,* 12 June 1926; *Labour Organization in Canada* (1926), 205; author's interview with Reginald Parkyn.

64 *Labour Organization in Canada* (1926), 205.

65 *Calgary Herald,* 25 June, 1926, 26 June 1926.

66 Ibid., 29 June 1926.

67 *Alberta Labor News,* 3 July 1926.

68 *Calgary Herald,* 4 Aug. 1926, 19 Aug. 1926, 23 Aug. 1926, 24 Aug. 1926. Adshead's immediate connection to the labour movement had been his spell as relief officer at the Provincial Labour Bureau in 1923. Ibid., 23 March 1923.

69 Ibid., 15 Sept. 1926; *Alberta Labor News,* 15 Sept. 1926; Scarrow, *Canada Votes,* 72.

70 *Calgary Herald,* 9 Sept. 1926, 13 Sept. 1926. Robert Parkyn's son later recalled that 'There were lots of labour people who wouldn't vote Labour, lots of guys who were digging sewers and vote Conservative and CGA – why, you wouldn't know.' Author's interview with Reginald Parkyn. See also Paul Craven and Tom Traves, 'The Class Politics of the National Policy, 1872-1930,' *Journal of Canadian Studies* 14, 3 (1979): 23-36.

71 *Calgary Herald,* 2 Oct. 1926, 18 Nov. 1926, 20 Nov. 1926, 25 Nov. 1926, 4 Dec. 1926.

72 Ibid., 11 Dec. 1926, 12 Dec. 1926, 16 Dec. 1926.

73 Ibid., 20 Jan. 1927.

74 *Alberta Labor News,* 30 April 1927.

75 Ibid., 16 Nov. 1929; George Latham, 'Alberta Labor Party and the Communists,' *Alberta Labor News: Labor Annual,* 2 Sept. 1929; *Calgary Herald,* 17 Nov. 1927, 19 Nov. 1927, 15 Dec. 1927; Ging G.G. Wong, *Calgary's Civic Government: A Structural History* (Calgary: Glenbow Archives Institute, 1978), 30-1. Fred White and Edith Patterson were elected in December 1928, John Russell and Robert Parkyn in 1929. In both cases, labour's overall representation remained at four seats on the twelve-seat council. *Calgary Herald,* 13 Dec. 1928, 21 Nov. 1929.

76 For example, see Foran, *Calgary,* 148.

77 *Alberta Labor News,* 11 Dec. 1926.

78 Ibid., 24 Nov. 1928; *Calgary Herald,* 16 Nov. 1928, 5 Dec. 1928, 16 Aug. 1925. For biographical details of Davison, see ibid., 11 Dec. 1926; Jean Leslie, 'Andrew Davidson, Mayor 1930-1945,' in *Good Morning, Your Worship: Mayors of Calgary, 1884-1975* (Calgary: Century Calgary Publications, 1975), 103-4.

79 *Alberta Labor News,* 2 Oct. 1926; GMA, M2239, United Mine Workers of America, District 18, box 4, file 20, Canadian Labor Party (Alberta Section), *Reports of Officers and Resolutions Submitted to the Fifth Convention* (10 Nov. 1928).

80 United Mine Workers of America, Canadian Labor Party, *Reports of Officers.*
81 Martina Hardwick, 'Alberta Labour, Labour Politics, and Labour Legislation, 1872-1936' (unpublished paper, University of Calgary, 1991). I wish to thank Martina Hardwick for making this paper available. See also *Union Label Guide of Calgary,* 2: 33; *Alberta Labor News,* 11 Aug. 1928; *Canadian Congress Journal* (Aug. 1922), 434-5.
82 However, see comments by Michael J. Piva in 'The Workers' Compensation Movement in Ontario,' *Ontario History* 67 (1975): 39-56, and also R.C.B. Risk, '"This Nuisance of Litigation": The Origins of Workers' Compensation in Ontario,' in *Essays in the History of Canadian Law,* ed. David H. Flaherty (Toronto: University of Toronto Press, 1983), 418-91.
83 CLP, *Reports of Officers and Resolutions Submitted to the Fifth Convention.* See also Eric Tucker, 'Making the Workplace "Safe" in Capitalism: The Enforcement of Factory Legislation in Nineteenth-Century Ontario,' *Labour/Le Travail* 21 (1988): 45-85.
84 *Calgary Herald,* 23 Nov. 1929.
85 Ibid., 27 Nov. 1929.

Epilogue

1 See David Bright, 'Conflicts between the State, the Unemployed and the Communist Party in Calgary, 1930-35,' *Canadian Historical Review* 78, 4 (1997): 537-65.
2 See C.B. Macpherson, *Democracy in Alberta: Social Credit and the Party System,* 2nd ed. (Toronto: University of Toronto Press, 1962); Alvin Finkel, *The Social Credit Phenomenon in Alberta* (Toronto: University of Toronto Press, 1988); Edward Bell, *Social Classes and Social Credit in Alberta* (Montreal: McGill-Queen's University Press, 1993). The 1935 election entered popular fiction in Bruce Allen Powe, *The Aberhart Summer* (Harmondsworth: Penguin, 1983).
3 Kenneth A. Wark, *A Report on Alberta Elections, 1905-1982* (Edmonton: n.p., 1983), 49-53.
4 A.J.E. Liesemer, a former labour candidate, did secure election as a CCF MLA in the provincial elections of 1944 and 1948. Wark, *Report on Alberta Elections,* 61, 66.
5 Edward Bell, 'Class Voting in the First Alberta Social Credit Election,' *Canadian Journal of Political Science* 23, 3 (990): 519-30; Larry Hannant, 'The Calgary Working Class and the Social Credit Movement in Alberta, 1932-1935,' *Labour/Le Travail* 15 (1985): 97-116.
6 Bell, 'Class Voting,' 525.
7 Quoted in John A. Irving, *The Social Credit Movement in Alberta* (Toronto: University of Toronto Press, 1959), 248.
8 Ibid., 266; author's interviews with various Calgarians (1992).
9 Finkel, *Social Credit Phenomenon,* 25; Alvin Finkel, 'Social Credit and the Unemployed,' *Alberta History* 31, 2 (1981): 14-22.
10 Wark, *Report on Alberta Elections,* 49.
11 *Calgary Herald,* 20 Aug. 1935.
12 See David Bright, 'A Lack of Brotherly Love: The Calgary Printers' Dispute of 1935,' *Prairie Forum* 19, 2 (1994): 207-30.
13 Canada, Royal Commission to Inquire into Industrial Relations in Canada (1919), closing remarks by Robert H. Parkyn (Calgary, 3 May 1919).
14 Ira Katznelson and Aristide R. Zolberg, eds., *Working-Class Formation: Nineteenth-Century Patterns in Western Europe and the United States* (Princeton: Princeton University Press, 1986).
15 E.P. Thompson, 'The Peculiarities of the English,' reprinted in his *The Poverty of Theory and Other Essays* (London: Merlin Press, 1978), 295.
16 *Bond of Brotherhood,* 2 Jan. 1904.

Bibliography

Abbreviations

CCA City of Calgary Archives
GMA Glenbow Museum Archives
NAC National Archives of Canada
PAA Provincial Archives of Alberta

Primary Sources

Union Minutes, Correspondence

American Federation of Musicians, Local 53. Minutes. GMA, M2193/M2937

Bricklayers and Stonemasons International Union, Local 2. Minutes. GMA, M2198

Brotherhood of Locomotive Firemen and Enginemen, Local 635. Minutes. GMA, M2201

Calgary Federation of Civic Employees. Papers. GMA, M2214

Calgary Labour Temple. Minutes. GMA, M2204/M4743

Calgary Trades and Labour Council. Minutes. GMA, M4743

Edmonton Trades and Labour Council. Minutes. PAA, 74.57

International Brotherhood of Electrical Workers, Locals 348 and 410. Minutes and Correspondence. GMA, M2214/M2215

International Typographical Union, Local 449. Minutes. GMA, M7070

Sheet Metal Workers Union, Local 254. Minutes. GMA, M2230

United Brotherhood of Carpenters and Joiners of America, Local 1055/1779. Minutes. GMA, M2241/M7227

United Mineworkers of America, District 18. Papers. GMA, M2239

Private Papers, Correspondence

David Ernest Black Papers. GMA, M98

Peter Turner Bone Papers. GMA, M109

Robert Borden Papers. NAC, MG26 H

Richard Burton Deane Papers. GMA, M311

I.S. Freeze Papers. GMA, M6141

John Gillespie Papers and Diary. GMA, M273/Film AB

Jack Hackman Papers. GMA, M3978

William Lyon Mackenzie King Papers. NAC, MG26 J

Wilfrid Laurier Papers. NAC, MG26 G

James Francis Melville Moodie Papers. GMA, M1157

Ada Ryan Papers. GMA, M3126

Walter Norman Smith Papers. GMA, M1157

Theodore Strom Papers and Memoirs. GMA, M1196

Frank White Diaries. GMA, M1302

Government Records and Documents

Alberta. Report of the Conference between the Unemployed Association of Alberta and the Provincial Government, 31 March 1925
Calgary. City of Calgary Civic Government. Papers. GMA, M1883
–. City Clerk Files. CCA, RG26
–. Report of Unemployment Conference, Calgary, 6 Nov. 1914
Canada. *Canadian Annual Review.* 1901-30
–. *Census of Canada.* 1891, 1901, 1911, 1921, 1931
–. *Census of Prairie Provinces.* 1906, 1916, 1926
–. *Census of the Three Provincial Districts of the North West Territories.* 1884-5
–. Evidence Given to the Royal Commission on Industrial Relations, 1919 (Calgary. 1-3 May 1919)
–. *National Industrial Conference.* 1919
–. *Royal Commission on Industrial Training and Technical Education.* Report of Commissioners. Ottawa: C.H. Parmalee, 1913
–. *Sessional Papers.* Annual Reports of the Department of the Interior
–. *Sessional Papers.* Annual Reports of the North-West Mounted Police, 'E' Division
–. Canadian Security Intelligence Service. Papers. RG146
–. Department of Labour. *Board of Inquiry into Cost of Living: Report of Board.* 2 vols. Ottawa: J. de L. Taché, 1915
–. Department of Labour. *Labour Gazette.* 1902-30
–. Department of Labour. *Labour Organization in Canada.* 1911-30
–. Department of Labour. Papers. NAC, RG27
–. Department of Labour. *Wages and Hours in Canada, 1901-1920.* Ottawa: J. de L. Taché, 1921
–. Department of Labour. *Wages and Hours of Labour in Canada, 1920-1930.* Ottawa: F.A. Acland, 1931
–. Immigration Branch. Papers. NAC, RG76
–. Royal Canadian Mounted Police. Papers. NAC, RG18

Proceedings and Reports

Calgary. *Annual Report of the City of Calgary.* 1902-30
Calgary Associated Charities Association. Papers. GMA, M2118
Calgary Chamber of Commerce. Annual Reports. GMA, M2260
Calgary Fire Brigade Department. Papers. GMA, M1881
Calgary Police. Charge Books. Calgary Police Archives
Calgary Trades and Labour Athletic Association. *Official Program and Souvenir of Labour Day 1914.* Calgary: Calgary Trades and Labour Council, 1914
Calgary Trades and Labour Council. *Souvenir of the 27th Annual Convention, Trades and Labour Congress of Canada.* Calgary: Calgary Trades and Labour Council, 1911
Canadian Labor Party (Alberta Section). Reports of Officers and Resolutions Submitted to the Fifth Convention. GMA, M2239
City of Calgary. Annual Reports. CCA, RG26
G.W.V.A. of Calgary Yearbook. 1919
Sons of England Benevolent Society, United Rose Lodge. Papers. GMA, M1660
The Origin of the One Big Union: A Verbatim Report of the Calgary Conference, 1919. Winnipeg: One Big Union, 1919
Trades and Labour Congress of Canada. *Annual Report of Proceedings.* 1900-30

Newspapers

Alberta Federationist
Alberta Labor News
Alberta Non-Partisan
Alberta Veteran
Albertan (title varies)
Bond of Brotherhood

Calgary Daily News
Calgary Herald
Calgary News-Telegram
Calgary Strike Bulletin
Canadian Congress Journal
Edmonton Bulletin
Edmonton Free Press
Industrial Canada
Manitoba Free Press
Monetary Times
Nor'wester
Nutcracker
Prairie (Illustrated)
Red Flag
Searchlight

Books and Articles

Adshead, H.B. *Pioneer Tales and Other Human Stories*. Calgary: n.p., 1924

Bensusan, S.L., ed. *Calgary*. Toronto: Hodder and Stoughton, 1912

Bezanson, Anne. 'Skill.' *Quarterly Journal of Economics* 36 (1922): 626-45

Bickersteth, John Burgon. *The Land of Open Doors*. 1914; reprint, Toronto: University of Toronto Press, 1976

Blue, John. *Alberta, Past and Present: Historical and Biographical*. 2 vols. Chicago: Pioneer Historical Publishing, 1924

Calgary: A Word to the Manufacturers. Calgary: n.p., 1908

Calgary, Alberta, Canada: Her Industries and Resources. Calgary: Burns and Elliott, 1885

Calgary Municipal Manual. 1900-30

Calgary, Sunny Alberta. Calgary: Jennings Publishing, 1911

Calgary, the City Phenomenal. Calgary: n.p., 1912

Calgary, the Land of Plenty. Calgary: Calgary City Council and Board of Trade, 1907

Calgary Typographical Union No. 449, 1902-1952. Calgary: n.p., 1952

Calgary Yearbook. Various years

Canadian Yearbook. Various years

Carman, Francis A. 'The Labour Party in Parliament.' *Dalhousie Review* 2, 4 (1923): 444-56

Conn, K.B. 'Employment and Unemployment in Canada: Its Measurement with Special Reference to 1919.' *Canadian Historical Review* 6, 3 (1925): 236-44

Constitution of the Grand Encampment of Manitoba IOOF and of Subordinate Encampments (1891)

Cummins, E.E. 'Political and Social Philosophy of the Carpenters' Union.' *Political Science Quarterly* 42, 3 (1927): 397-418

Davin, Nicholas Flood. *Homes For Millions: The Great Canadian Northwest: Its Resources Fully Described*. Ottawa: Brown Chamberlain, 1891

Dun and Bradstreet Reference Book. 1883-1930

Field, Frank W. *Capital Investments in Canada*. Montreal: Monetary Times, 1912

Fitzgerald, J.G. *Business Directory of Calgary, Alberta, Canada*. Calgary: Calgary Herald Publishing, 1883

Fryer, C.E. 'The Opposition to Oriental Labour.' *Journal of the Canadian Bankers' Association* 15, 3 (1908): 241-9

Gronlund's Calgary City Directory. Various years

Heide, A.J., ed. *Union Label Guide of Calgary*, vol. 2. Calgary: n.p., 1928

Henderson's Calgary City Directory. Various years

Irvine, J.A. *Souvenir of the Dominion Day Pageant*. Calgary: J.A. Irvine, 1908

King, Dr John S. *The Early History of the Sons of England Benevolent Society*. Toronto: Thos. Moore, 1891

Local 496, Golden Jubilee: 50 Years of Progress. Calgary: n.p., 1954

Longley, Hon. J.W. 'Socialism: Its Truths and Errors.' *Canadian Magazine* 6, 4 (1896): 297-304
MacRae, Archibald Oswald. *History of the Province of Alberta: Biographical.* 2 vols. Canada: Western Canada History, 1912
Nearing, Scott. 'The Labour Situation in Western Canada.' *Labor Monthly* 7, 5 (1925): 288-93
One Thousand Facts about Calgary. Calgary: One Hundred Thousand Club, 1909
Parker, C.W., ed. *Who's Who and Why,* vol. 2. Toronto: Canadian Press Association, 1912
Picturesque Calgary. Calgary: Calgary Daily Herald, 1905
Prosperous Calgary. Calgary: n.p., 1908
Subordinate Lodge Constitution: General Laws and Standing Regulations. Woodstock: Sentinel-Review Print, 1890
The Story of Calgary, Alberta, Canada: Progress, Resources, Opportunities. Calgary: n.p., 1914
Thwaite, Leo. *Porter's Progress of Nations: Alberta.* Chicago: Rand McNally, 1912
What Sunny Alberta Is Like. Calgary: n.p., 1911
Why Go to Canada? Calgary: Calgary Daily Herald, 1910
Williams, Whiting. *Mainsprings of Men.* New York: Charles Scribner's Sons, 1925

Interviews

Interviews conducted by David Bright and Shane Carmody. 'Working People of Calgary Oral History Project' (1992). GMA, RCT879
Interviews conducted by George Gooderham. GMA, M3973

Secondary Sources

Adelman, Melvin L. 'Baseball, Business and the Work Place: Gelber's Thesis Reexamined.' *Journal of Social History* 23, 2 (1989): 285-301
Airhart, Phyllis D. *Serving the Present Age: Revivalism, Progressivism, and the Methodist Tradition in Canada.* Montreal: McGill-Queen's University Press, 1992
Akers, David. 'Rebel or Revolutionary? Jack Kavanagh and the Early Years of the Communist Movement in Vancouver, 1920-1925.' *Labour/Le Travail* 30 (1992): 9-44
Allen, Richard. *The Social Passion: Religion and Social Reform in Canada, 1914-1928.* 1971; reprint, Toronto: University of Toronto Press, 1991
Altman, Morris. 'A Revision of Canadian Economic Growth, 1870-1910 (A Challenge to the Gradualist Interpretation).' *Canadian Journal of Economics* 20, 1 (1987): 86-113
Angus, Ian. *Canadian Bolsheviks: The Early Years of the Communist Party of Canada.* Montreal: Vanguard Publications, 1981
Applebaum, Herbert A. *Royal Blue: The Culture of Construction Workers.* New York: Holt Rinehart and Winston, 1981
Artibise, Alan F.J. 'Boosterism and the Development of Prairie Cities, 1871-1913.' In *Town and City: Aspects of Western Canadian Urban Development,* edited by Alan F.J. Artibise, 209-35. Regina: Canadian Plains Research Center, 1981
Asher, Robert. 'Union Nativism and the Immigrant Response.' *Labor History* 23, 2 (1982): 325-48
Askins, William R. 'Labor Unrest in Edmonton and District and Its Coverage by the Edmonton Press, 1918-1919.' MA thesis, University of Alberta, 1973
Avakumovic, Ivan. *The Communist Party in Canada: A History.* Toronto: McClelland and Stewart, 1975
Avery, Donald. *'Dangerous Foreigners': European Immigrant Workers and Labour Radicalism in Canada, 1896-1932.* Toronto: McClelland and Stewart, 1979
–. *Reluctant Host: Canada's Response to Immigrant Workers, 1896-1994.* Toronto: McClelland and Stewart, 1995
Babcock, D.R. *Alexander Cameron Rutherford: A Gentleman of Strathcona.* Calgary: University of Calgary Press, 1989
Babcock, Robert H. *Gompers in Canada: A Study in American Continentalism before the First World War.* Toronto: University of Toronto Press, 1974

Baker, William M. *Pioneer Policing in Southern Alberta: Deane of the Mounties, 1888-1914.* Calgary: Historical Society of Alberta, 1993

Barnett, George E. *Chapters on Machinery and Labor.* 1926; reprint, Carbondale: Southern Illinois University Press, 1969

Barrett, James R. 'Unity and Fragmentation on Chicago's South Side, 1900-1922.' *Journal of Social History* 18, 1 (1984): 37-55

Barrett, Michèle and Mary McIntosh. 'The "Family Wage": Some Problems for Socialists and Feminists.' *Capital and Class* 11 (Summer 1980): 5-72

Bassler, Gerhard P. 'The Enemy Alien Experience in Newfoundland.' *Canadian Ethnic Studies* 20, 3 (1988): 42-62

Battye, John. 'The Nine Hours Pioneers: The Genesis of the Canadian Labour Movement.' *Labour/Le Travailleur* 4 (1979): 25-56

Bedford, Judith Blanche. 'Prostitution in Calgary, 1905-1914.' *Alberta History* 29, 2 (1981): 1-11

–. 'Social Justice in Calgary: A Study of Urban Poverty and Welfare Development in the 1920s.' MA thesis, University of Calgary, 1981

Beeby, Dean. 'Industrial Strategy and Manufacturing Growth in Toronto, 1880-1910.' *Ontario History* 76, 3 (1984): 199-232

Bell, Edward. 'Class Voting in the First Alberta Social Credit Election.' *Canadian Journal of Political Science* 23, 3 (1990): 519-30

–. *Social Classes and Social Credit in Alberta.* Montreal: McGill-Queen's University Press, 1993

Belshaw, John Douglas. 'The Standard of Living of British Miners on Vancouver Island, 1848-1900.' *BC Studies* 84 (1989-90): 37-64

–. 'The British Collier in British Columbia: Another Archetype Reconsidered. *Labour/Le Travail* 34 (1994): 11-36

Benenson, Harold. 'Victorian Sexual Ideology and Marx's Theory of the Working Class.' *International Labor and Working Class History* 25 (1984): 1-23

Bennett, Tony, Graham Martin, Colin Mercer, and Janet Woollacott. *Culture, Ideology, and Social Process: A Reader.* London: B.T. Batsford, 1981

Benson, John. *Entrepreneurism in Canada: A History of 'Penny Capitalists.'* Lewiston, NY: Edwin Mellen Press, 1992

Bercuson, David J. 'Western Labour Radicalism and the One Big Union: Myths and Realities.' In *The Twenties in Western Canada,* edited by S.M. Trofimenkoff, 32-49. Ottawa: Queen's Printer, 1973

–. *Confrontation at Winnipeg: Labour, Industrial Relations, and the General Strike.* Montreal: McGill-Queen's University Press, 1974

–. 'Labour Radicalism and the Western Industrial Frontier, 1897-1919.' *Canadian Historical Review* 58, 2 (1977): 154-77

–. *Fools and Wise Men: The Rise and Fall of the One Big Union.* Toronto: McGraw-Hill Ryerson, 1978

–. 'Through the Looking Glass of Culture: An Essay on the New Labour History and Working-Class History in Recent Historical Writing.' *Labour/Le Travail* 7 (1981): 95-112

Berlanstein, Lenard R., ed. *Rethinking Labor History: Essays on Discourse and Class Analysis.* Urbana: University of Illinois Press, 1993

Bernstein, Irving. *The Lean Years: A History of the American Worker, 1920-1933.* Boston: Houghton Mifflin, 1960

Bertram, Gordon W. 'Economic Growth in Canadian Industry, 1870-1915: The Staple Model and Take-Off Hypothesis.' *Canadian Journal of Economic and Political Science* 29, 2 (1963): 162-84

Bertram, Gordon W., and Michael B. Percy. 'Real Wage Trends in Canada, 1900-1926: Some Provisional Estimates.' *Canadian Journal of Economics* 12, 2 (1979): 299-312

Black, Errol, and Tom Mitchell. 'Labour in Brandon Civic Politics: A Long View.' *Manitoba History* 23 (Spring 1992): 2-16

Bliss, Michael. *A Living Profit: Studies in the Social History of Canadian Business, 1883-1911.* Toronto: McClelland and Stewart, 1974

–. 'War Business as Usual: Canadian Munitions Production, 1914-1918.' In *Mobilization for Total War,* edited by N.F. Dreisziger, 45-55. Waterloo: Wilfrid Laurier University Press, 1981

–. *Northern Enterprise: Five Centuries of Canadian Business.* Toronto: McClelland and Stewart, 1987

Bodnar, John. *Immigration and Industrialization: Ethnicity in an American Mill Town, 1870-1940.* Pittsburgh: University of Pittsburgh Press, 1977

Bothwell, Robert, Ian Drummond, and John English. *Canada 1900-1945.* Toronto: University of Toronto Press, 1987

Bottomore, Tom. *Classes in Modern Society.* 2nd ed. London: HarperCollins Academic, 1991

Boudreau, David A. 'Militarism, Sport, and Social Control in Alberta, 1900-1920.' MA thesis, University of Calgary, 1985

Boudreau, Joseph A. 'Western Canada's "Enemy Aliens" in World War One.' *Alberta Historical Review* 12, 1 (1964): 1-9

Bourke, Joanna. *Working-Class Cultures in Britain, 1890-1960: Gender, Class, and Ethnicity.* London: Routledge, 1994

Bowker, Wilbur F. 'The Honourable Horace Harvey, Chief Justice of Alberta.' *Canadian Bar Review* 32, 9 (1954): 933-7

Bradbury, Bettina. 'Pigs, Cows, and Boarders: Non-Wage Forms of Survival among Montreal Families, 1861-1891.' *Labour/Le Travail* 19 (1987): 9-46

–. 'Gender at Work and Home: Family Decisions, the Labour Market, and Girls' Contributions to the Family Economy.' In *Canadian and Australian Labour History,* edited by Gregory S. Kealey and Greg Patmore, 119-40. St John's: AASLH/CCLH, 1990

–. *Working Families: Age, Gender, and Daily Survival in Industrializing Montreal.* Toronto: McClelland and Stewart, 1993

Brandes, Stuart D. *American Welfare Capitalism, 1880-1940.* Chicago: University of Chicago Press, 1970

Brandt, Gail Cuthbert. '"Weaving It Together": Life Cycle and the Industrial Experience of Female Cotton Workers in Quebec, 1910-1950.' *Labour/Le Travailleur* 7 (1981): 113-26

–. 'Postmodern Patchwork: Some Recent Trends in the Writing of Women's History in Canada.' *Canadian Historical Review* 72, 4 (1991): 441-70

Braverman, Harry. *Labor and Monopoly Capital: The Degradation of Work in the Twentieth Century.* New York: Monthly Review Press, 1974

Bray, Matthew. '"Fighting as an Ally": The English-Canadian Patriotic Response to the Great War.' *Canadian Historical Review* 61, 2 (1980): 141-68

Breen, David H. *The Canadian Prairie West and the Ranching Frontier, 1874-1924.* Toronto: University of Toronto Press, 1978

Bright, David. 'Bonds of Brotherhood? The Experiences of Labour in Calgary, 1903-1919.' MA thesis, University of Calgary, 1990

–. '"We Are All Kin": Reconsidering Labour and Class in Calgary, 1919.' *Labour/Le Travail* 29 (1992): 59-80

–. 'A Lack of Brotherly Love: The Printers' Conflict in Calgary, 1935.' *Prairie Forum* 19, 2 (1994): 207-30

–. 'Meatpackers' Strike at Calgary, 1920.' *Alberta History* 44, 2 (1996): 2-10

–. 'Conflicts between the State, the Unemployed, and the Communist Party in Calgary, 1930-1935.' *Canadian Historical Review* 78, 4 (1997): 537-65

–. 'The Cop, the Chief, the Hooker, and Her Life.' *Alberta History* 45, 4 (1997): 16-26

de Brou, Dave, and Bill Waiser, eds. *Documenting Canada: A History of Modern Canada in Documents.* Saskatoon: Fifth House Publishers, 1992

Brown, Robert Craig, and Ramsay Cook. *Canada, 1896-1921: A Nation Transformed.* Toronto: McClelland and Stewart, 1974

Buhle, Mari Jo. 'Gender and Labor History.' In *Perspectives on American Labor History: The Problems of Synthesis,* edited by. J. Carroll Moody and Alice Kessler-Harris, 55-79. De Kalb: Northern Illinois University Press, 1990

Buhle, Paul. 'E.P. Thompson and His Critics.' *Telos* 49 (1981): 127-37

Bullen, John. 'Hidden Workers: Child Labour and the Family Economy in Late-Nineteenth-Century Urban Ontario.' *Labour/Le Travail* 18 (1986): 163-87

Bumsted, J.M. '1919: The Winnipeg General Strike Reconsidered.' *Beaver* 74, 3 (1994): 27-44

Burgess, Joanne. 'Exploring the Limited Identities of Canadian Labour: Recent Trends in English Canada and in Quebec.' *International Journal of Canadian Studies/Revue internationale d'études canadiennes* 1-2 (Spring-Fall 1990): 149-73

Burnet, Jean, with Howard Palmer. *"Coming Canadians": An Introduction to a History of Canada's Peoples*. Toronto: McClelland and Stewart, 1988

Burr, Christina. 'Defending "The Art Preservative": Class and Gender Relations in the Printing Trades Unions, 1850-1914.' *Labour/Le Travail* 31 (1993): 47-74

Bussard, Lawrence H. 'The Early History of Calgary.' MA thesis, University of Calgary, 1935

Callinicos, Alex. *Making History: Agency, Structure, and Change in Social Theory*. Oxford: Polity Press, 1987

–. *Against Postmodernism: A Marxist Critique*. Oxford: Polity Press, 1989

Calvert, Peter. *The Concept of Class: An Historical Introduction*. London: Hutchinson, 1982

Campbell, Colin. 'The Stampede: Cowtown's Sacred Cow.' In *Stampede City: Power and Politics in the West*, edited by Chuck Reasons, 103-22. Toronto: Between the Lines, 1984

Cannadine, David. 'The Context, Performance, and Meaning of Ritual: The British Monarchy and the "Invention of Tradition," c. 1820-1977.' In *The Invention of Traditions,* edited by Eric Hobsbawm and Terence Ranger, 101-64. Cambridge: Cambridge University Press, 1983

Capling, M. Ann. 'The Communist Party of Canada in Alberta, 1922-1929.' MA thesis, University of Calgary, 1983

Caragata, Warren. *Alberta Labour: A Heritage Untold*. Toronto: Lorimer, 1978

Cassin, A. Marguerite, and Alison I. Griffith. 'Class and Ethnicity: Producing the Difference That Counts.' *Canadian Ethnic Studies* 13, 1 (1981): 109-29

Centennial City: Calgary, 1894-1994. Calgary: University of Calgary Press, 1994

Chambers, Edward J. 'Late-Nineteenth-Century Business Cycles in Canada.' *Canadian Journal of Economics and Political Science* 30, 3 (1964): 391-412

–. 'New Evidence on the Living Standards of Toronto Blue Collar Workers in the Pre-1914 Era.' *Histoire sociale/Social History* 13, 36 (1985): 285-314

Cherwinski, W.J.C. 'Honoré Joseph Jaxon, Agitator, Disturber, Producer of Puns to Make Men Think, and Chronic Objector ...' *Canadian Historical Review* 46, 2 (1965): 122-33

Clawson, Mary Ann. *Constructing Brotherhood: Class, Gender, and Fraternalism*. Princeton: Princeton University Press, 1989

Cobble, Dorothy Sue. *Dishing It Out: Waitresses and Their Unions in the Twentieth Century*. Urbana: University of Illinois Press, 1991

Conley, James R. 'Frontier Labourers, Crafts in Crisis, and the Western Labour Revolt: The Case of Vancouver, 1900-1919.' *Labour/Le Travail* 23 (1989): 9-38

Copp, Terry. *The Anatomy of Poverty: The Condition of the Working Class in Montreal, 1897-1929*. Toronto: McClelland and Stewart, 1974

Craig, Terence L. 'Frederick Philip Grove and the "Alien" Immigrant in the West.' *Journal of Canadian Studies* 20, 2 (1985): 92-100

Craven, Paul. 'King and Context: A Reply to Whitaker.' *Labour/Le Travailleur* 4 (1979): 165-86

–. *'An Impartial Umpire': Industrial Relations and the Canadian State, 1900-1911*. Toronto: University of Toronto Press, 1981

Craven, Paul, and Tom Traves. 'The Class Politics of the National Policy.' *Journal of Canadian Studies* 14, 3 (1979): 23-36

Creese, Gillian. 'Class, Ethnicity, and Conflict: The Case of Chinese and Japanese Immigrants, 1880-1923.' In *Workers, Capital, and the State in British Columbia: Selected Readings,* edited by Rennie Warburton and David Coburn, 55-85. Vancouver: UBC Press, 1988

Cross, Gary. *A Social History of Leisure since 1600.* N.p.: Venture Publishing, 1990

Cruikshank, Douglas, and Gregory S. Kealey. 'Canadian Strike Statistics, 1891-1950.' *Labour/Le Travail* 20 (1987): 85-145

Crysdale, S. *The Industrial Struggle and Protestant Ethics in Canada.* Toronto: Ryerson, 1961

Cumbler, John T. *Working-Class Community in Industrial America: Work, Leisure, and Struggle in Two Industrial Cities, 1880-1930.* Westport, CT: Greenwood Press, 1979

Damji, Alimohamed. 'Militancy to Passivism: The Calgary Labour Movement, 1919-1924.' MA thesis, University of Calgary, 1987

Dawley, Alan. *Struggles for Justice: Social Responsibility and the Liberal State.* Cambridge: Belknap Press, 1991

Dawson, J. Brian. 'The Chinese Experience in Frontier Calgary: 1885-1910.' In *Frontier Calgary: Town, City, and Region,* edited by A.W. Rasporich and Henry C. Klassen, 24-40. Calgary: McClelland and Stewart West, 1975

Day, Ian. *'Sorting the Men out from the Boys': Masculinity, a Missing Link in the Sociology of Sport.* Sheffield: PAVIC, 1990

DeLottinville, Peter. 'Joe Beef of Montreal: Working-Class Culture and the Tavern.' *Labour/Le Travailleur* 8/9 (1981-2): 9-40

Dempsey, Hugh A. *Calgary: Spirit of the West.* Saskatoon: Glenbow/Fifth House Publishers, 1994

Dempsey, Hugh A., ed. 'Calgary: A Century Ago.' *Alberta History* 32, 3 (1984): 28-30

–. 'Calgary and the Riel Rebellion.' *Alberta History* 33, 2 (1985): 7-18

–. 'Confessions of a Calgary Stenographer.' *Alberta History* 36, 2 (1988): 1-15

Denning, Michael. 'The End of Mass Culture.' *International Labor and Working Class History* 37 (Spring 1990): 4-40

Deprez, Paul. 'Pentland's Scarcity of Labour and the Industrial Revolution.' *Canadian Journal of Political and Social Theory* 3, 2 (1979): 95-100

Dews, Peter. *Logics of Disintegration: Post-Structuralist Thought and the Claims of Critical Theory.* London: Verso, 1987

Diggins, Patrick. 'Comrades and Citizens: New Mythologies in American Historiography.' *American Historical Review* 90, 3 (1985): 614-39

Drummond, Ian. 'Financial Institutions in Historical Perspective.' *Canadian Banker* 74 (1967): 150-8

Dubro, James, and Robin Rowland. *Undercover: Cases of the RCMP's Most Secret Operative.* Toronto: McClelland and Stewart, 1991

Dunk, Thomas W. *It's a Working Man's Town: Male Working-Class Culture in Northwestern Ontario.* Montreal: McGill-Queen's University Press, 1991

Eagle, John. *The Canadian Pacific Railway and the Development of Western Canada.* Montreal: McGill-Queen's University Press, 1989

Edwards, Richard. *Contested Terrain: The Transformation of the Workplace in the Twentieth Century.* New York: Basic Books, 1979

Ehrlich, Richard L., ed. *Immigrants in Industrial America, 1850-1920.* Charlottesville: University of Virginia Press, 1977

Emmons, David. *The Butte Irish: Class and Ethnicity in an American Mining Town, 1875-1925.* Urbana: University of Illinois Press, 1989

English, John. *The Decline of Politics: The Conservatives and the Party System, 1901-1920.* Toronto: University of Toronto Press, 1977

Ewen, Stuart. *Captains of Consciousness: Advertising and the Social Roots of the Consumer Culture.* Toronto: McGraw-Hill, 1976

Fay, E.R. 'The Early Years.' *Marxist Quarterly* 1 (Spring 1962): 13-21

Ferns, S.J., and H.S. Ferns. *Eighty-Five Years in Canada.* Winnipeg: Queenston House, 1978

Field, John. 'British Historians and the Concept of the Labor Aristocracy.' *Radical History Review* 19 (Winter 1978-9): 61-85

Fillmore, Nicholas. *Maritime Radical: The Life and Times of Roscoe Fillmore.* Toronto: Between the Lines, 1992

Fingard, Judith. *Jack in Port: Sailortowns of Eastern Canada.* Toronto: University of Toronto Press, 1982

Fink, Leon. 'Looking Backward: Reflections on Workers' Culture and Certain Conceptual Dilemmas within Labor History.' In *Perspectives on American Labor History: The Problems of Synthesis,* edited by J. Carroll Moody and Alice Kessler-Harris, 5-29. De Kalb: Northern Illinois University Press, 1990

–. 'Culture's Last Stand? Gender and the Search for Synthesis in American Labor History.' *Labor History* 34, 2-3 (1993): 178-89

Finkel, Alvin. 'Social Credit and the Unemployed.' *Alberta History* 31, 2 (1981): 14-22

–. 'The Rise and Fall of the Labour Party in Alberta, 1917-1942.' *Labour/Le Travail* 16 (1985): 61-96

–. *The Social Credit Phenomenon in Alberta.* Toronto: University of Toronto Press, 1988

Foran, Heather. 'Annie Gale.' In *Citymakers: Calgarians after the Frontier,* edited by Max Foran and Sheilagh Jameson, 196-207. Calgary: Historical Society of Alberta, Chinook Country Chapter, 1987

Foran, Max. 'The "Travis Affair."' *Alberta Historical Review* 19, 4 (1971): 1-7

–. *Calgary: An Illustrated History.* Toronto: Lorimer, 1978

–. 'The Boosters in Boosterism: Some Calgary Examples.' *Urban History Review* 8, 2 (1979): 77-82

–. 'The Civic Corporation and Urban Growth: Calgary, 1884-1930.' PhD diss., University of Calgary, 1981

Foster, John. 'British Imperialism and the Labour Aristocracy.' In *The General Strike 1926,* edited by Jeffrey Skelley, 3-57. London: Lawrence and Wishart, 1976

Fox, Paul W. 'Early Socialism in Canada.' In *The Political Process in Canada,* edited by J.H. Aitchison, 79-98. Toronto: University of Toronto Press, 1963

Francis, James M. 'Montana Business and Canadian Regionalism in the 1870s and 1880s.' *Western Historical Quarterly* 12, 3 (1981): 291-304

Friesen, Gerald. '"Yours in Revolt": The Socialist Party of Canada and the Western Labour Movement.' *Labour/Le Travailleur* 1 (1976): 139-54

–. *The Canadian Prairies: A History.* Toronto: University of Toronto Press, 1987

Gagan, David, and Rosemary Gagan. 'Working-Class Standards of Living in Late-Victorian Urban Ontario: A Review of the Miscellaneous Evidence on the Quality of Material Life.' *Journal of the Canadian Historical Association* (1990): 171-93

Galenson, Walter. *Rival Unionism in the United States.* New York: Russell and Russell, 1966

Geertz, Clifford. *The Interpretation of Culture.* New York: Basic Books, 1973

Gelber, Steven. 'Working at Playing: The Culture of the Workplace and the Rise of Baseball.' *Journal of Social History* 16 (Summer 1983): 3-20

Glassberg, David. *American Historical Pageantry: The Uses of Tradition in the Early Twentieth Century.* Chapel Hill: University of North Carolina Press, 1990

Glynn, Desmond. '"Exporting Outcast London": Assisted Emigration to Canada, 1886-1914.' *Histoire sociale/Social History* 15, 29 (1982): 209-38

Godelier, Maurice. 'Infrastructures, Societies, and History.' *Current Anthropology* 19, 4 (1978): 763-8

Goodwyn, Lawrence. *The Populist Movement: A Short History of the Agrarian Revolt.* Oxford: Oxford University Press, 1978

Gordon, David M., Richard Edwards, and Michael Reich. *Segmented Work, Divided Workers: The Historical Transformation of Labor in the United States.* Cambridge: Cambridge University Press, 1982

Gouldner, Alvin. *Wildcat Strike.* Yellow Springs, OH: Antioch Press, 1954

Graham, Roger. *Arthur Meighen.* Vol. 2. *And Fortune Fled.* Toronto: Clarke, Irwin, 1963

Gray, James H. *Red Lights on the Prairies.* Scarborough, ON: Signet, 1973

–. *The Roar of the Twenties.* Toronto: Macmillan, 1975

–. *R.B. Bennett: The Calgary Years.* Toronto: University of Toronto Press, 1991

Gray, Robert. *The Aristocracy of Labour in Nineteenth-Century Britain, c. 1850-1900.* London: Macmillan, 1981

–. 'Bourgeois Hegemony in Victorian Britain.' In *Culture: Ideology and Social Progress,* edited by Tony Bennett, Graham Martin, Colin Mercer, and Janet Woollacott, 235-50. London: B.T. Batsford, 1989

Greer, Alan. 'Wage Labour and the Transition to Capitalism: A Critique of Pentland.' *Labour/Le Travail* 15 (1985): 7-22

Grenke, Art. 'The German Community of Winnipeg and the English-Canadian Response to World War I.' *Canadian Ethnic Studies* 20, 1 (1984): 21-44

Grinder, Barbara. *Local Colour: A Commemoration of the 75th Anniversary of the Amalgamated Transit Union Local 583*. Calgary: n.p., 1990

Gruneau, Richard. *Class, Sports, and Social Development*. Amherst: University of Massachusetts Press, 1983

Guichon, M.M. 'Riley & McCormick.' Unpublished paper, n.d.

Gutman, Herbert G. *Work, Culture, and Society in Industrializing America: Essays in American Working-Class and Social History*. New York: Alfred A. Knopf, 1976

–. *Power and Culture: Essays on the American Working Class*. Edited by Ira Berlin. New York: New Press, 1987

Guttman, Allen. *From Ritual to Record: The Nature of Modern Sports*. New York: Columbia University Press, 1978

Haber, Samuel. *Efficiency and Uplift: Scientific Management in the Progressive Era, 1890-1920*. Chicago: University of Chicago Press, 1964

Hammerton, Elizabeth, and David Cannadine. 'Conflict and Consensus on a Ceremonial Occasion: The Diamond Jubilee in Cambridge, 1897.' *Historical Journal* 24 (1981): 111-46

Hanagan, Michael. 'New Perspectives on Class Formation: Culture, Reproduction, and Agency.' *Social Science History* 18, 1 (1994): 77-94

Hannant, Larry. 'The Calgary Working Class and the Social Credit Movement in Alberta, 1932-1935.' *Labour/Le Travail* 16 (1985): 97-110

Hareven, Tamara K. *Family Time and Industrial Time: The Relationship between the Family and Work in a New England Industrial Community*. Cambridge: Cambridge University Press, 1982

Hartland, Penelope. 'Factors in Economic Growth in Canada.' *Journal of Economic History* 15 (March 1955): 13-22

Hawkins, W.E. *Electrifying Calgary: A Century of Public and Private Power*. Calgary: University of Calgary Press, 1987

Haydu, Jeffrey. *Between Craft and Class: Skilled Workers and Factory Politics in the United States and Britain, 1890-1922*. Berkeley: University of California Press, 1988

Helmes, Richard C. 'Ideology and Social Control in Canadian Sport: A Theoretical Review.' In *Sport in the Sociocultural Process*, edited by Marie Hart and Susan Birrell, 207-32. Rev. ed. Dubuque, IA: W.C. Brown, 1981

Heron, Craig. 'Labourism and the Canadian Working Class.' *Labour/Le Travail* 13 (1984): 45-75

–. *Working in Steel: The Early Years in Canada, 1888-1935*. Toronto: McClelland and Stewart, 1986

Heron, Craig, and Bryan D. Palmer. 'Through the Prism of the Strike: Industrial Conflict in Southern Ontario, 1901-1914.' *Canadian Historical Review* 57, 4 (1977): 423-58

Heron, Craig, and Robert Storey, eds. *On the Job: Confronting the Labour Process in Canada*. Montreal: McGill-Queen's University Press, 1986

–. 'Work and Struggle in the Canadian Steel Industry, 1900-1950.' In *On the Job: Confronting the Labour Process in Canada*, edited by Craig Heron and Robert Storey, 210-44. Montreal: McGill-Queen's University Press, 1986

Himmelfarb, Gertrude. *The New History and the Old: Critical Essays and Reappraisals*. Cambridge: Belknap Press, 1987

–. *On Looking into the Abyss: Untimely Thoughts on Culture and Society*. New York: Vintage Books, 1995

Hinton, James. *The First Shop Stewards' Movement*. London: Allen and Irwin, 1973

Hobsbawm, Eric. *Labouring Men: Studies in the History of Labour*. London: Weidenfeld and Nicolson, 1964

–. *Workers: Worlds of Labour*. New York: Pantheon, 1984

Hobsbawm, Eric, and Terence Ranger, eds. *The Invention of Tradition*. Cambridge: Cambridge University Press, 1992

Hoffman, Charles. 'The Depression of the Nineties.' *Journal of Economic History* 16, 2 (1956): 137-64

Hoggart, Richard. *The Uses of Literacy.* Harmondsworth: Penguin, 1957

Hooke, A.J. *30 + 5: I Know, I Was There.* Edmonton: Co-op Press, 1971

Horrall, S.W. 'The (Royal) North-West Mounted Police and Prostitution on the Canadian Prairies.' *Prairie Forum* 10, 1 (1985): 105-27

Howell, Colin D.. 'Baseball, Community, and Class in the Maritime Provinces, 1870-1910.' *Histoire sociale/Social History* 22, 44 (1988): 205-86

–. *Northern Sandlots: A Social History of Maritime Baseball.* Toronto: University of Toronto Press, 1995

Howell, Nancy, and Maxwell L. Howell. *Sports and Games in Canadian Life: 1700 to the Present.* Toronto: Macmillan, 1969

Humphries, Jane. 'Class Struggle and the Persistence of the Working-Class Family.' *Cambridge Journal of Economics* 1 (1977): 241-58

Hunt, Lynn, ed. *The New Cultural History.* Berkeley: University of California Press, 1989

Hunter, Alfred A. *Class Tells: On Social Inequality in Canada.* Toronto: Butterworths, 1981

Iggers, George G. *Historiography in the Twentieth Century: From Scientific Objectivity to the Postmodern Challenge.* Hanover: Wesleyan University Press, 1997

Irving, John A. *The Social Credit Movement in Alberta.* Toronto: University of Toronto Press, 1959

Jacoby, Sanford. *Employing Bureaucracy: Managers, Unions, and the Transformation of Work in American Industry, 1900-1945.* New York: Columbia University Press, 1985

Jamieson, Stuart. *Times of Trouble: Labour Unrest and Industrial Conflict in Canada, 1900-1966.* Ottawa: Task Force on Labour Relations, 1968

Jasen, Patricia. 'Oddfellows in Early Calgary.' *Alberta History* 35, 3 (1987): 8-12

Jenkins, Keith, ed. *The Postmodern Reader.* London: Routledge, 1997

Jenson, Jane, and Rianne Mahon, eds. *The Challenge of Restructuring: North American Labor Movements Respond.* Philadelphia: Temple University Press, 1993

Jones, Gareth Stedman. *Languages of Class: Studies in English Working-Class History, 1832-1982.* Cambridge: Cambridge University Press, 1983

Joyce, Patrick, ed. *The Historical Meanings of Work.* Cambridge: Cambridge University Press, 1987

–. *Visions of the People: Industrial England and the Question of Class, 1848-1914.* Cambridge: Cambridge University Press, 1991

Katznelson, Ira. *City Trenches: Urban Politics and the Patterning of Class in the United States.* New York: Pantheon Books, 1981

–. 'Working-Class Formation and the State: Nineteenth-Century England in American Perspective.' In *Bringing the State Back In,* edited by Peter B. Evans, Dietrich Rueschemeyer, and Theda Skocpol, 257-84. Cambridge: Cambridge University Press, 1985

–. *Marxism and the City.* Oxford: Clarendon Press, 1992

–. 'The "Bourgeois" Dimension: A Provocation about Institutions, Politics, and the Future of Labor History,' *International Labor and Working Class History* 46 (1994): 7-31

Katznelson, Ira, and Aristide R. Zolberg, eds. *Working-Class Formation: Nineteenth-Century Patterns in Western Europe and the United States.* Princeton: Princeton University Press, 1986

Kaye, Harvey J., and Keith McClelland, eds. *E.P. Thompson: Critical Perspectives.* Philadelphia: Temple University Press, 1990

Kazin, Michael, and Steven J. Ross. 'America's Labor Day: The Dilemma of a Workers' Celebration.' *Journal of American History* 78, 4 (1992): 1,294-1,319

Kealey, Gregory S. 'Labour and Working-Class History in Canada: Prospects in the 1980s.' *Labour/Le Travailleur* 7 (1981): 116-35

–. '1919: The Canadian Labour Revolt.' *Labour/Le Travail* 13 (1984): 11-44

–. 'Work Control, the Labour Process, and Nineteenth-Century Canadian Printers.' In *On The Job: Confronting the Labour Process in Canada,* edited by Craig Heron and Robert Storey, 75-101. Montreal: McGill-Queen's University Press, 1986

–. 'Writing about Labour History.' In *Writing About Canada: A Handbook for Modern Canadian History,* edited by John Schulze, 145-74. Scarborough, ON: Prentice-Hall, 1990
–. *Toronto Workers Respond to Industrial Capitalism, 1867-1892.* 1980; reprint, Toronto: University of Toronto Press, 1991
–. 'State Repression of Labour and the Left in Canada, 1914-1920: The Impact of the First World War.' *Canadian Historical Review* 73, 3 (1992): 281-314
–. 'The Surveillance State: The Origins of Domestic Intelligence and Counter-Subversion in Canada, 1914-1921.' *Intelligence and National Security* 7, 3 (1992): 179-210
Kealey, Gregory S., and Bryan D. Palmer. *Dreaming of What Might Be: The Knights of Labor in Ontario, 1880-1900.* Toronto: New Hogtown Press, 1987
Kealey, Gregory S., and Peter Warrian, eds. *Essays in Canadian Working Class History.* Toronto: McClelland and Stewart, 1976
Kealey, Linda. 'Women and Labour during World War I: Women Workers and the Minimum Wage in Manitoba.' In *First Days, Fighting Days,* edited by Mary Kinnear, 76-99. Regina: Canadian Plains Research Center, 1987
–. '"No Special Protection – No Sympathy": Women's Activism in the Canadian Labour Revolt of 1919.' In *Class, Community, and the Labour Movement: Wales and Canada, 1850-1930,* edited by Deian R. Hopkins and Gregory S. Kealey, 134-59. Wales: LLAFUR/CCLH, 1989
–. 'Women in the Canadian Socialist Movement, 1904-1914.' In *Beyond the Vote: Canadian Women and Politics,* edited by Linda Kealey and Joan Sangster, 171-95. Toronto: University of Toronto Press, 1989
Kearney, Kathryn. 'Canadian Women and the First World War.' *Canadian Woman Studies* 3, 1 (1981): 95-6
Kessler-Harris, Alice. *Out to Work: A History of Wage-Earning Women in the United States.* Oxford: Oxford University Press, 1982
–. 'A New Agenda for American Labor History: A Gendered Analysis and the Question of Class.' In *Perspectives on American Labor History: The Problems of Synthesis,* edited by J. Carroll Moody and Alice Kessler-Harris, 217-34. De Kalb: Northern Illinois University Press, 1990
–. *A Woman's Wage: Historical Meanings and Social Consequences.* Lexington: University of Kentucky, 1990
Keyssar, Alexander. *Out of Work: The First Century of Unemployment in Massachusetts.* Cambridge: Cambridge University Press, 1986
Kidd, Bruce. *The Struggle for Canadian Sport.* Toronto: University of Toronto Press, 1996
Klassen, Henry C. 'Social Troubles in Calgary in the Mid-1890s.' *Urban History Review* 3, 74 (1974): 8-16
–. 'The *Bond of Brotherhood* and Calgary Workingmen.' In *Frontier Calgary: Town, City and Region,* edited by A.W. Rasporich and Henry C. Klassen, 267-71. Calgary: McClelland and Stewart West, 1975
–. 'Life in Frontier Calgary.' In *Western Canada: Past and Present,* edited by A.W. Rasporich, 42-57. Calgary: McClelland and Stewart West, 1975
–. 'Bicycles and Automobiles in Early Calgary.' *Alberta History* 24, 2 (1976): 1-8
–. 'In Search of Neglected and Delinquent Children: The Calgary Children's Aid Society, 1909-1920.' In *Town and City: Aspects of Western Canadian Urban Development,* edited by Alan F.J. Artibise, 375-92. Regina: Canadian Plains Research Center, 1981
–. 'I.G. Baker & Co. in Calgary, 1875-1884.' *Montana* 35, 3 (July 1985): 40-55
–. 'Family Businesses in Calgary to 1939.' In *Citymakers: Calgarians after the Frontier,* edited by Max Foran and Sheilagh Jameson, 303-19. Calgary: Historical Society of Alberta, Chinook Country Chapter, 1987
Knafla, Louis A. 'Violence on the Western Canadian Frontier: A Historical Perspective.' In *Violence in Canada: Sociopolitical Perspectives,* edited by Jeffrey Ian Ross, 10-39. Don Mills, ON: Oxford University Press, 1995
Knowles, K.G.J.C. *Strikes: A Study of Industrial Conflict.* Oxford: Basil Blackwell, 1954
Kooyman, Susan M. 'The Policies and Legislation of the United Farmers of Alberta Government, 1921-1935.' MA thesis, University of Calgary, 1981

Korpi, Walter, and Michael Shalev. 'Strikes, Industrial Relations, and Class Conflict in Capitalist Society.' *British Journal of Sociology* 30, 2 (1979): 164-87

Krause, Paul. *The Battle for Homestead, 1880-1892: Politics, Culture, and Steel.* Pittsburgh: University of Pittsburgh Press, 1992

Land, Hilary. 'The Family Wage.' *Feminist Review* 6 (1980): 55-77

Langford, Tom. 'Strikes and Class Consciousness.' *Labour/Le Travail* 34 (1994): 107-37

Laycock, David. *Democratic Thought in the Canadian Prairies, 1910 to 1945.* Toronto: University of Toronto Press, 1990

Leier, Mark. *Where the Fraser River Flows: The Industrial Workers of the World in British Columbia.* Vancouver: New Star Books, 1990

–. *Red Flags and Red Tape: The Making of a Labour Bureaucracy.* Toronto: University of Toronto Press, 1995

–. Workers and Intellectuals: The Theory of the New Class and Early Canadian Socialism.' In *Making Western Canada: Essays on European Colonization and Settlement,* edited by Catherine Cavanaugh and Jeremy Mouat, 133-53. Toronto: Garamond Press, 1996

Lenin, V.I. *'Left-Wing' Communism, an Infantile Disorder.* Moscow: Progress Publishers, 1950

Leslie, Jean. 'Andrew Davison, Mayor, 1930-1945.' In *Good Morning, Your Worship: Mayors of Calgary, 1884-1975.* Calgary: Century Calgary Publications, 1975

Lutz, John. 'After the Fur Trade: The Aboriginal Labouring Class of British Columbia, 1849-1890.' *Journal of the Canadian Historical Association* (1992): 69-93

McCall, Christopher. *Class, Ethnicity, and Social Inequality.* Montreal: McGill-Queen's University Press, 1990

McCalla Vickers, Jill. 'Feminist Approaches to Women in Politics.' In *Beyond the Vote: Canadian Women and Politics,* edited by Linda Kealey and Joan Sangster, 16-36. Toronto: University of Toronto Press, 1989

McCallum, Margaret. 'Corporate Welfarism in Canada, 1919-1939.' *Canadian Historical Review* 71, 1 (1990): 46-79

McCormack, A. Ross. 'Cloth Caps and Jobs: The Ethnicity of English Immigrants in Canada, 1900-1914.' In *Ethnicity, Power, and Politics in Canada,* edited by Jorgen Dahlie and Tissa Fernando, 38-55. Toronto: Methuen, 1981

–. 'The Western Working-Class Experience.' In *Lectures in Canadian Labour and Working-Class History,* edited by W.J.C. Cherwinski and Gregory S. Kealey, 115-26. St John's: CCLH/New Hogtown Press, 1985

–. 'Wobblies and Blanketstiffs: The Constituency of the IWW in Western Canada.' In *Lectures in Canadian Labour and Working-Class History,* edited by W.J.C. Cherwinski and Gregory S. Kealey, 101-14. St John's: CCLH/New Hogtown Press, 1985

–. *Reformers, Rebels, and Revolutionaries: The Western Canadian Radical Movement, 1899-1919.* 1977; reprint, Toronto: University of Toronto Press, 1991

McDonald, Robert A.J. 'Working-Class Vancouver, 1886-1914: Urbanism and Class in British Columbia.' *BC Studies* 69-70 (1986): 33-69

McDougall, Duncan. 'Canadian Manufactured Commodity Output, 1870-1915.' *Canadian Journal of Economics* 4, 1 (1971): 21-36

MacEwan, Grant. *Pat Burns: Cattle King.* Saskatoon: Western Producer Prairie Books, 1979

MacGregor, J.G. *A History of Alberta.* Edmonton: Hurtig, 1972

McIntosh, P.C. *Sport in Society.* London: C.A. Watts, 1968

McKay, Ian. 'History, Anthropology, and the Concept of Culture.' *Labour/Le Travailleur* 8/9 (1981-2): 185-241

–. 'Strikes in the Maritimes, 1901-1914.' *Acadiensis* 13, 1 (1983): 3-46

–. *The Craft Transformed.* Halifax: Holdfast Press, 1985

McKibbin, Ross. 'Why Was There No Marxism in Britain?' *English Historical Review* 99, 391 (1984): 297-331

MacKinnon, Catharine. *Toward a Feminist Theory of the State.* Cambridge: Harvard University Press, 1989

Mackintosh, W.A. 'Economic Factors in Canadian History.' *Canadian Historical Review* 4, 1 (1923): 12-25

MacLean, Una. 'The Famous Five.' *Alberta Historical Review* 10, 2 (1962): 1-4
McLennan, William M. *Sport in Early Calgary.* Calgary: Fort Brisebois Publishing, 1983
MacLeod, H.L. 'Properties, Investors, and Taxes: A Study of Calgary Real Estate Investment, Municipal Finances, and Property Tax Arrears, 1911-1919.' MA thesis, University of Calgary, 1977
McNaught, Kenneth. *A Prophet in Politics: A Biography of J.S. Woodsworth.* Toronto: University of Toronto Press, 1963
–. 'E.P. Thompson vs Harold Logan: Writing about Labour and the Left in the 1970s,' *Canadian Historical Review* 62, 2 (1981): 141-68
Macpherson, C.B. *Democracy in Alberta: Social Credit and the Party System.* 2nd ed. Toronto: University of Toronto Press, 1962
Maier, Charles S. 'Between Taylorism and Technocracy: European Ideologies and the Vision of Industrial Productivity in the 1920s.' *Journal of Contemporary History* 5, 2 (1970): 27-61
–. *Recasting Bourgeois Europe: Stabilization in France, Germany, and Italy in the Decade after World War I.* Princeton: Princeton University Press, 1975
–. 'The Factory as Society: Ideologies of Industrial Management in the Twentieth Century.' In *Ideas into Politics: Aspects of European History, 1880-1950,* edited by R.J. Bullen, 147-63. Totowa, NJ: Barnes and Noble, 1984
Mangan, J.A., and James Walvin, eds. *Manliness and Morality: Middle-Class Masculinity in Britain and America, 1800-1940.* New York: St Martin's Press, 1987
Mann, W.E. *Sect, Cult, and Church in Alberta.* Toronto: University of Toronto Press, 1955
Manson, Jack. *Bricks in Alberta.* Edmonton: Jack Manson/Alberta Masonry Institute, 1982
Mardiros, Anthony. *William Irvine: The Life of a Prairie Radical.* Toronto: Lorimer, 1979
Marks, Lynne. 'The Knights of Labor and the Salvation Army: Religion and Working-Class Culture in Ontario, 1882-1890.' *Labour/Le Travail* 28 (1991): 89-128
–. 'The "Hallelujah Lasses": Working-Class Women in the Salvation Army in English Canada.' In *Gender Conflicts: New Essays in Women's History,* edited by Franca Iacovetta and Mariana Valverde, 67-117. Toronto: University of Toronto Press, 1992
Marquis, Greg. 'Police Unionism in Early Twentieth-Century Toronto.' *Ontario History* 81, 2 (1989): 109-28
Marshall, David B. *Secularizing the Faith: Canadian Protestant Clergy and the Crisis of Belief, 1850-1940.* Toronto: University of Toronto Press, 1992
Marx, Karl. *The Eighteenth Brumaire of Louis Bonaparte.* 1859. Reprint, New York: International Publishers, 1963
Masson, Jack, and Peter Blaikie. 'Labour Politics in Alberta.' In *Society and Politics in Alberta: Political Research Papers,* edited by C. Caldarola, 271-83. Toronto: Methuen, 1979
Maw, Margaret. 'George Murdoch Biography, 1850-1919.' Unpublished paper, 1968
Meiksins, Peter F. 'Scientific Management and Class Relations: A Dissenting View.' *Theory and Society* 13, 1 (1984): 177-209
Melnyk, Bryan P. *Calgary Builds: The Emergence of an Urban Landscape.* Edmonton: Alberta Culture/Canadian Plains Research Center, 1985
Metcalfe, Alan. *Canada Learns to Play: The Emergence of Organized Sport, 1807-1914.* Toronto: McClelland and Stewart, 1987
Miliband, Ralph. *Parliamentary Socialism: A Study in the Politics of Labour.* 2nd ed. London: Merlin Press, 1972
–. *The State in Capitalist Society.* London: Quartet Books, 1979
Mitchell, Tom. '"A Square Deal for All and No Railroading": Labour and Politics in Brandon, 1900-1920.' *Prairie Forum* 15, 1 (1990): 45-66
–. '"To Reach the Leadership of the Revolutionary Movement": A.J. Andrews, the Canadian State, and the Suppression of the Winnipeg General Strike.' *Prairie Forum* 18, 2 (1993): 239-55
Montgomery, David. *Workers' Control in America.* Cambridge: Cambridge University Press, 1979
–. *The Fall of the House of Labor.* 1987; reprint, Cambridge: Cambridge University Press, 1989

Moorhouse, H.F. 'The Marxist Theory of the Labour Aristocracy.' *Social History* 3, 1 (1978): 61-83

Morris, Philip H., ed. *Canadian Patriotic Fund.* N.p., n.d.

Morton, Desmond. '"Kicking and Complaining": Postwar Demobilization in the Canadian Expeditionary Force, 1918-1919.' *Canadian Historical Review* 61, 3 (1980): 334-60

–. *When Your Number's Up: The Canadian Soldier in the First World War.* Toronto: Random House, 1993

Morton, Desmond, with Terry Copp. *Working People: An Illustrated History of the Canadian Labour Movement.* Rev. ed. Toronto: Deneau, 1987

Morton, Desmond, and Glenn Wright. 'The Bonus Campaign, 1919-1921: Veterans and the Campaign for Re-establishment.' *Canadian Historical Review* 64, 2 (1983): 147-67

–. *Winning the Second Battle: Canadian Veterans and the Return to Civilian Life, 1915-1930.* Toronto: University of Toronto Press, 1987

Morton, Suzanne. *Ideal Surroundings: Domestic Life in a Working-Class Suburb in the 1920s.* Toronto: University of Toronto Press, 1995

Morton, W.L. 'The Western Progressive Movement, 1919-1921.' In *Prophecy and Protest: Social Movements in Twentieth-Century Canada,* edited by Samuel D. Clark, J. Paul Grayson, and Linda M. Grayson, 115-29. Toronto: Gage, 1975

Mott, Morris K. 'The Problems of Professionalism: The Manitoba Amateur Athletic Association and the Fight against Pro Hockey, 1904-11.' In *Winter Sports in the West,* edited by E.A. Corbet and A.W. Rasporich, 132-42. Calgary: Historical Society of Alberta, 1990

Mouat, Jeremy. 'The Genesis of Western Exceptionalism: British Columbia's Hard-Rock Miners, 1895-1903.' *Canadian Historical Review* 71, 3 (1990): 317-45

Musson, A.E. 'Class Struggle and the Labour Aristocracy, 1830-1860.' *Social History* 1, 3 (1976): 335-56

Naylor, James. 'Toronto 1919.' Canadian Historical Association *Historical Papers* (1986): 33-55

–. 'Ontario Workers and the Decline of Labourism.' In *Patterns of the Past: Interpreting Ontario's History,* edited by Roger Hall, William Westfall, and Laurel Sefton MacDowell, 278-300. Toronto: Dundurn Press, 1988

–. 'Working-Class History in English Canada in the 1980s: An Assessment.' *Acadiensis* 19, 1 (1989): 156-69

–. *The New Democracy: Challenging the Social Order in Industrial Ontario, 1914-1925.* Toronto: University of Toronto Press, 1991

Naylor, R.T. 'The Canadian State, the Accumulation of Capital, and the Great War.' *Journal of Canadian Studies* 16, 3 (1982): 26-55

Neale, R.S. *Writing Marxist History: British Society, Economy, and Culture since 1700.* Oxford: Basil Blackwell, 1985

Nelson, Bruce C. 'Revival and Upheaval: Religion, Irreligion, and Chicago's Working Class in 1886.' *Journal of Social History* 25, 2 (1991): 233-53

Newton, Janice. 'From Wage Slave to White Slave: The Prostitution Controversy and the Early Canadian Left.' In *Beyond the Vote: Canadian Women and Politics,* edited by Linda Kealey and Joan Sangster, 217-36. Toronto: University of Toronto Press, 1989

Norrie, Kenneth, and Doug Owram. *A History of the Canadian Economy.* Toronto: Harcourt Brace Jovanovich, 1991

Oestreicher, Richard Jules. *Solidarity and Fragmentation: Working People and Class Consciousness in Detroit, 1875-1900.* Urbana: University of Illinois Press, 1986

Ostry, Bernard. 'Conservatives, Liberals, and Labour in the 1880s.' *Canadian Journal of Economics and Political Science* 27, 2 (1961): 141-61

den Otter, A.A. 'Transportation, Trade, and Regional Identity in the Southwestern Prairies.' *Prairie Forum* 15, 1 (1990): 1-23

Ozanne, Robert. *A Century of Labor-Management Relations at McCormick and International Harvester.* Madison: University of Wisconsin Press, 1967

Palmer, Bryan D. 'Class, Conception, and Conflict: The Thrust for Efficiency, Managerial Views of Labor, and the Working-Class Rebellion, 1903-1922.' *Review of Radical Political Economics* 7 (1975): 31-49

–. 'Most Uncommon Common Men: Craft and Culture in Crisis in Historical Perspective.' *Labour/Le Travailleur* 1 (1976): 5-31

–. *A Culture in Conflict: Skilled Workers and Industrial Capitalism in Hamilton, Ontario, 1860-1914.* Montreal: McGill-Queen's University Press, 1979

–. 'Working-Class Canada: Recent Historical Writing,' *Queen's Quarterly* 86 (1979): 594-616

–. 'Labour Protest and Organization in Nineteenth-Century Canada, 1820-1890.' *Labour/Le Travail* 20 (1987): 61-84

–. '"What the Hell": Or Some Comments on Class Formation and Cultural Reproduction.' In *Popular Cultures and Political Practices,* edited by Richard Gruneau, 33-42. Toronto: Garamond Press, 1988

–. *Descent into Discourse: The Reification of Language and the Writing of Social History.* Philadelphia: Temple University Press, 1989

–. *Working-Class Experience: Rethinking the History of Canadian Labour, 1800-1991.* 2nd ed. Toronto: McClelland and Stewart, 1992

–. *Capitalism Comes to the Backcountry: The Goodyear Invasion of Napanee.* Toronto: Between the Lines, 1994

Palmer, Howard. *Patterns of Prejudice: A History of Nativism in Alberta.* Toronto: McClelland and Stewart, 1982

–. 'William Irvine and the Emergence of Political Radicalism in Calgary, 1916-1921.' *Fort Calgary Quarterly* 7, 2 (1987): 2-19

Panitch, Leo, and Donald Swartz. *The Assault on Trade Union Freedoms: From Wage Controls to Social Contract.* Toronto: Garamond Press, 1993

Parker, Stanley. *The Sociology of Leisure.* London: George Allen and Irwin, 1979

Parr, Joy. *The Gender of Breadwinners: Women, Men, and Change in Two Industrial Towns, 1880-1950.* Toronto: University of Toronto Press, 1990

–. 'Gender History and Historical Practice.' *Canadian Historical Review* 76, 3 (1995): 354-76

Peach, Jack. *Days Gone By.* Saskatoon: Fifth House, 1993

Pelling, Henry. *The British Communist Party: A Historical Profile.* London: Adam and Charles Black, 1958

Pentland, H. Clare. 'The Development of a Capitalistic Labour Market in Canada.' *Canadian Journal of Economics and Political Science* 25, 4 (1959): 450-61

–. 'The Western Canadian Labour Movement.' *Canadian Journal of Political and Social Theory* 3 (1979): 53-78

–. *Labour and Capital in Canada, 1650-1860.* Toronto: Lorimer, 1981

Peterson, Larry. 'The One Big Union in International Perspective: Revolutionary Industrial Unionism, 1900-1925.' *Labour/Le Travailleur* 7 (1981): 115-31

Piva, Michael J. 'The Workers' Compensation Movement in Ontario.' *Ontario History* 67 (1975): 39-56

–. *The Condition of the Working Class in Toronto, 1900-1921.* Ottawa: University of Ottawa Press, 1979

–. 'Urban Working-Class Incomes and Real Incomes in 1921: A Comparative Analysis.' *Histoire sociale/Social History* 16, 31 (1983): 143-65

Powe, Bruce Allen. *Aberhart Summer.* Harmondsworth: Penguin, 1983

Price, Richard. *Masters, Unions, and Men: Work Control in Building and the Rise of Labour, 1830-1914.* Cambridge: Cambridge University Press, 1980

Rae, J.E. 'The Politics of Class: Winnipeg City Council in the Post-1919 Era.' In J.E. Rae, *Parties and Power: An Analysis of Winnipeg City Council.* Winnipeg: University of Winnipeg, n.d.

Ramirez, Bruno. 'Ethnic Studies and Working-Class History.' *Labour/Le Travail* 19 (1987): 45-8

Rancière, Jacques. 'The Myth of the Artisan: Critical Reflections on a Category of Social History.' *International Labor and Working Class History* 24 (1983): 1-25

Rasporich, A.W., and Henry C. Klassen, eds. *Frontier Calgary: Town, City, and Region.* Calgary: McClelland and Stewart West, 1975

Reid, Alistair. 'Politics and Economics in the Formation of the British Working Class: A Response to H.F. Moorhouse.' *Social History* 3, 3 (1978): 347-61

Reilly, Nolan. 'The General Strike in Amherst, Nova Scotia, 1919.' *Acadiensis* 9, 2 (1980): 56-77

Reimer, Chad. 'The Counterhegemonic Challenge of the 1919 Winnipeg General Strike.' *Prairie Forum* 18, 2 (1993): 219-37

Richards, John, and Larry Pratt. *Prairie Capitalism: Power and Influence in the New West.* Toronto: McClelland and Stewart, 1979

Rimlinger, Gaston V. 'The Legitimation of Protest: A Comparative Study in Labor History.' *Comparative Studies in Society and History* 2 (1959-60): 329-43

Risk, R.C.B. '"This Nuisance of Litigation": The Origins of Workers' Compensation in Ontario.' In *Essays in the History of Canadian Law,* edited by David H. Flaherty, 418-91. Toronto: University of Toronto Press, 1983

Roberts, Elizabeth. *Women's Work, 1840-1940.* London: Macmillan, 1979

Robin, Martin. *Radical Politics and Canadian Labour.* Kingston: Industrial Relations Centre, Queen's University, 1968

Rodney, William. *Soldiers of the International: A History of the Communist Party of Canada, 1919-1929.* Toronto: University of Toronto Press, 1968

Roome, Patricia. 'Amelia Turner.' In *Citymakers: Calgarians after the Frontier,* edited by Max Foran and Sheilagh Jameson, 225-46. Calgary: Historical Society of Alberta, Chinook Country Chapter, 1987

–. 'Amelia Turner and Calgary Labour Women, 1919-1935.' In *Beyond the Vote: Canadian Women and Politics,* edited by Linda Kealey and Joan Sangster, 89-117. Toronto: University of Toronto Press, 1989

Rose, Sonya O. *Limited Livelihoods: Gender and Class in Nineteenth-Century England.* Berkeley: University of California Press, 1992

Rosenthal, Star. 'Union Maids: Organized Women Workers in Vancouver, 1900-1915.' *BC Studies* 41 (1979): 36-55

Roy, Patricia E. 'British Columbia's Fear of Asians, 1900-1950.' *Histoire sociale/Social History* 13, 25 (1980): 161-72

Russell, Bob. *Back to Work? Labour, State, and Industrial Relations in Canada.* Scarborough, ON: Nelson, 1990

Samuel, Raphael. 'Workshop of the World: Steam Power and Hand Technology in mid-Victorian Britain.' *History Workshop* 3 (1977): 6-72

Sandiford, Keith A.P. 'Cricket and the Victorian Society.' *Journal of Social History* 16 (Winter 1983): 303-17

Sangster, Joan. 'Canadian Working Women in the Twentieth Century.' In *Lectures in Canadian Labour and Working-Class History,* edited by W.J.C. Cherwinski and Gregory S. Kealey, 59-78. St John's: CCLH/New Hogtown Press, 1985

–. '"Pardon Tales" from Magistrate's Court: Women, Crime, and the Court in Peterborough County, 1920-1950.' *Canadian Historical Review* 74, 2 (1993): 161-97

–. 'The Soft Ball Solution: Female Workers, Male Managers, and the Operation of Paternalism at Westclox, 1923-1960.' *Labour/Le Travail* 32 (1993): 167-99

–. *Earning Respect: The Lives of Working Women in Small-Town Ontario, 1920-1950.* Toronto: University of Toronto Press, 1995

Saul, S.B. *The Myth of the Great Depression, 1873-1896.* 2nd ed. London: Macmillan, 1985

Saville, John. 'The Ideology of Labourism.' In *Knowledge and Power in Politics: The Problem of Ideology,* edited by Robert Benewick, R.N. Berki, and Bhikhu Parekh, 213-26. London: George Allen and Unwin, 1973

Scarrow, Howard A. *Canada Votes: A Handbook of Federal and Provincial Election Data.* New Orleans: Hauser Press, 1962

Schulze, David. 'The Industrial Workers of the World and the Unemployed in Edmonton and Calgary in the Depression of 1913-1915.' *Labour/Le Travail* 25 (1990): 47-75

Scott, Bruce. 'A Place in the Sun: The Industrial Council at Massey-Harris, 1919-1929.' *Labour/Le Travailleur* 1 (1976): 158-92

Scott, Joan Wallach. *Gender and the Politics of History.* New York: Columbia University Press, 1988

Seager, Allen. 'Nineteen Nineteen: Year of Revolt.' *Journal of the West* 23, 4 (1984): 23-61

–. 'Class, Ethnicity, and Politics in the Alberta Coalfields.' In *'Struggle a Hard Battle': Essays on Working-Class Immigrants,* edited by Dirk Hoerder, 304-24. De Kalb: Northern Illinois University Press, 1986

–. 'Workers, Class, and Industrial Conflict in New Westminster, 1900-1930.' In *Workers, Capital, and the State in British Columbia: Selected Readings,* edited by Rennie Warburton and David Coburn, 117-40. Vancouver: UBC Press, 1988

Sen, Gita. 'The Sexual Division of Labor and the Working-Class Family: Towards a Conceptual Synthesis of Class Relations and the Subordination of Women.' *Review of Radical Political Economics* 12, 2 (1980): 76-86.

Senior, Hereward. 'Orangemen on the Frontier: The Prairies and British Columbia.' In *The Untold Story: The Irish in Canada.* Vol. 1, edited by Robert O'Driscoll and Lorna Reynolds, 417-22. Toronto: Celtic Arts of Canada, 1988

Sewell, William H., Jr. 'How Classes Are Made: Critical Reflections on E.P. Thompson's Theory of Working-Class Formation.' In *E.P. Thompson: Critical Perspectives,* edited by Harvey J. Kaye and Keith McClelland, 50-77. Philadelphia: Temple University Press, 1990

Sharp, Paul F. *The Agrarian Revolt in Western Canada.* Minneapolis: University of Minnesota Press, 1948

Shorter, Edward, and Charles Tilly. *Strikes in France, 1830-1960.* Cambridge: Cambridge University Press, 1974

Siemiatycki, Myer. 'Labour Contained: The Defeat of a Rank and File Workers' Movement in Canada, 1914-1921.' PhD diss., York University, 1986

Simon, Matthew. 'New British Investment in Canada, 1865-1914.' *Canadian Journal of Economics* 3, 2 (1970): 238-54

Smith, A.E. *All My Life: An Autobiography.* Toronto: Progressive Books, 1977

Smith, Donald B. 'Honoré Joseph Jaxon: A Man Who Lived for Others.' *Saskatchewan History* 34, 3 (1981): 81-101

–. 'Rip Van Jaxon: The Return of Riel's Secretary in 1884-1885 to the Canadian West, 1907-1909.' In *1885 and After: Native Society in Transition,* edited by F. Laurie Barron and James B. Waldram, 211-23. Regina: Canadian Plains Research Center, 1985

Sproule, Alfred Frederick. 'The Role of Patrick Burns in the Development of Western Canada.' MA thesis, University of Alberta, 1962

Stearns, Peter N. 'Measuring the Evolution of Strike Movements.' *International Review of Social History* 19, 1 (1974): 1-27

Steedman, Mercedes. 'Skill and Gender in the Canadian Clothing Industry, 1890-1940.' In *On the Job: Confronting the Labour Process in Canada,* edited by Craig Heron and Robert Storey, 152-76. Montreal: McGill-Queen's University Press, 1986

Steinberg, Marc W. 'The Re-Making of the English Working Class?' *Theory and Society* 20, 2 (1991): 173-97

Stelter, Gilbert A. 'The City-Building Process in Canada.' In *Shaping the Urban Landscape: Aspects of the Canadian City-Building Process,* edited by Gilbert A. Stelter and Alan F.J. Artibise, 1-29. Ottawa: Carleton University Press, 1982

Stolee, Leif Gordon. 'The Parliamentary Career of William Irvine, 1922-1935.' MA thesis, University of Alberta, 1969

Storey, Robert. 'Unionization versus Corporate Welfare: The "Dofasco Way."' *Labour/Le Travailleur* 12 (1983): 7-42

Stricker, Frank. 'Affluence for Whom? Another Look at Prosperity and the Working Classes in the 1920s.' *Labor History* 24 (Winter 1983): 5-33

Strong-Boag, Veronica. *The New Day Recalled: Lives of Girls and Women in English Canada, 1919-1939.* Toronto: Copp Clark Pitman, 1988

Struthers, James. *No Fault of Their Own: Unemployment and the Canadian Welfare State, 1914-1941.* Toronto: University of Toronto Press, 1983

–. *The Limits of Affluence: Welfare in Ontario, 1920-1970.* Toronto: University of Toronto Press, 1994

Suissa, Sydney. 'From Canvas Walls to Marble Halls: A History of the First Thirty Years of the *Calgary Herald.*' BA thesis, University of Calgary, 1983

Sutcliffe, Joseph Harry. 'Economic Background of the Winnipeg General Strike: Wages and Working Conditions.' MA thesis, University of Manitoba, 1972

Sutherland, Neil. '"We Always Had Things to Do": The Paid and Unpaid Work of Anglophone Children between the 1920s and the 1960s.' *Labour/Le Travail* 25 (1990): 105-41

Taraska, Elizabeth Ann. 'The Calgary Craft Union Movement, 1900-1920.' MA thesis, University of Calgary, 1975

Teeple, Gary. *Globalization and the Decline of Social Reform.* Toronto: Garamond Press, 1995

Thernstrom, Stephan. *Poverty and Progress: Social Mobility in a Nineteenth-Century City.* New York: Atheneum, 1973

Thomas, Lewis G. *The Liberal Party in Alberta: A History of Politics in the Province of Alberta, 1905-1921.* Toronto: University of Toronto Press, 1959

–. 'The Rancher and the City: Calgary and the Cattlemen, 1883-1914.' In *Ranchers' Legacy: Alberta Essays by Lewis G. Thomas,* edited by Patrick Dunae, 39-60. Edmonton: University of Alberta Press, 1986

Thomas, Lewis H., ed. *The Making of a Socialist: The Recollections of T.C. Douglas.* Edmonton: University of Alberta Press, 1981

Thompson, E.P. *The Poverty of Theory and Other Essays.* London: Merlin, 1978

–. *The Making of the English Working Class.* 1963; reprint, Harmondsworth: Pelican, 1986

–. *Customs in Common.* London: Merlin Press, 1991

Thompson, John Herd. *The Harvests of War: The Prairie West, 1914-1918.* Toronto: McClelland and Stewart, 1978

Thompson, John Herd, with Allen Seager. *Canada, 1922-1939: Decades of Discord.* Toronto: McClelland and Stewart, 1985

Thompson, Kenneth, ed. *Work, Employment, and Unemployment: Perspectives on Work and Society.* Milton Keynes: Open University Press, 1984

Thompson, Paul. *The Nature of Work: An Introduction to the Debate on the Labour Process.* London: Macmillan, 1983

Thorsen, Neils. 'The Traditional and the Modern Understanding of Consumption.' In *Consumption and American Culture,* edited by David Nye and Carl Pedersen, 5-17. Amsterdam: VU University Press, 1991

Tillotson, Shirley. '"We May All Soon Be 'First-Class Men'": Gender and Skill in Canada's Early-Twentieth-Century Urban Telegraph Industry.' *Labour/Le Travail* 27 (1991): 97-125

Trimberger, Kay. 'E.P. Thompson: Understanding the Process of History.' In *Vision and Method in Historical Sociology,* edited by Theda Skocpol, 211-43. Cambridge: Cambridge University Press, 1984

Tucker, Eric. 'Making the Workplace "Safe" in Capitalism: The Enforcement of Factory Legislation in Nineteenth-Century Ontario.' *Labour/Le Travail* 21 (1988): 45-85

Tucker, Robert C., ed. *The Marx-Engels Reader.* 2nd ed. New York: W.W. Norton, 1978

Turner Bone, P. *When the Steel Went Through: Reminiscences of a Railroad Engineer.* Toronto: Macmillan, 1947

Valverde, Mariana. *The Age of Light, Soap, and Water: Moral Reform in English Canada, 1885-1925.* Toronto: McClelland and Stewart, 1991

Voisey, Paul. 'The "Votes for Women" Movement.' *Alberta History* 23, 3 (1975): 10-23

–. 'Boosting the Small Prairie Town, 1904-1931: An Example from Southern Alberta.' In *Town and City: Aspects of Western Canadian Urban Development,* edited by Alan F.J. Artibise, 147-76. Regina: Canadian Plains Research Center, 1981

–. *Vulcan: The Making of a Prairie Community.* Toronto: University of Toronto Press, 1988

Walden, Keith. 'Speaking Modern: Language, Culture, and Hegemony in Grocery Window Displays, 1887-1920.' *Canadian Historical Review* 70, 3 (1989): 285-310

Ward, W. Peter. 'Class and Race in the Social Structure of British Columbia, 1870-1939.' *BC Studies* 45 (1980): 17-35

Wark, Kenneth A. *A Report on Alberta Elections, 1905-1982.* Edmonton: n.p., 1983

Warrian, Jim W. 'From Pluralism to Pluralism: The Political Experience of Organized Labour in Saskatchewan from 1900 to 1938.' MA thesis, University of Regina, 1985

Weber, Max. *The Protestant Ethic and the Spirit of Capitalism.* London: Irwin University Books, 1965

Wetherell, Donald G., with Irene Kmet. *Useful Pleasure: The Shaping of Leisure in Alberta, 1896-1932.* Regina: Canadian Plains Research Center, 1990

Whipp, Richard. '"A Time to Every Purpose": An Essay on Time and Work.' In *The Historical Meanings of Work,* edited by Patrick Joyce, 210-36. Cambridge: Cambridge University Press, 1987

Whitaker, Reginald. 'The Liberal Corporatist Ideas of Mackenzie King.' *Labour/Le Travailleur* 2 (1977): 137-69

–. 'Scientific Management as Political Ideology.' *Studies in Political Economy* 2 (1979): 75-108

Wilentz, Sean. *Chants Democratic: New York City and the Rise of the American Working Class, 1788-1850.* New York: Oxford University Press, 1984

Williams, Raymond. *The Long Revolution.* 1961; reprint, Harmondsworth: Pelican, 1973

–. 'Base and Superstructure in Marxist Cultural Theory.' *New Left Review* 82 (1973): 3-16

–. *Politics and Letters: Interviews with the New Left Review.* London: Verso, 1979

–. *Culture and Society, 1780-1950.* 1958; reprint, Harmondsworth: Penguin, 1984

Wilson, David A. *The Irish in Canada.* Ottawa: Canadian Historical Association, 1989

Wilson, R. Bruce. 'Business, Industry, and Commerce in Calgary, 1920-1930.' Unpublished paper, 1976

Wong, Ging G.G. *Calgary's Civic Government: A Structural History.* Calgary: Glenbow Archives Institute, 1978

Wood, Ellen Meiksins. 'The Politics of Theory and the Concept of Class: E.P. Thompson and His Critics.' *Studies in Political Economy* 9 (Fall 1982): 45-75

–. *The Retreat from Class: A New 'True' Socialism.* London: Verso, 1986

Wood, Walter S. *The Men Who Came Back: A Book of Memories.* Toronto: Ryerson Press, 1956

Wright, Cynthia. '"Feminine Trifles of Vast Importance": Writing Gender into the History of Consumption.' In *Gender Conflicts: New Essays in Women's History,* edited by Franca Iacovetta and Mariana Valverde, 229-60. Toronto: University of Toronto Press, 1992

Young, Walter D. *Democracy and Discontent: Progressivism, Socialism, and Social Credit in the Canadian West.* Toronto: Ryerson, 1969

Zeitlin, Jonathan. '"Rank and Filism" in British Labour History: A Critique.' *International Review of Social History* 34 (1989): 42-61

Zerker, Sally. *The Rise and Fall of the Toronto Typographical Union, 1832-1972: A Case Study of Foreign Domination.* Toronto: University of Toronto Press, 1982

Zieger, Robert H. *American Workers, American Unions, 1920-1985.* Baltimore: Johns Hopkins University Press, 1986

Index